A Jewish Jesuit in the Eastern Mediterranean

In *A Jewish Jesuit in the Eastern Mediterranean*, Robert John Clines retraces the conversion and missionary career of Giovanni Battista Eliano, the only Jewish-born member of the Society of Jesus. He high-lights the lived experience of conversion, and how converts dealt with others' skepticism of their motives. Clines uses primary sources, includ-ing Eliano's personal letters, missionary reports, and autobiography, together with scholarship on conversion in the early modern Mediterra-nean world, to illustrate how false and sincere conversion often mirrored each other in outward performance. Devout converts were not readily taken at face value and needed to prove themselves in the moment and over the course of their lifetimes. Consequently, Eliano's story underscores that the mystical, introspective nature of religious belief and the formulation of new spiritual selves came into direct confrontation with the ways in which converts needed to present them-selves to others in an age of political and religious turmoil.

Robert John Clines is a scholar of the history and culture of the early modern Mediterranean world. A recipient of a Rome Prize from the American Academy in Rome, he has also held fellowships from the U.S.-Italy Fulbright Commission, the Andrew W. Mellon Foundation, and the University of Cambridge.

A Jewish Jesuit in the Eastern Mediterranean

Early Modern Conversion, Mission, and the Construction of Identity

ROBERT JOHN CLINES

Western Carolina University

CAMBRIDGE
UNIVERSITY PRESS

CAMBRIDGE
UNIVERSITY PRESS

University Printing House, Cambridge CB2 8BS, United Kingdom

One Liberty Plaza, 20th Floor, New York, NY 10006, USA

477 Williamstown Road, Port Melbourne, VIC 3207, Australia

314–321, 3rd Floor, Plot 3, Splendor Forum, Jasola District Centre,
New Delhi – 110025, India

79 Anson Road, #06–04/06, Singapore 079906

Cambridge University Press is part of the University of Cambridge.

It furthers the University's mission by disseminating knowledge in the pursuit of
education, learning, and research at the highest international levels of excellence.

www.cambridge.org
Information on this title: www.cambridge.org/9781108485340
DOI: 10.1017/9781108756419

First published 2020

Printed in the United Kingdom by TJ International Ltd, Padstow Cornwall

A catalogue record for this publication is available from the British Library.

ISBN 978-1-108-48534-0 Hardback

Cambridge University Press has no responsibility for the persistence or accuracy
of URLs for external or third-party internet websites referred to in this publication
and does not guarantee that any content on such websites is, or will remain,
accurate or appropriate.

Contents

Acknowledgments

Writing a book is hard. I certainly would not have completed this project without the legion of support that I have received over the past decade. This book began as a doctoral thesis at Syracuse University under the direction of Dennis Romano. Dennis is a wonderful mentor who pushes me to interrogate the past and think more complexly about what exactly I am trying to do with the source material. This book would not exist without his kind words, insights, and advice, which extend well past my dissertation defense and continue even as I type this. His sustained counsel, tips for rethinking things, knack for getting me unstuck, and willingness to scold me when I need to think more (or think less) have been immeasurably helpful, and no thanks can do them justice. Likewise, Junko Takeda remains a close reader of my work and reminds me constantly what the Mediterranean is, what it is not, and why it is such a fascinating place (or idea!) to study.

Ed Muir has pushed me to rethink everything and to always question what I've rethought; and he is a constant beacon of light in an often dark and dreary sea of half-cooked ideas and wholly undercooked written words. Bronwen Wilson introduced me to a broader definition of conversion and she pushes me to think more abstractly while never losing sight of the importance of the subjects we study. Stella Nair continues to cheer on my work and provide me with insights into worlds I had never even considered. I now know more about space and place – to say nothing of the world beyond the Mediterranean – than I ever thought I would.

I also have to thank Abdulhamit Arvas, who completely bent my disciplinary will by pushing me more toward the theoretical and literary texts that often scared and scarred me as a student. The same goes for

Paul Yachnin, who does not shy away from thrusting literature on unsuspecting historians. I never even considered I would have to think about Shakespeare and Marlowe to understand Eliano, but here we are.

I also want to thank the group of unapologetic Mediterraneanists who organically and periodically came together at the American Academy in Rome over meals and Negronis. None of them is both a historian and an early modernist, and this turned out to be a wonderful thing. They rattled me temporally and methodologically, which hurt at the time but has borne wonderful fruits. Thanks especially go to Mary Beard, Caroline Cheung, Hussein Fancy, Leon Grek, Jessica Marglin, Barry Strauss, and Joseph Williams.

The same goes for the Mediterraneanists who have heard my conference papers and whose papers have given me much to consider. At the core of this group are Megan Armstrong, Allyson Poska, Brian Sandberg, and Junko Takeda. But, much like the Mediterranean itself, this group's landscape is amorphous and its members ever-changing, yet it remains forever itself. Our scholarly crowdsourcing at various conferences has been one of my most enjoyable and formative experiences as a scholar. Thank you, and I'll see you all soon at whichever conference calls us together next.

I am grateful for my supportive colleagues in the Department of History and the International Studies Program at Western Carolina University. While I was away in places as far afield as Cambridge, Florence, and Rome, they picked up my slack by advising my students and shouldering the extra service burden. Also, my students at WCU deserve special recognition. Their enthusiasm for all things historical and their undying perspicacity are a constant reminder that good history does not have to be complicated. It just needs to be about the people and their stories.

Essential to this project was access to Eliano's papers, which are held at the Archivum Romanum Societatis Iesu, the Jesuit archive in Rome. Simply put, this project does not exist without the help of archivist Mauro Brunello. Not only did Mauro help me locate the sources I wanted, but he often brought me materials I did not know existed. A good archivist is a tired historian's best friend. Thanks go to Camilla Russell for her enthusiasm for the project over the years and her firm belief that Eliano "deserves a book."

At Syracuse University, I received generous funding from the Department of History, the Maxwell School of Citizenship and Public Affairs, and the Moynihan Institute of Global Affairs. This funding allowed me to conduct preliminary archival research. I also received generous support from Western Carolina University in the form of research grants from the College of Arts and Sciences and the Graduate School.

Several institutions have also been central to this book's completion, as well as my continued intellectual growth. I received a Fondazione Lemmermann Fellowship for the Study of Roman Culture, which allowed for some preliminary archival work in Rome, as well as a Fulbright to Italy. The hardest part of a project of this scope is finding the time to think and write. I was able to think thoughts and write words thanks to the generous support of the Andrew W. Mellon Foundation, which allowed me to participate in the Academy for Advanced Study in the Renaissance, directed by Ed Muir and Regina Schwartz. I also found ample time for reflection and writing at Selwyn College, Cambridge, thanks to a jointly-funded Post-Doctoral grant from the Early Modern Conversions Project, the Social Sciences and Humanities Research Council of Canada, and the Center for Research in the Arts, Social Sciences, and Humanities (CRASSH) at the University of Cambridge. Special recognition goes to Simon Goldhill, former director of CRASSH, who gave me an outsider's perspective on early modernity that has radically altered what I think I do.

I am forever indebted to the American Academy in Rome, where I was a Rome Prize Fellow in 2016–2017. In addition to providing me the time to finish a draft of this book, the Academy was a wonderful environment to try out new ideas, take intellectual risks, and learn so much about a city I thought I knew so well. In addition to the wonderful community of Fellows and Residents, the Academy works because of its staff. President Mark Robbins stressed the importance of collaboration and the need for the Arts and Humanities in trying times. Thanks also to the Rome Sustainable Food Project for keeping me well fed. I was also fortunate enough to be a Fellow at the American Academy in Rome under the directorship of two wonderful scholars and people, Kim Bowes and John Ochsendorf. Both, in their own ways, shaped my intellectual outlook through their kindness and candidness. Also, thanks go to Lindsay Harris, who was the Andrew W. Mellon Professor-in-Charge of the Humanities; no matter my state of despair, Lindsay remained enthusiastic about my work. Lastly, I remain in awe of the hard work of the Drue Heinz Librarian, Sebastian Hierl, and his staff. They strove to ensure that the Library had the books we needed and did everything they could to get them when it didn't.

At Cambridge University Press, I thank my editor, Beatrice Rehl, for her belief and enthusiasm in this project from the very beginning.

Her continued support and excitement for how the book has developed over time means the world. Likewise, Eilidh Burrett has provided further help and enthusiasm for a project I must admit I took too long to write. I also want to thank the book's two blind reviewers. Their feedback compelled me to reconsider much about Eliano, conversion, and the Mediterranean. Without them, this book simply wouldn't be what it is. I owe a world of thanks to my production editor Sarah Lambert and project manager Sindhu Ayyappan for overseeing the final stages of this book. I am also forever indebted to Beth Morel, my copyeditor, for keeping a close eye on the manuscript and preventing me from embarrassing myself any more than necessary.

I thank the respective editors for permission to reprint revised versions of two essays: "How to Become a Jesuit Crypto-Jew: The Self-Confessionalization of Giovanni Battista Eliano through the Textual Artifice of Conversion," *The Sixteenth Century Journal* 48:1 (Spring 2017): 3–26; and "Wayward Leadership and the Breakdown of Reform on the Failed Jesuit Mission to the Maronites, 1577-1579," *Journal of Early Modern History* 22:4 (Summer 2018): 215–37.

Lastly, special thanks go to my parents, Dennis and Laura, for a lifetime of support and for giving me the confidence to believe that I can be whatever I want.

I dedicate this book to my partner, harshest critic, and biggest fan, my wife, Lisa. She has given me nothing but support, advice, proof reading, and love over the years. She has followed me halfway around the world, just so I can sit around, read, look at old things, and write about them. Thank you for not taking it personally when I disappear for hours on end to read, write, and think. I love you and I like you.

My apologies to whomever I have forgotten; given how many people have helped me along the way, this is nothing short of an inevitability. I could not have written this book without you, so thank you. That said, this book's shortcomings and infelicities are completely my own.

Introduction

On 9 September 1553, Giovanni Battista Eliano, a twenty-three-year-old novice at the Collegio Romano, the Jesuit college in Rome, stepped out into the city with a number of his seminarian peers. The Collegio Romano was just a short walk from the ancient Roman Forum and not too far from the Jesuits' current liturgical hub, the Church of the Gesù. While we know Eliano's destination – Campo de' Fiori, one of the major open squares of early modern Rome – his route remains a mystery. This is partly due to the tortuous labyrinth of Rome's medieval streets that allows foot traffic to follow a variety of itineraries that intersect and overlap yet lead to any number of sites throughout the city's historic center known as the Campo Marzio, the Field of Mars. For first-time visitors and seasoned pros alike, the Campo Marzio is an easy place in which to get turned around, as the streets seem to pull one to nowhere, or – often enough – exactly where one started.

While we may never know how Eliano got to Campo de' Fiori, or what motivated him to take the route he did, or where he might have stopped along the way, we know exactly why he went there. It was Rosh Hashanah, the Jewish New Year, and Eliano was off to participate in the burning of the Talmud, an ancient corpus of Jewish civil and ceremonial law central to rabbinical Judaism. The Roman Inquisition had ordered it be burned because of fears that the Talmud fomented obstinacy against papal efforts to convert the Jews.[1] The burning of the Talmud was part of a larger process to compel the Jews to either convert or accept their social

---

[1] Kenneth R. Stow, "The Burning of the Talmud in 1553, in Light of Sixteenth-Century Catholic Attitudes Toward the Talmud," *Bibliothèque d'Humanisme et Renaissance* 34:3

ostracism. This came in a fuller form in 1555, when Pope Paul IV's bull
Cum nimis absurdum established Rome's Jewish Ghetto, a stone's throw
from both Campo de' Fiori and the Collegio Romano.[2]

For the city's Jews, all of this was surely reason for lament. But for
Rome's Catholics, like Eliano and his peers, participating in or cheering
on the burning of Jewish books meant proclaiming their role in the
church's effort to safeguard its claim to universal truth in the face of its
Protestant, Jewish, and Muslim rivals. It should not surprise anyone that
young Jesuit novices like Eliano threw themselves headlong into the mob
of people at Campo de' Fiori and pushed their way to the front of the
crowd to ensure they got their hands on one of those heretical texts and
personally saw to it that it found its way into the conflagration. We can
imagine Eliano, a dutiful Jesuit in training, holding the text aloft and
launching it into the pile that was to be ignited in a show of the Catholic
Church's effort to purge resistance. Then, after a series of prayers and
cheers as the embers once possessing Hebrew script floated into the late
summer air, Eliano and his companions would have ambled back toward
the Collegio Romano and continued on as if this were just one of many
activities that made up their daily lives.

In the years that followed, Eliano continued his studies. He was
ordained a Jesuit priest on 1 March 1561. Over the course of his career
in the Society of Jesus, Eliano dedicated himself to many of the Jesuits'
ministries: he taught Arabic and Hebrew; preached throughout the city;
heard confessions from Eastern Christian pilgrims; and helped to open an
Arabic and Syriac printing press. He also conducted missions to Egypt
and Lebanon, which will make up the bulk of this book's narrative.

On the surface of things, the burning of the Talmud on 9 September
1553 was not a particularly significant or even rare event in early modern
Rome, and it fits in well with Eliano's other activities as a Jesuit over the
subsequent four decades of his life. Nevertheless, it is a microcosm
of the conflictual nature of religious identity formation in the early
modern Mediterranean that this book attempts to interrogate. And this

---

(September 1972): 435–49; Kenneth R. Stow, "The Papacy and the Jews: Catholic
  Reformation and Beyond," *Jewish History* 6:1/2 (January 1, 1992): 257–79.
[2] On Jewish conversion to Catholicism and the Ghetto in the early modern period, see David
  Berger, "*Cum Nimis Absurdum* and the Conversion of the Jews," *The Jewish Quarterly
  Review*, New Series, 70:1 (July 1, 1979): 41–9; Kenneth R. Stow, *Theater of
  Acculturation: The Roman Ghetto in the Sixteenth Century* (Seattle: University of
  Washington Press, 2001); Kenneth R. Stow, *Jewish Life in Early Modern Rome:
  Challenge, Conversion, and Private Life* (Aldershot: Ashgate, 2007).

examination centers on Eliano, for there is more to the story here than tracing the career of an average Jesuit or in exploring his activities in Rome or missions to the Christian communities of the Eastern Mediterranean. This is because, as much as it was just one event of many in which the Catholic Church declared its position regarding the Jews, the burning of the Talmud on 9 September 1553 mattered more for Eliano than it did for the other Jesuit novices, and acts such as this would remain central to how Eliano constructed his Catholic identity. But why? For one, Eliano was fluent in Hebrew and Arabic. Second, before beginning his novitiate, Eliano had been all over the Mediterranean with his father and grandfather. Lastly, Eliano had had a rather intimate relationship with the Talmud since the tender age of seven. And this was because, unlike any of his companions who burned the Talmud that day and unlike any other member of the early modern Society of Jesus, Giovanni Battista Eliano was born a Jew.

Eliano's status as the only Jewish-born Jesuit and the decades he spent confronting that reality provide us with the opportunity to explore the ways in which one convert experienced and engaged with both the evolutions of his own identity as well as the larger fluctuations of religious culture in the early modern Mediterranean. The goal of this book is to trace Eliano's experience as a Jewish convert who became a Jesuit missionary with the hope of better understanding exactly what it was like to be a convert and what that experience tells us about the place of religious conversion in the early modern Mediterranean.

In particular, this book follows Eliano's lifelong struggle with his conversion to ask a series of questions about the nature of conversion as a lived experience. How did converts reconcile their religious pasts and religious presents to formulate a sense of belonging? How did their interactions with others and the acts they performed in everyday life inform their understanding of their converted selves?[3] How did the entanglement of their pre- and post-conversion identities change over time because of the continual negotiations, shifting loyalties, and

---

[3] Felicia Hughes-Freeland and Mary M. Crain, *Recasting Ritual: Performance, Media, Identity* (London: Routledge, 1998); Matthew Causey and Fintan Walsh, *Performance, Identity, and the Neo-Political Subject* (London: Routledge, 2013); Matt Tomlinson, *Ritual Textuality Pattern and Motion in Performance* (New York: Oxford University Press, 2014); Rachel Tsang and Eric Taylor Woods, *The Cultural Politics of Nationalism and Nation-Building: Ritual and Performance in the Forging of Nations* (London: Routledge, 2014); Matt Omasta and Drew Chappell, *Play, Performance, and Identity: How Institutions Structure Ludic Spaces* (London: Routledge, 2015).

ambiguous identities that pervaded the early modern Mediterranean?[4] In essence, this book asks, how can we discern what it meant to be a convert through tracing the ways in which Eliano negotiated his Jewishness, what I define as the burden of his Jewish past and the impossibility of disentangling it from his own sense of his Catholic self? Furthermore, how did his confrontation with this religious past take place in a world where conversion was often doubted or equated with renegadism and crypto-religion?

This need to negotiate one's entangled pre- and post-conversion identities to prove one's sincerity is central to understanding conversion in the early modern Mediterranean. The answers to the questions I posed in the previous paragraph will help us better understand how converts attempted to prove their sincerity in a world where the most frequent accusation was that a conversion took place for reasons beyond faith.[5] Eric Dursteler has declared the early modern period the "golden age of the renegade," with hundreds of thousands of individuals traversing religious boundaries for reasons beyond soteriology.[6] Cultural chameleons such as the polymath Leo Africanus, the Moroccan Jew Samuel Pallache, the Venetian convert to Islam Beatrice Michiel, and many others all prove that people crisscrossed the fluid religious and cultural borders

[4] This notion of ambiguous identities is in part informed by the work of Etienne Balibar and Immanuel Wallerstein, who jointly argue that identity is continuously constructed against an array of identities, both those of others as well as potential identities that individuals could claim, which are deeply entangled and cannot be sustained without the fictive existence of other constructed identities, hence rendering all identities ambiguous but nevertheless integral parts of human interaction. While their work focuses on the modern period, their insights into identity as a continuously constructed but nevertheless very real sense of the self suggest that humans experienced conflict in their efforts to make sense of their own experiences, which in turn shaped their sense of themselves and others. See their *Race, Nation, Class: Ambiguous Identities* (London: Verso, 1991).

[5] Jeffrey S. Shoulson, *Fictions of Conversion: Jews, Christians, and Cultures of Change in Early Modern England* (Philadelphia: University of Pennsylvania Press, 2013).

[6] Eric Dursteler, *Renegade Women: Gender, Identity, and Boundaries in the Early Modern Mediterranean* (Baltimore, MD: Johns Hopkins University Press, 2011), 111. Cf. Gino Benzoni, *Venezia e i turchi: scontri e confronti di due civiltà* (Milan: Electa, 1985); Pedro García Martín, Emilio Solá Castaño, and Germán Vázquez, *Renegados, viajeros y tránsfugas: comportamientos heterodoxos y de frontera en el siglo XVI* (Madrid: Fugaz, 2000); Emilio Solá Castaño, *Un Mediterráneo de piratas: corsarios, renegados y cautivos* (Madrid: Tecnos, 2004); Lucetta Scaraffia, *Rinnegati: per una storia dell'identità occidentale* (Rome: Laterza, 2002); Bartolomé Bennassar and Lucile Bennassar, *Les chrétiens d'Allah: l'histoire extraordinaire des renégats, XVIe et XVIIe siècles* (Paris: Perrin, 2008); Valentina Oldrati, "Renegades and the Habsburg Secret Services in the Aftermath of Lepanto: Haci Murad and the Algerian Threat as a Case Study," *Journal of Iberian and Latin American Studies* 24:1 (January 2, 2018): 7–26.

of the Mediterranean for all sorts of reasons. And this in turn made life quite difficult for converts like Eliano.[7] As we will see, such as when a Portuguese *converso* living as a Jew in Egypt conspired to have Eliano arrested, Eliano himself had to confront renegadism and crypto-Judaism in a very real way because of the impossibility of disentangling his Jewish past and conversion from his Catholic identity.[8]

It is also important, while attempting to answer the questions this book poses, to remember that Eliano lived not only in the golden age of the renegade, but also in a world of forced and coerced conversions of Muslims and Jews,[9] as well as institutional attempts to ensure that those conversions were sincere and not simply the result of opportunism or pragmatism.[10] As a former Jew, Eliano's life was colored by those tensions. Moreover, Eliano came of age in a post-Reformation Italy that

---

[7] Natalie Zemon Davis, *Trickster Travels: A Sixteenth-Century Muslim Between Worlds* (New York: Hill and Wang, 2006); Mercedes García-Arenal and Gerard Albert Wiegers, *A Man of Three Worlds: Samuel Pallache, a Moroccan Jew in Catholic and Protestant Europe*, trans. Martin Beagles (Baltimore, MD: Johns Hopkins University Press, 2007); Sanjay Subrahmanyam, *Three Ways to Be Alien: Travails and Encounters in the Early Modern World* (Waltham, MA: Brandeis University Press, 2011); Eric Dursteler, *Renegade Women: Gender, Identity, and Boundaries in the Early Modern Mediterranean* (Baltimore, MD: Johns Hopkins University Press, 2011), 1–33.

[8] Lewis R. Rambo, *Understanding Religious Conversion* (New Haven, CT: Yale University Press, 1993), 5–8.

[9] Norman Roth, *Conversos, Inquisition, and the Expulsion of the Jews from Spain* (Madison: University of Wisconsin Press, 2002); François Soyer, *The Persecution of the Jews and Muslims of Portugal: King Manuel I and the End of Religious Tolerance (1496–7)* (Leiden: Brill, 2007); José Pedro Paiva, "Vescovi ed ebrei/nuovi cristiani nel Cinquecento portoghese," in *Riti di passaggio, storie di giustizia*, ed. Vincenzo Lavenia and Giovanna Paolin (Pisa: Edizioni della Normale, 2011), 67–85; Maria Filomena Lopes de Barros and José Alberto Rodrigues da Silva Tavim, "Cristãos(ãs)-Novos(as), Mouriscos(as), Judeus e Mouros. Diálogos em trânsito no Portugal moderno (séculos XVI–XVII)," *Journal of Sefardic Studies* 1 (2013): 1–45.

[10] Adriano Prosperi, *Tribunali della coscienza: inquisitori, confessori, missionari* (Turin: G. Einaudi, 1996); Michael Alpert, *Crypto-Judaism and the Spanish Inquisition* (New York: Palgrave, 2001); Helen Rawlings, *The Spanish Inquisition* (Malden, MA: Blackwell, 2006); Henry Charles Lea, *The Inquisition in the Spanish Dependencies: Sicily, Naples, Sardinia, Milan, the Canaries, Mexico, Peru, New Granada* (Cambridge: Cambridge University Press, 2010); David L Graizbord, *Souls in Dispute: Converso Identities in Iberia and the Jewish Diaspora, 1580–1700* (Philadelphia: University of Pennsylvania Press, 2013); Mercedes García-Arenal and Fernando Rodríguez Mediano, eds., *The Orient in Spain: Converted Muslims, the Forged Lead Books of Granada, and the Rise of Orientalism* (Leiden: Brill, 2013); Elizabeth R. Wright, *The Epic of Juan Latino: Dilemmas of Race and Religion in Renaissance Spain* (Toronto: University of Toronto Press, 2016).

saw conversion as central to promoting the church,[11] yet conversions needed to be monitored closely, lest the triumphalism of early modern missionary Catholicism break down.[12]

Eliano also lived at the edge of and traveled throughout the Eastern Mediterranean, which was dominated by the Ottomans.[13] As a consequence, he operated in a world that believed that the allure of Islam posed a fundamental challenge to the very integrity of pure Christian society and would initiate the irreversible recalibration of the essence of Christians, what Eliano's contemporaries called "turning Turk."[14] Europeans' fascination with and fear of this religious permeability led to mythical cults of the renegade, crypto-Jew, and Turk. European intellectual culture often centered on vilifying these religious others;[15] at the same time, these

[11] Lance Lazar, *Working in the Vineyard of the Lord: Jesuit Confraternities in Early Modern Italy* (Toronto: University of Toronto Press, 2005); Rosemary Lee, "Theologies of Failure: Islamic Conversion in Early Modern Rome," *Essays in History* (January 2012): 59–74; Peter Mazur, *Conversion to Catholicism in Early Modern Italy* (London: Routledge, 2016).

[12] E. Natalie Rothman, *Brokering Empire: Trans-Imperial Subjects Between Venice and Istanbul* (Ithaca, NY: Cornell University Press, 2012), 122–62. Pilar Huerga Criado, "Cristianos nuevos de origen ibérico en el Reino de Nápoles en el siglo XVII," *Sefarad* 72:2 (2012): 351–87; Gennaro Varriale, "Tra ll Mediterraneo e il fonte battesimale: Musulmani a Napoli nel XVI secolo," *Revista de historia moderna. Anales de la Universidad de Alicante* 31 (2013): 91–108; Pilar Huerga Criado, "La Inquisicion romana en Napoles contra los judaizantes, 1656–1659," *Monográfico* 6:9 (2017): 303–22.

[13] Tijana Krstić, *Contested Conversions to Islam: Narratives of Religious Change in the Early Modern Ottoman Empire* (Stanford, CA: Stanford University Press, 2011); Tobias Graf, *The Sultan's Renegades: Christian-European Converts to Islam and the Making of the Ottoman Elite, 1575–1610* (Oxford: Oxford University Press, 2017).

[14] Lucia Rostagno, *Mi faccio turco: esperienze ed immagini dell'Islam nell'Italia moderna* (Rome: Istituto per l'Oriente C.A. Nallino, 1983); Daniel J. Vitkus, "Turning Turk in Othello: The Conversion and Damnation of the Moor," *Shakespeare Quarterly* 48:2 (July 1, 1997): 145–76; Mustafa Soykut, "The Development of the Image 'Turk' in Italy Through 'Della Letteratura de' Turchi' of Giambattista Dona," *Journal of Mediterranean Studies* 9:2 (November 1999): 175–203; Giovanni Ricci, *Ossessione turca: in una retrovia cristiana dell'Europa moderna* (Bologna: Il mulino, 2002); Daniel J. Vitkus, *Turning Turk: English Theater and the Multicultural Mediterranean, 1570–1630* (New York: Palgrave Macmillan, 2003); Gennaro Varriale, *Arrivano li turchi: guerra navale e spionaggio nel Mediterraneo (1532–1582)* (Novi Ligure: Città del silenzio, 2014).

[15] Ottmar Hegyi, *Cervantes and the Turks: Historical Reality Versus Literary Fiction in La Gran Sultana and El Amante Liberal* (Newark, DE: Juan de la Cuesta, 1992); Emilio Solá Castaño and José F. de la Peña, *Cervantes y la Berbería: (Cervantes, mundo turco-berberisco y servicios secretos en la época de Felipe II)* (Madrid: Fondo de Cultura Economica, 1996); Michèle Longino, *Orientalism in French Classical Drama* (Cambridge: Cambridge University Press, 2002); Nancy Bisaha, *Creating East and*

captivating figures spurred travel accounts[16] and even plays that allowed individuals as far away as London to come face-to-face with "real life" renegades, crypto-Jews, Moors, and Turks.[17]

But there is something missing here – namely, how converts dealt with these pervasive anxieties. Eliano's story will compel us to question to what extent renegadism, crypto-religion, and turning Turk presented problems for converts who were not shapeshifting, opportunistic renegades. In other words, what if we admitted that many converts were not dissimulators but were actually motivated to convert out of a sense of religiosity? Perhaps Eliano's story will force us to rethink whether his conversion to Catholicism was more akin to those stemming from overseas missions, syncretic but nevertheless sincere, than it was those of crypto-Jews and renegades.[18] Or, perhaps, Eliano's life will allow for a richer understanding of the ways in which individuals and communities embraced new faiths or confronted those whose strong convictions

---

West: Renaissance Humanists and the Ottoman Turks (Philadelphia: University of Pennsylvania Press, 2004); Margaret Meserve, *Empires of Islam in Renaissance Historical Thought* (Cambridge, MA: Harvard University Press, 2008); Marina Formica, *Lo specchio turco: immagini dell'altro e riflessi del sé nella cultura italiana d'età moderna* (Rome: Donzelli, 2012); Jo Ann Cavallo, *The World beyond Europe in the Romance Epics of Boiardo and Ariosto* (Toronto: University of Toronto Press, 2013).

[16] Gerald MacLean, *Looking East: English Writing and the Ottoman Empire Before 1800* (New York: Palgrave Macmillan, 2007); Goran V. Stanivukovic, ed., *Remapping the Mediterranean World in Early Modern English Writings* (New York: Palgrave Macmillan, 2007); Matthew Dimmock, *Mythologies of the Prophet Muhammad in Early Modern English Culture* (Cambridge: Cambridge University Press, 2013).

[17] Daniel J. Vitkus, ed., *Three Turk Plays from Early Modern England: Selimus, A Christian Turned Turk, and The Renegado* (New York: Columbia University Press, 2000); Daniel J. Vitkus, ed., *Piracy, Slavery, and Redemption: Barbary Captivity Narratives from Early Modern England* (New York: Columbia University Press, 2001); Linda McJannet, *The Sultan Speaks: Dialogue in English Plays and Histories about the Ottoman Turks* (New York: Palgrave Macmillan, 2006); Janet Adelman, *Blood Relations: Christian and Jew in the Merchant of Venice* (Chicago: University of Chicago Press, 2008); Ian Smith, *Race and Rhetoric in the Renaissance: Barbarian Errors* (New York: Palgrave Macmillan, 2009); Robert Henke and Eric Nicholson, eds., *Transnational Mobilities in Early Modern Theater* (Farnham: Ashgate, 2016).

[18] Louise M Burkhart, *The Slippery Earth: Nahua-Christian Moral Dialogue in Sixteenth-Century Mexico* (Tucson: University of Arizona Press, 1989); Dominique Deslandres, *Croire et faire croire: les missions françaises au XVIIe siècle (1600–1650)* (Paris: Fayard, 2003); Osvaldo F. Pardo, *The Origins of Mexican Catholicism: Nahua Rituals and Christian Sacraments in Sixteenth-Century Mexico* (Ann Arbor: University of Michigan Press, 2006); Mark Z. Christensen, *Translated Christianities: Nahuatl and Maya Religious Texts* (University Park: Pennsylvania State University Press, 2014); Cécile Fromont, *The Art of Conversion: Christian Visual Culture in the Kingdom of Kongo* (Chapel Hill: University of North Carolina Press, 2014).

contrasted their own.[19] Eliano's experiences, such as a Jesuit washing a Jewish Eliano's feet, should lead us to probe further the larger nexus of motivations beyond pragmatism for why individuals converted, as well as to unpack individuals' efforts to recalibrate the meaning of their beliefs in their confrontations with others.[20] While it is difficult, if not impossible, to prove the veracity of belief and its relationship to individuals' consciousness and sense of belonging in society, this book heeds Lewis Rambo's reminder that "we must take the religious sphere seriously" if we are ever to get a full picture of the nature of conversion in the early modern Mediterranean.[21]

Likewise, the fact that Eliano lived in the golden age of the renegade allows us to pose questions about the intersection of internal belief on one hand and the very public nature of religious self-representation on the other. For example, to what extent were Eliano's lifelong attempts to reconcile his Jewishness and Catholicness a vertiginous experience in which his internal sense of himself was destabilized by his continual need to come to grips with the reality of his Jewish past in everyday life? How did this inform the ways in which he embarked on a new religious future with its own system of ideas, signs, and methods of belonging, especially since he could not simply erase his religious past?[22] How did

---

[19] Eric Zimmer, "Jewish and Christian Hebraist Collaboration in Sixteenth Century Germany," *The Jewish Quarterly Review*, New Series, 71:2 (October 1, 1980): 69–88; Gregory Hanlon, *Confession and Community in Seventeenth-Century France* (Philadelphia: University of Pennsylvania Press, 1993); R. Po-chia Hsia and Hartmut Lehmann, eds., *In and Out of the Ghetto: Jewish-Gentile Relations in Late Medieval and Early Modern Germany* (Cambridge: Cambridge University Press, 1995); Ole Peter Grell and R. W. Scribner, eds., *Tolerance and Intolerance in the European Reformation* (Cambridge: Cambridge University Press, 1996); Keith P. Luria, "Separated by Death? Burials, Cemeteries, and Confessional Boundaries in Seventeenth-Century France," *French Historical Studies* 24:2 (Spring 2001): 185–222; Keith P. Luria, *Sacred Boundaries: Religious Coexistence and Conflict in Early-Modern France* (Washington, DC: Catholic University of America Press, 2005); Benjamin J. Kaplan, *Divided by Faith: Religious Conflict and the Practice of Toleration in Early Modern Europe* (Cambridge, MA: Belknap Press of Harvard University Press, 2007).

[20] Simon Ditchfield and Helen Smith, eds., *Conversions: Gender and Religious Change in Early Modern Europe* (Manchester: Manchester University Press, 2017).

[21] Lewis R. Rambo, *Understanding Religious Conversion* (New Haven, CT: Yale University Press, 1993), 10–11.

[22] Clifford Geertz, "Religion as a Cultural System," in Geertz, *The Interpretation of Cultures: Selected Essays* (New York: Basic Books, 1973), 87–125. Cf. Richard Trexler, *Public Life in Renaissance Florence* (New York: Academic Press, 1980); Edward Muir, *Civic Ritual in Renaissance Venice* (Princeton, NJ: Princeton University Press, 1981).

the boundaries between the reality of his conversion as he experienced it and the ways in which he was expected to present it to others blur? How did Eliano craft a conversion narrative that allowed him to prove to others that he was not a crypto-Jew? How did he eliminate the spiritual dizziness that overcomes the convert in the effort to find meaning?[23] In other words, this book attempts to explore how converts lived in a world in which renegadism and crypto-religion created anxieties about religious disintegration. It likewise analyzes how they embarked on what Henri Paul Pierre Gooren has called a "conversion career," a lifelong, evolving process by which converts could outwardly confirm their inward sense of belonging in a new religious group to those with whom they interacted.[24] By looking at what convinced Eliano to convert as well as how he grappled with the legacy of his Jewishness over the course of his lifetime, this book illuminates what the very subjective and personal nature of spiritual conversion looked like when it was performed in the theater of everyday life.

It also examines the ways in which individuals constructed a narrative of their conversions both for themselves and for others. The study of conversion narratives is hardly new. But most conversion narratives, as useful as they are, provide information about the convert's worldview when the text was written, not necessarily what the convert had experienced in the past or over the course of the convert's larger life experience.[25] Likewise, inquisitorial records – often a major source for the voices of converts accused of apostasy or crypto-religion – were written by inquisitors. They are also quite episodic, that is to say, individuals usually appeared before the Inquisition once or twice, and were never heard from again. Even Carlo Ginzburg's famous Menocchio is a shadowy figure whose voice appears only in fits and starts throughout the story, and always through the filter of his inquisitorial adversaries.[26]

[23] Massimo Leone, *Religious Conversion and Identity: The Semiotic Analysis of Texts* (London: Routledge, 2004), x–xiii. Quote is from p. xii. Cf. Henri Paul Pierre Gooren, *Religious Conversion and Disaffiliation: Tracing Patterns of Change in Faith Practices* (New York: Palgrave Macmillan, 2010), 43–52.

[24] Henri Paul Pierre Gooren, *Religious Conversion and Disaffiliation: Tracing Patterns of Change in Faith Practices* (New York: Palgrave Macmillan, 2010).

[25] Peter Mazur and Abigail Shinn, eds., "Conversion Narratives in the Early Modern World," special edition of *Journal of Early Modern History* 17:5–6 (2013): 427–595.

[26] Carlo Ginzburg, *The Cheese and the Worms: The Cosmos of a Sixteenth-Century Miller* (Baltimore, MD: Johns Hopkins University Press, 1980).

While useful in the aggregate, conversion narratives and inquisitorial records are limited in their use for constructing individual converts' life histories. Eliano, however, is different. He traveled throughout the Eastern Mediterranean both before and after his conversion; he produced volumes of letters and missionary reports detailing his efforts with the Christians of the Ottoman Empire; and he wrote an autobiography a year before his death. The variety and chronological scope of his writings allow us to take a new direction in the study of conversion in the early modern Mediterranean. By looking at Eliano's conversion narrative not as a single text but as a textual corpus, how he experienced his conversion in the moment as well as over the course of his lifetime will come into focus.

By moving beyond the episodic and fragmentary reconstructions of the conversionary experience toward a lifelong exploration of it through Eliano's career as a Jesuit missionary, this book aims to accomplish two goals regarding our understanding of conversion in the early modern Mediterranean. First, it illuminates the ways that a seemingly sincere convert confronted a world of doubt, renegadism, cross-cultural anxiety, and crypto-religion.[27] In turn, Eliano's experiences and reflections elucidate that converts had to come to terms with the place of their religious pasts in their lives if they were ever to settle their religious identities for themselves as well as for those who doubted them. Second, by tracing Eliano's experiences as he described them in the moment and over the course of his lifetime, his conversion becomes more than simply an act that was carried out or even something that was intermittently contemplated over time. Rather, Eliano's conversion will be discussed in the pages that follow as a fundamental reorientation and redefinition of the self. It was both an intimate experience in the moment as well as a process of integration that continued to recur and evolve through Eliano's confrontations with others.[28]

This book examines Eliano's conversion as neither a single act nor a spasmodic reminder that he was different; rather, reading Eliano's disparate writings as a cohesive conversion narrative suggests that conversion

---

[27] I qualify Eliano's conversion because it is of course impossible to fully know to what extent his conversion was sincere. That said, because Eliano spent nearly forty years in the Society of Jesus, a religious order known for its intellectual and spiritual rigor, it seems highly unlikely that Eliano was simply passing himself off as a sincere convert.

[28] Diane Austin-Broos, "The Anthropology of Conversion: An Introduction" in *The Anthropology of Religious Conversion*, ed. Andrew Buckser and Stephen D. Glazier (Lanham, MD: Rowman & Littlefield, 2003), 1–12.

was a persistent source of anxiety as well as a lifelong pursuit of soteriological and ontological security.[29] In sum, this book offers a new way of thinking about conversion in the early modern Mediterranean: it argues that, because renegadism and sincere conversion often mirrored each other quite closely, devout converts were not readily taken at face value and needed to prove themselves in the moment and over the course of their lifetime; consequently, the deeply mystical and introspective nature of religious belief that spurred new spiritual selves came into direct confrontation with the ways in which converts needed to present themselves to others in the golden age of the renegade.[30]

This tension between Eliano's internal sense of himself and how he presented it to others in everyday life also calls into question how we explore the nature of early modern religious culture more generally, which has hitherto tended to focus on the consolidation of religious belief and practice that centered on the strengthening of the bonds between religious institutions and territorial states.[31] While this method of studying early modern religious change originally began as a means of understanding Christianity in the era of the Reformation, it has also been successfully employed in studies on Sunni Islam in the Ottoman Empire, Eastern Rite Christianity, and Mediterranean Jewry – in other words, all of the religious groups that Eliano encountered in his lifetime – rendering the religious landscape of the early modern Mediterranean a quite

---

[29] Keith P. Luria, "Conversion and Coercion: Personal Conscience and Political Conformity in Early Modern France," *The Medieval History Journal* 12:2 (July 1, 2009): 221–47.

[30] Moshe Sluhovsky, *Becoming a New Self: Practices of Belief in Early Modern Catholicism* (Chicago: University of Chicago Press, 2017).

[31] This process has often been called confessionalization. I do not use this term in the text, as I do not want its many complexities to deter from the narrative or to lose a reader who is less familiar with its many historiographical wrinkles. For an introduction to confessionalization, readers can consult Heinz Schilling, "Confessionalization in the Empire," in Schilling, *Religion, Political Culture, and the Emergence of Early Modern Society: Essays in German and Dutch History* (Leiden: Brill, 1992), 205–46; Wolfgang Reinhard, "Gegenreformation als Modernisierung? Prolegomena einer Theorie des konfessionellen Zeitalters," *Archiv für Reformationsgeschichte* 68 (1977): 226–51; Reinhard would later re-address these themes, revising and concentrating on the modernizing aspects of the Society of Jesus in "Reformation, Counter-Reformation, and the Early Modern State," in *The Counter-Reformation: The Essential Readings*, ed. David Luebke (Malden, MA: Blackwell, 1999), 105–28. For more recent discussions of the paradigm and its continued usefulness, see Ute Lotz-Heumann, "The Concept of 'Confessionalization': A Historiographical Paradigm in Dispute," *Memoria y Civilización* 4 (2001): 93–114; John M. Headley, Hans J. Hillerbrand, and Anthony J. Papalas, eds., *Confessionalization in Europe, 1555–1700: Essays in Honor and Memory of Bodo Nischan* (Aldershot: Ashgate, 2004).

dynamic one indeed.[32] Likewise, such as when Eliano falls out of favor
with his French patrons in Egypt, one of the hallmarks of early modern
religious identity was the interweaving of religious zealotry and political
allegiance, which subsequently played itself out through the ways in
which individuals attempted to navigate the larger pan-Mediterranean
imperial rivalries that were both political and religious in nature.[33] Often
at the center of these religious and political conflicts were of course
missionaries like Eliano, who strove to convert individuals and communities in the name of strengthening and expanding the reach of their
respective faiths and polities. We also now have a clearer picture of
missionary tactics as well as the ways in which missionaries saw themselves as agents of religious and political change.[34] Accordingly, Eliano's

---

[32] Bernard Heyberger, *Les chrétiens du Proche-Orient au temps de la Réforme catholique:
Syrie, Liban, Palestine, XVIIe–XVIIIe siècles* (Rome: Bibliothèque des Écoles Françaises
d'Athènes et de Rome, 1994); Daniel Goffman, *The Ottoman Empire and Early Modern
Europe* (Cambridge: Cambridge University Press, 2002); Tijana Krstić, *Contested
Conversions to Islam: Narratives of Religious Change in the Early Modern Ottoman
Empire* (Stanford, CA: Stanford University Press, 2011); David B. Ruderman, *Early
Modern Jewry: A New Cultural History* (Princeton, NJ: Princeton University Press,
2010); Jonathan Ray, *After Expulsion: 1492 and the Making of Sephardic Jewry* (New
York: New York University Press, 2013).

[33] Paolo Prodi, ed. *Disciplina dell'anima, disciplina del corpo e disciplina della società tra
medioevo ed età moderna* (Bologna: Società editrice il Mulino, 1994); Katharine Jackson
Lualdi and Anne T. Thayer, eds., *Penitence in the Age of Reformations* (Aldershot:
Ashgate, 2000), particularly Ronald Rittgers, "Private Confession and Religious
Authority in Reformation Nurnberg" (49–70), Jodi Bilicoff's "Confession, Gender,
Life-Writing: Some Cases (mainly) from Spain" (169–183), and Michael Maher's
"Confession and Consolation: The Society of Jesus and Its Promotion of the General
Confession" (184–200). See also Wietse de Boer, *The Conquest of the Soul: Confession,
Discipline, and Public Order in Counter-Reformation Milan* (Leiden: Brill, 2001); Marc
R. Forster, *The Counter-Reformation in the Villages: Religion and Reform in the
Bishopric of Speyer, 1560–1720* (Ithaca, NY: Cornell University Press, 1992); Forster,
"The Elite and Popular Foundations of German Catholicism in the Age of
Confessionalism: The Reichskirche," *Central European History* 26:3 (January 1, 1993):
311–25; Forster, *Catholic Revival in the Age of the Baroque: Religious Identity in
Southwest Germany, 1550–1750* (Cambridge: Cambridge University Press, 2001);
Philip Benedict, *Christ's Churches Purely Reformed: A Social History of Calvinism*
(New Haven, CT: Yale University Press, 2002); Andrew Pettegree, *Reformation and the
Culture of Persuasion* (Cambridge: Cambridge University Press, 2005).

[34] John M. Headley, "Geography and Empire in the Late Renaissance: Botero's Assignment,
Western Universalism, and the Civilizing Process," *Renaissance Quarterly* 53:4 (2000):
1119–55; Jonathan Chaves, "Inculturation Versus Evangelization: Are Contemporary
Values Causing Us to Misinterpret the 16–18th Century Jesuit Missionaries?," *Sino-
Western Cultural Relations Journal* 22 (January 2000): 56–60; Bernadette Majorana,
"Une pastorale spectaculaire: missions et missionnaires jésuites en Italie (XVIe–XVIIIe
Siècle)," *Annales. Histoire, Sciences Sociales* 57:2 (March 1, 2002): 297–320; Paolo

missionary efforts in the Ottoman Empire will be at the center of this book's narrative.

But studying religious culture purely in its collective sense has diminished the centrality of the actions and thoughts of individuals who confronted religious change and grappled with its implications for their own identities. Eliano's reflections on his conversion suggest that religious culture in the early modern Mediterranean was about more than individuals wandering about blindly adhering to the religious and imperial blocs to which they belonged. Such a view puts too much emphasis on institutionally forced or communally driven constructions of identity, as well as the mechanisms and strategies employed by religious societies in the name of conformity. It likewise ignores the interpersonal and acculturative nature of religious change, both in terms of individual conversions and the ways in which particular religions themselves changed over time.

Eliano's lifelong confrontation with his Jewishness therefore suggests that understanding the true nature of early modern religious culture hinges on unpacking the unique experiences of individuals who confronted religious change. For converts like Eliano, becoming Catholic was often an introspective struggle with the totality of one's religious past as well as the extension of internalized religious beliefs into lived experiences and performances in the theater of the everyday.[35] Furthermore, as we will see throughout this book, the norms of conformity shifted; being a Jewish-born Jesuit meant very different things in 1550 and in 1580. This compelled Eliano to search for new means of proving that his religious past was in the past. For example, how Eliano presented his Jewishness as the source of his missionary toolkit shifted quite dramatically, but always in accordance with expected social norms that he and his fellow Catholics created. Thus, religious identity and how it intersected with political and social institutions centered on individuals engaging in a recursive, dialogic exchange with one another that provided individuals with a sense of

---

Broggio, "La questione dell'identità missionaria nei gesuiti spagnoli dei xvii secolo," *Mélanges de l'École Française de Rome. Italie et Méditerranée* 115:1 (May 2003): 227–61; Allan Greer, *Mohawk Saint: Catherine Tekakwitha and the Jesuits* (Oxford: Oxford University Press, 2005); Alison Forrestal and Seán Alexander Smith, eds., *The Frontiers of Mission: Perspectives on Early Modern Missionary Catholicism* (Leiden: Brill, 2016).

[35] Susan C. Karant-Nunn, *The Reformation of Feeling: Shaping the Religious Emotions in Early Modern Germany* (Oxford: Oxford University Press, 2010). Scholars have also addressed how the senses played a role in one's ability to experience and participate in religion. See Wietse de Boer and Christine Göttler, eds., *Religion and the Senses in Early Modern Europe* (Leiden: Brill, 2013).

belonging while also contributing to a richer understanding of what their given faiths were.

This is not to suggest that Eliano proves Jacob Burckhardt's point that the early modern period birthed the modern individual, as appealing to our sensibility as that thesis might be.[36] Individual agency was not unfettered or without some semblance of expectation in how individuals presented themselves to the wider world,[37] as early modern religious life was certainly a collective experience.[38] But exploring Eliano's persistent, evolving confrontation with his Jewishness allows us to probe the ways in which religious belief was central to an early modern individual's consciousness and understanding of the self in social settings. It also elucidates that religious convictions were in dialogue with how individuals represented themselves to others.[39] Eliano's conversion as he lived it therefore nuances our understanding of individuals' religious choices and their lifelong negotiations of identity by reminding us that human actors were as essential to religious identity as were the larger institutional structures to which they professed belonging.

My interrogation of Eliano's conversion, missionary efforts, and identity construction derives in part from Anthony Giddens's theory of structuration and his exploration of the interrelationship between

---

[36] Jacob Burckhardt, *The Civilization of the Renaissance in Italy (1860)* (New York: Penguin, 1958). Cf. John Jeffries Martin, *Myths of Renaissance Individualism* (New York: Palgrave Macmillan, 2004); Hannah Chapelle Wojciehowski, *Group Identity in the Renaissance World* (Cambridge: Cambridge University Press, 2011).

[37] Stephen Greenblatt, *Renaissance Self-Fashioning: From More to Shakespeare* (Chicago: University of Chicago Press, 1980); Lisa Jardine, *Worldly Goods: A New History of the Renaissance* (New York: Norton, 1996).

[38] Richard Trexler, *Public Life in Renaissance Florence* (New York: Academic Press, 1980); for cross-confessional groups, see Gregory Hanlon, *Confession and Community in Seventeenth-Century France* (Philadelphia: University of Pennsylvania Press, 1993); for the dynamics of class and collective religious life in confraternities, see Christopher F. Black, *Italian Confraternities in the Sixteenth Century* (Cambridge: Cambridge University Press, 1989) and Nicholas Terpstra, *Lay Confraternities and Civic Religion in Renaissance Bologna* (Cambridge: Cambridge University Press, 1995); for the Protestant arena, cf. Raymond Mentzer and Andrew Spicer, eds., *Society and Culture in the Huguenot World: 1559–1685* (Cambridge: Cambridge University Press, 2002).

[39] Harry Berger has also explored the notion of self-representation, which centers on a more recursive understanding of how individuals portrayed themselves both as individuals and as participants in a collective understanding of how individuals should be received. See Harry Berger, *Fictions of the Pose: Rembrandt against the Italian Renaissance* (Stanford, CA: Stanford University Press, 2000); Berger, *The Absence of Grace: Sprezzatura and Suspicion in Two Renaissance Courtesy Books* (Stanford, CA: Stanford University Press, 2000).

consciousness and self-definition in social settings.[40] Giddens's explication of the evolution of the self, and the self's reflexive and recursive relationship with other selves in social settings, hinges in part on a co-evolution and mutual edification of the self and social institutions. Giddens suggests that, while individuals' actions are not wholly compulsory, they are "'made to happen' by the modes of reflexive monitoring of action which individuals sustain in circumstances of co-presence." This points to a more complex understanding of the various ways in which a figure like Eliano constructed his identity in concert with dynamic socio-religious shifts.[41]

The key, then, to understanding how Eliano confronted the complexity and ramifications of his decision to convert is recognizing the inherently ephemeral and evolutionary nature of religious identity and individuals' continual efforts to self-define in the presence of others. In short, shifts in collective definition, which are the products of social interactions, continually stimulated new forms of self-representation that produced shifts in collective definitions. Such a method of exploring Eliano's conversion, missionary career, and effort to construct a fuller sense of himself allows us to see conversion, religious change, and cross-cultural interaction as evolutionary processes rather than static forms.

This book presents Eliano's conversionary journey as both a profoundly religious experience and a series of quotidian and lifelong performances that were staged between Eliano and those whom he encountered in the streets, churches, homes, courts, prisons, printing houses, monasteries, markets, and ships in places as far afield as Rome, Venice, Cyprus, Alexandria, the Egyptian desert, Cairo, Tripoli, the mountains of Lebanon, and even the middle of the Mediterranean Sea itself.[42] While the Mediterranean has a rich historiographical tradition, only recently has the scholarship made room for individual agency in the larger historical vicissitudes of the Middle Sea. This reluctance to see the individual as integral to Mediterranean history of course lies at the very font of the modern historiography of the Mediterranean, Fernand Braudel's *The Mediterranean and the Mediterranean World in the Age of Philip II.* Braudel famously claimed that the actions of individuals were

[40] Anthony Giddens, *The Constitution of Society: Outline of the Theory of Structuration* (Berkeley: University of California Press, 1984).
[41] Ibid., 64.
[42] Yi-Fu Tuan, *Space and Place: The Perspective of Experience* (Minneapolis: University of Minnesota Press, 1977); Dell Upton, "Architecture in Everyday Life," *New Literary History* 33:4 (2002): 707–23.

little more than "surface disturbances, crests of foam that the tides of history carry on their strong backs."[43] As anyone who has spent any time with Braudel's tome knows, the reign of his book's eponymous protagonist is relegated to the relatively short third part of the work, and Braudel always discusses it with skepticism. Braudel's trivialization of human agency even led Oswyn Murray, the English editor of Braudel's *The Mediterranean in the Ancient World*, to quip that Braudel would have seen little difference between the worlds of the Sea's infamous King Philips: of Macedon (r. 359–36 BC) and of Spain (r. AD 1556–98).[44]

Such claims, however, betray the varied and fragmented cultural diversity across time and space that underscores the Mediterranean's overarching geo-historical unity. Peregrine Horden and Nicholas Purcell's *The Corrupting Sea*, for example, recognizes the larger structures to which Braudel wedded his history while also appreciating the Sea's fragmentation that was often manipulated by human agency.[45] Since the publication of *The Corrupting Sea* in 2000, the Mediterranean basin can no longer be treated as just a bowl of determinism in which individuals were mostly the reactionary victims of structures beyond their control.[46] Rather, we should appreciate the unique cultural developments of say, the early modern period. And we should study topics such as religio-imperial ambition and the role of monarchs in shaping the early modern Mediterranean.[47] Doing so allows us to better appreciate the ways in

---

[43] Fernand Braudel, *The Mediterranean and the Mediterranean World in the Age of Philip II*, vol. 1 (New York: Harper & Row, 1972), 21.

[44] Fernand Braudel, *The Mediterranean in the Ancient World* (London: Allen Lane, 2001), xx.

[45] Peregrine Horden and Nicholas Purcell, *The Corrupting Sea: A Study of Mediterranean History* (Malden, MA: Blackwell, 2000). On geography and religion, see pp. 401–60.

[46] A. T. Grove and Oliver Rackham, *The Nature of Mediterranean Europe: An Ecological History* (New Haven, CT: Yale University Press, 2001); William V. Harris, ed., *Rethinking the Mediterranean* (Oxford: Oxford University Press, 2004); Maria Fusaro, Colin Heywood, and Mohamed-Salah Omri, eds., *Trade and Cultural Exchange in the Early Modern Mediterranean: Braudel's Maritime Legacy* (London: Tauris Academic Studies, 2010); Teofilo F. Ruiz, Geoffrey Symcox, and Gabriel Piterberg, *Braudel Revisited: The Mediterranean World, 1600–1800* (Toronto: University of Toronto Press, 2010); Peregrine Horden and Sharon Kinoshita, eds., *A Companion to Mediterranean History* (Malden, MA: Wiley Blackwell, 2014); Brian A. Catlos and Sharon Kinoshita, *Can We Talk Mediterranean?: Conversations on an Emerging Field in Medieval and Early Modern Studies* (Cham, Switzerland: Palgrave Macmillan, 2017).

[47] Barbara Fuchs, *Mimesis and Empire: The New World, Islam, and European Identities* (Cambridge: Cambridge University Press, 2001); Barbara Fuchs and Emily Weissbourd, eds., *Representing Imperial Rivalry in the Early Modern Mediterranean* (Toronto: University of Toronto Press, 2015); Céline Dauverd, *Imperial Ambition in the Early*

which individuals such as Eliano saw their world and molded it in turn. Despite all of this, Braudel's suspicion of lives that "were as short and as short-sighted as ours" still looms large.[48] This has led to resistance to digging much deeper into the history of events beyond the larger structures of the early modern period and how collective identities were formulated in turn. After all, Braudel cautioned us that "after the true Renaissance, came the Renaissance of the poor, the humble, eager to write, to talk of themselves and of others. This precious mass of paper distorts, filling up the lost hours and assuming a false importance."[49]

Yet Eliano's mass of paper, along with its purported distortions and false importance, is what most interests me, and is where this book aims to contribute to our understanding of the history of the Mediterranean. Horden and Purcell have made a clear distinction between history *in* versus history *of* the Mediterranean, that is to say, in an admittedly oversimplified way, exploring one topic that took place within the Mediterranean versus making a transhistorical claim about the Middle Sea.[50] First, this book does explore Eliano's actions *in* the Mediterranean, e.g., burning the Talmud in Rome; dressing like a Maronite villager in Lebanon or as a Venetian silk merchant in Alexandria; likening his survival of a shipwreck off Cyprus to Paul of Tarsus's off Malta.

But these episodes that mostly take place *in* the Eastern Mediterranean, hence this book's title, reveal something central to the history *of* the Mediterranean as a whole. The story of Eliano's life underscores that individuals' actions and reactions were part and parcel of the larger environmental, geological, political, religious, commercial, and cultural interconnectivities of the early modern Mediterranean. After all, we should remember that the early modern Mediterranean – which saw the

---

Modern Mediterranean: Genoese Merchants and the Spanish Crown (Cambridge: Cambridge University Press, 2016); Brian A. Catlos and Sharon Kinoshita, *Can We Talk Mediterranean?: Conversations on an Emerging Field in Medieval and Early Modern Studies* (Cham, Switzerland: Palgrave Macmillan, 2017).

[48] Fernand Braudel, *The Mediterranean and the Mediterranean World in the Age of Philip II*, vol. 1 (New York: Harper & Row, 1972), 21.

[49] Ibid.

[50] Peregrine Horden and Nicholas Purcell, *The Corrupting Sea: A Study of Mediterranean History* (Malden, MA: Blackwell, 2000), 9. Cf. Michelle Hamilton, ed., *In and of the Mediterranean: Medieval and Early Modern Iberian Studies* (Nashville, TN: Vanderbilt University Press, 2015).

stirrings of global imperial expansion,[51] sea-wide religious change,[52] and even dramatic climatic shifts[53] – was a sea in crisis, and one that compelled its inhabitants to come to terms with an ever-changing world.[54] If we admit that Eliano's lifelong journey of dealing with his conversion hinged on a dialogue with these larger structures of the Mediterranean, we can better probe to what extent those admittedly biased personal views were equally integral to Mediterranean history as were patterns of transhumance.[55] Therefore, just as David Abulafia has recently posited that "the human hand has been more important in moulding the history of the Mediterranean than Braudel was ever prepared to admit," this book uses Eliano's experiences as a convert and missionary to problematize the notion that individuals were simply products of the early modern Mediterranean world and proposes instead that we see them as agents of change and shapers of the Middle Sea's historical trajectory.[56]

As a result, much of this book emphasizes Eliano's grappling with his entangled Jewish and Catholic identities because of what it illuminates about the ways in which converts lived life in the early modern Mediterranean. It operates on the level of the familiar – family, friends, fellow Jesuits, other Catholics, former co-religionists, and the various other peoples with whom he interacted – that was integral to the shaping and performing of his identity. In this sense, this is not a book about the rhetoric of conversion as a socio-political ideal or even about conversionary methods.[57] It is about

---

[51] I. Metin Kunt and Christine Woodhead, eds., *Süleyman the Magnificent and His Age: The Ottoman Empire in the Early Modern World* (London: Longman, 1995); Daniel Goffman, *The Ottoman Empire and Early Modern Europe* (Cambridge: Cambridge University Press, 2002); Charles H. Parker and Jerry H. Bentley, eds., *Between the Middle Ages and Modernity: Individual and Community in the Early Modern World* (Lanham, MD: Rowman & Littlefield, 2007); Charles H. Parker, *Global Interactions in the Early Modern Age, 1400–1800* (Cambridge: Cambridge University Press, 2010); Giancarlo L. Casale, *The Ottoman Age of Exploration: Spices, Maps and Conquest in the Sixteenth-Century Indian Ocean* (Oxford: Oxford University Press, 2010).

[52] See note 32 about confessionalization as a pan-Mediterranean phenomenon.

[53] Faruk Tabak, *The Waning of the Mediterranean, 1550–1870: A Geohistorical Approach* (Baltimore, MD: Johns Hopkins University Press, 2008).

[54] William Bouwsma, *The Waning of the Renaissance, 1550–1640* (New Haven, CT: Yale University Press, 2000); Geoffrey Parker and Lesley M. Smith, *The General Crisis of the Seventeenth Century* (London: Routledge & Kegan Paul, 1978).

[55] Fernand Braudel, *The Mediterranean and the Mediterranean World in the Age of Philip II*, vol. 1 (New York: Harper & Row, 1972), 85–102.

[56] David Abulafia, *The Great Sea: A Human History of the Mediterranean* (New York: Oxford University Press, 2011).

[57] For such an important study, see Emily Michelson, "Conversionary Preaching and the Jews in Early Modern Rome," *Past & Present* 235:1 (May 2017): 68–104.

how one convert lived his conversion in the macrocontext of the Mediterranean's sinuous networks of intellectual exchange, trade, communication, religion, and empire. This world was central to Eliano's story and reminds us that his lifelong wrestling with his conversion and its ramifications for his identity occurred within the larger contexts in which he and everyone else lived.[58] Through Eliano's story, we can approach a better understanding of the experience of early modern converts, come to terms with how individuals reflected on and shaped religious change, and underscore the individual life histories that composed the cultural landscape of the early modern Mediterranean. By probing how one individual continuously strove to become a new self, we can approach the ways in which individual lives were the forgers of new cultural milieux in the Mediterranean's myriad theaters of the everyday.

Lastly, scholars of the Society of Jesus, Jesuit missions, and early modern Catholicism more generally should find Eliano's story as presented here to be instructive.[59] Much of what follows hinges on the ways

---

[58] Lewis R. Rambo, *Understanding Religious Conversion* (New Haven, CT: Yale University Press, 1993), 22–27.

[59] There is much work already done on these topics, including Jesuit missions to Eastern Rite Christians. For those works, see Alison Forrestal and Seán Alexander Smith, eds., *The Frontiers of Mission: Perspectives on Early Modern Missionary Catholicism* (Leiden: Brill, 2016). On Jesuit missions to the Christian Orient, see Henri Fouqueray, "La mission de France a Constantinople durant l'ambassade de M. de Césy," *Études* 113 (1907): 70–101; Pietro Pirri, "Sultan Yahya e P. Claudio Acquaviva," *Archivum Historicum Societatis Iesu* 13 (1944): 62–76; Carmelo Capizzi, "Un gesuita italiano di fine Cinquecento per i Maroniti," *Studi e Ricerche Sull'oriente Christiano* 1 (1978): 19–36; Vincenzo Ruggieri, "Constantinopoli vista da P. Giulio Mancinelli S.J. (1583–1585)," *Revue des études byzantines* 60:1 (2002): 113–31; Adina Ruiu, "Conflicting Visions of the Jesuit Missions to the Ottoman Empire, 1609–1628," *Journal of Jesuit Studies* 1:2 (March 12, 2014): 260–80; Robert John Clines, "Jesuit Thalassology Reconsidered: The Mediterranean and the Geopolitics of Jesuit Missionary Aims in Seventeenth-Century Ethiopia," *Mediterranean Historical Review* 31:1 (January 2, 2016): 43–64; Clines, "Fighting Enemies and Finding Friends: The Cosmopolitan Pragmatism of Jesuit Residences in the Ottoman Levant," *Renaissance Studies* 31:1 (February 1, 2017): 66–86. For a fuller discussion of the trajectory of this historiography, see Clines, "The Society of Jesus and the Early Modern Christian Orient," *Jesuit Historiography Online*, December 2016. For the larger picture of the Jesuit missionary endeavors of the early modern period, see Dauril Alden, *The Making of an Enterprise: The Society of Jesus in Portugal, Its Empire, and Beyond, 1540–1750* (Stanford, CA: Stanford University Press, 1996); Ines G. Županov, *Disputed Mission: Jesuit Experiments and Brahmanical Knowledge in Seventeenth-Century India* (New Delhi: Oxford University Press, 1999); Jonathan Chaves, "Inculturation Versus Evangelization: Are Contemporary Values Causing Us to Misinterpret the 16–18th Century Jesuit Missionaries?," *Sino-Western Cultural Relations Journal* 22 (January 2000): 56–60; Dominique Deslandres, *Croire et faire croire: les missions françaises au*

in which Eliano represented his Jewishness over the course of his missionary career as proof of his unique ability to serve the Society of Jesus in its goal of bringing Tridentine Catholicism to the Eastern Mediterranean. Eliano used the apostolic mission of the Society of Jesus as a stage upon which to reconcile the entanglement of his Jewish and Catholic identities. While not every Jesuit would have needed to do this to the same extent, missionary activity was a conduit through which Jesuits proved themselves to their superiors and explored their own spiritual development. Therefore, reading missionary letters as autobiographical, discursive, and performative texts is a keen reminder that we should see Jesuit missionaries as individuals who wrestled with where they fit within the larger, evershifting structures of the Society of Jesus and early modern Catholicism more generally.[60] This prompts us to see missionary reports as interpersonal and subjective documents that did more than report what missionaries did and saw. In this regard, I read Eliano's texts in light of Peter Burke's counsel that "[t]o read these personal documents, particularly the more self-conscious autobiographies, between the lines, a cultural historian needs to acquire the skills of a literary critic, more especially the kind of critic who has a sense of history, an interest in anthropology, and a concern with 'Renaissance self-fashioning.'"[61] By looking at Eliano's writings as a corpus of deeply personal quasi-literary texts, we can better understand who he thought he was as a result of his religious past, his introspective immersion in Ignatian spirituality, and his efforts as a missionary. In so doing, Eliano's missionary epistles and self-reflections

---

XVIIe siècle (1600–1650) (Paris: Fayard, 2003); Paolo Broggio, *Evangelizzare il mondo: le missioni della Compagnia di Gesù tra Europa e America (secoli XVI–XVII)* (Rome: Carocci, 2004); Liam Matthew Brockey, *Journey to the East: The Jesuit Mission to China, 1579–1724* (Cambridge, MA: Belknap Press of Harvard University Press, 2007); Luke Clossey, *Salvation and Globalization in the Early Jesuit Missions* (Cambridge: Cambridge University Press, 2008); Michela Catto, Guido Mongini, and Silvia Mostaccio, eds., *Evangelizzazione e globalizzazione: le missioni gesuitiche nell'età moderna tra storia e storiografia* (Rome: Società editrice Dante Alighieri, 2010); R. Po-chia Hsia, *A Jesuit in the Forbidden City: Matteo Ricci, 1552–1610* (Oxford: Oxford University Press, 2010); Marc André Bernier, Clorinda Donato, and Hans-Jürgen Lüsebrink, eds., *Jesuit Accounts of the Colonial Americas: Intercultural Transfers, Intellectual Disputes, and Textualities* (Toronto: University of Toronto Press, 2014); Micah True, *Masters and Students: Jesuit Mission Ethnography in Seventeenth-Century New France* (Montreal: McGill-Queen's University Press, 2015).

60 Adriano Prosperi, *La vocazione: storie di gesuiti tra cinquecento e seicento* (Turin: Einaudi, 2016). Prosperi also mentions Eliano at some length. See pp. 131–8.

61 Peter Burke, *The Historical Anthropology of Early Modern Italy: Essays on Perception and Communication* (Cambridge: Cambridge University Press, 2005), 20–1.

become windows into his psyche that allow us to probe the entangled layers of his sense of himself.[62]

In the pages that follow, Eliano's efforts to come to terms with the deeper meaning of his conversion and the entanglement of his Jewish and Catholic identities shed light on the challenges that converts faced in their efforts to secure their place within their new faiths. Because conversion blurred boundaries and did little to assuage the fear that one's co-religionist today may not be thus tomorrow, converts like Eliano faced continuous, ever-changing, and new obstacles.[63] The many anecdotes that make up Eliano's story – hiding from Jews in the hull of a ship; convincing his superiors that he only met with his Jewish sister to convert her; likening himself to Elijah, John the Baptist, or Paul of Tarsus – should compel us to reconsider the complex ways in which converts constructed their identities within the fluid, polyvalent, and contradictory nexus of cross-cultural interactions that was the early modern Mediterranean.[64]

These events and how they affected Eliano's identity formation are laid out across seven chapters. Chapter 1 begins with his exposure to a world of cross-cultural exchange and his intellectual formation under the tutelage of his grandfather, Elijah Levita, the famed scholar of biblical Hebrew and tutor of Christian Kabbalists. It also follows the years surrounding his conversion to Catholicism and entry into the Society of Jesus, concluding with his first confrontation with his Jewish past in Venice and en route to Egypt, where he was sent on a mission to the Coptic Orthodox Church. This mission and Eliano's confrontations with his Jewishness are the subject of Chapter 2. While working with the Copts, certain Jews, angry with Eliano for having converted, accused him of blaspheming Islam and converting to Catholicism under spurious

---

[62] Carolyn A. Barros, *Autobiography: Narrative of Transformation* (Ann Arbor: University of Michigan Press, 1998); D. Bruce Hindmarsh, *The Evangelical Conversion Narrative: Spiritual Autobiography in Early Modern England* (Oxford: Oxford University Press, 2012); John M. McManamon, *The Text and Contexts of Ignatius Loyola's Autobiography* (New York: Fordham University Press, 2013).

[63] On cross-cultural interaction as a crisis, see Sanford Budick and Wolfgang Iser, eds., *The Translatability of Cultures: Figurations of the Space Between* (Stanford, CA: Stanford University Press, 1996), in particular Sanford Budick, "Crises of Alterity: Cultural Untranslatability and the Experience of Secondary Otherness," 1–22.

[64] Sanjay Subrahmanyam, "Connected Histories: Notes Towards a Reconfiguration of Early Modern Eurasia," *Modern Asian Studies* 31:3 (July 1, 1997): 735–62; Michael Werner and Bénédicte Zimmermann, "Beyond Comparison: Histoire Croisée and the Challenge of Reflexivity," *History and Theory* 45:1 (February 1, 2006): 30–50. Also, cf. Niels Steensgaard, "The Seventeenth-Century Crisis and the Unity of Eurasian History," *Modern Asian Studies* 24:4 (October 1, 1990): 683–97.

circumstances. They bribed the Ottoman governor, resulting in Eliano's arrest and flight from Egypt.

Chapters 3 and 4 explore Eliano's work with the Maronite Christians of Lebanon. Chapter 3 begins with a brief sketch of Eliano's time as preacher and professor of Hebrew and Arabic at the Jesuit college in Rome (1563–78), which coincided with increasing skepticism of Jewish-lineage members within the Society of Jesus. The chapter then turns to Eliano's first foray in Lebanon, when he was overlooked as superior because he was a convert and was relegated to interpreter and translator for the mission's superior, Tommaso Raggio. After they were recalled because of Raggio's inexperience, Eliano was sent back to Lebanon. That mission is the subject of Chapter 4, which stresses that Eliano hinged his successes with the Maronites on his textual and pastoral skills that were grounded in his knowledge of Semitic languages as well as knowledge of colloquial Arabic, both sharpened in his Jewish youth. This allowed Eliano to bolster his status as Jesuit by emphasizing his Jewishness while successfully distancing himself from anxieties that he was a crypto-Jew.

Chapters 5 and 6 sketch out Eliano's second stint in Egypt in 1582–5. Chapter 5 follows Eliano's efforts to transfer the work he was conducting with the Maronites to Egypt. It also positions Eliano's larger efforts within the diplomatic networks of the burgeoning French empire. Chapter 6 discusses the Coptic synod that Eliano convoked as well as the mission's subsequent unraveling. While the synod was never formally adopted by the Copts, the real issue in this chapter was Eliano's Jewish birth: a Portuguese Jew named David Moze, who was associated with one of Eliano's political enemies, purportedly had evidence that Eliano aimed to overthrow Ottoman authority in Egypt. The mission's breakdown and the confrontation with the Jews that led to his arrest are reminders that Eliano's Jewish past, however helpful it might have been in allowing him to scour religious texts and engage in theological debates, was always potential fodder for accusations of renegadism and opportunism.

The seventh and final chapter examines Eliano's letters concerning the Copts written in retirement, as well as his 1588 autobiography. Because Eliano could no longer leave Italy, he used his knowledge of biblical exegesis to recast his conversion in his autobiography as akin to that of biblical Jews, in order to demonstrate to his superiors that his conversion was sincere and that it was his purity in spirit, not his birth, that mattered. These final documents stress Eliano's continual need to present himself as a Catholic despite his Jewish birth, as he knew that death was imminent.

What becomes apparent throughout Eliano's story is that the central strands of the religious experience – introspective and performative; soteriological and ontological; theological and socio-cultural; immediate and lifelong – were mutually dependent shapers of identity. Eliano's journey from Jewish youth to Jesuit missionary suggests that the early modern Mediterranean was as much a structural burden on individual and collective identities as it was the product of individual actions in the moment and over time. In short – through the lens of Eliano's religious conversion, career as a Jesuit missionary, and lifelong reflections on and representations of the entanglement of his Jewish and Catholic identities – this book challenges us to nuance our understanding of the ways in which individuals constructed and performed richer senses of themselves and in turn became agents of change in the early modern Mediterranean.[65]

---

[65] John M. Headley, "Geography and Empire in the Late Renaissance: Botero's Assignment, Western Universalism, and the Civilizing Process," *Renaissance Quarterly* 53:4 (2000): 1119–55; Maria Georgopoulou, *Venice's Mediterranean Colonies: Architecture and Urbanism* (Cambridge: Cambridge University Press, 2001); Bronwen Wilson, *The World in Venice: Print, the City and Early Modern Identity* (Toronto: University of Toronto Press, 2005); Virginia H. Aksan and Daniel Goffman, eds., *The Early Modern Ottomans: Remapping the Empire* (Cambridge: Cambridge University Press, 2007); M. Pinar Emiralioğlu, *Geographical Knowledge and Imperial Culture in the Early Modern Ottoman Empire* (Farnham: Ashgate, 2014); Mark Rosen, *The Mapping of Power in Renaissance Italy: Painted Cartographic Cycles in Social and Intellectual Context* (Cambridge: Cambridge University Press, 2015); Palmira Johnson Brummett, *Mapping the Ottomans: Sovereignty, Territory, and Identity in the Early Modern Mediterranean* (Cambridge: Cambridge University Press, 2015).

Becoming a Jewish Jesuit: Eliano's Early Years

That young Jew about whom I have written ... [is] very intelligent and judicious, and very well versed in Hebrew Scriptures. ... He will easily learn Latin as he has already mastered Italian, Spanish, German, Moorish and Turkish, in addition to Hebrew; he has also been to Cairo and Jerusalem, etc. ... He can be an instrument for helping others.[1]

– André des Freux, Superior of the Jesuit Residence
in Venice, to Ignatius of Loyola

I was in a constant state of mortification as I desired to speak to the Jews, to convince them of their falsity, to teach them the truth of the Christian faith, to hear the many insults that they always say against the faith and against those who leave Judaism.[2]

– Giovanni Battista Eliano to the Jesuit Community in Rome

Though sparsely documented, Eliano's Jewish youth and early years in the Society of Jesus are central to understanding the role that his Jewishness played throughout his missionary career. Through reconstructing the context around him, the general experiences of Jews in Rome and Venice, as well as understanding the key figures in his early years and what we know about his time as a Jesuit seminarian, we can approximate what Eliano might have experienced as a Jewish youth, Christian neophyte, and young Jesuit priest. This will in turn illuminate the ways in which his Jewish past and conversion as well as the larger religious and political shifts of the early modern Mediterranean shaped his experiences

---

[1] *Litterae quadrimestres ex universis, praeter Indiam et Brasiliam. Tomus primus (1546–1552)* (Rome: Monumenta Historica Societatis Iesu, 1894), 441–2.
[2] ARSI, *Epp. NN 86*, fol. 212v./MPO 2, 99.

as a missionary. In short, we can only come to understand Eliano's maturation as a Jesuit missionary once we get to know, as best we can, Eliano as a Jew.

ELIANO'S EARLY CHILDHOOD, 1530–1537

According to his 1588 autobiography, which I will discuss at further length in Chapter 7, Eliano was born in Rome in 1530.[3] While he would often refer to himself as Eliano Romano or Giovanni Battista Romano, his family was in fact not Roman. His father, Yitzchaq ben Yehiel, was a Bohemian merchant who spent much of his time traveling on business throughout the Levant and Egypt. His mother, Hanah, born in Padua, was the daughter of the Ashkenazi scholar Elijah Levita (1469–1549), one of the most prolific Jewish scholars of the early modern period, producing pivotal grammatical and lexicographical works, as well as Yiddish poetry such as the chivalric epic *Bovo-Bukh*. That his well-traveled maternal grandfather was Ashkenazi and his mother was born in Padua demonstrate that his mother's family was also of Eastern Euro-pean extraction and had been in Italy for only two generations, and in Rome for only one. It is also possible that Italian was not the language he spoke at home, as he explained in 1583 that he and his sister spoke to each other in German when they met up in Egypt.[4] While Eliano may have taken the name Romano because he was born in Rome, from the perspective of Rome's historic Jewish community, the oldest in Europe, Eliano and his family were outsiders and probably struggled to blend in with the Jews who had been in Rome since at least the second century before Christ and who were often ambivalent toward foreign Jews.[5] While Eliano never reflects on this, perhaps because he was only a young child, Eliano's experience of being an outsider among outsiders must have informed the ways in which he never quite felt as though he fit into the

---

[3] ARSI, *Hist. Soc. 176*, fol. 119. His exact birthdate is unknown.

[4] ARSI, *Gall. 98 I*, fol. 103v./MPO 4, 94.

[5] On the various elements of the Jewish community in Rome, see Kenneth R. Stow, *Jewish Life in Early Modern Rome: Challenge, Conversion, and Private Life* (Aldershot: Ashgate, 2007). The historiography on ancient diasporic Judaism is extensive. On the earliest Jewish community in Rome, see Silvia Cappelletti, *The Jewish Community of Rome: From the Second Century B.C. to the Third Century C.E.* (Leiden: Brill, 2006). Cf. Erich S. Gruen, *Diaspora: Jews Amidst Greeks and Romans* (Cambridge, MA: Harvard University Press, 2002).

Jewish community of his home city and, as we will see, other Jewish communities with whom he interacted.

The next piece of information that Eliano gives us, and that we can state with any concreteness, is that, at the age of seven, Eliano moved to Venice with his grandfather and older brother, Yusef, in 1537, while his parents and sister remained in Rome. Before delving into that experience, it is important to understand exactly who Elijah Levita was and how his own past informed Eliano's later experiences.

RENAISSANCE HUMANISM, CHRISTIAN KABBALLAH, AND THE BIRTH OF THE ERUDITE ELIANO

Elijah Levita is best known for his collaborations with Christian intellectuals, which provided his grandsons access to a quite cosmopolitan world. Looming large among Levita's numerous Christian associates was Egidio da Viterbo (1469–1532), who was superior of the Augustinians, a cardinal, and a leading reformer under popes Julius II, Leo X, Adrian VI, and Clement VII.[6] Egidio was so influential within the church that, upon Adrian's death in 1523, many considered Egidio likely to be the next pope. Beginning in 1514, when Egidio asked Levita to provide him with copies of the Kabbalistic works of Eleazar of Worms (1178–1238), Levita guided the cardinal in his Hermetic and Kabbalistic studies as well as his immersion in the Neoplatonic texts of such heavyweights as Marsilio Ficino and Giovanni Pico della Mirandola.[7] This textual meeting of the minds between the two most famous members of the Platonic Academy of Florence,[8] a Catholic cardinal, and a Jewish rabbi represents an attempt

---

[6] John W. O'Malley, *Giles of Viterbo on Church and Reform* (Leiden: Brill, 1968); Francis Xavier Martin and John E. Rotelle, *Friar, Reformer and Renaissance Scholar: Life and Work of Giles of Viterbo, 1469–1532* (Villanova, PA: Augustinian Press, 1992).

[7] Brian Copenhaver and Daniel Stein Kokin, "Egidio da Viterbo's Book on Hebrew Letters: Christian Kabbalah in Papal Rome," *Renaissance Quarterly* 67:1 (2014): 1–42; Gérard Weil, *Élie Lévita humaniste et massorète (1469–1549)* (Leiden: Brill, 1963), 74–5. On the legacy of Jewish mysticism *sui generis* as well as in Christian thought, see Karl-Erich Grözinger and Joseph Dan, *Mysticism, Magic, and Kabbalah in Ashkenazi Judaism* (Berlin: Walter de Gruyter, 1995).

[8] On the Platonic Academy of Florence, see Brian Copenhaver and Charles Schmitt, *Renaissance Philosophy* (Oxford: Oxford University Press, 1992); Arthur Field, *The Origins of the Platonic Academy of Florence* (Princeton, NJ: Princeton University Press, 1988); James Hankins, *Humanism and Platonism in the Italian Renaissance* (Rome: Edizioni di storia e letteratura, 2003). On Ficino and his impact, see Charles Edward Trinkaus, *In Our Image and Likeness: Humanity and Divinity in Italian Humanist*

to reconcile – or at least ignore – religious differences in the name of triangulating three great intellectual traditions: Neoplatonism, Christian humanism, and Jewish mysticism.[9]

For quite different reasons, neither Levita nor his patrons planned on switching faiths. His patrons and intellectual peers seemed to have deep religious convictions, especially Egidio,[10] who wanted to use Levita's skills in his exploration of what Ficino had called the *Prisca Theologia*, the belief that all previous theologies could lead to a deeper understanding of the one true theology (which was, for Egidio, Christian theology).[11] For his part, Levita's work is devoid of religious concerns, which, as Deena Aranoff posits, "may explain the great ease with which he worked with the Christians of his day. It may also explain his failure to convert."[12] Rather, his relationship with Egidio da Viterbo centered on his desire to collaborate in the name of humanistic learning.[13] And this exposure to a diversity of religious and intellectual traditions was central to how Levita nurtured Eliano, and – probably contrary to what he would have hoped – was likely part of the reason he decided to abandon Judaism and join the Jesuits given the Society of Jesus's reputation for intellectual perspicacity and rigor.

Yet, Egidio's theological concerns and Levita's religious ambivalence did not result in a disconnect between patron and client. Rather, both saw their relationship as mutually fruitful: Egidio provided Levita with a modest stipend and living quarters in his palace for more than a decade

---

Thought (Chicago: University of Chicago Press, 1970); Michael Allen, *The Platonism of Marsilio Ficino: A Study of His Phaedrus Commentary, Its Sources and Genesis* (Berkeley: University of California Press, 1984); Paul Oskar Kristeller, *Marsilio Ficino and His Work after Five Hundred Years* (Florence: Leo S. Olschki, 1987); Denis J.-J. Robichaud, *Plato's Persona: Marsilio Ficino, Renaissance Humanism, and Platonic Traditions* (Philadelphia: University of Pennsylvania Press, 2018). On Pico and Ficino together and their importance for the growth of Neo-Platonism in Christian Humanist thought, see Amos Edelheit, *Ficino, Pico and Savonarola: The Evolution of Humanist Theology 1461/2–1498* (Leiden: Brill, 2008).

[9] Robert J. Wilkinson, *Orientalism, Aramaic, and Kabbalah in the Catholic Reformation: The First Printing of the Syriac New Testament* (Leiden: Brill, 2007), 30.

[10] John W. O'Malley, *Giles of Viterbo on Church and Reform* (Leiden: Brill, 1968).

[11] Maria Muccillo, *Platonismo ermetismo e "Prisca theologia": ricerche di storiografia filosofica rinascimentale* (Florence: L. S. Olschki, 1996); Michael Allen, Valery Rees, and Martin Davies, eds., *Marsilio Ficino: His Theology, His Philosophy, His Legacy.* (Leiden: Brill, 2002).

[12] Deena Aranoff, "Elijah Levita: A Jewish Hebraist," *Jewish History* 23:1 (March 2009): 29.

[13] Ibid., 30. On language translation and cultural exchange as a form of conversion, see Peter Burke and R. Hsia, eds., *Cultural Translation in Early Modern Europe* (Cambridge: Cambridge University Press, 2007).

in exchange for Levita's tutelage, and Levita received the financial support and intellectual freedom necessary to pursue his scholarship.[14] More important, the two men – both born in 1469 – seemed to have struck up a deep friendship. The two even huddled together in Egidio's palace in May 1527, when Emperor Charles V's troops mutinied and sacked Rome as recompense given their lack of pay. One can still see German graffiti in the Vatican as well as in the Villa Farnesina, the Sienese banker Agostino Chigi's pleasure palace decorated by masters of the High Renaissance such as Sebastiano del Piombo, Raphael, and Giulio Romano. Further, some of these mutinous troops were the *Landsknechte*, flamboyantly dressed mercenaries who oftentimes were supporters of Martin Luther's break from Rome. For them, the pope was the Antichrist and Rome was a den of thieves; sacking Rome was as much about being paid as it was doing God's work.[15]

The Sack of Rome, which occurred just three years prior to Eliano's birth, had a significant impact on Italian cultural and political life and ushered in a period of heightened anxiety concerning the place of the Catholic Church in the wider world. Much of that apprehension would ebb by century's end as Charles – and his son Philip II – eventually reconciled themselves with the papacy and forged a strong Habsburg–papal alliance.[16] But the sack's psychological impact, coupled with ongoing challenges to papal authority in the form of Protestantism,[17] should not be discounted as factors in the larger tensions that Eliano eventually faced. Likewise, Egidio and Levita's hiding together in the cardinal's palace reminds us that intellectual and cultural exchange was not immune to the religious and political conflicts of the day.[18]

---

[14] Gérard Weil, *Élie Lévita humaniste et massorète (1469–1549)* (Leiden: Brill, 1963), 87–107.

[15] Ibid., 107. Judith Hook, *The Sack of Rome 1527*, 2nd ed. (Basingstoke: Palgrave Macmillan, 2004); Michael Edward Mallett and Christine Shaw, *The Italian Wars 1494–1559: War, State and Society in Early Modern Europe* (New York: Routledge, 2012), 160–4. For a contemporary account of the Sack of Rome, see Luigi Guicciardini, *The Sack of Rome*, trans. James H. McGregor (New York: Italica Press, 2008).

[16] Thomas Dandelet, *Spanish Rome, 1500–1700* (New Haven, CT: Yale University Press, 2001).

[17] Diarmaid MacCulloch, *The Reformation* (New York: Viking, 2004); Lawrence P. Buck, *The Roman Monster: An Icon of the Papal Antichrist in Reformation Polemics* (Kirksville, MO: Truman State University Press, 2014); Carlos M. N. Eire, *Reformations: The Early Modern World, 1450–1650* (New Haven, CT: Yale University Press, 2016).

[18] This is of course nothing new, as seen in Ryan Szpiech, *Medieval Exegesis and Religious Difference: Commentary, Conflict, and Community in the Premodern Mediterranean* (New York: Fordham University Press, 2016). Nevertheless, the early modern period

That Levita lived with a cardinal also suggests that his family was not subject to undue restrictions and pressures that Rome's Jews faced. While the Roman Ghetto was not established until 1555, there was still a significant level of tension between the papacy and Rome's Jews. But Levita, a non-Roman Jew and an intellectual heavyweight, seems to have been protected, as far as an Eastern European Jew could be, from the mutual anxieties that plagued the relationships between Italy and its Jews. But one can imagine how a figure like Levita could have been resented among Rome's Jews for the liberties that came with having such powerful Christian patrons.

Moreover, Levita's relationships to which he introduced his grandsons after he became their full-time guardian in 1537 were met with rebuke because they directly challenged the religio-political status quo. Despite Levita's lukewarm attitude toward Catholicism, some rabbis feared that Levita teetered awfully close to the edge of crypto-Christianity by living in the palace of a cardinal and spending his days reconciling texts such as the Talmud with Neoplatonic Christian theology. He felt compelled to defend himself, albeit unapologetically: "If I do not explain it, they will learn it anyway from my compositions, which they have in their hands and which everyone can understand."[19] Witnessing his grandfather defend himself against fellow Jews' attacks may very well have been as instructive as book-printing ventures, as Eliano would have to defend himself against similar reproofs that eventually came his way once he became Catholic. Levita's – and in time, young Eliano's – collaborators were also not free from scrutiny simply because they were Christian potentates. A wide array of once well-received texts, such as Egidio da Viterbo's *Libellus*,[20] were heavily dissected for theological imperfections after the Protestant

would usher in a new period of challenges to these relationships. Cf. Erika Rummel, *The Confessionalization of Humanism in Reformation Germany* (Oxford: Oxford University Press, 2000); Heiko Augustinus Oberman and Dennis D. Martin, *Masters of the Reformation: The Emergence of a New Intellectual Climate in Europe* (Cambridge: Cambridge University Press, 2008).

[19] Quoted in Gérard Weil, *Élie Lévita humaniste et massorète (1469–1549)* (Leiden: Brill, 1963), 20–6. The quote can be found on page 21. It can also be found in Christian D. Ginsburg's translation of the *Masoret Ha-Masoret: Jacob ben Chajim ibn Adoniah's Introduction to the Hebrew Bible and Massoreth Ha-Massoreth of Elias Levita* (New York: Ktav Pub. House, 1968), 98.

[20] Brian Copenhaver and Daniel Stein Kokin, "Egidio da Viterbo's Book on Hebrew Letters: Christian Kabbalah in Papal Rome," *Renaissance Quarterly* 67:1 (2014): 38.

Reformation put a strain on any intellectual pursuits that might further undermine the Catholic Church's claim to universal religious truth.[21] This is the tumultuous world of intellectual exchange and religious anxieties that Levita introduced to Eliano.

ELIANO'S EARLY CONFRONTATIONS WITH INTELLECTUAL EXCHANGE AND RELIGIOUS DIFFERENCE

In addition to introducing his grandsons to intellectual exchange between Christians and Jews, Levita also introduced them to the life of Venice's Jews. While Eliano's family perhaps did not fit into Rome's Jewish community and Rome's Jews were hardly unfettered, there were limits placed on the Jews in Venice that did not exist in Rome in the 1530s – namely, being forced to live in the Jewish Ghetto. In 1516, the Venetian Senate decreed that all Jews must live within the confines of the Ghetto, "to prevent such grave disordered and unseemly occurrences" that might arise should Christians and Jews live side by side. Furthermore, the Jews were barred from leaving the Ghetto at night, lest they cause "the greatest discontent and the deepest displeasure on the part of Jesus Christ."[22] While the Venetian authorities were not always so restrictive in their treatment of the Jews, such as how their liberal policies concerning intellectual freedom fostered many of Levita's book-printing ventures, we should not underestimate how jarring it must have been for a seven-year-old to live in a ghetto for the first time because of

---

[21] On censorship in early modern Catholic culture, see Peter Godman, *The Saint as Censor: Robert Bellarmine Between Inquisition and Index* (Leiden: Brill, 2000); Stefania Tutino, *Empire of Souls: Robert Bellarmine and the Christian Commonwealth* (Oxford: Oxford University Press, 2010). On doubt and religious tensions, particularly concerning cross-confessional learning and the deconstruction of knowledge, see Carlo Ginzburg, *The Cheese and the Worms: The Cosmos of a Sixteenth-Century Miller* (Baltimore, MD: Johns Hopkins University Press, 1980); Ingrid D. Rowland, *Giordano Bruno: Philosopher/Heretic* (Chicago: University of Chicago Press, 2008); Stefania Tutino, *Shadows of Doubt: Language and Truth in Post-Reformation Catholic Culture* (Oxford: Oxford University Press, 2014); Stefania Tutino, *Uncertainty in Post-Reformation Catholicism: A History of Probabilism* (Oxford: Oxford University Press, 2018). For Spain, cf. Lu Ann Homza, *Religious Authority in the Spanish Renaissance* (Baltimore, MD: Johns Hopkins University Press, 2000). For the Empire, see Ute Lotz-Heumann and Matthias Pohlig, "Confessionalization and Literature in the Empire, 1555–1700," *Central European History* 40:1 (March 1, 2007): 35–61.

[22] "The 'Geto at San Hieronimo,' 1516" in David Chambers and Brian Pullan, eds., *Venice: A Documentary History, 1450–1630* (Toronto: University of Toronto Press, 2001), 338–9.

his socially and legally entrenched religious inferiority. From a very early age, Eliano was forced to confront, via his grandfather's collaborations and the realization of his social ostracism, that his positive interactions with religious others were often counterpoints to heresy and apostasy as latent possibilities. More acutely, Eliano had to confront such challenges not simply to intellectual and cultural exchange itself, but how such exchanges reflected the fluid state of his own religiosity and where he fit into society.

This continued during his youth spent with his grandfather. Eliano gives us few further details of his first years in Venice. The next topic of his youth in his later autobiography is his time collaborating with the Reformed theologian and book printer Paul Fagius in the imperial free city of Isny im Allgäu in Württemberg in 1541. Forty-seven years later, Eliano looked back on this moment in time and referred to Fagius not as a collaborator or even a brilliant scholar, which he certainly was; no, he was "a great heretical preacher."[23] Yet, while he later recast Fagius as a religious enemy because Eliano was an aging Jesuit when he wrote his autobiography, Eliano's time in Germany provides us with some of the most concrete evidence for the ways in which his Jewish youth shaped his later life and informed his missionary work. First, although Eliano was an Ashkenazi Jew, the Jewish experience in the early modern Holy Roman Empire was foreign to Eliano. Being in Germany would have provided him with further opportunities to unpack his family's past, his experiences as an itinerant Jew, and the deeper meaning of the spectrum of Jewish experiences in a now religiously fragmented Christendom.[24] Second, in addition to expanding his understanding of early modern Jewry and Reformed Protestantism, the eleven-year-old Eliano and his older brother, Yusef, worked alongside Levita and Fagius to produce a wide array of texts.[25] Third, Eliano sharpened his technical skills in the then century-old process of book printing – a technology that had

[23] ARSI, *Hist. Soc. 176*, fol. *119*.
[24] Eric Zimmer, "Jewish and Christian Hebraist Collaboration in Sixteenth Century Germany," *The Jewish Quarterly Review*, New Series, 71:2 (October 1, 1980): 69–88; R. Po-chia Hsia and Hartmut Lehmann, eds., *In and out of the Ghetto: Jewish-Gentile Relations in Late Medieval and Early Modern Germany* (Cambridge: Cambridge University Press, 1995); Dean Phillip Bell and Stephen G. Burnett, eds., *Jews, Judaism, and the Reformation in Sixteenth-Century Germany* (Leiden: Brill, 2006); Dean Phillip Bell, *Jewish Identity in Early Modern Germany: Memory, Power and Community* (London: Routledge, 2016).
[25] Deena Aranoff, "Elijah Levita: A Jewish Hebraist," *Jewish History* 23:1 (March 2009): 20.

completely revolutionized the dissemination of knowledge – by working on the production of his grandfather's *Bovo-Buch*, which Fagius stamped.[26]

This collaboration between young Eliano and a Reformed preacher who had broken from Rome – which must have been so instrumental in his textual erudition and ability to rip off scriptural references at will in his epistolary exchanges – suggests that Eliano honed his ability to navigate a world of multiple faiths, nations, and languages in his youth. But the challenges that he and his grandfather faced – ranging from moving into the Venetian Ghetto to being accused of heresy for working with Christians – are also reminders that Eliano was exposed at a very young age to a world of scrutiny, doubt, ostracization, censorship, and the latent fear of religious contamination that would color how his Jewishness informed his missionary career.[27]

After their time in Germany, Eliano, Yusef, and Levita returned to Venice to be reunited with the boys' parents and sister. Eliano and Levita also worked on other printing ventures, such as the 1544 edition of the *Sefer Rûaḥḥen*, a grammar written by the twelfth-century Spanish Jew Judah ben Saul ibn Tibbon. At some point, most likely 1545, during one of his father's commercial ventures Eliano moved to Constantinople with his parents for a year and a half. Shortly after they returned to Venice, his father's business permanently then took the family to Egypt, "where we hoped to make great profit in commerce."[28] Helping his father in his mercantile ventures was a dramatic change from the work he had been doing with his grandfather. Yet, his travels to Constantinople and Egypt would be essential to his later missionary work, as they allowed him to gain at least a basic understanding of the various mercantile communities and networks there, as well as to learn Arabic, the main language he would eventually use while on mission.

---

[26] Elizabeth L. Eisenstein, *The Printing Press as an Agent of Change: Communications and Cultural Transformations in Early Modern Europe* (Cambridge: Cambridge University Press, 1979).

[27] Michael T. Walton and Phyllis J. Walton, "In Defense of the Church Militant: The Censorship of the Rashi Commentary in the Magna Biblia Rabbinica," *The Sixteenth Century Journal* 21:3 (October 1, 1990): 385–400.

[28] ARSI, *Hist. Soc. 176*, fol. 120.

THE END OF ELIANO'S YOUTH

While in Egypt working for his father, Eliano entered into a period of crisis that resulted from the slow unraveling of the security of his youth. In 1548, the news arrived that his brother, Yusef, who had remained in Venice, had converted to Catholicism and taken the name Vittorio.[29] The family immediately returned to Venice to convince Vittorio to abandon Catholicism, but he remained staunch in his newfound faith. The trip that began as a family crisis quickly turned tragic for Eliano, as Levita died the following January.[30] The broken family returned to Cairo, without Vittorio.

Vittorio's conversion and Levita's death must have had a profound impact on the teenage Eliano. In particular, seeing his brother convert and trying to decide how to react – fraternal sympathy or indignation at the apparent betrayal, perhaps both – are poignant reminders that conversion was a part of life in the early modern Mediterranean. But, he tells us, while conversion was common, it was not necessarily accepted: "among the Jews, our house, which now has a member of the family that is Christian, will remain infamous." So, Eliano explained, when the family returned to Egypt, they disowned Vittorio for his conversion, as "we all agreed that we did not want to show our infamy to the Jews of Cairo."[31] As foreigners again, the last family secret they wanted exposed was Vittorio's apostasy. Given his previously close relationship with his brother and the bond they shared with the now-deceased Levita, the family's decision to erase Vittorio from memory so soon after Levita's death must have been jarring, especially when we remember that he spent so much of his youth with Vittorio and seems to have looked up to him.

Following Vittorio's apostasy and Levita's death, Eliano remained true to his family, and to his Jewish faith. He accompanied his widowed

---

[29] Born in 1528, two years before Giovanni Battista, Vittorio converted sometime between 1544 and 1546. The family learned about it shortly thereafter. Among his many accolades, Vittorio collaborated with Francesco Zanetti on the publication of a Hebrew Bible in 1578, and, in the same year, an edition of Robert Bellarmine's *Institutiones linguae hebraicae*. Vittorio also became a censor of Jewish books in Cremona. See ELIANO, Vittorio, in *Dizionario biografico degli italiani*, vol. 42 (Rome: Istituto della enciclopedia italiana), 475–7; Robert A. Maryks, *The Jesuit Order as a Synagogue of Jews: Jesuits of Jewish Ancestry and Purity-of-Blood Laws in the Early Society of Jesus* (Leiden: Brill, 2010), 66; Shlomo Simonsohn, *The Jews in the Duchy of Milan: A Documentary History of the Jews of Italy* (Jerusalem: Israel Academy of Sciences and Humanities, 1982), 1324–5; 1354.
[30] ARSI, *Hist. Soc. 176*, fol. 120.   [31] Ibid.

grandmother from Egypt to Jerusalem "where she wanted to live out her final days." While there, he prayed "to the Lord to forgive my brother, that he would find himself, and return to Judaism."[32] Within a span of two years, he witnessed his brother's conversion and abandonment of the family, the death of his grandfather-cum-teacher, and his grandmother's desire to die on pilgrimage. While it is hard to know exactly how Eliano felt given that his reflections were written decades later, being forced to juggle a mixed bag of emotions regarding his family and faith must have weighed heavily on his mind and instilled in him a sense that his Jewish faith was as central to his identity as were his family bonds. We can infer this because, upon leaving Jerusalem, Eliano did not return to Egypt to be with his parents and sister. Rather, he relocated to Venice to become a rabbi, just like his grandfather.

Despite this, his youth was grounded in neither strict Jewish ortho-doxy nor the rejection of difference. His grandfather had trained him to work with a wide array of collaborators, and his travels throughout the eastern Mediterranean assisting on his father's commercial enterprises introduced him to individuals from all walks of life. So, no matter how zealously Jewish Eliano might have been in the summer of 1551, one of the first people he connected with upon arriving in Venice was his Christian brother, Vittorio. Moreover, while he was there studying to become a rabbi, Eliano was, if nothing else, the grandson of Elijah Levita. He soon began frequenting the Benedictine community at San Gregorio, where he and his brother debated scripture with the monks. Vittorio had also introduced him to the superior of the Jesuit residence, André des Freux.

Eliano could not help but to discuss his exegetical conversations with rabbis. Given Eliano's upbringing, this was hardly a sign that he was distancing himself from Judaism. Rather, it was his intellectual curiosity being piqued. Yet, the rabbis did not provide him with theological counterpoints or wish to engage with him intellectually – to his ire, surely. They simply lambasted him for discussing scripture with Chris-tians. Such dismissal of what he saw as legitimate scriptural inquiry cooled his desire to become a rabbi. By 1 September, to Vittorio's joy, Eliano had abandoned his studies and moved into the Jesuit residence; he was baptized on 21 September, taking Giovanni Battista – John the Baptist – as his Christian name. He quickly entered the Society of Jesus

---

[32] Ibid.

once Ignatius of Loyola, the founder of the Jesuits, gave his assent to the admission of a Jewish convert.

Eliano's becoming a Jesuit is unprecedented, as he was the only Jewish convert to enter the order in the early modern period. Yet, the means by which he converted were not at all uncommon. And the pressures he experienced later in his efforts to grapple with the legacy of his Jewishness and its role in shaping his Catholic identity were hardly an anomaly: a Jew comes to befriend a well-to-do Christian, who in turn guides that person through conversion and dedication to spreading the faith, including to other Jews; but he or she nevertheless is under constant scrutiny to prove the veracity of the conversion, and often uses Jewishness as utilitarian evidence of sincerity.[33] One such case that paralleled Eliano's quite closely – at roughly the same time and also in Venice – was that of the Jewish-born Christian glassblower Marc'Antonio degli Eletti, born Isaac; in 1569, he explained to the Inquisition that he had decided to become Christian after Pietro di Lorenzo Loredan (1505–68), a Venetian nobleman with whom Marc'Antonio had become familiar, urged him to hear a conversionary sermon in the Church of Santi Giovanni e Paolo. When defending his conversion, Marc'Antonio explained that "I have been baptized for no purpose other than the saving of my soul, and so I wish to persevere to the end, and I will accept death for the faith as readily as any other good fortune, and I hope to be the means of bringing other Jews to the light of the holy Christian faith."[34]

Like Marc'Antonio, Eliano tells us little about what motivated him to convert beyond stating that he had embraced Christ. But such a motive for conversion – conscience – is untestable beyond one's word, which is what makes conversion such a contentious process. Thus, his word alone would come to cause Eliano much grief because, simply put, one cannot definitively prove that type of sincerity. This is clear in the case of Marc'Antonio as well, who defended the veracity of his conversion before skeptical inquisitors by claiming that he would work to convert other Jews. Eliano's past as the grandson of a Jewish intellectual who

---

[33] E. Natalie Rothman, *Brokering Empire: Trans-Imperial Subjects Between Venice and Istanbul* (Ithaca, NY: Cornell University Press, 2012), 122–62. On networks with non-converts and godparents, see pp. 139–44; on surveillance and safeguarding against apostasy or opportunism, see pp. 157–62.

[34] "Testimony of Marc'Antonio degli Eletti, formerly Isaac, son of Mira and Mandolino Pugliese, to the Inquisition in Venice, 15 November 1569," in David Chambers and Brian Pullan, eds, *Venice: A Documentary History, 1450–1630* (Toronto: University of Toronto Press, 2001), 339–40.

collaborated mostly with Christians, the son of a cosmopolitan merchant, and the brother of a convert turned censor of Hebrew books shows that conversions were not simply motivated by conscience, but that one's religiosity was often enmeshed in one's life history and was not antithetical to the opportunities that a new religious future could provide. This reality intimates that skepticism followed converts wherever they went.

ELIANO'S ENTRY INTO THE SOCIETY OF JESUS

The other element in unpacking the interrelationship of Eliano's Jewish past and his Catholic identity is his entry into the Society of Jesus. Unfortunately, none of Eliano's writings from the 1550s explains exactly why he decided to join the Jesuits instead of another order. His autobiography, however, gives us some insight into his decision. By the beginning of September 1551, he had moved into the Jesuit residence. Eliano claims that he found himself "in great confusion, seeing myself in a state where I was neither Jewish nor Christian, for having, from one sect and from the other, reasons for and against [each faith]."[35] Causing much of the confusion, Eliano claimed, was the warmth of Christian brotherhood that he experienced while living among the Jesuits. One night, a Jesuit came to him with warm water and offered to wash his feet. Taken aback, Eliano asked him why he would want to wash the feet of a Jew. The Jesuit replied, "It is our custom here, that when a stranger comes to us, in the example of Christ, who washed the feet of the disciples, we wash his feet." Eliano "did not sleep at all that night, as I thought about this and ruminated over many truths" that he had begun to accept from the Jesuits in their numerous conversations and meditations.[36] For Eliano, the Jesuits did not see him as a Jew, but as a fellow man, a guest in their residence. This is in stark contrast to many of his experiences as a youth, as he had often felt out of place among Jews in Rome and Venice; and he must have remembered that it was his grandfather's Christian collaborators who were most receptive to him. When coupled with the rich theological and exegetical conversations that occurred in the Jesuit residence and the Jesuits' willingness to hear him out, Eliano felt accepted, and he fit in intellectually. He must have felt at home for the first time since the death of Elijah Levita.

---

[35] ARSI, *Hist. Soc. 176*, fols. 124–25.   [36] ARSI, *His. Soc. 176*, fol. 124.

Despite the staunch Judaism of his parents, which must have weighed on his conscience as he left Judaism behind, his Jewish youth was as central to becoming a Jesuit as were the Catholic teachings to which Vittorio had introduced him. Even his mentor in Venice, André des Freux, recognized that Eliano's uniqueness as a Jewish convert could help the young Society's ministries. Just five days after Eliano's baptism, des Freux wrote to Ignatius to tell him of "that young Jew of twenty years, about whom I have previously written." For des Freux, Eliano's conversion and entry into the Society of Jesus was a boon for the Jesuits because Eliano was "very intelligent and judicious, and very well versed in Hebrew Scriptures." Des Freux believed that Eliano could soon prove to be a great asset in the Jesuits' ministries in Europe and beyond, as Eliano already knew "Italian, Spanish, German, Moorish and Turkish, in addition to Hebrew; he has also been to Cairo and Jerusalem, etc." In short, des Freux believed, Eliano's unique skill set meant that "he can be an instrument for helping others."[37]

Soon after Eliano's baptism on 21 September 1551, Ignatius requested that Eliano be transferred to Rome to begin his novitiate and to instruct fellow Jesuits in Hebrew at the Collegio Romano. When Eliano left Venice for Rome with André des Freux, neither the Collegio Romano nor the Society of Jesus was the large-scale operation that now comes to mind when one thinks of Jesuit educational and missionary networks. Rather, the Society was barely a decade old, and the Collegio Romano was a fledgling institution with few students – Eliano puts his cohort at about eighteen students – that had just been founded the year prior to Eliano's arrival in Rome.[38] This meant that the first generation of students had a rather warm relationship with Ignatius, who closely oversaw the goings-on of the college, which John O'Malley has called "the apple of Ignatius's eye."[39] Eliano explained that Ignatius had a hands-on approach to those first few cohorts: "having arrived in Rome, Our Reverend Father Ignatius showed me much tenderness, and he explained that I must study with diligence."[40] Eliano seemed to have been a

---

[37] *Litterae quadrimestres ex universis, praeter Indiam et Brasiliam. Tomus primus (1546–1552)* (Rome: Monumenta Historica Societatis Iesu, 1894), 441–2.

[38] On the first few years of the Collegio Romano and its growth during Eliano's time there, see Ricardo García Villoslada, *Storia del Collegio romano dal suo inizio (1551) alla soppressione della Compagnia di Gesù (1773)* (Rome: Pontificia Università Gregoriana, 1954), 19–47.

[39] John O'Malley, *The First Jesuits* (Cambridge, MA: Harvard University Press, 1993), 233.

[40] ARSI, *Hist. Soc. 176*, fol. 128.

conscientious pupil indeed: shortly after his arrival, Ignatius put Eliano's and other Jesuits' talents on display during a public literary exhibition in the city, which aimed to demonstrate the intellectual prowess of the Collegio; Eliano showed off his skills in Hebrew and Arabic.[41] Eliano soon proved himself worthy of a faculty position – a chair in Hebrew – thereby becoming a colleague of his Jesuit mentor in Venice, André des Freux, who held a chair in Greek.[42] It was likewise in this period that, in 1553, Eliano participated in the public burning of the Talmud at Campo de' Fiori, a public declaration through expurgation that he no longer considered himself Jewish.

In addition to the intellectual formation he received at the Collegio Romano, his immersion in the religious landscape of early modern Rome, and his first public declarations of his having distancing himself from Judaism, Eliano also would have been trained in a deep, meditative spirituality that was rooted in Ignatius's own conversionary experience that led to the foundation of the Society of Jesus.[43] Ignatius's journey from Basque courtier to Catholic mystic was its own type of conversion that informed the types of introspection typical of the Society of Jesus.[44] Like Eliano, Ignatius too had to confront his own ordeals, such as being expelled from Jerusalem or pulled before the Inquisition for his questionable mysticism. Thus, as Eliano came to terms with his Jewishness and its place in his intellectual and spiritual formation, it was Ignatius who would serve as a type of conversionary guide. While Ignatius was not a Jewish convert, his struggles prompt us to recognize that one's religious identity was rarely ever without issue given the larger religious and imperial tensions that pervaded the early modern Mediterranean.

---

[41] Ricardo García Villoslada, *Storia del Collegio romano dal suo inizio (1551) alla soppressione della Compagnia di Gesù (1773)* (Rome: Pontificia Università Gregoriana, 1954), 28.

[42] Ibid., 30.

[43] J. Michelle Molina, *To Overcome Oneself: The Jesuit Ethic and Spirit of Global Expansion, 1520–1767* (Berkeley: University of California Press, 2013).

[44] Ignatius's biography is well known, and so I do not recount it here. For a full biography of Ignatius of Loyola, see Pierre Émonet, *Ignatius of Loyola: Legend and Reality*, trans. Thomas M. McCoog (Philadelphia, PA: Saint Joseph's University Press, 2016). For contemporary accounts, see Luís Gonçalves da Câmera, "Reminiscences," in Ignatius of Loyola, *Personal Writings, Reminiscences, Spiritual Diary, Select Letters Including the Text of The Spiritual Exercises* (London: Penguin Books, 1996), 3–64; Pedro de Ribadeneira, *The Life of Ignatius of Loyola* (St. Louis, MO: Institute of Jesuit Sources, 2014).

Conversion, then, was not simply switching faiths, but was a deeply spiritual, introspective experience that stimulated an intense period of reflection and recalibration of the self. It is important that we keep in mind that Eliano's conversion was an emotional and spiritual journey that often manifested itself through his public and outward confrontations with others. While private meditation and public self-representation may seem contradictory or unrelated, Eliano's edification under the supervision of a deeply spiritual man who underwent an emotional revolution in his efforts to come to know God elucidates that the outward expression of conversion was always in dialogue with internal struggles; and Ignatius stressed this when he emphasized that the introspective deliberation over one's past sins and how one conducted oneself in the world were deeply intertwined. In this sense, Ignatius's and Eliano's conversions are not nearly as dissimilar as they might first appear, rendering Ignatius an ideal guide to help Eliano in his internal struggles as well as the external, interpersonal negotiations of his conversion.

ELIANO AND THE *CONVERSO* JESUITS

Another motivation for Eliano's decision to enter the Society of Jesus as well as his ability to flourish as a Jesuit was the preponderance of *converso*, i.e., Jewish-lineage, Jesuits.[45] When Eliano entered the Society of Jesus, most other Catholic religious orders, such as the Carmelites and Jeronymites, had already begun rejecting men of Jewish lineage.[46] In an age of increasing anxieties concerning the Jews, their conversions were certainly desired. Yet, because their conversions were not always viewed as sincere, Catholic leaders were not eager to admit them into the priesthood. The Jesuits, therefore, were uniquely hospitable toward Jewish-ancestry novices.[47] Much of this rested with Ignatius of Loyola. It has been suggested that Ignatius had distant Jewish relatives, rendering

---

[45] James W. Reites, *St. Ignatius of Loyola and the Jews* (St. Louis, MO: American Assistancy Seminar on Jesuit Spirituality, 1981), 28.

[46] Jodi Bilinkoff, *The Avila of Saint Teresa: Religious Reform in a Sixteenth-Century City* (Ithaca, NY: Cornell University Press, 1989); Sophie Coussemacker, "L'ordre de Saint Jerome en Espagne, 1373–1516" (Ph.D. diss., Université de Paris X, 1994).

[47] Marc Rastoin, "Les chrétiens d'origine juive dans la Compagnie naissante," *Christus* 211 (2006): 357–63.

Ignatius himself a *converso* by the definitions of the day.[48] Even though this may never be fully proved, Ignatius had an affinity for and associated with Jewish converts and *conversos*, and he admitted them into his inner circle because he saw their status as a reflection of Christ's and Paul's Judaism.[49] These views seem to have carried over to his perspective on Eliano: In addition to approving Eliano's admission to the Society,[50] Ignatius personally requested that Eliano be sent to Rome to study under his supervision.[51]

Another *converso* who came to serve as a mentor to Eliano was Diego Laínez.[52] Laínez's *converso* status was well known, suggesting that not only did Ignatius not see it as a problem, but saw it as some mark of distinction.[53] Laínez was born in Almazán in Castile in 1512. After his studies at Alcalá, Laínez traveled to Paris, where he befriended Ignatius and helped organize the first group that would eventually become the Society of Jesus. Following Ignatius's death in 1556 and his 1558 election as the second Superior General of the Society of Jesus, Laínez served as Eliano's mentor in the same fashion as Ignatius had. Later claims by Jesuit anti-Jewish polemicists such as Benedetto Palmio that *converso* leaders like Laínez doled out preferential treatment to other *conversos* were hyperbolic in scale. And the notion that Laínez's election and generalate

---

[48] Kevin Ingram, "Secret Lives, Public Lies: The Conversos and Socio-Religious Non-Conformism in the Spanish Golden Age" (Ph.D. diss., University of California, San Diego, 2006), 87–8.

[49] Robert Aleksander Maryks, "Ignatius of Loyola and the Converso Question," in Maryks, *A Companion to Ignatius Loyola: Life, Writings, Spirituality, Influence* (Leiden: Brill, 2014), 84–102; Pedro de Ribadeneyra, *Vita del P. Ignatio Loiola Vita Del P. Ignatio Loiola fondatore della religione della Compagnia di Giesù ... nuovamente tradutta dalla spagnuola nell'italiana da Giovanni Giolito de' Ferrari* (Venice, 1586). On Ribadeneyra's *converso* legacy, see José Gómez-Menor, "La progenie ebrea del padre Pedro de Ribadeneyra S.I. (hijo del jurado de Polendo Alvaro Fusillo Ortiz de Cisneros)," *Sefarad* 36 (1976): 307–32. All of this should be contrasted, of course, with Ignatius's well-known anti-Jewish stance. See James Reites, S.J., "St. Ignatius of Loyola and the Jews," *Studies in the Spirituality of the Jesuits* 13:4 (1981): 13–17.

[50] Eusebio Rey, "San Ignacio de Loyola y el problema de los 'cristianos nuevos,'" *Razón y Fe* 153 (1956): 173–87.

[51] James Reites, S.J., *St. Ignatius of Loyola and the Jews* (St. Louis, MO: American Assistancy Seminar on Jesuit Spirituality, 1981), 28.

[52] Robert A. Maryks, *The Jesuit Order as a Synagogue of Jews: Jesuits of Jewish Ancestry and Purity-of-Blood Laws in the Early Society of Jesus* (Leiden: Brill, 2010), 55; John O'Malley, *The First Jesuits* (Cambridge, MA: Harvard University Press, 1993), 30–2.

[53] Fellow Jesuit *converso* Jerome Nadal knew well of Laínez's legacy, and many of Laínez's relatives were prosecuted for apostasy. See Enrique Sanz, "Los Laínez y la limpieza de sangre," *Perficit* 17 (1993): 65–71.

were the product of the politicking of what Palmio called the "*Converso* Triumvirate" of Laínez, Jerome Nadal, and Juan de Polanco is equally exaggerated.[54] Such accusations also suggest that, despite the openness of Ignatius and Laínez, not every member of the Society of Jesus was so keen on Jewish-lineage members holding positions of influence – more on this in Chapter 3. Nevertheless, as a *converso* who was fully cognizant of the pressures that came with being a New Christian amid debates concerning blood purity, Laínez was the perfect mentor for Eliano and the two did strike up a close bond.[55]

Eliano would eventually come to befriend another Jesuit *converso*, Cristóbal Rodríguez, when they were paired to conduct a mission to the Coptic Orthodox Church in 1561, just months after Eliano's ordination. Born in the Guadalajaran town of Hita in 1521, Rodríguez entered the Society in 1554 under the sponsorship of Francisco Borja (another *converso*) after having studied theology at Sigüenza. He earned a doctorate in theology at Alcalá, served as professor of theology at the Jesuit college in Gandía after 1555, and served as rector there in 1556. From 1557 to 1559 he was rector of the Jesuit college at Valladolid and vice-provincial of Castile.[56] More important, Rodríguez, like Laínez, had grown up under Spanish royal policies that increasingly emphasized blood purity as well as increasing skepticism within the Society concerning the authority of the so-called *Converso* Triumvirate.[57]

The presence of *conversos* in the Society of Jesus and the Jesuits' openness toward Jewish-lineage members were important for Eliano on two levels. First and foremost, it meant that he felt welcomed. Rather than just being accepted into the Society provisionally or with a certain level of scrutiny, he was openly embraced by numerous *conversos* with whom he

---

[54] Robert A. Maryks claims that it was quite common for *conversos* – and by extension the Jewish-born Eliano – to bond over their shared Jewish heritage. Maryks, *The Jesuit Order as a Synagogue of Jews: Jesuits of Jewish Ancestry and Purity-of-Blood Laws in the Early Society of Jesus* (Leiden: Brill, 2010), 90–100, 129–43. ARSI, *Institutum 106*, fols. 92–132. This polemic, written probably by Palmio between 1584 and 1589, attacks New Christians and positions them as a destabilizing force within the Society of Jesus

[55] Norman Roth, *Conversos, Inquisition, and the Expulsion of the Jews from Spain* (Madison: University of Wisconsin Press, 2002); Renée Levine Melammed, *A Question of Identity: Iberian Conversos in Historical Perspective* (New York: Oxford University Press, 2004); Kevin Ingram, ed., *The Conversos and Moriscos in Late Medieval Spain and Beyond* (Leiden: Brill, 2009).

[56] For an extended biography of Cristóbal Rodríguez, see the biographical sketch in *MPO* 2, 327–8.

[57] Albert A. Sicroff, *Les controverses des statuts de "pureté de sang" en Espagne du XVe au XVIIe siècle* (Paris: Didier, 1960).

felt some affinity; while they themselves were not converts, they understood the challenges that came with having Jewish blood and could aid him in his efforts to grapple with those pressures. Second, as Eliano had spent much of his youth not fitting in because he had always felt like a stranger without a home, no religious order offered Eliano, the academically gifted and well-traveled grandson of a famous Jewish rabbi, the type of welcoming, enriching, and intellectually stimulating environment quite like the Society of Jesus.

CONFRONTING HIS JEWISH PAST: ELIANO'S FIRST CALL TO MISSION

After a decade in Rome studying under Ignatius and Laínez, Eliano was ordained a priest on 1 March 1561. Some time prior to Eliano's ordination, a Coptic deacon named Abraham had arrived in Rome bearing a letter in which Coptic Patriarch of Alexandria Gabriel VII rendered obedience to Pope Pius IV.[58] Pius believed that this was the perfect opportunity for a Jesuit mission to Egypt. Laínez, however, was less sure. While missions to Eastern Rite Christians were a great opportunity to extend the Society's reach and in turn strengthen his authority, Laínez felt that Abraham was enticing the papal curia with a feigned promise that the Copts would convert solely to gain some financial support.[59] This was not an unfounded claim by any stretch, as Eastern Rite delegates often did travel to Rome under what their Catholic hosts would see as false pretenses. The Copts in particular had flirted with Rome since the mid-fifteenth century, such as sending a delegation to the Council of Florence, but this usually went nowhere.[60]

However, Laínez felt great pressure from Pius, who saw himself as papal prince par excellence.[61] Under his immediate predecessors, the

---

[58] Alastair Hamilton, *The Copts and the West, 1439–1822: The European Discovery of the Egyptian Church* (Oxford: Oxford University Press, 2006), 58.

[59] On the Copts in Ottoman Egypt, see Febe Armanios, *Coptic Christianity in Ottoman Egypt* (Oxford: Oxford University Press, 2011).

[60] Alastair Hamilton, *The Copts and the West, 1439–1822: The European Discovery of the Egyptian Church* (Oxford: Oxford University Press, 2006), 49–57.

[61] For more on the concept of the papal prince, especially in the period of the Counter-Reformation, see Paolo Prodi, *The Papal Prince* (Cambridge: Cambridge University Press, 1987); also, for the concept of the religious nature of a world empire and the idea of a princely state and mission being inextricably intertwined, see Luke Clossey's "Faith in Empire: Religious Sources of Legitimacy for Expansionist Early-Modern

Catholic Church had regained much of the territory lost to the first waves of the Reformation. Superficially, the Peace of Augsburg of 1555 seemed like a concession that recognized the existence and political legitimacy of Lutheranism. However, the Peace effectively ended years of religious warfare in the Empire until the outbreak of the Thirty Years' War.[62] The conclusion of a defensive Catholicism thereby allowed the papal-imperial camp to go on an evangelizing offensive for the next half-century.[63] By Pius's assumption of the papal tiara on 6 January 1560, the process of Catholic renewal was well under way, and expanding the influence of the Catholic Church became his personal goal. Under his watch, the Council of Trent – to which Laínez was an important papal theologian – met for the first time in ten years, reconvening on 18 January 1562.[64] Pius and leading cardinals saw the council as a sign that the church, staunch in its reforms and militant in implementing them,[65] was entering a period of resurgence.[66] Further, Pius made it clear that he

States," in *Politics and Reformations: Communities, Polities, Nations, and Empires*, ed. Christopher Ocker et al. (Leiden: Brill, 2007), 571–87.

[62] Geoffrey Parker, *The Thirty Years' War*, 2nd ed. (London: Routledge, 1997); Peter Wilson, *The Thirty Years War: Europe's Tragedy* (Cambridge, MA: Harvard University Press, 2009).

[63] This theme of the Peace of Augsburg (1555) and the implementation of *cuius regio, eius religio* as the means by which Catholic (and Protestant territories) were able to expand and consolidate their religious and political authorities is outlined in Heinz Schilling, "Confessionalization: Historical and Scholarly Perspectives of a Comparative and Interdisciplinary Paradigm," in *Confessionalization in Europe, 1555–1700: Essays in Honor and memory of bodo Nischan*, ed. M. Headley, H. J. Hillerbrand, and A. J. Papalas (Aldershot: Ashgate, 2004), 21–36. The theme of a resurgent Catholicism throughout Europe is also addressed in R. Hsia, *The World of Catholic Renewal, 1540–1770*, 2nd ed. (Cambridge: Cambridge University Press, 2005), specifically chapters "The Triumphant Church" and "The Militant Church," 43–81.

[64] John W. O'Malley, *Trent: What Happened at the Council* (Cambridge, MA: Belknap Press of Harvard University Press, 2013), 168–204.

[65] The extent to which Trent was "implemented" is of course up for debate. There are numerous case studies, too many to name, that discuss the relative successes and failures of Catholic reform after Trent or to what extent reform occurred without it. See, as examples, Marc R. Forster, *The Counter-Reformation in the Villages: Religion and Reform in the Bishopric of Speyer, 1560–1720* (Ithaca, NY: Cornell University Press, 1992); Wietse de Boer, *The Conquest of the Soul: Confession, Discipline, and Public Order in Counter-Reformation Milan* (Leiden: Brill, 2001); Francesco C. Cesareo, "The Episcopacy in Sixteenth-Century Italy," in *Early Modern Catholicism: Essays in Honour of John W. O'Malley, S.J.*, ed. Kathleen M. Comerford and Hilmar M. Pabel (Toronto: University of Toronto Press, 2001), 67–83.

[66] See Robert Bireley, *The Refashioning of Catholicism, 1450–1700: A Reassessment of the Counter Reformation* (Washington, DC: Catholic University of America Press, 1999). The three-armed approach to Catholic reform (the papacy, Trent, and the Jesuits) is

believed that the Society of Jesus was the best tool for converting the Copts because of the very work of Laínez as father general.[67] Pius's martial views for the ways in which Catholic reform should take place did not settle well with Laínez, and he worried about coming into conflict with Pius concerning the Copts, as the Society of Jesus could fall out of Pius's favor.[68] Given that the two-year interregnum between Ignatius's death and his election as father general had caused tensions between the Jesuits and general administration of the church, Laínez did not want to draw Pius's ire.

Despite his superior's misgivings, Eliano, who had been to Egypt to assist his father in his commercial ventures and claimed to have first-hand knowledge of the geopolitical and cultural landscape of Ottoman Egypt, was convinced that this mission should take place. In the spring of 1561, Eliano told Laínez that "the very day that [Coptic envoy Abraham] was here with Your Paternity, I read the letters of the Patriarch. I have been unable to stop thinking about this mission, praying to the Lord over how important it is. For this reason, I have compelled myself to write this." Eliano also believed that the letter that Abraham bore was indeed from Patriarch Gabriel. Eliano felt that the overtures of obedience and the desires to convert were true. While almost surely the Copts' claims of threats, dangers, and obstacles under Ottoman rule were overblown, Eliano seemed to believe (or stressed to Laínez for his own ends) that they were under duress, and he wanted to offer them solace through spiritual aid.[69]

Eliano also provided his superior with a more substantial list of reasons why this mission should be carried forth. First and foremost, Eliano explained that the letter that Abraham brought from Gabriel,

---

highlighted in Hubert Jedin's seminal article: "Catholic Reformation or Counter-Reformation?," in *The Counter-Reformation: The Essential Readings*, ed. David Martin Luebke (Malden, MA: Blackwell, 1999), 21–46.

[67] On Laínez and his generalate, see Paul Oberholzer, S.J., ed., *Diego Laínez (1512–1565) and His Generalate: Jesuit with Jewish Roots, Close Confidant of Ignatius of Loyola, Preeminent Theologian of the Council of Trent* (Rome: Institutum Historicum Societatis Iesu, 2015).

[68] MHSI, *Lainii Monumenta*, "Lainii Vitae Summarium," vii–xii.

[69] ARSI, *Gall. 98 I*, fol. 5r. Bruce Alan Masters posits that while some Christians and most Jews were "ambivalent" toward the new Ottoman rulers in relation to the previous Mamluk regime, Egypt "witnessed an outpouring of Islamic legal polemic against the Christians that led, on occasion, to mob attacks on the remaining Coptic churches and monasteries. An increasing rate of conversion further reduced the Copts to an isolated minority." See Bruce Alan Masters, *Christians and Jews in the Ottoman Arab World: The Roots of Sectarianism* (Cambridge: Cambridge University Press, 2001), 41–2.

which "was signed by around twenty bishops," explained that the Copts "have had this faith in the Roman See since Pope Sylvester [r. 314–35]." Further, "the gifts that [Abraham] brought from the patriarch are of no small value, like a cross of pure gold and some reliquaries, etc., the kindness of the ambassador, which I have long experienced in him," as well as "his desire to leave his son here as a pledge of honesty, so that he not be suspected of falsehood."[70] For these reasons, Eliano believed that "notwithstanding the dangers and trials, it seems necessary to send men on this mission." As for himself, Eliano explained that "I have offered myself in writing this, as I always offer my opinion. Nor in this do I say that I desire to go there, because I after having seen Your Paternity's inclination that I not go, I have persuaded myself that I am most inept and useless."[71] A mission to the Copts would be quite difficult, as overtures to the Copts had almost always fallen on deaf ears; and (as hindsight will show us in due course) Laínez was right to be skeptical.[72]

Despite his obsequiousness, Eliano represented himself as the ideal Jesuit for this mission. While he may have been naïve or perhaps coy regarding the Copts' willingness to submit to Rome so easily, Eliano saw this as a means of proving himself to his superiors so shortly after his ordination. And, despite his humble acquiescence in accepting his superior's doubts concerning his skills as a missionary, Eliano clearly had spent much time thinking about this mission and longed to go to Egypt. Furthermore, it would take place in a land he had visited and had claimed to know well. The viability of the mission aside, such frankness on Eliano's part allows us to probe his mind-set as he jumped at this opportunity to prove his mettle just months after his ordination, as being sent to Egypt would allow him to prove to his superiors that his utility extended beyond language instruction. While Eliano does not explicitly couch it in the language of his own conversion, his insistence that his prayers have steeled his desire to convert the Copts is partly driven by his effort to prove to his superior that he was fit and ready to conduct a mission.

And it seems that, despite his apprehensions, Laínez believed that Eliano's experiences in Egypt rendered him ideal for this mission. Laínez therefore announced that the Society of Jesus would conduct a mission to Egypt.[73] Pius then notified Cristóbal Rodríguez that he was selected as

---

[70] ARSI, *Gall. 98 I*, fol. 5r./MPO 2, 317.   [71] ARSI, *Gall. 98 I*, fol. 5v./MPO 2, 318.
[72] Alastair Hamilton, *The Copts and the West, 1439–1822: The European Discovery of the Egyptian Church* (Oxford: Oxford University Press, 2006).
[73] ARSI, *Rom. 127*, fol. 25r./MPO 2, 36.

papal nuncio to Gabriel, and that Eliano and a third Jesuit, Alfonso Bravo, were to be his missionary coadjutors.[74] Eliano's desire to serve on this mission and Laínez's eventual decision to send him and another *converso* illustrate that Laínez, like des Freux and Ignatius, saw Eliano's Jewishness as an important tool for converting the Copts. For Eliano, it was an opportunity to prove to his superiors, and to himself, that his Jewish past could be central to how he served the Society. The ways in which his Jewish and Catholic identities would entangle themselves in Egypt will be discussed at greater length in Chapter 2. Before that could occur, Eliano needed to travel to Egypt. As was the case for many in the early modern period, Eliano did so via Venice and its maritime empire. For Eliano, this presented, in no small way, an opportunity to cut his teeth as a Jesuit missionary; but it also forced him to encounter the burdens of his Jewishness.

CONFRONTING HIS JEWISHNESS AS A JESUIT: ELIANO'S RETURN TO THE WORLD OF EARLY MODERN VENICE

Eliano, Rodríguez, and Bravo arrived in Venice on 16 July 1561.[75] Most likely, it was the first time Eliano had visited Venice since his conversion ten years prior. As Eliano knew Venice well from his youth, its maze of canals, alleys, and people rendered it the perfect place to get his bearings as a Jesuit missionary. Eliano would traverse routes familiar to him, as he would visit the old Jesuit residence where he lived, and he would walk down the same streets he had with his grandfather on their way out of the Ghetto to any number of printing houses with which they were collaborating. It was the perfect stage for Eliano: "in this city, it seems to me that it will be quite easy to perform all of our Society's ministries. And there is great need of them, because no one attends to them." Furthermore, "there are Lutherans ... Jews, Moors, Greeks, and men of seemingly every nation who have need [of ministry]," and it would be Eliano who would provide those services.[76] By textually remapping Venice's religious diversity and showing a thorough knowledge of how these various people

---

[74] Bravo played little part in the mission and is rarely mentioned in the missionary reports, but I have included him in the story throughout. He was born in Trigueros in Andalusia around 1540 and entered the Society of Jesus in 1554. He too apparently knew at least some Arabic. For more, see a short biography of Bravo in *MPO* 2, 319–20.

[75] ARSI, *Epp. NN 86*, fol. 212r./*MPO* 2, 96.

[76] ARSI, *Epp. NN 86*, fol. 82r./*MPO* 2, 74–75.

viewed one another, Eliano reassured his skeptical mentor and superior that the mission was safe in his hands.

But there was one problem, of course – namely, that Eliano had learned of Venice's intricacies as a Jew. While he aimed to demonstrate to Laínez that he possessed an uncanny penchant for negotiating the borders between faiths, his ability to unpack the complexities of Venice also exposed him to the potential accusation that he was a catalyst for the erosion of religious identities. He therefore needed to go to extra lengths to ensure Laínez that, should he undo any borders around any faiths, it would not be Catholicism.[77] Furthermore, Eliano's use of *nation* – the common, if not invariable, term that appears in a goodly number of writings, of many genres, in all its linguistic manifestations – shows that Eliano understood the very real boundaries that people had constructed around these groups and his need to tiptoe around those boundaries.[78] Yet, as one who had traversed such finite and staunchly defended boundaries, he was nevertheless proof of their elasticity.[79]

Expressing his ability to put pressures on the borders of faiths through conversion exposed Eliano to the accusation – which would come from the Jews in Egypt, as we will see in Chapter 2 – that he had a knack for eroding religious communities for personal gain. On one hand, Eliano's descriptions of Venice's diversity and the fruits that could come from his time there would stem from the utility of his religious past. On the other hand, such utilitarianism, while not necessarily incompatible with true conviction, meant that his conversion and dedication to the mission could appear to some to be proof that he was nothing more than an opportunistic crypto-Jew.[80] Laínez was commanding Eliano to perform the very

---

[77] For more on this process, see Tijana Krstić, *Contested Conversions to Islam: Narratives of Religious Change in the Early Modern Ottoman Empire* (Stanford, CA: Stanford University Press, 2011).

[78] Some exceptions notwithstanding, the word "nation," regardless of language, was the most prevalent way to discuss one's larger cultural group identity. The four most dominant languages concerning travel and identity in the early modern Mediterranean, deriving from the Latin (*natio*), are Italian (*nazione/natione*), Spanish (*nación*), Portuguese (*nação*), and French (*nation*). They all articulate this cross-linguistic and cross-cultural perception of the nation as a fixed collective identity. Eric Dursteler describes this as an "unofficial nation" in the eponymous chapter "The Unofficial Nation: Banditi, Schiavi, Greci" in Dursteler, *Venetians in Constantinople: Nation, Identity, and Coesistence in the Early Modern Mediterranean* (Baltimore, MD: Johns Hopkins University Press, 2006), 61–102.

[79] Benedict Anderson, *Imagined Communities* (London: Verso, 1991).

[80] On this question of using one's religious past to formulate a future identity, see Eric Dursteler, *Venetians in Constantinople* (Baltimore, MD: Johns Hopkins University Press,

tasks that would assuredly draw the ire of his former co-religionists. In essence, whether Eliano wanted to admit it or not, being a Jewish-born Jesuit in the very city where he converted, awaiting a ship to carry him to the Ottoman Empire, where he planned to evangelize, did not look innocuous to everyone. Given the deeply entangled ways in which individuals viewed, discussed, questioned, and verified conversion and apostasy in the golden age of the renegade, Eliano's life choices looked an awful lot like opportunism and dissimulation.[81]

This preoccupation with the ways in which his motivations were viewed continued during an unexpected postponement of their departure from Venice. During the delay, Eliano reassured Laínez of his dedication to the mission, as he and his companions "all travel with the same will and desire to work for Christ with which we left Rome." And as their departure approached, Eliano, Rodríguez, and Bravo "said confession and renewed our vows, and we have made other exhortations so that we may know the good that God and Your Paternity have done for us." Eliano expressed his gratitude for Laínez's mentorship and decision to send him on the mission through his "efforts according to all the virtues and observation of [the Society's] rules, so that Our Lord God may carry forth all that we desire for this mission."[82] There is something more here than a Jesuit reassuring his superior of the mission's viability. The context in which it took place – in Venice, the city of Eliano's conversion – compels us to rethink what seem like fairly typical declarations of a Jesuit missionary. By grappling with his religious journey, stating that he and his companions renewed their vows, and claiming that he possessed the same missionary fervor that had convinced Laínez to call the mission in the first place, Eliano was making a declaration of where he stood not simply as a Jesuit but along a spectrum of religious possibilities.

Eliano continued this show of loyalty to Laínez and the mission by explaining that they "will do what we must" to "observe the rules and constitutions of the Society ... since this pilgrimage is our college." He further hoped that eventually God would "deem it proper to give us a firm

2006), 23–40; E. Natalie Rothman, "Becoming Venetian: Conversion and Transformation in the Seventeenth-Century Mediterranean," *Mediterranean Historical Review* 21:1 (June 1, 2006): 39–75; E. Natalie Rothman, *Brokering Empire: Trans-Imperial Subjects Between Venice and Istanbul* (Ithaca, NY: Cornell University Press, 2012).

[81] Sanjay Subrahmanyam, *Three Ways to Be Alien: Travails and Encounters in the Early Modern World* (Waltham, MA: Brandeis University Press, 2011).

[82] ARSI, *Epp. NN 86*, fol. 83r./MPO 2, 76.

place in Cairo, and consequently in those lands many other houses and colleges."[83] This passage allows us to enter Eliano's mind in terms of how he desired to present himself as both a Jesuit and sincere convert. First, the reassurance that he and his companions "will do what we must" in their efforts to observe the *Constitutions*, the main set of objectives of the Society of Jesus as laid out by Ignatius himself, shows that Eliano felt the need to reassure his superior that no obstacle would stand in his way in his efforts.[84] Likewise, the expression "this pilgrimage is our college" echoes the Jesuit principle that they would go anywhere, at any time. It reflects Ignatius's belief, laid bare in the *Spiritual Exercises*, that religious experience was an introspective, meditative, and sensory one that took place as much between the ears as in dialogue with the outside world.[85]

It also repeats the sentiment of the famous expression of Ignatius's close associate, member of the so-called *Converso* Triumvirate, and reformer of Jesuit education whom Eliano had probably met, Jerome Nadal: "the world is our house."[86] Eliano had more at stake, however, than simply following orders. Rather, the words "mission," "journey," and "pilgrimage" were used almost interchangeably in the early decades of the Society because the missionary experience was as much an effort to reform others' souls as it was a journey for the missionary himself to reflect on his own religiosity.[87] Thus, for Eliano this necessarily included thinking about the role that his Jewish past played in his journey toward becoming a Catholic and a Jesuit.

Such reflection while he was stuck in Venice was not simply the product of Eliano's intellectual formation under Ignatius – it had much

---

[83] ARSI, *Epp. NN 86*, fol. 83r./*MPO* 2, 76.

[84] Ignatius Loyola, *The Constitutions of the Society of Jesus* (St. Louis, MO: Institute of Jesuit Sources, 1970).

[85] On religion and the senses, see Wietse de Boer and Christine Göttler, eds., *Religion and the Senses in Early Modern Europe* (Leiden: Brill, 2013). On the Jesuits in particular, see Jeffrey Chipps Smith, *Sensuous Worship: Jesuits and the Art of the Early Catholic Reformation in Germany* (Princeton, NJ: Princeton University Press, 2002); Robert John Clines, "By Virtue of the Senses: Ignatian Aestheticism and the Origins of Sense Application in the First Decades of the Gesù in Rome" (master's thesis, Miami University, 2009).

[86] Jonathan Wright, *God's Soldiers: Adventure Politics, Intrigue, and Power: A History of the Jesuits* (New York: Doubleday, 2004), 51.

[87] Luke Clossey, *Salvation and Globalization in the Early Jesuit Missions* (Cambridge: Cambridge University Press, 2008), 14. See also Adriano Prosperi, "L'Europa cristiana e il mondo: alle origini dell'idea di missione," *Dimensioni e problemi della ricerca storica* 2 (1992): 189–220.

more immediacy than that. Word on the street was that a number of Jews were displeased with his presence in the city, which compelled Rodríguez to restrict Eliano's movement.[88] And once they were able to board the ship for Alexandria on 20 September 1561, Rodríguez and Bravo found their shipboard lodgings, but Eliano was unable to join them until departure, because he "always stays inside so that he can remain better hidden from the Jews."[89] It is unclear who these Jews were, whether they were family members or simply Jews frustrated that he had become a Jesuit. Regardless, having to remain in hiding must have weighed heavily on Eliano, and must have given him occasion to dissect the ways that his Jewish past might derail the mission. His contemplation of the implications of his Jewishness hinges on how Eliano read Venice, not simply as a field for evangelization, but as the place where he renounced his family and faith. Hiding from the Jews of Venice compelled him to mull over both his daily exchanges with others as well as with the physical souvenirs of his conversion. Venice was home to the tokens of a world he had left behind: sites, languages, people, and neighborhoods of his religious past. But that religious past still existed as the seed out of which he grew into a Catholic.

Generally speaking, it is assumed that the lion's share of scrutiny of Jewish converts, as in the case of Marc'Antonio degli Eletti and the Inquisition, came from fellow Christians.[90] And Eliano was surely attempting to present himself in the best light before Laínez and Pius. At this moment, however, Eliano's forced sequester points to how converts also faced pressures from their former religious kinsmen who questioned converts' – or, as they saw them, apostates' – motives and sincerity, especially given the perception that Jewish converts to Catholicism used their former faiths to excel in their new ones. This was clearly the case for Eliano, as well as his brother; Vittorio was using the education that he received from their grandfather in the employ of the Catholic Church as a censor of Hebrew books.[91]

---

[88] Alastair Hamilton, *The Copts and the West, 1439–1822: The European Discovery of the Egyptian Church* (Oxford: Oxford University Press, 2006), 59.

[89] ARSI, *Epp. NN.* 86, fol. 86rv./*MPO* 2, 80.

[90] E. Natalie Rothman, *Brokering Empire: Trans-Imperial Subjects Between Venice and Istanbul* (Ithaca, NY: Cornell University Press, 2012), 157–62.

[91] For more on religious ambiguity, especially concerning the amalgam of friction points between Christianity and Judaism from the perspective of Jews, see David B. Ruderman, *Early Modern Jewry: A New Cultural History* (Princeton, NJ: Princeton University Press, 2010), 159–89. For the role of Jewish converts in the censorship of Hebrew

A few precautionary words from Rodríguez before departure exposed further uneasiness, and show that this mission faced numerous challenges, including keeping Eliano's true identity under wraps. Rodríguez informed Laínez that accompanying his previous letter from 13 September was a crib sheet, *ad cautelam* (for precaution), containing codes for various terms, lest suspicious eyes uncover the more sensitive details of the mission.[92] Compounded by fears of having Eliano exposed as a former Jew (and, to a lesser extent, Rodríguez as a *converso*), using code allowed the Jesuits to communicate candidly but clandestinely with Laínez and Pius, lest the missionaries find themselves imperiled. The inclusion of the Latin expression *ad cautelam* encapsulates the Jesuits' outlook and Eliano's state of mind as he proceeded to return to Egypt, this time as a Christian: while they might have believed that they were serving God, they nevertheless understood that even the slightest misstep or leak of information could have negative consequences. Most important of all was ensuring that Eliano not run into issues with anyone who might have reason to obstruct the mission because of Eliano's convert status. They embraced their duty, but still shared some of the angst that Laínez held about the prospects for the mission, in part because of their Jewish legacy.

The hope was that departing for Alexandria would allow Eliano time to collect himself and leave all of this behind him. However, the Venetian Senate was reluctant to dispatch a flotilla with foreigners aboard because of the Ottomans' refusal to condemn corsairs who seized non-Venetians who were not protected by the Capitulations of 1540 that ended the Ottoman-Venetian war for Corfù. As a result, departure was delayed

---

books – including Vittorio Eliano – see Amnon Raz-Krakotzkin, *The Censor, the Editor, and the Text: The Catholic Church and the Shaping of the Jewish Canon in the Sixteenth Century* (Philadelphia: University of Pennsylvania Press, 2007). This so-called expertise of one's past faith would have also been the case for Muslim converts to Christianity. See Natalie Zemon Davis, *Trickster Travels: A Sixteenth-Century Muslim Between Worlds* (New York: Hill and Wang, 2006).

[92] ARSI, *Epp. NN 86*, fols. 87r–88v./*MPO* 2, 82. While the letter from 13 September from Rodríguez to Laínez is now lost, the code itself has survived and is inventoried as ARSI, *Fondo Gesuitico 678/21/4*. It contains code names for the missionaries, geographic locations, Ottoman and European officials in Egypt, Greeks, Jews, and even doctrinal matters like the Sacraments, Purgatory, the Filioque clause of the Creed, and the observation of the Sabbath. For example, "The Roman Church" is "house," and "Rome" is "vineyard." My personal favorite code name is for "The Turks": "our brother friends." See also *MPO* 2, 47–49 for a published version of the code.

even further.[93] Then, a torrential storm blocked all ships from leaving the lagoon. Finally, on 24 September, they received word that departure was imminent, perhaps by the end of the month. A week later, on 1 October, they set sail.[94] Departing Venice, however, did not prove to be the respite that Eliano had desired.

GOING ABROAD AS A JEWISH JESUIT: ELIANO'S JOURNEY TO EGYPT

While Eliano might have hoped that he had abandoned his issues regarding the Jews in Venice, it did not take long to reckon that the galley was a veritable floating Venice. Rodríguez related to Laínez that "there are many men on the ship, Jews, Greeks, Renegades and many Turks; but we do not work with them, as we observe the order of Your Paternity and [Papal Secretary] Monsignor Fioribello, but also because there is no hope of doing anything with them."[95] Instead, Rodríguez explained that he, Eliano, and Bravo prayed every day "for the Church, the Supreme Pontiff, the council, the cardinals and prelates and the clergy, the religious, the Society, the reduction of heretics, infidels, schismatics, and for our mission, and for other things for which we are obliged."[96] That is not to say Rodríguez would have refused any who came to confess to him or even embrace Catholicism. The problem was, as far as Rodríguez saw it,

---

[93] ARSI, *Epp. NN 86*, fol. 85r./*MPO* 2, 78. The fear of enslavement of Christians at the hands of Turkish and Barbary corsairs was quite high by the late sixteenth century, as the Venetian fleet was not nearly what it had been 100 years prior. Moreover, this time period (especially after the Battle of Lepanto in 1571, though this is debated as well) saw the decline of the Turkish fleet and the rise of piracy and Christian slavery. For more on Christian slavery, see Robert Davis, *Christian Slaves, Muslim Masters: White Slavery in the Mediterranean, the Barbary Coast, and Italy, 1500–1800* (New York: Palgrave Macmillan, 2003), and Davis, *Holy War and Human Bondage: Tales of Christian-Muslim Slavery in the Early-Modern Mediterranean* (Santa Barbara, CA: Praeger/ABC-CLIO, 2009). For investigations of the relative decline of the Ottoman navy (and Mediterranean navies and galley warfare in general) after Lepanto, see John F. Guilmartin, *Gunpowder and Galleys: Changing Technology and Mediterranean Warfare at Sea in the Sixteenth Century* (Cambridge: Cambridge University Press, 1974) and Guilmartin, "Ideology and Conflict: The Wars of the Ottoman Empire, 1453–1606," *Journal of Interdisciplinary History* 18:4 (Spring 1988): 721–47.

[94] Rodríguez explains on 30 September that they would leave the following day: ARSI, *Epp. NN 86*, fol. 90rv./*MPO* 2, 85. The departure of the ship from Venice on 1 October 1561 was verified in two letters. See ARSI, *Ital. 119*, fol. 136rv./*MPO* 2, 85 and ARSI, *Epp. NN 86*, fol. 93r./*MPO* 2, 87.

[95] ARSI, *Epp. NN 86*, fol. 93r./*MPO* 2, 87.   [96] ARSI, *Epp. NN 86*, fol. 93r./*MPO* 2, 87.

whether any potential convert could be trusted given the pervasiveness of renegadism. This was particularly the case with one individual who had once been Christian but had "succumbed to the danger of turning Turk." While Rodríguez wanted to help this young man in his return to the faith, "it was quite difficult to forgive him."[97] He also feared letting Eliano's presence be too well known, an admission that evangelization was as much about zeal as it was pragmatism.

Despite orders from Laínez, and even in spite of Rodríguez's doubts concerning whether their shipmates could be converted, Eliano could not help but obsess over the Jews aboard the ship, an important step toward Eliano's seeing this mission as about more than converting the Copts: "I deeply desired to remain unknown because of what I used to be, so I did not speak about the faith in Hebrew or with the Jews." However, Eliano felt that keeping silent allowed the Jews to stew in their ignorance, leaving him "in a constant state of mortification as I desired to speak to the Jews, to convince them of their falsity, to teach them the truth of the Christian faith, to hear the many insults that they always say against the faith and against those who leave Judaism." Eliano also took these insults personally, as he believed that the Jews' attacks on Christianity were "against me to hurt me, knowing that I hear them but – at least so it seems to them – do not have the ardor to reply. But God is the true judge, and he will lift them from that perverse obstinacy."[98]

Eliano's candidness here points to his preoccupation with his religious past in a way unique to him among the Jesuits. But it also reflects his internal struggle between fear of exposure that would jeopardize the mission on one hand and mortification at such a missed opportunity to convert the Jews on the other. While this ship was carrying him to Egypt to convert the Copts, it was a microcosm of his experiences in Venice, and he obsessed over converting Jews to prove that he was no longer Jewish. There is an ironic level of obstinacy in this, as Eliano seems to be more concerned with proving that he is not Jewish than in following orders. While the two are obviously not mutually exclusive, Eliano was cautious about any questions tied to his status as a former Jew, mainly because he was preoccupied with the Jews' accusations that he was an apostate and an opportunist.

Eliano's concern with the place of conversion in interactions between Christians and Jews did not stop there. He met two youths on the ship

[97] ARSI, *Epp. NN 86*, fol. 98v./*MPO* 2, 104.
[98] ARSI, *Epp. NN 86*, fol. 212v./*MPO* 2, 99.

who lived "under Jewish names; one was named Joseph, the other Solomon; but it was already known aboard the ship that they had previously been baptized." Eliano was comforted by other Christians' actions, for "between kindness, rebuffs from other Christians, and even threats such as those telling them that 'If I find that you have returned to Judaism, I will have you killed,' they were so thoroughly reduced that one confessed to me on the ship, and the other was unable to collect himself because of the rebukes of the Christians." The issue, however, was that, despite their desire to live as Christians, "they were insulted and teased and threatened by the Jews," which compelled them to live outwardly as Jews but inwardly as Christians.[99]

Eliano felt no need to hide just how hard it was to be a convert, how real were the long-term struggles for neophytes attempting to transition into their new faiths, and how immediate were the pressures to conform or renege on one's conversion. When juxtaposed with his desire to out himself as a former Jew in the name of converting the Jews after he believed they were insulting him, his reflection on these two youths exposes that Eliano wanted to position himself as uniquely equipped in preventing baptized Jews from apostatizing and protecting new Christians from their former co-religionists' insults. Despite being sent to Egypt to work with the Copts, he felt that his work as a Jewish-born Jesuit should include converting other Jews and protecting neophytes from their detractors. By couching it fully in the language of the conversion struggle, Eliano lays bare his own preoccupation with his conversion and the toll it could take on his psyche.

This realization on Eliano's part – as well as his forthrightness in sharing this deliberation with fellow Jesuits – reminds us that his superiors and peers saw his Jewish past as a potential asset because all recognized conversion as a complex process laden with the burden of belonging and the temptations of lapsing. His own religious journey and his confrontation with it in Venice and on a Venetian ship were proof of his unique ability to help converts in their movement toward full acceptance into the faith. And he deemed it necessary to remind fellow Catholics how useful this skill was, especially given Rodríguez's inability to gauge whether potential converts could be trusted, to say nothing of the fact that he knew no Arabic. And while Bravo seems to have known some Arabic, he was the most junior. This left Eliano with the overwhelming responsibility

---

[99] ARSI, *Epp. NN 86*, fol. 212r./*MPO 2*, 97.

of communicating with locals in Egypt and ensuring that all documents were translated efficiently, not to mention correctly.

Being thrust into such a position of responsibility surely put the newly ordained Eliano in a trying position: he was propelled to the fore of the mission as its main conduit of communication because he had been to Egypt and knew Arabic. But he learned it while he was Jewish, a reminder that his Jewishness would always play a central role in formulating his Jesuit identity. His reflections aboard the ship reveal that he would have to come to terms with exactly what it meant to be a Jewish-born Jesuit and the many layers that comprised the tumultuous religious landscape of the early modern Mediterranean: linguistic polyvalence, an assortment of nations and faiths, individuals' attempts to categorize each other, and individuals' desires to express where they belonged along the religio-cultural spectrum of the Mediterranean. Eliano's journey from Jew to Christian neophyte to Jesuit missionary, and the impossibility of divorcing those identities from one another, rendered him a go-between through whom we see conversion – his and others' – as a friction point where individuals interacted, performed their religious identities, and shifted the borders of their respective faiths. And for figures like Eliano, their religious identities were precarious, fragile, and potential sources for their own undoing.

CONCLUSION

The first thirty-two years of Eliano's life had taught him that movements within, between, and across faiths were hardly ever without issue. He was born to Eastern European Jews in Rome; he had to learn to navigate the Venetian Ghetto at seven years old; he spent time in Germany and the Ottoman Empire learning the ins and outs of the Jewish diaspora, book production, and pan-Mediterranean commerce; he went from disillusioned rabbi-in-training to warmly welcomed neophyte to Jesuit priest; he returned to Venice as a Jesuit and attempted to use his Jewishness as proof of his unique ability to convince any and all to embrace Catholicism. He must have thought that, if he could stay firm in his efforts with the Copts, he would succeed in Egypt.

But as the next chapter shows, this would not be the case. In fact, Eliano would first face this reality at the next port of call, the Venetian island of Zakynthos, off the coast of the Greek Morea.[100] While there, the

---

[100] ARSI, *Epp. NN 86*, fol. 94r./*MPO 2*, 89.

Jesuits encountered a group of Ethiopian Copts who were less than receptive to the Jesuits' overtures. Eliano found the Ethiopians' rites and practices rather odd; and their irreverence toward the papacy and the institutions of the church offended Eliano. One Ethiopian was particularly adamant about his beliefs, and even told the Jesuits that they were evil for their blasphemous and inexcusable loyalty to the man who was nothing more than the bishop of Rome. The Jesuits were shocked by such insolence. Despite Eliano's claim that they were amicable toward them, the Ethiopians on Zakynthos were openly hostile, and accused Eliano, Rodríguez, and Bravo of being depraved heathens, intent on corrupting true believers with a false form of Christianity.[101] If this encounter were any indication of things to come, then the Copts in Egypt would be equally obstinate, and Laínez's misgivings regarding the mission would come to fruition. This disorienting experience forced Eliano to reevaluate how they would proceed with the Copts of Egypt, who might be just as hostile as these Ethiopians, even more so. More pointedly, it would portend Eliano's failure to convert the Copts, something for which he believed he was uniquely skilled.

Moreover, the next chapter also serves as a poignant reminder that religious identities were vigorously defended against conversion and apostasy in such everyday interactions as this one. But this intransigence would not come from the Copts alone. Rather, if there were anything that should have signaled to Eliano the way his return to Egypt would unfold, it was his sequester in Venice and his struggles to remain silent aboard the ship despite the Jews' taunts and mockery. Eliano would soon find that the pressures he faced as a Jewish convert would be more pronounced in Egypt than they were in Venice. And this is because Egypt was home to his deceased father's creditors as well as Jewish family members, who were, in his own words, "infamous" for having Christian kin.

---

[101] ARSI, *Epp. NN 86*, fol. 94rv./*MPO* 2, 89–90.

2

Jesuit Missionary or Jewish Renegade? Eliano's Confrontation with His Jewish Past

Concerning my mother: neither do I desire to speak to her, nor does she want to see me. As it has been told to me, she said that she did not want me to come here, as she thinks that having a Christian son is against her honor. And so, we agree: 'Woe unto them who call evil good, and good evil.'[1]

         – Giovanni Battista Eliano to Diego Laínez

Several Jews have begun to give us grief, falsely demanding ancient debts, which they say that [Eliano] owes them, as he was a Jew and a Moor in various times ... to threaten him and get what they want, they say that ... he should be tried by the law of the Turks, according to which he should be obliged to turn Turk or be burned.[2]

         – Cristóbal Rodríguez (written by Eliano) to Diego Laínez

At first glance, the logistics and planning of Eliano's work with the Copts suggest that it was like any other Jesuit mission. It required strong leadership and theological acumen, hence the choice of the theology professor and administrator Cristóbal Rodríguez as superior and papal nuncio.[3] In addition to his position as papal nuncio, Rodríguez was given the juridical authority of a Jesuit provincial, which included the power to open colleges in Egypt on the model of those throughout Europe.[4]

---

[1] ARSI, *Epp. NN 86*, fol. 211r./MPO 2, 94.
[2] ARSI, *Epp. NN 86*, fol. 114r./MPO 2, 133.
[3] ARSI, *Gall. 98 I*, fol. 9v./MPO 2, 39–40.
[4] ARSI, *Gall. 98 I*, fol. 10v./MPO 2, 42. For more on Jesuit colleges and educational foundations, see Filippo Iappelli, ed., *Alle origini dell'università dell'Aquila: cultura, università, collegi gesuitici all'inizio dell'età moderna in Italia meridionale: Atti del convegno internazionale ... L'Aquila, 8–11 Novembre 1995* (Rome: Institutum Historicum S.I., 2000); Maurizio Sangalli, *Università, accademie, gesuiti: cultura e*

With these powers, the Jesuits were to extend the reach of the church; and beyond anything else, the Jesuits should stress doctrinal reform and participation in the Sacraments.[5] Of course, Diego Laínez explained, "Among dogmas, the first issue ... is the primacy of Saint Peter and his successors," that is to say, compelling the Copts to submit to Pius.[6] These directives would not have been out of place on any Jesuit mission to the Americas or Goa.

However, this mission's success would hinge on more than Rodríguez's theological prowess or his and Eliano's ability to convince the Copts of the errors of their ways through a doctrinal tutorial and an emphasis on papal primacy. Rather, as Laínez told Francisco Borja, the mission would depend on Eliano: "He has spent time in much of that country and he knows Arabic" because of his experiences as a merchant there in his teens.[7] Laínez and others saw this as the ideal way to convince the Copts to embrace Catholicism. After all, it was Ignatius and Laínez who supported and mentored Eliano when he joined the Society of Jesus, and – as his burning of the Talmud as a neophyte showed – he was willing to do whatever he was asked.[8] But that does not mean that everyone agreed with Ignatius and Laínez that Eliano wanted to convert the Copts because of his dedication to the Society's apostolic mission. And this would become manifest throughout his time in Egypt, as evidenced by Eliano

---

religione a Padova tra Cinque e Seicento (Trieste: LINT, 2001); Luca Testa, *Fondazione e primo sviluppo del Seminario Romano (1565–1608)* (Rome: Pontificia Università Gregoriana, 2002); Manfred Hinz and Danillo Zardin, eds., *I gesuiti e la Ratio Studiorum* (Rome: Bulzoni Editore, 2004); Paul F. Grendler, *The University of Mantua, the Gonzaga & the Jesuits, 1584–1630* (Baltimore, MD: Johns Hopkins University Press, 2009).

[5] ARSI, *Gall. 98 I*, fol. 10v./MPO 2, 40–1.

[6] ARSI, *Institut. 187*, fol. 52v./MPO 2, 45. For more on papal primacy, see Klaus Schatz, *Papal Primacy: From Its Origins to the Present* (Collegeville, MN: Liturgical Press, 1996).

[7] ARSI, *Hisp. 98*, fols. 335v–336r. Alastair Hamilton suggests that although Rodríguez seemed a logical choice, in retrospect it was an "unfortunate" one because Rodríguez "knew no Arabic and had little experience of travel. He was above all a schoolmaster and a dogmatist – a combination which would prove ill-suited to a mission of such delicacy." But this ignores Rodríguez's administrative skills, which were integral to the mission. It also downplays Eliano's previous time in Egypt. See Hamilton, *The Copts and the West, 1439–1822: The European Discovery of the Egyptian Church* (Oxford: Oxford University Press, 2006), 58–9.

[8] While it seems sincere, Laínez in particular was hard pressed to believe him. After all, he too was a *converso*. See Robert Maryks, "'A True Israelite in Whom There Is Nothing False': The Controversy over the Jewish Ancestry of Diego Laínez," in *Diego Laínez (1512–1565) and His Generalate,* ed. Paul Oberholzer (Rome: Bibliotheca Instituti Historici Societatis Iesu, 2015), 424–7.

and Rodríguez's correspondence with fellow Jesuits, above all with Laínez, the majority of which is in Eliano's hand.[9]

This is because many of the Jews he encountered on this mission – including family members – believed he was an apostate, an opportunist, and a renegade who employed the skills sharpened in his youth to serve Catholicism, to the detriment of Judaism. And this warranted retribution. From his arrival in Alexandria on 4 November 1561 to his return to Rome two years later, Eliano was compelled to face the reality that coming to terms with his Jewish past hinged on confronting his former co-religionists, his family included, and combating their accusations of renegadism. In his interactions with others, he continually had to lay bare the boundaries between his Jewish past and Jesuit present even though these two realities could never fully be disentangled because both were central to his identity as well as his evangelizing efforts. This is not to say that his attempts to bifurcate his Jewish and Catholic identities were fictive representations; however sincere he may have been, some would always look upon him with skepticism and his past was something he could never escape.

Proving he was no longer Jewish despite the centrality of his Jewishness to his Catholic identity thus remained central to how he represented himself to others. This reality is best encapsulated in Laínez's directive to limit interactions with Jews and to "guard yourselves against [your identities] being discovered by them and then having to contend with them."[10] Laínez wanted to ensure that Eliano's family's presence and

---

[9] Rodríguez signed the letters, as he was the mission's superior. However, they are overwhelmingly in Eliano's hand and contain personal information that suggests that Eliano wrote the letters with Rodríguez's approval and final signature. Eliano also wrote his own correspondences with Laínez and with former colleagues at the Collegio Romano.

[10] ARSI, *Institut. 187*, fol. 53r./*MPO* 2, 46. For more on Ottoman Jews and their relationship with Ottoman officials, see David B. Ruderman, *Early Modern Jewry: A New Cultural History* (Princeton, NJ: Princeton University Press, 2010), especially 26–9, 81–5. For more on the Jewish-*converso* legacy (Muslim-*morisco* as well), see the various contributions in Kevin Ingram, ed., *The Conversos and Moriscos in Late Medieval Spain and Beyond* (Leiden: Brill, 2009). See also François Soyer, *The Persecution of the Jews and Muslims of Portugal: King Manuel I and the End of Religious Tolerance (1496–7)* (Leiden: Brill, 2007). For the Judeo-Spanish experience in the Ottoman world, see Annette Benaim, *Sixteenth-Century Judeo-Spanish Testimonies: An Edition of Eighty-Four Testimonies from the Sephardic Responsa in the Ottoman Empire* (Leiden: Brill, 2012). For the relationship of Christians and Jews in the Ottoman Empire, see Bruce Alan Masters, *Christians and Jews in the Ottoman Arab World: The Roots of Sectarianism* (Cambridge: Cambridge University Press, 2001), 68–97. While Masters covers a period beginning forty years after the current mission under

his status as a convert would not become a problem for the mission or for Eliano's safety. As Eliano's letters will show, he was torn: on one hand, he desired to serve the Society and prove his dedication to the faith via the skills he had sharpened in his Jewish youth; on the other, he feared that, should accusations of renegadism lead to an actual attack, the reason he was chosen for the mission – his Jewishness – could very well be the mission's undoing.[11]

ELIANO'S EARLY CONFRONTATIONS WITH HIS JEWISH PAST

Shortly after the Jesuits arrived in Alexandria on 4 November 1561, Eliano set off for Cairo to engage in preliminary talks with Patriarch Gabriel while Rodríguez and Bravo secured protection and assistance from European diplomats and merchants in Alexandria. In a letter to Laínez, written in Cairo on 12 November, Eliano discussed his unease in traveling alone from Alexandria to Cairo, as he was concerned that "I would have been easily recognized by the Jews." To keep his identity under wraps, he traveled with a group of Christian merchants.[12] Upon his arrival, Eliano was a guest in the home of the Venetian Consul, Lunardo Emo; while there, Eliano said Mass for Emo and his Catholic merchant associates.[13]

After spending some time in Emo's company, Eliano set out to meet Gabriel in early November 1561. In their first meeting, Eliano and Gabriel discussed the Jesuits' joy in having safely arrived in Egypt, and Gabriel was pleased to hear of Abraham's positive experience in Rome.[14] However warm these greetings might have been, Eliano was concerned about two issues that could affect the mission – namely, the Copts' resistance to Catholic doctrine and his Jewish past. These anxieties tell us much about Eliano's frame of mind coming off the experiences with both the Ethiopians and the Jews during his travels in Venetian lands, as well as how this first mission was to be a key element of Eliano's efforts to make sense of his Jewishness. Eliano explained to Laínez that "truly it will be a bit difficult in the beginning ... but who will be able to stand against

---

investigation, he offers important insights into how Europeans, Eastern Rite Christians, Jews, and Muslims co-mingled and navigated their cultural differences.

[11]   MHSI, *Polanci complementa*, II, p. 628; ARSI, *Epp. NN 86*, fol. 71rv.; ARSI, *Epp. NN 86*, fol. 72rv.

[12]   ARSI, *Epp. NN 86*, fol. 210r./MPO 2, 92.   [13]   Ibid.

[14]   ARSI, *Epp. NN 86*, fol. 210v./MPO 2, 92–3.

our Lord God, and his holy church, and his faithful ministers? I pray therefore, as I believe that Your Paternity will not miss the opportunity to pray with warmth for this very important mission."[15] In an attempt to assuage his superior's concerns (and perhaps his own), Eliano pointed to his belief that, as one of God's and the church's faithful ministers, Eliano could ultimately overcome his personal obstacles and convince the Copts to acquiesce to his overtures of union.

On one hand, this is in lockstep with the typical rhetoric that pervades Jesuit missionary letters and the immediate issues that missions faced;[16] on the other hand, Eliano's experiences with the Jews in Venice's maritime empire point to his ambiguous status as a convert. This comes through when he relayed to Laínez on 12 November, barely a week after arriving in Egypt, that he had learned that an unnamed family member "recognized me without me knowing it was him; early this morning, the [Venetian] consul [Emo], to ensure that [this relative] not expose me, ordered him to appear, asking him if he knew me."[17] As we saw in Chapter 1, Eliano's family had relocated to Egypt permanently in the late 1540s because of his father's business ventures, but also perhaps because of the increased pressures Jews faced in the Papal States.[18]

---

[15] ARSI, *Epp. NN 86*, fol. 210v./*MPO* 2, 93.

[16] Issues of fluidity in the Mediterranean, particularly in religion, are important to bear in mind here. Maria Fusaro explains that the early modern Mediterranean was a "world whose keywords are exchange and fluidity, where the frontiers between empires and states, cultures and religions were ever permeable." See Maria Fusaro, "After Braudel: A Reassessment of Mediterranean History between the Northern Invasion and the *Caravane Maritime*," in *Trade and Cultural Exchange in the Early Modern Mediterranean: Braudel's Maritime Legacy*, ed. Maria Fusaro, Colin Heywood, and Mohamed-Salah Omri (London: Tauris Academic Studies, 2010), 1–22. Likewise, Jerry Brotton explains that "nation states and emerging global empires set the political agenda, and the fluidity of religious encounters and exchanges between east and west had hardened into the programmatic belief systems of Catholicism, Protestantism, and Islam. This signalled the birth of the modern institution of the state and the concomitant rise of nationalism." See Jerry Brotton, *The Renaissance Bazaar: From the Silk Road to Michelangelo* (Oxford: Oxford University Press, 2010), 122. See also Molly Greene, *A Shared World: Christians and Muslims in the Early Modern Mediterranean* (Princeton, NJ: Princeton University Press, 2000), 78–109. This fluidity in religious identity has also been extended to gendered elements of non-Christians, particularly Muslims. see Joseph Allen Boone, *The Homoerotics of Orientalism* (New York: University of Columbia Press, 2014).

[17] ARSI, *Epp. NN 86*, fol. 211r./*MPO* 2, 94.

[18] David Berger, "*Cum Nimis Absurdum* and the Conversion of the Jews," *The Jewish Quarterly Review* 70:1 (July 1, 1979): 41–9; Daniele Santarelli, *Il papato di Paolo IV nella crisi politico-religiosa del cinquecento* (Rome: Aracne editrice, 2008). On Moze, see *MPO* 4, 440.

This relative explained to Emo that he did know who Eliano was and that he had spoken to Eliano's widowed mother concerning her son's presence in Cairo.[19] This troubled Emo, who "kept me in hiding." There was some relief when another relative "doubted that anything would come of it." Despite his family's potential challenge to his identity, Eliano waxed rhetorical: "'If God is for us, who is against us?' And all the more so, the consul is on our side. Also, the Jews here do not have much authority, so they say."[20] At this moment, Eliano attempted to downplay any plots against him by suggesting that the Jews were politically impotent. Furthermore, Eliano informed Laínez that his Jewish family members were uninterested in bringing attention to themselves, lest they be shamed for having a Christian relative. One family member was particularly keen to avoid any scandal: "Concerning my mother: neither do I desire to speak to her, nor does she want to see me. As it has been told to me, she said that she did not want me to come here, as she thinks that having a Christian son is against her honor. And so, we agree: 'Woe unto them who call evil good, and good evil.'"[21]

Despite attempting to downplay his Jewish past, it was clearly a source of great bewilderment, as his claim that he did not wish to speak to his family suggests that he desired to convince Laínez that his only focus was his work with the Copts. And the two scriptural passages he quotes in this letter, Romans 8:31 ("If God is for us, who is against us?") and Isaiah 5:20 ("Woe unto them who call evil good, and good evil") are oppositional and hostile toward anyone unwilling to accept Eliano's Christian identity. By attempting to assuage any fear that his Jewish family could impede the mission, he unconsciously betrayed how much it informed his sense of self. This dilemma over his conversion and family struggle compelled him to write to fellow Jesuits in Rome that same November: "I have found some of my family members here, both Jews and those who were made Christian; but I wish that I had not found them." He also assured his fellow Jesuits that their presence was no obstacle, but a test of faith that he would overcome: "Yet still, even from this God will find fruit for his glory."[22] For now, hoping that his Jewish past was behind him, he turned his focus to the Copts.

---

[19] Eliano never says when his father had died.
[20] ARSI, *Epp. NN 86*, fol. 211r./MPO 2, 94.   [21] Ibid.
[22] ARSI, *Epp. NN 86*, fol. 213r./MPO 2, 101–2.

ELIANO'S EFFORTS WITH THE COPTS

Soon after Eliano wrote these letters concerning his struggles with his Jewish relatives, Rodríguez and Bravo joined him in Cairo. The three spent the rest of November discussing matters of union with the patriarch and leading Coptic theologians. Eliano and Rodríguez felt that Gabriel was receptive to some sort of communion with Rome but remained reluctant to accept papal primacy or to send a delegation to Trent.[23] After nearly two months of discussion, Gabriel agreed to send representatives to the council, perhaps in the following year.[24] Aside from this, the Jesuits had other reasons to be hopeful. The Copts welcomed them and gave them great liberty in observing their rites and customs.[25] Some Copts were also open to teaching Arabic to Rodríguez and Bravo.[26]

In addition to Emo's support and Gabriel's agreement to send a delegation to Trent, December saw the French consul Guillaume Gardiolles ease the Jesuits' fears regarding their safety: he procured a janissary – one of the elite soldiers of the Ottoman Empire – to be the Jesuits' personal bodyguard.[27] Gardiolles and the patriarch were also on friendly terms, and he used his influence with Gabriel to convince him that the Jesuits desired to serve the Copts' spiritual needs, and that the Copts should let the Jesuits remain among the community.[28] This was a needed push, as Gabriel remained unsure if he could trust the Jesuits or if their presence would cause concern among the Armenians and the Syriac Orthodox Church of Antioch (colloquially known as the Jacobites), with whom the Copts were in autocephalous communion.[29]

There were other challenges regarding the Copts' willingness to work with the Jesuits. For one, Eliano noticed that the Copts seemed fearful of Kara Şahin Mustafa Pasha, the governor of Egypt.[30] Ostensibly, he was supposed to execute the will of the sultan, Suleiman, which included the

---

[23] ARSI, *Epp. NN 86*, fol. 104r./*MPO* 2, 108–9.

[24] ARSI, *Epp. NN 86*, fol. 104r./*MPO* 2, 109.

[25] ARSI, *Epp. NN 86*, fol. 110r./*MPO* 2, 112.   [26] Ibid.

[27] ARSI, *Epp. NN 86*, fol. 109r.*MPO* 2, 120.

[28] ARSI, *Epp. NN 86*, fol. 111r./*MPO* 2, 114. Janissaries, originally the elite bodyguards of the sultan, were normally Balkan Christian slaves pressed into military service and trained from their youth. For more on Janissaries in Ottoman Egypt, see Andre Raymond, "Soldiers in Trade: The Case of Ottoman Cairo," *British Journal of Middle Eastern Studies* 18:1 (1991): 16–37. This letter is also copied and inventoried as ARSI, *Epp. NN 86*, fols. 102r–103v.

[29] ARSI, *Epp. NN 86*, fol. 112r./*MPO* 2, 129.

[30] In their correspondence, Eliano often referred to him as Semin Ali Pasha. Semin appears to be a Latinization of Şahin.

protection of religious minorities. And given the centuries of coexistence between Christians and Muslims in Egypt that the Ottomans inherited from the Mamluks when they conquered Egypt in 1517, this generally was the case, as the Ottomans often went to great lengths to protect the rights of their religious minorities.[31] However, while it is unclear whether Gabriel speciously claimed this to convince the Jesuits to assist him, Gabriel suggested that in practice the pasha tended to rule autocratically with little regard for policies coming from Constantinople; further, the pasha was purportedly inimical toward the Coptic community given that he favored the economically prosperous Greeks, and he feared any ties between Europeans and indigenous Christians under his rule.[32] Gabriel therefore seemed unwilling to do much that would draw the pasha's ire, which included working too closely with Catholics.[33]

After a month of discussions, Eliano believed that the patriarch was dissimulating and accusing the pasha of tyranny as a pretense to avoid talks of union: "But [Gabriel] has the voice of Jacob and the hands of Esau, because he always replies that he has the will [to discuss union], but then he gives many excuses and impediments, especially the fear of many [Copts] who oftentimes give him offense and condemn him before the pasha" for showing any interest in working with the Jesuits.[34] Such division within the Coptic community and the use of purported Ottoman oppression to deceive the Jesuits laid bare the Copts' own internal issues as well as Gabriel's own tenuous position within the community.[35] This suggested to the Jesuits that the Copts' overtures of

[31] Michael Winter, *Egyptian Society Under Ottoman Rule, 1517–1798* (London: Routledge, 1992), 193–218.

[32] Michael Winter, *Egyptian Society Under Ottoman Rule, 1517–1798* (London: Routledge, 1992), 31–6. On the pasha, Winter explains that "central Ottoman government gave him complete authority, which is reflected even in the structure and phrasing of imperial edicts. Although formally the edicts express the sultan's personal wish concerning even the most trifling matters, such as a raise in the pay of a common soldier, the decrees in fact confirm the pasha's proposals" (31–2). On the Greeks in the Ottoman realm, see Tom Papademetriou, *Render unto the Sultan Power, Authority, and the Greek Orthodox Church in the Early Ottoman Centuries* (Oxford: Oxford University Press, 2015).

[33] Tensions between the Copts, the Ottomans, and the local Muslim population of Egypt were quite normal, given that the Copts were technically a protected minority, but were nevertheless distrusted by local populations offended by their religious practices. One case in particular – a Coptic pilgrimage to Jerusalem – stands out. See Febe Armanios, *Coptic Christianity in Ottoman Egypt* (Oxford: Oxford University Press, 2011), 91–115.

[34] ARSI, *Epp. NN 86*, fol. 112r./*MPO* 2, 129.

[35] This is particularly the case in the struggles between the clergy and the community's lay leaders, known as archons. For a brief introduction to this, see Febe Armanios, *Coptic*

union were not sincere, or they were divided on how far they were willing to work with Catholics.

In late January 1562, as Eliano grew frustrated over Gabriel's nearly two months of balks, an unnamed Copt was leaning toward converting to Islam. Gabriel, ever cognizant of Ottoman prohibitions on apostasy from Islam as well as the pasha's allegedly negative views of the Copts, claimed that attempting to prevent or reverse a conversion to Islam would put him and the convert in danger, as punishment could include the execution of both men.[36] Gabriel presented this as a direct threat to the community and, by extension, his authority. While Christian conversions to Islam were rarely coerced, socio-economic and cultural pressures had caused intermittent conversions to Islam over the centuries.[37] With Copts unevenly disbursed throughout Egypt, Ethiopia, and other locales such as Cyprus, Gabriel intimated that he could not sit idly by and watch the slow disintegration of his community through conversion to Islam.

Almost immediately, "the patriarch was condemned to the judge of the Turks for having prevented a Christian from turning Turk. And while we have begged him many times to let us carry out our work, he delays it by saying 'the first day of Lent we will go to the Desert of Saint Anthony, where we will have space to work without perturbation.'"[38] There is

---

Christianity in Ottoman Egypt (Oxford: Oxford University Press, 2011), and on the background to the archons in particular, see 26–31.

[36] Reneged conversions to and from Islam and subsequent martyrdom are the subject of "Between the Turban and the Papal Tiara: Orthodox Christian Neomartyrs and Their Impresarios in the Age of Confessionalization," the fifth chapter of Tijana Krstić, *Contested Conversions to Islam: Narratives of Religious Change in the Early Modern Ottoman Empire* (Stanford, CA: Stanford University Press, 2011), 121–42. Likewise, "Championing a Communal Ethos: The Neo-Martyrdom of St. Salib in the Sixteenth Century," the second chapter of Febe Armanios's recent work, demonstrates how these martyr stories functioned as means of communal solidarity in the face of Ottoman authoritarianism and even Catholic efforts at unity. See Febe Armanios, *Coptic Christianity in Ottoman Egypt* (Oxford: Oxford University Press, 2011), 41–64. On conversion to Islam as an aspect of Ottoman statecraft, see Marc David Baer, *Honored by the Glory of Islam: Conversion and Conquest in Ottoman Europe* (New York: Oxford University Press, 2011).

[37] On these centuries-long developments, see Wilson B. Bishai, "The Transition from Coptic to Arabic," *The Muslim World* 53 (1963): 145–50; Donald P. Little, "Coptic Conversion to Islam under the Baḥrī Mamlūks, 692–755/1293–1354," *Bulletin of the School of Oriental and African Studies* 39 (1976): 552–69; Jason R. Zaborowski, *The Coptic Martyrdom of John of Phanijōit: Assimilation and Conversion to Islam in Thirteenth-Century Egypt* (Leiden: Brill, 2005); Tamer El-Leithy, "Coptic Culture and Conversion in Medieval Cairo, 1293–1524 A.D." (Ph.D. diss., University of Michigan, 2005).

[38] ARSI, *Epp. NN 86*, fol. 114r./*MPO* 2, 132.

some apprehensiveness in Eliano's letters, though, which suggest that he did not fully believe that Gabriel was in as much danger as he claimed. However, this turn of events also comes on the heels of dealing with his family's sense of disgrace concerning his presence in Egypt. This is a reminder that the religious choices of one person often had larger ramifications for the honor of the collective whole, whether that be a family unit or an entire community.[39] After all, Eliano's public rejection of his family in the form of the burning of the Talmud was a direct affront to them, and did not go unnoticed.[40] The patriarch's fear of the pasha, its genuineness notwithstanding, was also a convenient excuse for Eliano to flee Cairo and avoid his own troubles.

While Eliano does not directly link these events in his letter, he nevertheless remained confident that he could save the Copts in part because of the very Jewishness that had caused him perturbation. Rather than explicitly state this to Laínez, however, Eliano relied on an exegetical link between scripture and his own proficiency as an evangelist: "I have hope that the Omnipotent God will make children of Abraham from these stones; and thus, we will go to the desert, we will work often with Abraham and with another [Coptic theologian], whom the patriarch trusts most, as they are the most lettered." Eliano did not undertake this journey without unease, though: "The greatest impediment is the great ignorance that exists among them."[41] Eliano prayed to Laínez that "God grant by his mercy – so that this their ignorance come to an end through our holy mother the Roman church – all that is necessary for the health [of their souls]. And may your Paternity – for the love of God – always ensure to commend this to all our fellow fathers and brothers in their prayers."[42]

---

[39] On honor and shame in the Mediterranean, see Michael Herzfeld, "Honour and Shame: Problems in the Comparative Analysis of Moral Systems," *Man* 15 (1980): 339–51; Michael Herzfeld, *Poetics of Manhood: Contest and Identity in a Cretan Mountain Village* (Princeton, NJ: Princeton University Press, 1985); David D. Gilmore, ed., *Honor and Shame and the Unity of the Mediterranean* (Washington, DC: American Anthropological Association, 1987); Robert A. Nye, *Masculinity and Male Codes of Honor in Modern France* (Berkeley: University of California Press, 1998).

[40] Elizabeth S. Cohen, "Honor and Gender in the Streets of Early Modern Rome," *The Journal of Interdisciplinary History* 22:4 (1992): 597–625. On the defense of honor, see Edward Muir, *Mad Blood Stirring: Vendetta & Factions in Friuli during the Renaissance* (Baltimore, MD: Johns Hopkins University Press, 1993), 165–66; Elizabeth Horodowich, *Language and Statecraft in Early Modern Venice* (New York: Cambridge University Press, 2011), 117–18.

[41] ARSI, *Epp. NN 86*, fol. 114r./*MPO* 2, 132.

[42] ARSI, *Epp. NN 86*, fol. 114r./*MPO* 2, 132.

While Eliano couches this in the language of God's power to convert the Copts through the truth of the Gospel message as he hoped to deliver it in the desert – to say nothing of the elements of Catholic doctrine that needed to be addressed – this passage allows Eliano to cast his Jewishness as a tool for converting the Copts. In his call to God to aid him in his efforts, Eliano referred to Matthew 3:9 and Luke 3:8, "I tell you that out of these stones God can raise up children for Abraham," an expression that alludes to John the Baptist preparing the way for the coming of Christ by preaching to and baptizing the multitude in the wilderness of Jordan, replete with the exegetical prophesy of Isaiah 40:3–5.[43] The recipient of this letter, Laínez, would recognize the scriptural reference to the actions of Eliano's baptismal namesake (i.e., Giovanni Battista), and see that Eliano presented himself as the Copts' John the Baptist, a Jewish-born evangelist come to renew the Copts' faith in the deserts of Egypt. In essence, while Gabriel used Ottoman reprisals as a means of dissimulating, Eliano believed that he would succeed in winning the Copts for Rome just as John the Baptist prepared the people for the coming of Christ. Nevertheless, however much he presented it as a mechanism for evangelization by likening himself to biblical Jewish evangelists, Eliano's Jewishness again became a problem.

A JEWISH CHALLENGE TO ELIANO'S CATHOLIC IDENTITY

While some of his family wished, like he did, that they not interact, other Jews were more than willing to challenge Eliano. And once it was clear that he had no intention of ever returning to Judaism, some felt that the only recourse left was to punish him for his apostasy. In late January 1562, just as the Jesuits were planning the journey to the desert, rumors began to swirl that a number of Jews – it is not ever clear who exactly they were, but they claimed to be his deceased father's creditors – were plotting to have Eliano arrested, as they were "falsely demanding ancient debts, which they say that [Eliano] owes them, as he was a Jew and a Moor in various times."[44]

---

[43] Isaiah 40:3–5: "The voice of one crying in the wilderness: 'Prepare the way of the Lord; Make His paths straight. Every valley shall be filled and every mountain and hill brought low; The crooked places shall be made straight and the rough ways smooth; And all flesh shall see the salvation of God.'"

[44] ARSI, *Epp. NN 86*, fol. 114r./*MPO* 2, 133.

The issue with his father's debts was only part of the problem. The accusation that he had been a Muslim at some point meant that Eliano could theoretically be tried under "the law of the Turks, according to which he should be obliged to turn Turk or be burned."[45] While such accusations of religious subterfuge were not wholly uncommon given the frequency with which individuals converted for motives other than conviction, Eliano knew that this was no idle threat or the saber rattling of disgruntled Jews.[46] Rather, "we have learned that the source of this is that some Jews know who [Eliano] is, and they incite this [intrigue], offering money [to the qadi, the Turkish judge] in order to persecute him." Furthermore, "not only the Turks but also the Jews are powerful, as they say, to do what they wish with the judges,"[47] given the Jews' commercial influence in the Ottoman Empire.[48] In turn, Lunardo Emo deemed it best that "because of the rancor and malice of the Jews," Eliano should "remain indoors for now until we depart for the desert with the patriarch, where we will spend Lent."[49]

There is more to the letter than the Jesuits relaying to Laínez the vicissitudes of mission. Rather, while this letter is signed by Rodríguez and discusses Eliano in the third person, it is in Eliano's hand; despite his claims that he was ready for the mission and that his Jewish past would only work to his benefit, Eliano underestimated the Jews' hostility toward him, or at the very least downplayed it lest Laínez send someone else. Further, having to write out the fact that his own religious past was the potential cause of the mission's undoing is beyond the typical problems

---

[45] Ibid.

[46] Lucia Rostagno, *Mi faccio turco: esperienze ed immagini dell'Islam nell'Italia moderna* (Rome: Istituto per l'Oriente C.A. Nallino, 1983); Perez Zagorin, *Ways of Lying: Dissimulation, Persecution, and Conformity in Early Modern Europe* (Cambridge, MA: Harvard University Press, 1990); John Jeffries Martin, *Venice's Hidden Enemies: Italian Heretics in a Renaissance City* (Berkeley: University of California Press, 1993); Loretta T. Johnson Burns, "The Politics of Conversion: John Calvin and the Bishop of Troyes," *The Sixteenth Century Journal* 25:4 (1994): 809–22; Mary Elizabeth Perry, *The Handless Maiden: Moriscos and the Politics of Religion in Early Modern Spain* (Princeton, NJ: Princeton University Press, 2005); Jon R. Snyder, *Dissimulation and the Culture of Secrecy in Early Modern Europe* (Berkeley: University of California Press, 2012); David L. Graizbord, *Souls in Dispute: Converso Identities in Iberia and the Jewish Diaspora, 1580–1700* (Philadelphia: University of Pennsylvania Press, 2013).

[47] ARSI, *Epp. NN 86*, fol. 114r./*MPO* 2, 133.

[48] See Haim Gerber, "Jews and Money-Lending in the Ottoman Empire," *The Jewish Quarterly Review* 72:2, New Series (October 1, 1981): 100–18. Gerber does not conclusively claim that Jews predominated in the profession, but they nevertheless held a significant place in it.

[49] ARSI, *Epp. NN 86*, fol. 114r./*MPO* 2, 133.

that missionaries faced. Also weighing on Eliano was the potential strain that any Jewish plot might have on his relationship with his superior and mentor Rodríguez, a *converso* who had his own reasons to fear Jewish reprisals. Even though generations had passed, the Sephardim communities that settled in Ottoman urban centers after their expulsion from Iberia at the end of the fifteenth century had forged a collective memory that hinged on the sufferings of their ancestors; and they often saw *conversos* like Rodríguez as traitors.[50] Rodríguez surely was sympathetic to Eliano's struggles, but he also needed to protect the mission, reminding us of the limits of the collective identities purportedly shared by those labeled *conversos* or *moriscos*, which were as much constructed, essentializing labels as they were experienced identities.[51]

While Rodríguez admired Eliano's tenacity and believed he was dedicated to the mission, he had to set aside his empathy for Eliano and think about the mission's viability. He asked Eliano to write to Laínez that "if you suggest that it will be necessary, may Your Paternity send Father Gieronimo Valentiano, who has spent the past year in Gandía and who knows how to speak and write Arabic ... if [Eliano] is unable to remain for the aforementioned reasons."[52] One can hardly imagine the difficulty with which Eliano had to inquire about his possible replacement. Eliano had assured his superior that his Jewish past would not be an issue, and that the mission would only find success because of the unique skills that his time in Egypt had given him; now, however, that mercantile past and debts incurred therein were potentially his undoing. Here was Eliano,

---

[50] Jonathan Ray, *After Expulsion: 1492 and the Making of Sephardic Jewry* (New York: New York University Press, 2013).

[51] Renée Levine Melammed, *A Question of Identity: Iberian Conversos in Historical Perspective* (New York: Oxford University Press, 2004); Kevin Ingram, "Secret Lives, Public Lies: The Conversos and Socio-Religious Non-Conformism in the Spanish Golden Age" (Ph.D. diss., University of California, San Diego, 2006); Donald Maddox, *Fictions of Identity in Medieval France* (Cambridge: Cambridge University Press, 2006); David L. Graizbord, *Souls in Dispute: Converso Identities in Iberia and the Jewish Diaspora, 1580–1700* (Philadelphia: University of Pennsylvania Press, 2013); Jeffrey S. Shoulson, *Fictions of Conversion: Jews, Christians, and Cultures of Change in Early Modern England* (Philadelphia: University of Pennsylvania Press, 2013); Maria Filomena Lopes de Barros and José Alberto Rodrigues da Silva Tavim, "Cristãos(ãs)-Novos(as), Mouriscos(as), Judeus e Mouros. Diálogos em trânsito no Portugal moderno (séculos XVI–XVII)," *Journal of Sefardic Studies* 1 (2013): 1–45; Karoline P. Cook, *Forbidden Passages: Muslims and Moriscos in Colonial Spanish America* (Philadelphia: University of Pennsylvania Press, 2016).

[52] ARSI, *Epp. NN 86*, fol. 114r./MPO 2, 133.

just short of three months after having arrived, writing to Laínez that perhaps he should be replaced to save the mission from his Jewishness.

Eliano would not be deterred so easily. In an addendum to the letter concerning his possible replacement, Eliano explained that "it seems that it would be a great imperfection because of fear if we did not, with softness, try to help [the Jews] and prevent them from doing evil; and in this [effort to convert them], if we suffered any danger that came to us, it would be through God's mercy."[53] Further, Eliano explained that, because he was the reason the Jews were trying to undo the mission, he would not subject Rodríguez and Bravo to the Jews' threats: "at the very least, I alone can work with them."[54]

RENEWED EFFORTS WITH THE COPTS

Eliano's desire to remain in Cairo and face his Jewish ghosts would have to wait, however, as Rodríguez feared allowing Eliano to circulate freely. In the meantime – between the surfacing of the Jewish intrigues in late January 1562 and departure for the desert on 2 March – the Jesuits continued to correspond with Gabriel. Once this letter of submission was sent to Rome and papal authority over the Copts was established, the Jesuits believed, they could begin instituting doctrinal reforms; in the end, their efforts would result in one great triumph for the Catholic Church.[55] However, they did not fully grasp the differences between Catholic and Coptic ecclesiologies or the nature of Gabriel's authority. Whereas Catholic teaching held that papal authority came from God alone via the pope's election through the power of the Holy Spirit, the Coptic patriarch was more first among equals than divinely inspired supreme arbiter in matters of faith.[56] Greeks had taught Catholics this lesson regarding the horizontal nature of Orthodox Christian ecclesiology in the fifteenth century, when a similar accord with a Greek delegation that was struck at the Council of Florence fell on deaf ears upon the delegation's return home; but that lesson did not appear to stick.[57]

---

[53] ARSI, *Epp. NN 86*, fol. 115r./*MPO* 2, 135.   [54] Ibid.
[55] ARSI, *Epp. NN 86*, fol. 116r./*MPO* 2, 137.
[56] Febe Armanios, *Coptic Christianity in Ottoman Egypt* (Oxford: Oxford University Press, 2011), 22–5.
[57] Deno J. Geanakoplos, "The Council of Florence (1438–1439) and the Problem of Union between the Greek and Latin Churches," *Church History* 24:4 (December 1, 1955): 324–46; Joseph Gill, *The Council of Florence* (Cambridge: Cambridge University Press, 1961); Martin Anton Schmidt, "The Problem of Papal Primacy at the Council of

Further complicating matters was the shadowy presence of the archons, influential and wealthy lay Copts.[58] Gabriel was also bound by other Coptic clerics, and in a sense, whenever he consulted his theologians and bishops, Gabriel was not asking for advice; he was asking for permission.[59] There is also the question of how sincere the Copts truly were in accepting papal authority in the first place, something Eliano, despite widespread Coptic resistance, was reluctant to admit.

To gauge institutional opinion regarding Pius, Gabriel consulted Isaac, Coptic archbishop of Nicosia. Isaac lambasted him for even entertaining the idea of papal primacy. Isaac could provide Gabriel with unique insight into papal overreach in local Christian communities. Under Isaac's leadership, the Copts on Venetian Cyprus had witnessed Catholic intrusion into their religious life firsthand. Minority religious communities such as Copts, Greeks, and Maronites were often caught in the middle of the jurisdictional struggle between the papacy and Venice, and Isaac felt that anything that looked like submission to Rome would lead to the complete capitulation of the community's already tenuous autonomy.[60] Gabriel

Florence," *Church History* 30:1 (March 1, 1961): 35–49; Henry Chadwick, *East and West: The Making of a Rift in the Church: From Apostolic Times until the Council of Florence* (Oxford: Oxford University Press, 2003).

[58] On the lay archons, see Febe Armanios, *Coptic Christianity in Ottoman Egypt* (Oxford: Oxford University Press, 2011), 26–31.

[59] For more on the structures of the Coptic Church in Ottoman Egypt, see Febe Armanios, *Coptic Christianity in Ottoman Egypt* (Oxford: Oxford University Press, 2011), 22–31. Armanios directly discusses the decline of the office of the patriarchate from the Fatimid period (969–1171) through the Mamluk period and into Ottoman rule after 1517 on pp. 22–3.

[60] ARSI, *Epp. NN 86*, fol. 116r./*MPO* 2, 138; Benjamin Arbel, *Cyprus, the Franks and Venice, 13th–16th Centuries* (Aldershot: Ashgate, 2000), particularly the articles focused on the Venetian period: "Régime colonial, colonisation et peuplement: le cas de Chypre sous la domination vénitienne" and "Résistance ou collaboration? Les chypriotes sous la domination vénitienne." For more on religious dynamics between Venice and religious minorities as they played out in Venice and the *stato da mar* in the early modern period, see Massimo Costantini and Aliki Nikiforou, eds., *Levante veneziano: aspetti di storia delle Isole Ionie al tempo della Serenissima* (Rome: Bulzoni, 1996); Nicolas Karapidakis, *Civis fidelis: l'avènement et l'affirmation de la citoyenneté corfiote (XVIème–XVIIème siècles)* (Frankfurt: P. Lang, 1992); Chrysa Maltezou, ed., *Venezia e le Isole Ionie* (Venice: Istituto Veneto di scienze lettere ed arti, 2005); Sally McKee, *Uncommon Dominion: Venetian Crete and the Myth of Ethnic Purity* (Philadelphia: University of Pennsylvania Press, 2000); Maddalena Redolfi, *Venezia e la difesa del Levante: da Lepanto a Candia 1570–1670* (Venice: Arsenale, 1986); Antonio Santosuosso, "Religious Orthodoxy, Dissent and Suppression in Venice in the 1540s," *Church History* 42:4 (December 1973): 476–85; Maria Tiepolo, ed., *I greci a Venezia* (Venice: Istituto veneto di scienze lettere ed arti, 2002).

claimed that "the archbishop of Cyprus wanted him to burn their anointing oil, saying that the Copts were united with the Franks."[61] Eliano questioned why Isaac would say this, "as I have said many times that His Holiness does not wish to change anything in their ceremonies, as it is union with the Roman Catholic Church that is necessary for their salvation." Eliano read this not as a miscommunication but as dissimulation, as "I have not been able to return to them to get them to sign the letter, as it seems to me that they have hidden themselves away, often making excuses for not meeting with us to discuss this [letter.]"[62] Nevertheless, the hope was that, once removed from the challenges of Cairo – both the Copts' fears of the Ottomans and the Jesuits' issues with the Jews – some sort of dialogue could manifest itself in the Egyptian desert. It would also give Eliano free rein to come out of hiding, put his Jewish past behind him, and work with the Copts.

Finally, on 2 March 1562, the Jesuits and Gabriel left Cairo for the desert monastery of Saint Anthony the Great. Eliano believed that, if they could convince Gabriel to submit to Rome, the community would follow suit. By 9 March, however, Eliano had been disabused of that notion: he lamented that the Copts were mired in "great ignorance" and that correcting a people "so firm in their opinions and errors" was an insurmountable obstacle.[63] The Jesuits were also mortified to discover that Copts living in rural villages often waited months to baptize their newborns.[64] They implored Gabriel to order collective baptisms at once, but he was reluctant because of Muslim reprisals against large Coptic celebrations like mass communal baptisms, as such an attack would not have been without precedent.[65] In hopes that they could buttress their position with the Copts, Eliano told Gabriel that they did not fear the Ottoman rulers or the local population, "but he feared that the Moors would kill us in the streets."[66]

---

[61] ARSI, *Epp. NN 86*, fol. 116r./*MPO* 2, 138.   [62] Ibid.

[63] ARSI, *Epp. NN 86*, fol. 118r./*MPO* 2, 140.   [64] Ibid.

[65] This is not unique for Coptic Christians, or, for that matter, any *dhimmī* population. Febe Armanios recounts a Muslim reaction to an overt expression of Coptic identity when, in 1748, Muslims forced the disbanding of a procession headed to the Holy Land from Egypt. *Dhimmī* were banned from ostentatious displays of religious identity, and open celebrations of baptism would have fallen into this category. Christian displays during Lent were particularly seen as suspect, and their suppression was endemic. See Febe Armanios, *Coptic Christianity in Ottoman Egypt* (Oxford: Oxford University Press, 2011), 3–4.

[66] ARSI, *Epp. NN 86*, fol. 118r./*MPO* 2, 140.

The Jesuits would not acquiesce. Eliano was particularly forceful in his desire to baptize the children of Egypt: "I responded to him that we would willingly travel throughout his diocese, as it is more than 20 days to Ethiopia, where there are innumerable Christians with unbaptized children, and that we will have no fear, neither of the danger nor of the work therein, of doing this for the greater service of God."[67] Very quickly, this debate about baptizing youths morphed from a means of safeguarding Coptic souls into a referendum on Eliano's ability to convert the Copts: "[Gabriel] agreed [to allow us to baptize youths]. May we thus proceed, with divine aid, and may there be great fruit, not only in [the baptisms], but also in persuading them and letting them know how important their union with the Holy Roman Mother Church is, which is why we have come." Eliano was confident that, through his efforts, "[Gabriel] and the rest of his little lambs may more easily bring themselves into union with the church."[68] Much as in previous letters, Eliano wanted to remind Laínez that he had nothing but faith in his abilities. With his Jewish past lurking in the background, Eliano needed to reassure Laínez that this mission would not falter.

This, however, would soon prove empty. Within a month of arriving in the desert, the Jesuits were back in Cairo. On 7 April 1562, writing from Cairo, Eliano sent off a series of letters to Pius, papal secretary Antonio Fioribello, and Laínez. These letters, which often border on vitriol and diatribe, illuminate that, as the Copts resisted, Eliano remained steadfast in his efforts and desired to continue the mission despite its obstacles. But his distress is equally apparent. Eliano voiced his frustration to Pius that Gabriel "conceded that Catholic principle of obedience to the Apostolic See," but then would "change his mind often without cause, to agree without condoning, or perhaps to hide the dissimulation with which Abraham had shown in Rome, or to reclaim the vestments that he had left for fear of the Moors in the Venetian Consul's house until he left for the desert."[69] Eliano further explained that "I have come to know of this dissimulation of Abraham and even of the patriarch," who explained that, while he had sent Abraham to Rome with a letter of recommendation, "he went with only this, not to render obedience."[70] Given that it was Eliano who implored Laínez to send him on this mission because he believed that the letter was indeed a declaration of obedience, Eliano's

---

[67] Ibid.   [68] ARSI, *Epp. NN 86*, fol.118r/MPO 2, 140.
[69] ARSI, *Epp. NN 86*, fol. 120r./MPO 2, 143-4.
[70] ARSI, *Epp. NN 86*, fol. 120r./MPO 2, 144.

naïveté in believing that the Copts would convert so easily could potentially be a major blow to Eliano's credibility before his superiors; his desire to carry out this mission and show his zeal had perhaps gotten the best of him.

Eliano was undeterred, and wanted Pius to know that the mission was not a failure; rather, although they were "in danger of death on our journeys amidst these Moors," they would continue to work to convert the Copts "so that with divine favor we can achieve this holy union that is so necessary for their souls, and to which we were sent by Your Holiness."[71] While he is writing on Rodríguez's behalf, Eliano put himself to the fore of the mission when he wrote to Pius "may Our Lord God by his mercy turn these stones into sons of Abraham," the same biblical reference used to remind Laínez of his personal affinity with John the Baptist.[72]

This pattern continues in his April letter to Monsignor Antonio Fioribello, Pius's secretary. Eliano explained that the patriarch had designated two men to meet with Eliano: Abraham (the envoy sent to Rome) and another theologian named George, "whom they say is among the most intelligent."[73] At first, just as Eliano had explained previously, these theologians seemed as though they had influenced Gabriel to come to some sort of agreement on union with the Jesuits, and Gabriel explained that he would agree to sign an agreement so long as "a priest, named Gabriel, his personal assistant, transcribed them; and afterward he would sign it."[74] But this did not settle well with Eliano, for "we know that that priest is young, ignorant, and quite inimical toward Catholics, as he always attempts to harm us without cause, even if we always embrace him." Even Patriarch Gabriel was aware of his young assistant's penchant for insulting the Jesuits, to the point that, according to Eliano, "the Patriarch called him 'Judas.'"[75]

Eliano begged the patriarch to let anyone but the young priest write the agreement. Despite his own misgivings, Gabriel ignored Eliano's request. Once Gabriel's young assistant refused to transcribe the document so that Gabriel could read and sign it, Eliano and Rodríguez realized that the mission was imperiled; without the patriarch's cooperation, there would be no theological debates, there would be no Coptic delegation to Trent,

[71] ARSI, *Epp. NN 86*, fol. 120rv./*MPO* 2, 144.
[72] ARSI, *Epp. NN 86*, fol. 120v./*MPO* 2, 144-5.
[73] ARSI, *Epp. NN 86*, fol. 121r./*MPO* 2, 146.
[74] ARSI, *Epp. NN 86*, fol. 121v./*MPO* 2, 148.   [75] Ibid.

and there would be no union. Eliano lamented to Fioribello that the "Copts do not want to hear it, nor any other clear reason; and even if there is some erudition in the letters that they sent ... I judge it doubtful that they were composed by them."[76] Thus, "after having spent nineteen days in the monastery of Saint Anthony, seeing that every day they proved themselves to be more pertinacious," Eliano lamented to Fioribello, "we judged it best to return to Cairo."[77]

In recounting their failures in the desert to Laínez, Eliano likewise showed his frustration with the Copts. While often including sections copied almost verbatim from the letters sent to Pius and Fioribello, Eliano's letters to Laínez include passages not present in the other letters that are much more personal in tone, reflecting the pair's close relationship. To start, Eliano outlined for Laínez the tensions between Gabriel and his assistant, and that the young theologian had accused Eliano and Rodríguez of attempting to confuse and deceive the patriarch because of his old age and lack of theological training, and he declared that they should immediately return to Rome.[78] He also told Laínez how the patriarchal assistant rejected the "the councils and the true Catholic faith." Further, Eliano reacted negatively to the young theologian's attitude and told Gabriel, "I would not work with him (and only with intelligent men) and that he should call on [Abraham and George] or someone else who was at Saint Anthony where we were. And so, we left him with affection."[79] Eliano wanted to ensure his superior that this theological gridlock was not for a lack of trying. Rather, it needed to be clear that the Copts' intransigence, not anything he failed to do, was what caused the mission to go awry. Furthermore, Eliano hammered home the point that he was doing everything he could to convince the Copts of the risk to their souls.

This is quite apparent when writing to Laínez of the resumption of talks the following day. For Eliano, this discussion was as much about trying to save the Copts' souls as it was Eliano's efforts to prevent the unraveling of the mission. After the younger Gabriel continued to deny basic Catholic theology, Eliano explained that such views rendered the Copts outside of the grace of "His Holiness, the Vicar of Christ, and the whole Catholic Church" as their views "were against the Gospels, the councils, and the whole faith; that if they did not abandon [these errors],

---

[76] ARSI, *Epp. NN 86*, fol. 122v./MPO 2, 151.   [77] Ibid.
[78] ARSI, *Ep. NN 86*, fol. 149v./MPO 2, 166.
[79] ARSI, *Epp. NN 86*, fol. 149v./MPO 2, 166–7.

that it would be impossible to save them."[80] Eliano was quite frustrated at this point, especially when the Copts explained that "they did not have to think about it, because they believed they had the true faith that they have inherited from their ancestors; therefore, they did not desire to change or search for another [faith]." Despite his agitation, Eliano wanted to keep working: "so that we do not close the door [on union] and so that we delay negotiations, I said to the patriarch that it would be better to deal with this later with more learned [Copts]."[81] The "more learned Copts" that the Jesuits had in mind were the monks of the monastery; Eliano hoped that they would convince Gabriel and the others to reengage in talks of union. However, this encounter did not go according to plan: "The more I tried, the more pertinacious" the Copts showed themselves to be, and the monks "blasphemed the faith, the councils, and the Apostolic See; I am omitting the insults that they said against us when they called us heretics, crazies, etc. These were the caresses and modesty that the brothers showed us."[82]

The troubles did not stop there. Eliano had come to learn from Venetian consul Lunardo Emo that Abraham had either doctored or completely forged Gabriel's letter to convince Pius to give him an audience, and that the patriarch, seeing Pius solely as his peer, never had any designs for submission to Rome.[83] Emo's discovery struck a nerve with Eliano. As we saw in Chapter 1, Coptic duplicity – why Laínez was reluctant to call the mission – was coming to fruition. This was a problem for Eliano, as he had convinced Laínez to order the mission in the first place. In revealing this turn of events to Laínez, Eliano deviated from how he related this discovery to Pius and Fioribello, whom he simply informed that Abraham lied. Instead, Eliano reminded Laínez of all that had been done for Abraham, including the "warmth that His Holiness and the Most Reverend Cardinals and Monsignor Fioribello had shown Abraham in Rome, and we on our travels and here serving [their needs], as servants doing everything that he wished, and so often to our discomfort and expense." Nevertheless, "he has only dissimulated, as I said, and remains obstinate in so many errors, which I cannot even write, as it would be too prolix."[84]

[80] ARSI, *Epp. NN 86*, fol. 149v./MPO.167.
[81] ARSI, *Epp. NN 86*, fol. 150r./MPO 2, 168.
[82] ARSI, *Epp. NN 86*, fol. 127v./MPO 2, 157.   [83] Ibid.
[84] ARSI, *Epp. NN 86*, fol. 128r./MPO 2, 158.

Eliano's rambling anger concerning Abraham and his claim that he cut his rant short in the name of avoiding verbosity demonstrate a certain level of embarrassment on Eliano's part. He had assured Laínez and others that they could trust Abraham and that the mission would find success because of his knowledge of Arabic and his previous experiences in Egypt. Yet, Abraham had duped Eliano when he told him that he, like Eliano, had turned to Rome and embraced the Catholic faith. Eliano, however, did not want his superior to worry or doubt his ability to see the mission through: "But may it all be to the greater glory of God."[85] Eliano's juxtaposition of Abraham's deception with his firm desire to continue the mission and do whatever Laínez deemed necessary shows that Eliano did not want his superior to think that Abraham had gotten the best of him, even though he clearly had.

By 13 May, matters had not improved, as the Jesuits had returned to Alexandria. While there, Eliano wrote to Laínez to inform him that the mission was dying down and that, should any fruit come from a Jesuit presence there, it would come in the form of a college to be established at a later date. Eliano believed that a college would "persuade the Copts, Greeks, and the Franks of the truth."[86] That, however, would have to wait, as Eliano and Rodríguez had determined that their time in Egypt had come to an end, as the Copts' "obstinacy is so great that not only the patriarch but all the others say that they will never leave their sect, in which are many heresies, and that they will have nothing to do with the pope, because he is not the head of the church, but only the Franks." By that point, it had been three months since the last meeting with Gabriel and his advisors, because "every time that we interact, they demonstrate themselves more heretical and schismatic, that it was better not to interact anymore."[87] They tried to stay busy in Alexandria, but they found the Latin merchant community to be ambivalent about the Jesuits' presence.[88]

---

[85] Ibid.   [86] ARSI, *Epp. NN 86*, fol. 135r./MPO 2, 178.

[87] ARSI, *Epp. NN 86*, fol. 138v./MPO 2, 200.

[88] Ibid. On the Latin community of Egypt, see Charles A. Frazee, *Catholics and Sultans: The Church and the Ottoman Empire, 1453–1923* (Cambridge: Cambridge University Press, 1983). Frazee explains (p. 62) that "The Latin faith was represented in Egypt by French, Catalan and Venetian merchants who had come there to trade ... Latin Catholics lived in Egypt for the sake of profit. Most were young men without families who intended to spend only a few years in the Orient before returning home. Their interest in religion was not high. For them, the Sunday Eucharist was more a social than a religious event, which allowed them to learn the latest news from Western Europe, and to discuss the arrival and departure of ships and the prices obtained for cargoes."

While the mission to the Copts was at a dead end, Eliano was not ready to return to Italy, but desired an opportunity in another missionary theater: "From here, one can go to Goa and Ethiopia." If not there, Eliano reminded Laínez that, since they were only 300 miles from Cyprus, he would embrace the opportunity to work in the service of the Catholic archbishop of Nicosia, Filippo Mocenigo.[89]

Throughout the summer, he continued to reach out to the Copts, and even met one last time in mid-June with Gabriel, who again shunned these overtures. By August, Eliano felt that "with these Copts being so pertinacious, Your Reverence understood that it would be wise to send us to India or Ethiopia, since we are essentially halfway there." Eliano was worried, however, that Laínez would read this as a plea to abandon his work; thus, Eliano explained that "I continue to write to you about India not because I am resistant to obedience," but because he still held the desire with which "I entered and have always had in the Society, and now my desire is stronger seeing what is needed there ... with divine favor I will be able to serve, according to the obedience that you will demand, as far away as Japan."[90]

Eliano's admission of his failure with the Copts and his desire to be sent to the far corners of the Jesuit's missionary network point to both the educational formation he received at the Collegio Romano as well as his need to prove to Laínez his steadfast desire to serve.[91] It is also telling that Eliano claims that his yearning to be sent as far away as Japan is not a reflection of his disobedience – a tendency that had surfaced in his grappling with the Jews aboard the boat carrying him to Egypt – but rather is evidence of his dedication to the Society.[92] This mission had unraveled under his watch for the reason that Laínez did not want to call it in the first place – doubts concerning the Copts' willingness to accept papal authority. Eliano therefore needed another opportunity to prove to his superior that he was fit to serve. There was one issue above all,

---

[89] ARSI, *Epp. NN 86*, fol. 135r./MPO 2, 178.

[90] ARSI, *Epp. NN 86*, fol. 138r./MPO 2, 192.

[91] Kirstin Noreen, "Ecclesiae militantis triumphi: Jesuit Iconography and the Counter-Reformation," *The Sixteenth Century Journal* 29:3 (October 1, 1998): 689–715. On that educational foundation, see John O'Malley, *The First Jesuits* (Cambridge, MA: Harvard University Press, 1993), 200–42.

[92] On the Jesuits in Japan, see J. F. Moran, *The Japanese and the Jesuits: Alessandro Valignano in Sixteenth-Century Japan* (London: Routledge, 1993); Takao Abé, *The Jesuit Mission to New France: A New Interpretation in the Light of the Earlier Jesuit Experience in Japan* (Leiden: Brill, 2011).

however, that compelled Eliano to desire to leave Egypt at once: his Jewish past.

THE CONSEQUENCES OF ELIANO'S CONVERSION

On 21 October, as the Jesuits were preparing to leave Egypt, "certain Jews with some Turks seized [Eliano], and led him to the qadi, the Turkish judge; the Jews threatened that they would have him burned. Before the qadi, they demanded a debt of 324 and a half ducats and showed a Jewish bill from his father and from him from years prior." Lunardo Emo quickly "freed him with great diligence after having spent 30 ducats. They begged the Pasha in Cairo to hear the case, to give us some time, and also because justice will better be served under the authority of the Magnificent Venetian Consul [Emo]."[93] Emo even went so far as to write to Doge Girolamo Priuli to secure further assistance for Eliano.[94]

This account, written in Eliano's hand on 27 October 1562, suggests that Eliano was no longer in any real danger. Nevertheless, he was seized by Turkish soldiers who were spurred on by his Jewish detractors who saw him as a renegade who converted to avoid paying his family's debts. And while the Jews secured his arrest by claiming that Eliano had made a false profession to Islam and then turned face and blasphemed Muhammed, Eliano was sure that the Jews wanted him arrested because he "had burned the Talmud and had done many other things against them."[95]

As we saw in the introduction, Eliano had originally burned the Talmud in 1553 with a neophyte's zeal, as he desired to prove that he had distanced himself from his Jewish past. As far as the Jews seemed to read this act, however, he had successfully done the opposite: to them, Eliano only proved that he was a treacherous renegade who faked being Christian to avoid the reality of his Judaism. He was a religious opportunist who used the commercial cosmopolitanism of Venice, the openness of the Jesuits, and the authority of the Catholic Church to avoid old family debts; and he was living proof that their community was in peril, as his apostasy, decision to become a Jesuit, and burning of the Talmud put the Jews one step closer to extinction. For, if Eliano could be integrated into Catholicism that easily, and his brother and several other

---

[93] ARSI, *Epp. NN 86*, fol. 143r./*MPO* 2, 216–17.
[94] ASVe, *Senato–Dispacci del Console ad Alessandria*, fasc. 1 n. 35./*MPO* 2, 218–19.
[95] ARSI, *Epp. NN 86*, fol. 143r./*MPO* 2, 217.

family members could so easy convert, what would stop the rest of his family, or even all the Jews, from following suit?[96] For these reasons, as Rodríguez would eventually write in the final report of the mission, Eliano faced "many trials and persecutions by the Jews."[97] Lest these persecutions continue, on 26 November 1562, barely a year after having arrived in Alexandria, Eliano disguised himself, boarded a Venetian merchant vessel in the dark of night, and headed home. Eliano's return voyage, however, centered as much on his struggles with his Jewishness as had his time in Egypt.

ELIANO'S CYPRIOT INTERLUDE

On 19 December 1562, Eliano wrote to Laínez from Paphos on the southwest coast of Cyprus – one of Venice's most important holdings in its Mediterranean empire – that he had arrived there after the ship carrying him from Egypt had succumbed to a storm. He told Laínez that he had fled Egypt "because of the Jews' effort to persecute me, claiming that I owed them a sum of money." Eliano reassured Laínez that this accusation "is so false that, as far I can recall, nothing could be falser." Rather, Eliano believed that the Jews had bribed the Ottomans solely "to kill me. If I had been presented before the judge of the Moors and they had determined that I had been Jewish and was made Christian, they would have obliged me, according to their law, either to become a Moor or to be burned."[98]

It is peculiar that Eliano stated that his conversion from Judaism to Christianity would have caused the Ottoman qadi to order his execution, as Jewish conversions to Christianity were both not infrequent and were not illegal under Ottoman law. In this instance, Eliano omitted the Jews' actual accusation made months before Eliano's arrest and flight – namely, that "he was a Jew and a Moor in various times," which would have been a violation of Ottoman law against apostasy from Islam.[99] Eliano's decision to omit this suggests that he did not want his superiors in Rome to

---

[96] For more on the loss of religious kinfolk to other faiths as transgressions, see Benjamin J. Kaplan, *Divided by Faith: Religious Conflict and the Practice of Toleration in Early Modern Europe* (Cambridge, MA: Belknap Press of Harvard University Press, 2007), 266–93.

[97] ARSI, *Epp. NN 86*, fol. 157v./MPO 2, 307.

[98] ARSI, *Epp. NN 86*, fol. 214r./MPO 2, 233.

[99] ARSI, *Epp. NN 86*, fol. 114r./MPO 2, 133.

know that his flight had been precipitated by the Ottomans' belief that he was a Muslim at one point, as this might prevent Laínez from ever sending Eliano back to the Ottoman Empire.

To assuage these anxieties, Eliano told Laínez that the Venetians were of great help in securing his freedom and assisting in his departure from Egypt: after his liberation, he "dressed as a merchant, and I was accompanied by the vice-consul and another merchant; we walked together through customs and the port, where there are always Jews." He then elaborated on his experiences at sea: "I boarded the ship, where I hid in a room while we were in port because of the Jews who came and went. Finally, after we set sail, I exposed myself on the ship, where there were more than twenty Jews, who were mightily confused" by his presence.[100] Eliano's juxtaposition of his fear of the Jews with his desire to let them know who he was mirrors his yearning to confront the Jews on the ship carrying him to Alexandria from Venice; while the Jews were the cause of his departure and the mission's failure (a fear held from the very beginning), his bold challenge to them was a reminder of the emptiness of their accusations of renegadism and the strength of his dedication to the Society's ministries.

This dedication to the Society of Jesus was immediately put to the test, Eliano told Laínez, as the next event on this journey was a torrential storm at sea that caused the ship to capsize and crash into Cyprus's southern coast near Paphos. Eliano explained that "through the goodness of Jesus Christ, even though I was already prepared to make myself accountable to God, I never failed that night and that morning to perform the work of our blessed Society; and thus, that night many confessed to me, giving themselves over to God, by his mercy." After many confessed to Eliano, he explained that, as they all feared death, he "gathered them in His holy glory, as they were all truly contrite, which gave me in that moment such great consolation."[101] By thrusting himself into action in this perilous moment, Eliano hoped to reaffirm that the Jews' accusations against him were wholly baseless.

This was only half the process of doing so, for Eliano's next bold step was to console more than just fellow Christians who floated amid the shattered pieces of the ship. Rather, nothing would better distance him from the Jews' accusation of religious dissimulation and prove the truth of his conversion than converting Jews. This shipwreck provided Eliano

[100] ARSI, *Epp. NN 86*, fol. 214r./*MPO* 2, 233.
[101] ARSI, *Epp. NN 86*, fol. 214r./*MPO* 2, 234.

with this very opportunity, as "escaping from our ship was a Jew who, nearly killed at sea, was exhorted to become a Christian." Eliano explained that, after the danger subsided, the young Jew agreed to convert, as he believed that Christ had intervened to save his life. Eliano planned to baptize him in Nicosia as soon as possible.[102]

Once ashore, Eliano attempted to secure a Coptic delegation to the Council of Trent, as Gabriel had written to Isaac, the Coptic archbishop of Nicosia, requesting that he travel to Italy for the council. Eliano explained to Laínez that he planned to travel to Nicosia to convince Isaac to travel to Trent, as "I believe that it will bear great fruit for those [Coptic] souls, if he goes [to Trent] as he promised."[103] Eliano's desire to continue to work on converting the Copts demonstrates that Eliano did not want the Jews' ability to expel him from Egypt to be a reason to abandon hope. Rather, as he was now safe from their attacks in Venetian territory, he could attempt to soften one of the key figures who had convinced Gabriel to resist the Jesuits in the first place.

That is not to say that Eliano was not struggling with his difficult time in Egypt. After all, he had fled Egypt in duress and had nearly perished at sea. And Eliano admitted that he was wrestling with "the nature of our purpose and other matters in my prayers, and I strive to say Mass every day, which, as I am able, I have not failed to do, always turning my eyes toward my desire to be obedient." Despite the ministries that he had been able to carry forth on Cyprus, Eliano explained that he missed his brothers in Rome. He also implored Laínez "and all the other fathers and brothers to pray to God for my wretched self."[104] Here, we see a nearly broken Eliano. Confronting his religious past, family struggles, failures with the Copts, arrest, flight, and near death at sea had exhausted him. Rather than exuding confidence, Eliano simply and humbly desired that his fellow Jesuits pray that he find the wherewithal to confront any obstacle that came his way, including the ability to trek across Cyprus in the dead of winter so soon after a shipwreck that had nearly killed him.

On 9 January 1563, Eliano again wrote to Laínez of his activities on Cyprus. Staying at the residence of the Venetian archbishop of Nicosia, Filippo Mocenigo, Eliano reported that Mocenigo's vicar general, Andrea Stanca, "has welcomed me and shows me much warmth." However,

---

[102] ARSI, *Epp. NN 86*, fol. 215r./MPO 2, 235–6.
[103] ARSI, *Epp. NN 86*, fol. 215r./MPO 2, 235.
[104] ARSI, *Epp. NN 86*, fol. 215r./MPO 2, 236–7.

Eliano was eager to leave: "I hope that within a month or a bit less, a boat will leave for Venice."[105] But Eliano did not want his superior to imagine that he dallied about the island: "by the grace of God, I never fail to observe our rule, as much as I can, in preaching, hearing confession, and spending time well."[106] He was also pleased to report that twenty youths would be sent "to Rome to be instructed; and they are of diverse nations: Greeks, Copts, Maronites, Jacobites, Armenians; and as [Stanca] told me and as I have seen, they are quite bright; I hope that Our Lord God will be greatly served in [the education of these youths]."[107]

Due to the Mediterranean's wintry unpredictability, however, Eliano and these youths were still on Cyprus in March, and it was unclear when they would be able to leave. On 15 March, he wrote to Laínez that he had been in contact with Isaac, the Coptic archbishop of Nicosia. In their meeting, Eliano informed Isaac that Gabriel had wanted him to travel to Trent to participate in the council. At first, Isaac did not believe Eliano. However, when Eliano showed him Gabriel's letters in the company of others, Isaac publicly "kissed them and read them aloud with tears in his eyes. He responded that he would willingly do whatever the patriarch wished if he were healthy and younger, and had the ability, and had something to give to His Holiness."[108] Eliano saw this for what it was: "His responses to everything were sufficient, and he declared his desire to come; but he did not actually desire it ... he told me in secret that the patriarch is crazy and stupid, and that if he wanted to leave the [Coptic] faith, they would depose him."[109] While clearly converting the Copts would not happen via Isaac, Eliano was at least able to report that the twenty youths promised by the vicar would still travel to Rome, where they would be lodged in the German College.[110]

Eliano was also dismayed that he had still not baptized the Jewish youth who promised to convert: "Since the shipwreck, a young Jew who miraculously survived has wanted to become Christian. And as he has persevered in this, even though I did not have bread, to say nothing of clothing and other things for myself, seeing that this soul was so well disposed toward the faith, I put him [and his needs] before myself."[111] Cyprus was no place for a Jewish-born catechumen, however: "I wanted

[105] ARSI, *Epp. NN 86*, fol. 216r./*MPO* 2, 243.
[106] ARSI, *Epp. NN 86*, fol. 216r./*MPO* 2, 243–4.
[107] ARSI, *Epp. NN 86*, fol. 216r./*MPO* 2, 244.
[108] ARSI, *Epp. NN 86*, fol. 217r./*MPO* 2, 258–9.
[109] ARSI, *Epp. NN 86*, fol. 217r./*MPO* 2, 259. [110] Ibid.
[111] ARSI, *Epp. NN 86*, fol. 220r./*MPO* 2, 263.

to baptize him here, but because it will be difficult – because of the little edification that he will receive from the Greeks and because it is too close to Turkey, where any wind of temptation will compel him to return to vomit – it seemed better to everyone to bring him to Venice, which I will do."[112] This passage, along with the reference to 2 Peter 2:22 ("Of them the proverbs are true: 'A dog returns to its vomit'"),[113] points to the larger challenges that converts faced in fighting the temptations of recidivism. It underscores how Eliano confronted the instability of Mediterranean identities that were informed in no small part by larger imperial and religious structures that compelled individuals to come to terms with their own identities.[114]

It is significant that Eliano did not shy away from discussing the challenges that converts like himself and this young catechumen faced in their religious journeys, such as his own "great hunger and thirst to be in the companion of our brothers, as I have been alone now for four months. But by the grace of God I will do my best to live as if I were in Rome."[115]

---

[112] Ibid.

[113] 2 Peter 2:22 is itself a reference to Proverbs 26:11: "As a dog returns to its vomit, so fools repeat their folly."

[114] This type of self-reflection and concern with the construction of collective identities is prevalent in early modern literature concerning travel and experience in the Mediterranean world. New historicist research on early modern Mediterranean identities has stressed that scholarly reliance on binaries such as Self/Other, West/East, Colonizer/Colonized tends to break down under scrutiny. Daniel Vitkus explains that "religious and racial affiliations are unstable, giving the audience a sense of Jewish, Muslim, and Christian identities as interchangeable roles in a Machiavellian marketplace where identity was a slippery matter indeed, and where ... various forms of foreignness (or religious difference) were blurred, or in some cases, indistinguishable." The question of alterity and the prevalence of polyvalent Others in the Mediterranean transformed it from a geographic place of conflict into an intellectual, shared space. This self-proclaimed "post-Braudelian" intellectual approach to seeing the Mediterranean Sea as a space of unity and common experience allows us to view the permeability of identity juxtaposed with the firmness with which such identities are defended by figures like Giovanni Battista Eliano. See Daniel J Vitkus, *Turning Turk: English Theater and the Multicultural Mediterranean, 1570–1630* (New York: Palgrave Macmillan, 2003), 195. See also Goran V. Stanivukovic, ed., *Remapping the Mediterranean World in Early Modern English Writings* (New York: Palgrave Macmillan, 2007). In this collection, contributors attempt to "examine how early modern English imagination conceptualized the intermingling categories of sameness and difference, of otherness and familiarity, which were produced through complete and often ambiguous contacts between Renaissance England and the Mediterranean, especially the eastern Mediterranean" (p. 1). Not only do they attempt to see the Mediterranean as place where English could project imperialist fantasies, but it also brought real Mediterranean concerns to the fore.

[115] ARSI, *Epp. NN 86*, fol. 217r./MPO 2, 259.

This expression, as well as his telling Laínez that "I thirst to see again, by the Grace of God, that blessed city and its many holy servants," illuminates that Eliano felt no need to hide that confronting his Jewish past – which was both the source of his missionary toolkit as well as proof for the Jews of his renegadism – had exhausted him. It is likewise a declaration that, for him, being with fellow Jesuits would provide him with the solace that he sorely lacked because of his isolation in a world foreign from what he had come to see as home, the Collegio Romano.[116] Eliano got his wish two months later, when he departed Nicosia during Holy Week, arriving in Venice on 26 June.[117] From Venice, he set off for Trent to reconnect with Laínez. He then returned to Rome.[118]

THE END OF THE MISSION

While Eliano wintered on Cyprus, Rodríguez and Bravo tied up loose ends in Egypt. With no directives, Rodríguez was unsure whether they should return to Italy or reengage with the Copts.[119] By February, Rodríguez had heard from a Florentine merchant, Francesco Vifali, that their presence in Rome was requested. Nonetheless, without anything official from Laínez or Pius, he and Bravo stayed put.[120] Later in the month, he learned of Eliano's shipwreck but did not know whether Eliano had survived.[121] Eventually, he received orders to return to Italy. It is unclear what Rodríguez and Bravo achieved between Rodríguez's last letter sent to Rome (21 February 1563) and Lunardo Emo's dispatch to Doge Girolamo Priuli announcing their departure on 29 March.[122] Rodríguez's diary gives very little evidence of what occurred in Egypt after Eliano's departure. Rodríguez outlined his efforts to liberate a Portuguese Jesuit, Fulgencio Freire, who had been imprisoned in Cairo after his arrest in Moka, modern-day Yemen.[123] But beyond this, the mission to the Copts

---

[116] ARSI, *Epp. NN 86*, fol. 220r./*MPO* 2, 263.

[117] ARSI, *Ital. 123*, fol. 49r./*MPO* 2, 271.

[118] Eliano relays in his 1588 autobiography that he left Cyprus during Holy Week. (ARSI, *Hist. Soc. 176 I*, fol. 145). Easter was 21 April 1563, so Eliano would have left Cyprus for Venice sometime between 14 April and 20 April 1563.

[119] ARSI, *Epp. NN 86*, fol. 169r./*MPO* 2, 251.   [120] Ibid.

[121] ARSI, *Epp. NN 86*, fol. 170r./*MPO* 2, 253.

[122] ASVe, *Senato-Dispacci del Console ad Alessandria*, fasc. 1. N. 36./*MPO* 2, 265.

[123] BNCR, Sala manoscritti, *Fondo Gesuitico n. 1636./MPO* 2, 272–99. It gives great detail about the pair's personal views of the mission, their take on the interactions with the Copts, and the discussion of Fulgencio Freire. It also goes into far greater detail

ends. By 8 May, Rodríguez and Bravo were in Venice, seven weeks ahead of Eliano.

Cristóbal Rodríguez finished the final report of the mission soon after his return to Italy. In hindsight, Rodríguez lamented, the mission was doomed from the beginning: "If what the said Abraham said and did in Rome were true and not false, this mission would have been most felicitous for the health of those unhappy souls. But as it seems, and as the patriarch told us, everything was dissimulation and fiction, affirming to us that they never had it in mind to unite themselves with the Roman Church, as Abraham had suggested."[124] Rodríguez gave a brief overview of the failed mission: they engaged the Copts for nine months, but deliberations over doctrine and papal primacy went nowhere. He excoriated the Copts for their "pertinacity, malice, and ignorance, and above all great deceitfulness in practice."[125] He condemned Patriarch Gabriel for his resistance to papal authority. The Copts were not the only ones to receive Rodríguez's ire: "so many Moors, Jews, renegades, heretics, schismatics" remained obstinate despite the Jesuits' efforts.[126] The Greeks received the most acerbic condemnation: they were "so obstinate in their heresies and hatred for the Roman Church that they, as they say, more readily desired to become Turks than render obedience to the Holy Roman Church."[127] Despite the mission's failure, he praised his, Bravo's, and Eliano's dedication to the spiritual well-being of anyone who let the missionaries offer them solace, in order that they "convert those wretched people to our holy faith."[128] There were some successes, such as their ability to convert five German Lutherans and to convince a handful of renegades to return to Catholicism. Such anecdotes lay bare that, while this mission's failure was not their doing, it was a failure nevertheless.

CONCLUSION

The Copts' refusal to convert notwithstanding, the complex religious landscape of the eastern Mediterranean was a direct challenge to

concerning the daily disputes and theological discussions they had with the Copts, which are long elaborations on the accounts from letters sent to Rome, which are addressed earlier in this chapter.

[124] ARSI, *Epp. NN 86*, fol. 155r./MPO 2, 300–1.
[125] ARSI, *Epp. NN 86*, fol. 155r./MPO 2, 301.
[126] ARSI, *Epp. NN 86*, fol. 155v./MPO 2, 302.
[127] ARSI, *Epp. NN 86*, fols. 156r–157v./MPO 2, 305.
[128] ARSI, *Epp. NN 86*, fol. 155v./MPO 2, 302.

Eliano's sense of himself. This centered on the very real fact that his Jewish past complicated his status as a Jesuit. On one hand, his Jewish youth provided him with a unique ability to engage with the Copts because of his commercial experience in Egypt and his knowledge of Arabic. On the other hand, certain Jews saw him as a renegade, which nearly prevented him from leaving Egypt alive. Eliano's need to come to terms with the dual meanings of his Jewishness stemmed from a tacit recognition that becoming Catholic was far more difficult than simply being baptized. Furthermore, as we saw with the Christian youths living as Jews, the Copt who waffled between Christianity and Islam, and the Jew whose baptism Eliano delayed for fear of backsliding, converts could and often did return to the faiths of their births; and even if they did not, they surely thought about it. This put further strain on Eliano, as his arrest was both punishment for conversion and a rather strong nudge to accept the truth of his Judaism. This compelled him to grapple with what conversion meant beyond its ramifications for his own spiritual formation and efforts as a missionary. Rather, he needed to better consider how others perceived his conversion and how to confront their reactions in turn.[129]

The fluidity of conversion and its myriad challenges to religious identities are encapsulated in the case of the Venetian consul Lunardo Emo's dragoman, who desired to convert to Catholicism.[130] In his description of the Jesuits' efforts to convert him, Rodríguez called him a "Greek Turk." This dragoman hesitated to convert because of his fear of retribution from either Greeks or Muslims (or perhaps from both given that he was somehow both?).[131] The fact that a Greek Turk desired to become Catholic once it was deemed safe – to say nothing of the fact that a Greek Turk could exist in the first place – stresses the delicate lines between faiths that individuals had to navigate in their efforts to convert, come to terms with their religious pasts, and

---

[129] Benjamin J. Kaplan, *Divided by Faith: Religious Conflict and the Practice of Toleration in Early Modern Europe* (Cambridge, MA: Belknap Press of Harvard University Press, 2007), 292. Kaplan suggests that it was at least 20 percent in Augsburg and would have been roughly the same elsewhere. With Jewish converts, relapses were also constant fears. See Vincent Parello, "Inquisition and Crypto-Judaism: The 'Complicity' of the Mora Family of Quintanar de la Orden (1588–1592)," in *The Conversos and Moriscos in Late Medieval Spain and Beyond*, ed. Kevin Ingram (Leiden: Brill, 2009), 187–210.

[130] E. Natalie Rothman, "Interpreting Dragomans: Boundaries and Crossings in the Early Modern Mediterranean," *Comparative Studies in Society and History* 51:4 (2009): 771–800.

[131] ARSI, *Epp. NN 86*, fol. 157r./MPO 2, 306.

construct their identities. Eliano's own struggles to downplay his Jewish past while still relying on it as a means of converting others suggest that the religious fluidity of the early modern Mediterranean as it played out in the theater of the everyday compelled individuals like Eliano to articulate where they stood on the spectrum of religious identities in part because their motives fell under scrutiny too easily. Ambiguous and contradictory identities such as Jewish Jesuit or Greek Turk, and the enigmatic ways in which such figures used their religious pasts, elucidate the inherent paradox of conversion and individuals' concomitant defenses of the hazy, porous, and ever-changing borders of religious identities.

Further, Eliano's acknowledgment that relapses and doubts were part and parcel of conversion shows us that, at least in the 1560s, he did not feel the need to hide the difficulties of his own conversion from fellow Jesuits because they did not see his Jewishness as an obstacle to his ability to carry out his duties. It is an unspoken admission on Eliano's part that conversions were never complete, in so far as they remained integral to how individuals understood themselves and constructed a place within their new faiths. This prompts us to appreciate that the religious lives of baptized converts living as Jews, Copts torn between Islam and Christianity, Greek Turks, or even a Jewish Jesuit were not contested because conversion was deemed impossible. Rather, the diffusion of the borders of faiths, the ease and frequency of conversion and recidivism, and the simple inability to verify one's sincerity – no matter how true it might be – are all reminders that individuals strove to position themselves within and to defend borders between faiths that were too amorphous to define but nevertheless too important to ignore.

In the case of Eliano, the fact that he employed his Jewishness to help others embrace Catholicism is evidence enough that conversion is rife with challenges long after it is "complete," and that religious identities, even for non-converts, were rarely settled. On one hand, Jesuits like André des Freux embraced him because his Jewish past provided the Society of Jesus with a unique talent who could aid in its ever-expanding ministries. In this sense, there was nothing wrong with him being a Jewish Jesuit. On the other hand, certain Jews accused him of renegadism because his Jewishness represented an epistemological and ontological challenge to their own sense of themselves. Of course, the Jews were not alone in this. Whether it was the weeding out of dissent in

Catholic Europe,[132] royal efforts to eradicate Catholicism in early modern England,[133] or the pasha's reaction to Gabriel VII stopping a Copt from converting to Islam, religious communities and their believers needed to create deterrents against apostasy or to encourage recidivism, lest their communities continue to unravel at the fringes of the faith and convert themselves out of existence.

As he returned to Rome in the summer of 1563, Eliano believed that he had done his very best to serve the Society of Jesus, even if his family's embarrassment and the Jews' resentment of his apostasy had caused him to flee Egypt. Yet, as Eliano left Egypt and Cyprus behind him, it was now clear to him that his Jewish past did more than provide him with a set of practical tools that he could use in his ministries and to embrace the larger rhetoric of an evolving Society and early modern Catholic Church. He would continue to confront accusations that his conversion was not sincere. As this chapter and Chapter 1 have shown, these accusations first came from Jews. As we shall see in the following chapters, fellow Catholics soon came to dissect his Jewishness in the wake of the Society of Jesus's shifting views of its Jewish-lineage members. In turn, Eliano's grappling with the entanglement of his Jewishness and his Catholic identity would continue to evolve.

---

[132] Carlo Ginzburg, *The Cheese and the Worms: The Cosmos of a Sixteenth-Century Miller* (Baltimore, MD: Johns Hopkins University Press, 1980); Paolo Prodi, ed., *Disciplina dell'anima, disciplina del corpo e disciplina della società tra medioevo ed età moderna* (Bologna: Società editrice il Mulino, 1994); Peter Godman, *The Saint as Censor: Robert Bellarmine Between Inquisition and Index* (Leiden: Brill, 2000); Lu Ann Homza, *Religious Authority in the Spanish Renaissance* (Baltimore, MD: Johns Hopkins University Press, 2000); Ingrid D. Rowland, *Giordano Bruno: Philosopher/Heretic* (Chicago: University of Chicago Press, 2008).

[133] Eamon Duffy, *The Stripping of the Altars: Traditional Religion in England, c.1400–c.1580* (New Haven, CT: Yale University Press, 1992); For the Society of Jesus in the reign of Elizabeth, see Robert E. Scully, S.J., *Into the Lion's Den: The Jesuit Mission in Elizabethan England and Wales, 1580–1603* (St. Louis, MO: Institute of Jesuit Sources, 2011).

3

Jesuit Anti-Judaism and the Fear of Eliano's Jewishness on the First Mission to the Maronites of Lebanon

[Y]ea there are there for Greece and al the East people, Syrians, Arabians, Aethiopians, namely father Baptista Romanus, of a Rabbine among the Jewes a christian doctor, and these many yeares a Jesuite, excellent in al those tonges of the East.[1]

– Gregory Martin, *Roma Sancta*

What bothers me most, is that he does not recognize the work I do, as he thinks that I have nothing to do here, as he has said several times that I am here to be his interpreter and that I am to do nothing else.[2]

– Giovanni Battista Eliano to Everard Mercurian

After his time at the Council of Trent,[3] Eliano returned to Rome, where he resumed teaching Hebrew at the Collegio Romano; Pius IV requested that the Jesuits create a chair in Arabic as well as provide and print Arabic translations of the decrees of the Council of Trent. Eliano was selected for these roles,[4] which proves that his skills in Semitic languages, mastered in his Jewish youth as a rabbi-in-training and merchant's son traveling throughout the Mediterranean, remained central to his place within the Collegio Romano and the Catholic Church's efforts to convert Eastern

---

[1] Gregory Martin, *Roma Sancta* (1581) (Rome: Edizioni di Storia e Letteratura, 1969), 69.
[2] ARSI, *Gall. 106*, fol. 114r./*MPO 1*, 72.
[3] On Trent, see John W. O'Malley, *Trent: What Happened at the Council* (Cambridge, MA: Harvard University Press, 2013).
[4] Ricardo García Villoslada, *Storia del Collegio romano dal suo inizio (1551) alla soppressione della Compagnia di Gesù (1773)*. (Rome: Pontificia Università Gregoriana, 1954), 71–2.

Rite Christians in the years following his return from Egypt. Thus, in the 1560s, his Jewish past was integral to his Catholic identity and how he contributed to the Society of Jesus.

Over time, however, Eliano's Jewishness ceased to be evidence for some of his unique abilities to contribute to the Jesuits' apostolic mission, as institutional shifts within the Society of Jesus began to undercut the Jesuits' initial openness to Jewish-lineage members. This led Jesuit leaders to question whether Eliano's Jewish birth prevented him from ever being a sincere Jesuit. As this and the following chapter will show, Eliano had to confront the reality that some Jesuits, like his family had in the 1560s, believed he was a crypto-Jew. Because he could not hide his Jewish birth, Eliano had to recalibrate the nature of his Jewishness and more forcefully present it as central to his Catholic identity and how it could be best employed in his missionary efforts in the Ottoman Empire, even more so than he did in the 1560s.

ELIANO'S JEWISHNESS AND HIS MINISTRIES IN ROME AFTER THE COPTIC MISSION

While the period between Eliano's return to Rome in late 1563 and his departure for Lebanon in 1578 is another sparsely documented part of his life, we can, much like we did for his youth, reconstruct the context of his experiences in Rome through descriptions of the Jesuits in the city. We likewise have anecdotes concerning Eliano, in particular those from the English Catholic priest Gregory Martin, whose 1581 *Roma Sancta* depicts the Jesuits as servants to the spiritual needs of everyday Romans as well as the city's countless pilgrims, especially those who would have come to the city for the Jubilee Year of 1575.[5] Thomas Lucas also has illuminated that the Jesuits had a keen sense of how to integrate themselves into urban spaces like Rome, whose population density and diversity of people allowed for ample opportunities for reforming individuals and saving souls.[6] Jesuits like Eliano conducted a wide array of ministries,

---

[5] On the 1575 Jubilee and Pope Gregory's efforts to revamp Rome for the arrival of pilgrims, see Jack Freiberg, "The Lateran Patronage of Gregory XIII and the Holy Year 1575," *Zeitschrift Für Kunstgeschichte* 54:1 (1991): 66–87. For the subsequent Jubilee of 1600, cf. Clare Robertson, *Rome 1600: The City and the Visual Arts under Clement VIII* (New Haven, CT: Yale University Press, 2016).

[6] On Jesuit urbanism, see Thomas M. Lucas, *Saint, Site, and Sacred Strategy: Ignatius, Rome and Jesuit Urbanism* (Vatican City: Biblioteca apostolica vaticana, 1990); Thomas M. Lucas, *Landmarking: City, Church & Jesuit Urban Strategy* (Chicago: Loyola Press, 1997).

such as running confraternities and providing catechetical education.[7] Their work did not stop there, as they also ran hospitals, orphanages, and prisons; ministered to the sick and dying; and reformed prostitutes.[8]

Further, as the Jesuits slowly became a fixture of Rome's religious landscape, Eliano was to be more than just a bookish academic. The centerpiece of the Jesuits' efforts in Rome and Eliano's participation in them was to be their mother church, the Gesù, which was under construction but nevertheless a functioning religious space during this time in Eliano's life. Gregory Martin explains that the Gesù was "very large and fayre" despite "being but halfe built," and already provided "Masses, and preaching, and confessions, etc." to all comers.[9] In early modern Rome, preaching and confession were the two most frequent ministries that all of the religious orders (e.g., the Carthusians, the Carmelites, the Oratorians, the Capuchins, the Theatines, and the Jesuits) provided. But the Jesuits were masters of the confessional, "first for skil in al cases of conscience; secondly for languages, bycause there come thither to be confessed the Catholikes of al countries that come to Rome."[10]

Martin claimed as well that the Society of Jesus was so well renowned for its skilled confessors that Jesuits heard the greatest number of confessions at St. Peter's. In fact, the Jesuits were selected above the other orders to hear confessions at the half-built St. Peter's because they alone could ensure that "there is of every countrie one father at the lest, as of Ingland, Polland, Flaunders, and so forth: and of some mo, as of Italie, France Spayne."[11] Clearly, if we are to believe Martin, the Jesuits were the most dynamic, skilled, and diversified order at the papacy's disposal and therefore dominated the confessional. While the Jesuits' rivals might have disagreed with Martin's suggestion that the Jesuits possessed a monopoly of Rome's religious services, there is no denying the place of the Jesuits in the penitential and spiritual life of the Eternal City. And Eliano fit right in, in no small part because of his Jewishness: "yea there are there for Greece and al the East people, Syrians, Arabians, Aethiopians, namely father Baptista Romanus, of a Rabbine among the Jewes a christian doctor, and these many yeares a Jesuite, excellent in al those tonges of the East."[12] Eliano is, in Martin's description of Jesuit confessors active at

---

[7] Lance Lazar, *Working in the Vineyard of the Lord: Jesuit Confraternities in Early Modern Italy* (Toronto: University of Toronto Press, 2005).

[8] John O'Malley, *The First Jesuits* (Cambridge, MA: Harvard University Press, 1993), 165–99.

[9] Gregory Martin, *Roma Sancta* (1581) (Rome: Edizioni di Storia e Letteratura, 1969), 58.

[10] Ibid., 69.   [11] Ibid.   [12] Ibid.

St. Peter's, the only Jesuit mentioned by name, suggesting that Eliano was well known for his linguistic prowess and the uniqueness of his skills in "those tonges of the East."

When Martin discussed the Catholic Church's efforts to convert the Jews of Rome through preaching, he again refers to Eliano.[13] Every Saturday, the Jews of Rome heard conversionary sermons in San Benedetto in Arenula, the oratory of the Confraternita della Santissima Trinità dei Pellegrini, which was about halfway between the Jewish Ghetto and Campo de' Fiori, where Eliano had burned the Talmud in 1553, and it was not too far from the Collegio Romano and the Gesù.[14] Usually, Martin explains, "there come up into the pulpit two excellent men, one after another, for the space of two houres. The one and the first, a Jesuite or some other of greate skil and good spirit, to move: the other, a great Rabbine sometime of their owne, but now these manie years a zealous and learned Christian, named maister Andreas," the converted rabbi from Fez, Andrea de Monte.[15] Martin makes note that there were others who were present in the city with the skills to contribute to the conversion of the Jews: "of the which Christian Rabbines (by the way) there are in Rome fower very famous, one a Dominican fryer, an other a Jesuite, the third Reader of the Hebrew in *Sapientia*, that is the universitie: and the fourth, this M. Andreas."[16] The Jesuit is most likely Eliano, as he was the only Jewish-born Jesuit; likewise, while Martin does not explicitly state that Eliano preached to the Jews in San Benedetto in Arenula, given that he already had a reputation for his work with the city's Eastern Rite Christian visitors and the fact that Martin noted him among the four famous converts, it would not be surprising if Eliano were among the Jesuits selected to give one of these conversionary sermons.[17]

---

[13] On Conversionary sermons in Rome, see Emily Michelson, "Conversionary Preaching and the Jews in Early Modern Rome," *Past & Present* 235:1 (May 2017): 68–104.

[14] Ibid., 78. San Benedetto in Arenula was torn down in the 1580s and replaced with the current Chiesa della Santissima Trinità dei Pellegrini, consecrated in 1616. On the Jewish Ghetto, see Kenneth R. Stow, *Theater of Acculturation: The Roman Ghetto in the Sixteenth Century* (Seattle: University of Washington Press, 2001).

[15] Gregory Martin, *Roma Sancta* (1581) (Rome: Edizioni di Storia e Letteratura, 1969), 78. On De Monte, See Fausto Parente, "DE MONTE, Andrea," in *Dizionario biografico degli italiani*, 38 (Rome: Istituto della Enciclopedia italiana, 1990).

[16] Gregory Martin, *Roma Sancta* (1581) (Rome: Edizioni di Storia e Letteratura, 1969), 78.

[17] Ibid. There is some speculation as to which Jesuit Martin refers in this case. Some, such as Piet van Boxel, have postulated that it is in fact not Eliano but Antonio Possevino, whose work with the Jews Martin mentions on p. 82, and who was widely suspected of being a *converso* in his own lifetime. However, Martin calls these four men "Christian Rabbines," which suggests that they were converts, if not former rabbis themselves.

Even so, Eliano would have surely been used as an exemplar in those sermons given by fellow Jesuits or by figures like Andrea de Monte; like Eliano had done when attempting to convert Jews aboard the ships to and from Egypt, Andrea de Monte too relied on his Jewishness and empathy for converts' struggles to convince Jews to convert. Thus, converts' willingness to use their Jewishness as an expression of the truth of Catholicism became a mechanism for augmenting the church; Eliano's Jewishness remained central to how his fellow Catholics viewed him and how he represented himself to both Catholics and others, including the Jews: while he was "these many yeares a Jesuite," he would always be "of a Rabbine among the Jewes." Rather than shun them as a mark of shameful difference, Eliano could embrace his conversion and dexterity in "al those tonges of the East" as a marker of distinction. He used his Jewishness to construct for himself a place within the Society of Jesus as an "instrument for helping others," as André des Freux had described him in 1551.[18]

Despite having fled Egypt in 1562 because of Jewish accusations that he bounced between Judaism, Islam, and Christianity according to need, Eliano found an apostolic niche. So too did other Jewish-lineage Jesuits. Under Diego Laínez's successor as father general, Francisco Borja (r. 1565–72), Jesuits of Jewish lineage continued to hold positions of prominence, such as Borja's selection of Cristóbal Rodríguez as provincial of Tuscany even though the Coptic mission had failed under his leadership.[19] In sum, the 1560s and early 1570s were a prosperous time

---

It is possible he meant anyone of Jewish blood, but this runs counter to how he refers to converts elsewhere in the work. This opens the possibility, though it does not definitively prove, that Eliano was the Jesuit in question, even if he did not actually preach to the Jews himself. In fact, Emanuele Colombo suggests that Eliano did preach to the Jews. Such ambiguities as this run throughout Martin's quite detailed text, rendering him both one of our most useful and most frustrating sources for Rome in the pontificate of Gregory XIII. For more on this debate surrounding which Jesuits worked toward the conversion of the Jews, see Emanuele Colombo, "The Watershed of Conversion: Antonio Possevino, New Christians, and Jews," in *'The Tragic Couple': Encounters between Jews and Jesuits*, ed. James William Bernauer and Robert A. Maryks (Leiden: Brill, 2014), 25–42; Piet van Boxel, *Jewish Books in Christian Hands: Theology, Exegesis and Conversion under Gregory XIII (1572–1585)* (Vatican City: Biblioteca Apostolica Vaticana, 2016). I thank Emily Michelson for these references as well as for her pioneering work in Catholic designs for the Jews of Rome. See her "Conversionary Preaching and the Jews in Early Modern Rome," *Past & Present* 235:1 (May 2017): 68–104.

[18] *Litterae quadrimestres ex universis, praeter Indiam et Brasiliam. Tomus primus (1546–1552)* (Rome: Monumenta Historica Societatis Iesu, 1894), 441–2.

[19] Robert A. Maryks, *The Jesuit Order as a Synagogue of Jews: Jesuits of Jewish Ancestry and Purity-of-Blood Laws in the Early Society of Jesus* (Leiden: Brill, 2010), 100–15.

for Jesuits of Jewish ancestry like Eliano. After 1572, however, this would all begin to change.

THE RISE OF ANTI-JEWISH SENTIMENT WITHIN THE SOCIETY OF JESUS

While Eliano was ostensibly in a position to benefit from his Jewish past through teaching, textual work, preaching, and hearing confessions, the place of Jewish-lineage Jesuits within the Society – both Eliano as well as *conversos*, the descendants of converts – slowly began to shift. As we saw in Chapter 1, Eliano was admitted to the Society because of Ignatius of Loyola's openness toward admitting a Jewish convert and his own relationships with *conversos* as well as the belief shared between Ignatius and André des Freux that Eliano's Jewishness could be employed to the Society's benefit. Recall that many of the early Jesuits, such as Diego Laínez and Cristóbal Rodríguez, were themselves *conversos*. However, in this period when Eliano was most active in Rome, leading Jesuits' views regarding Jewish-lineage members began to shift away from Ignatius's acceptance toward a skepticism grounded in the fairly widespread Catholic belief that Jewish blood was so tainted that baptism could not fully purify it, and any Jewish-lineage Christians only appeared zealous to hide their secret Judaism.[20] This shift eventually led to de facto discrimination and, four years after Eliano's death, de jure repudiation of men of Jewish ancestry.

This process began in earnest in 1572–73 with the death of Diego Laínez's successor as father general – Francisco Borja, a *converso* and the third in an exclusive line of Spaniards to hold the high office – and the hotly contested election of his successor at the Third General Congregation of the Society of Jesus. Debates over Borja's successor stimulated the conflation of ideological shifts and political rivalries among leading Jesuits on one hand with rising anxieties concerning crypto-Judaism in the Society of Jesus and Catholic society more generally on the other.[21]

---

[20] Albert A. Sicroff, *Les controverses des statuts de "pureté de sang" en Espagne du XVe au XVIIe siècle* (Paris: Didier, 1960).

[21] A general exploration of this process is discussed in Thomas M. Cohen, "Racial and Ethnic Minorities in the Society of Jesus," in *The Cambridge Companion to the Jesuits*, ed. Thomas Worcester (Cambridge: Cambridge University Press, 2008), 199–205. Cf. Michael Alpert, *Crypto-Judaism and the Spanish Inquisition* (New York: Palgrave, 2001); Jonathan Irvine Israel, *Diasporas within a Diaspora: Jews, Crypto-Jews and the World Maritime Empires (1540–1740)* (Leiden: Brill, 2002); Renée Levine Melammed,

The previous two vicars general, Laínez and Borja, had both been elected father general; so when Borja died, it was assumed that Juan de Polanco – vicar general, one of Ignatius's closest confidants, secretary to the first three fathers general, and arguably the most influential and respected Jesuit at the time – would be selected as the fourth superior general of the Society of Jesus.

However, Italian and Portuguese Jesuits were increasingly at odds with their Spanish peers who monopolized leadership positions within the Jesuit curia in Rome. They feared that Polanco's election would continue the trend of Spanish dominance, thereby locking them out of key positions. However, opposing Polanco outright was risky because of his influence as well as the fear that it would vex Philip II of Spain and his close ally Pope Gregory XIII (r. 1572–85). To prevent Polanco's election, his opponents reminded Gregory that many important Spanish Jesuits, Polanco included, were *conversos*.[22] They intimated that the crypto-Judaism that the church had been trying to eradicate was on the cusp of percolating to the very top of the Society of Jesus and would taint Gregory's efforts at Catholic renewal.[23]

Heretics or Daughters of Israel?: The Crypto-Jewish Women of Castile (New York: Oxford University Press, 2002); Vincent Barletta, *Covert Gestures: Crypto-Islamic Literature as Cultural Practice in Early Modern Spain* (Minneapolis: University of Minnesota Press University, 2005).

[22] On the evolution of the sixteenth-century papacy on the question of Jews and Jewish converts, see David Berger, "*Cum Nimis Absurdum* and the Conversion of the Jews," *The Jewish Quarterly Review*, New Series, 70:1 (July 1, 1979): 41–9; Kenneth R. Stow, "The Papacy and the Jews: Catholic Reformation and Beyond," *Jewish History* 6:1/2 (January 1, 1992): 257–79; Daniele Santarelli, *Il papato di Paolo IV nella crisi politico-religiosa del Cinquecento* (Rome: Aracne editrice, 2008).

[23] Stefania Pastore, *Un'eresia spagnola: spiritualità conversa, alumbradismo e inquisizione (1449–1559)* (Florence: L.S. Olschki, 2004); L. P. Harvey, *Muslims in Spain, 1500 to 1614* (Chicago: University of Chicago Press, 2005); A. Katie Harris, *From Muslim to Christian Granada: Inventing a City's Past in Early Modern Spain* (Baltimore, MD: Johns Hopkins University Press, 2007); Kevin Ingram, ed., *The Conversos and Moriscos in Late Medieval Spain and Beyond* (Leiden: Brill, 2009); Marie Theresa Hernández, *The Virgin of Guadalupe and the Conversos: Uncovering Hidden Influences from Spain to Mexico* (New Brunswick, NJ: Rutgers University Press, 2014); Mercedes Garcia-Arenal and Gerard Albert Wiegers, eds., *The Expulsion of the Moriscos from Spain: A Mediterranean Diaspora* (Leiden: Brill, 2014). This process was, of course, also taking place in Portugal at the same time, and caused anxieties within the Portuguese church. However, the Portuguese Jesuits presented it as a purely Spanish problem. On the Portuguese and their religious minorities, see François Soyer, *The Persecution of the Jews and Muslims of Portugal: King Manuel I and the End of Religious Tolerance (1496–7)* (Leiden: Brill, 2007).

In the wake of this disquiet, Gregory urged the congregants to deliberate over whether a Jewish-lineage father general would perpetrate the Society's ruin. Unwilling to oppose the pope, those who would have supported Polanco slowly moved away from him. While Polanco's election seemed all but certain just months prior, the congregation eventually elected Everard Mercurian (1514–80), from the Spanish Netherlands, as a compromise candidate who broke the perceived Spanish hold on the highest office in the Society but continued the trend of having a subject of Philip II – Gregory's close ally – as superior general.[24]

Mercurian immediately proved himself to be inimical toward Jesuits of Jewish ancestry, or at the very least felt much institutional pressure to do so. The most blatant example of Mercurian's anti-Jewish housecleaning was his decision to move Polanco from Rome to a lesser clerical post in Sicily.[25] Even Benedetto Palmio, Polanco's bitter rival as well as an anti-Jewish polemist who coined the epithet "*Converso* Triumvirate" mentioned in Chapter 1, felt that this was a dramatic fall from grace given Polanco's relationships with the first three fathers general and his standing on the eve of the Third General Congregation.[26] Other Jewish-lineage Jesuits consequently chose to distance themselves from Mercurian and the Jesuit curia, lest they too be ostracized: Jerome Nadal, the great reformer of Jesuit education, retired to Tivoli outside Rome and eventually Austria;[27] Pedro de Ribadeneyra, former provincial of Tuscany and Sicily (and biographer of Ignatius), returned to his native Toledo.[28]

---

[24] Robert A. Maryks, "'A True Israelite in Whom There Is Nothing false': The Controversy over the Jewish Ancestry of Diego Laínez," in *Diego Laínez (1512–1565) and His Generalate*, ed. Paul Oberholzer (Rome: Bibliotheca Instituti Historici Societatis Iesu, 2015), 424–7.

[25] ARSI, *Vitae 164*, fols. 42–5.

[26] Robert A. Maryks, *The Jesuit Order as a Synagogue of Jews: Jesuits of Jewish Ancestry and Purity-of-Blood Laws in the Early Society of Jesus* (Leiden: Brill, 2010), 123; ARSI, *Vitae 164*, fol. 45.

[27] ARSI, *Vitae 164*, fol. 45. For more on Nadal, see William V. Bangert and Thomas M. McCoog, *Jerome Nadal, S.J., 1507–1580: Tracking the First Generation of Jesuits* (Chicago: Loyola University Press, 1992).

[28] Robert A. Maryks, *The Jesuit Order as a Synagogue of Jews: Jesuits of Jewish Ancestry and Purity-of-Blood Laws in the Early Society of Jesus* (Leiden: Brill, 2010), 123; *Patris Petri de Ribadeneira, Societatis Iesu sacerdotis, confessiones, epistolae aliaque scripta inedita*, vol. 1, ed. D. Restrepo, S.J. and Joannes Vilar, S.J. (Madrid: La editorial ibérica, 1920), 782.

Mercurian's successor as father general, Claudio Acquaviva (r. 1581–1615), only exacerbated the tenuous place of Jewish-lineage Jesuits.[29] Over the course of his quite lengthy generalate, Acquaviva pushed for the limitation and eventual expulsion of Jesuits of Jewish heredity in the name of purifying the Society. He also appointed three major opponents of Jewish-lineage Jesuits to various important posts in the Jesuit curia: Paul Hoffaeus (*admonitor* to the father general), Lorenzo Maggio (assistant general), and Manuel Rodrigues (also assistant general).[30] Acquaviva likewise clandestinely began instructing provincials not to admit anyone suspected of having Jewish heritage and to investigate potential novices' bloodlines.[31] Finally, the Fifth General Congregation of the Society of Jesus in 1593 decreed that no one of Jewish ancestry could enter the Society of Jesus, and all current non-ordained Jesuits of Jewish lineage were to be expelled. Nadal, Cristóbal Rodríguez (d. 1581), and Polanco did not live to see the full extent of Acquaviva's anti-*converso* campaign. Others sought to hide their Jewish heredity, and Ribadeneyra never mentioned Laínez's Jewish ancestry in his biography, lest his legacy be ruined.[32] Those who were not expelled because of their professed status no longer held important posts, and were relegated to academic and clerical positions, whereas some opted instead to leave the Society.[33]

The sentiments of men like Mercurian and Acquaviva would affect Eliano, but not in the sense that he would be outright condemned or even expelled from the Society – namely, because Eliano had been an ordained

---

[29] There was a sizable group within the Jesuits that was against these measures, but it was no longer the most powerful faction. See Robert A. Maryks, *The Jesuit Order as a Synagogue of Jews: Jesuits of Jewish Ancestry and Purity-of-Blood Laws in the Early Society of Jesus* (Leiden: Brill, 2010), 125–8; 159–214.

[30] Ibid., 143–6.   [31] ARSI, *Inst. 184/II*, fol. 347rv.

[32] Antonio Possevino, himself probably a *converso*, refused to ignore Laínez's *converso* legacy in his praise for the late father general. Possevino openly defended *conversos*, Laínez included, in his writings. For an overview of the defense of Laínez's New Christian status, see Robert A. Maryks, "'A True Israelite in Whom There Is Nothing false': The Controversy over the Jewish Ancestry of Diego Laínez," in *Diego Laínez (1512–1565) and His Generalate*, ed. Paul Oberholzer (Rome: Bibliotheca Instituti Historici Societatis Iesu, 2015); Thomas M. Cohen, "Nation, Lineage, and Jesuit Unity in Antonio Possevino's Appeal to Everard Mercurian (1576)," in *A Companhia de Jesus na península ibérica nos séculos XVI e XVII: Espiritualidade e cultura. Actas do colóquio internacional* (Porto: Instituto de Cultura Portuguesa da Faculdade de Letras; Centro Inter-universitário de História da Espiritualidade, Universidade do Porto, 2004), 543–61. For further discussion of Possevino, see John Patrick Donnelly, "Antonio Possevino and Jesuits of Jewish Ancestry," *Archivum Historicum Societatis Iesu* 55 (1986): 3–31.

[33] ARSI, *Inst. 186e*, fol. 355v.

priest since 1561 and anti-Jewish actions remained de facto in nature until 1593. Such policies likewise depended on individual provincials' cooperation as well as the ever-present tension between principles and pragmatism. Nevertheless, Eliano faced the reality that some within the Society – the fathers general in particular – were systematically undercutting the influence of Jewish-lineage Jesuits.

This major shift in how Jewish-lineage Jesuits were viewed meant, first, that Eliano could no longer use his own struggles with conversion as evidence that he empathized with the challenges of changing faiths, as we saw with the two Jews living as Christians or the Jew he wished to baptize in Nicosia. If he presented conversion as anything but easy and finite, he would surely open himself up to accusations of crypto-Judaism. More pointedly, everyone knew full well that he was born Jewish, meaning that he could not hide his Jewish past in the same manner that Ribadeneyra or Nadal attempted. And given that Gregory Martin's account of Eliano's activities stemmed from his time in Rome in the late 1570s, after the election of Mercurian, it is clear that Eliano was hardly a marked man for being a convert but continued to use his Jewish past as a means of securing a place for himself within the Society of Jesus.

Yet, to do so, Eliano had to find a way to reconcile his Jewishness with the expectations placed on him as a Jesuit priest. In this regard, Eliano returned more forcefully to des Freux's claim that he could be useful because of his linguistic and textual skills: going forward, Eliano grounded his ability to contribute to the Society of Jesus in teaching Hebrew and Arabic, producing and editing texts in Semitic languages, and hearing confessions. He also engaged in exegetical metaphors that underscored the Jewishness that he shared with key biblical figures who defended the faith and spread the Word, such as the prophet Elijah, John the Baptist, and Paul.

THE UTILITY OF ELIANO'S JEWISHNESS
AND THE CALL TO MISSION IN LEBANON

Eliano's first major opportunity to sharpen how he presented his Jewishness occurred when he was sent to Lebanon in 1578. The decision to send Eliano there followed Syriac Maronite Patriarch of Antioch Mihail ar-Ruzzy's (r. 1567–81) lament to Pope Gregory XIII on 10 September 1577 that a schismatic patriarchal vicar named Dawud had begun naming bishops without Mihail's approval.[34] Dawud, whom Mihail described as a man "with little fear of God," had also condemned Mihail before the Ottomans for having purportedly permitted the construction of a chapel without approval. Ottoman guards stormed the patriarchal monastery and arrested many of Mihail's supporters. Once Mihail composed himself and absorbed what had happened, he swiftly excommunicated Dawud and his conspirators.[35] Mihail was able to prevent any further damage from Dawud's attempted schism and the Ottoman reprisals quickly lessened once it was clear he had not violated Ottoman law. But he feared further internal challenges to his authority. While it is unclear how frequent this was the case given the general peace between Ottomans and their subjects, Mihail claimed that the Ottomans had ransacked monasteries and imposed heavy taxes on Maronite monks, who "had been molested greatly, and I find myself continually vexed because of them."[36] Mihail told Gregory that should episodes like Dawud's attempted schism and Ottoman intervention into Maronite life continue, the Maronites "will be in trouble, and no patriarch will want to live like this."[37]

Many within the curia felt that these sorts of tribulations were not new to the Maronites, and Gregory believed that this Eastern Rite Catholic community was on the precipice of apostasy due to its perceived poverty and lack of sustained communication with Rome.[38] That is not to say that

---

[34] For a broader sketch of Maronite history, see Pierre Dib, *History of the Maronite Church* (Detroit: Maronite Apostolic Exarchate, 1971); Matti Moosa, *The Maronites in History* (Syracuse, NY: Syracuse University Press, 1986). A good collection of sources on Rome and the Maronites in the Middle Ages is Bernard Ghobaïra al-Ghaziri, *Rome et l'eglise syrienne-maronite d'Antioche (517–1531): Théses, documents, lettres* (Beirut: Khalil Sarkis, 1906). Two contemporary accounts of the Maronites were printed in the seventeenth century: See Girolamo Dandini, *Missione apostolica al patriarca, e maroniti del Monte Libano* (Cesena: Neri, 1656); Paul Naaman and Antonius Faustus Naironus, *Essai sur les maronites: leur origine, leur nom et leur religion: par Fauste Nairon de Bane maronite, Rome 1679* (Kaslik, Lebanon: Universite Saint Esprit de Kaslik, 2006).

[35] ARSI, *Gall. 95 II*, fol. 23r./MPO 1, 43.

[36] ASV, *A.A.ARM I–XVIII*, 1761./MPO 1, 47–8.

[37] ARSI, *Gall. 95 II*, fol. 23r./MPO 1, 43.

[38] Kamal S. Salibi, "The Maronites of Lebanon under Frankish and Mamluk Rule (1099–1516)," *Arabica* 4:3 (September 1957): 296–303. Bruce Masters, *Christians and Jews in the Ottoman Arab World: The Roots of Sectarianism* (Cambridge: Cambridge University Press, 2001), 43. See also Sami Kuri's discussion of the Maronites in the introduction to *MPO 1*, 51–4. See also Pierre Rondot, *Les institutions politiques du Liban: Des communautés traditionnelles à l'état moderne* (Paris: Institute d'études de L'Orient contemporain, 1947); Pierre Raphael, *Le rôle du Collège Maronite romain dans*

no links had been maintained between Rome and Lebanon. On the contrary, the Maronites sent a delegation to the Fifth Lateran Council (1512–17) – which opened with a moving oration by Egidio da Viterbo, the powerful patron of Eliano's grandfather Elijah Levita – to reaffirm their recognition of papal authority.[39] But Dawud's failed schism demonstrates how fragmented and disunited the community could become, often due to clan-based infighting.[40] Typically, the Ottomans provided general toleration to their religious minorities; and claims by Christians of Ottoman oppression were often hyperbolic to procure Catholic aid. Yet, the crackdown stemming from Dawud's failed schism elucidates that the tension between Ottoman consolidation of power on one hand and the preservation of the liberties of minority communities like the Maronites on the other often did result in conflict.[41]

To assist Mihail in his struggles, Gregory decided that the Society of Jesus would be the ideal order to conduct a mission to Lebanon.[42] Antonio Carafa, the Cardinal Protector of the Maronites, agreed, and promised to do everything within his power to safeguard the Maronites

---

l'orientalisme aux XVIIe et XVIIIe siècles (Beirut: Univserité Saint Joseph, 1950); Etienne de Vaumas, *La répartition de la population au Liban introduction à la géographie humaine de la république libanaise* (Cairo: Impr. de l'Institute français d'archéologie orientale, 1953); Sélim Abou, "Le bilinguisme arabe-français au Liban; essai d'anthropologie culturelle" (Ph.D. diss., University of Paris, 1962); Jean-Claude Berchet, *Le voyage en Orient: Anthologie des voyageurs français dans le Levant au XIXe siècle* (Paris: R. Laffont, 1985); William W. Harris, *Lebanon: A History, 600–2011* (New York: Oxford University Press, 2012).

[39] Robert J. Wilkinson, *Orientalism, Aramaic, and Kabbalah in the Catholic Reformation: The First Printing of the Syriac New Testament* (Leiden: Brill, 2007), 11–28.

[40] Kamal S. Salibi, "The Muqaddams of Bšarrī: Maronite Chieftains of the Northern Lebanon 1382–1621," *Arabica* 15:1 (February 1968): 63–86.

[41] Muḥammad 'Adnān Bakhīt, *The Ottoman Province of Damascus in the Sixteenth Century* (Beirut: Librairie du Liban, 1982); I. Metin Kunt, *The Sultan's Servants: The Transformation of Ottoman Provincial Government, 1550–1650* (New York: Columbia University Press, 1983); Rifa'at Ali Abou-El-Haj, *Formation of the Modern State: The Ottoman Empire, Sixteenth to Eighteenth Centuries* (Albany: State University of New York Press, 1991); I. Metin Kunt and Christine Woodhead, eds., *Süleyman the Magnificent and His Age: The Ottoman Empire in the Early Modern World* (London: Longman, 1995); Colin Imber, *The Ottoman Empire, 1300–1650: The Structure of Power* (London: Palgrave Macmillan, 2002); Abdul-Rahim Abu-Husay, *The View from Istanbul: Lebanon and the Druze Emirate in the Ottoman Chancery Documents, 1546–1711* (London: Centre. for Lebanese Studies; I.B. Tauris, 2004); Stefan Winter, *The Shiites of Lebanon Under Ottoman Rule, 1516–1788* (Cambridge: Cambridge University Press, 2010).

[42] ARSI, *Gall. 95 II*, fol. 26rv./*MPO 1*, 57–9; on Catholic missions more generally, see Alison Forrestal and Seán Alexander Smith, eds., *The Frontiers of Mission: Perspectives on Early Modern Missionary Catholicism* (Leiden: Brill, 2016).

for generations to come.[43] The two called upon Everard Mercurian in the hope that the Jesuits could find the type of success with the Maronites that they had found elsewhere. Given his linguistic skills and his knowledge of the Ottoman Empire and its extensive diplomatic and religious networks, the ideal Jesuit to conduct this mission was Eliano. And for Mercurian, there was no doubt that he would send Eliano, along with two other Jesuits, Tommaso Raggio and Mario Amato.

As for the logistics of the mission, guiding the Jesuits' work were two papal bulls that Gregory issued, *Benedictus Deus* and *Semper Judicavimus*. In the first bull, Gregory wanted to ensure that Eliano, Raggio, and Amato implored the Maronites to reform their doctrinal errors as well as their liturgical practices. To achieve this goal, Gregory demanded that the Maronites have copies of the decrees of the Council of Trent, which, as mentioned, Eliano had translated into Arabic in 1564.[44] With *Semper Judicavimus*, Gregory announced the dispatch of Eliano, Raggio, and Amato to Lebanon.[45] Gregory had little doubt that the legates would find success with the Maronites, thereby both guaranteeing their resistance to outside threats and bringing an end to the fracturing of the community from within.

Carafa had similar hopes. In late February 1578, he expressed his satisfaction with Mihail's overtures for help and his profession of faith,[46] and implored the patriarch to observe *Benedictus Deus* and *Semper Judicavimus*, and any bulls that might follow, as they demonstrated nothing but the integrity and truth of the Catholic faith. After another brief reminder that the Maronites should take to heart all previous papal bulls, decrees, and councils – specifically those of Pope Innocent III and the Fourth Lateran Council – Carafa gave his closing salutations and anticipated nothing short of the complete eradication of the tribulations threatening the Maronites.[47]

It was clear to the Jesuits, then, that they were tasked with reforming a Christian community that was poor and uneducated, but nevertheless loyal to Rome. Given the larger context in which the Maronite mission was to take place, Eliano would remain central to this mission. His time in Egypt as well as the countless confessions from Eastern Rite Christians he

---

[43] ARSI, *Gall.* 95 II, fol. 28r./MPO 1, 60.   [44] ARSI, *Gall.* 95 II, fol. 29v./MPO 1, 51–2.
[45] ARSI, *Gall.* 95 II, fol. 24r./MPO 1, 55–6.
[46] ARSI, *Gall.* 95 II, fol. 28r./MPO 1, 59–60.
[47] ARSI, *Gall.* 95 II, fol. 28b./MPO 1, 62.

had heard in Rome rendered him uniquely skilled to see this mission through. As the only Arabic speaker in the group, the only one with any experience of the Ottoman Empire, and the only one having conducted a prior mission, it was clear from the onset that Eliano should have taken the lead.

Once they did arrive, in June 1578, Eliano was taken aback by the pervasive illiteracy among the Maronite bishops and priests, and it was immediately obvious that he would have to shoulder the burden of the linguistic and textual work.[48] In a letter to Mercurian written soon after arriving in Tripoli, Eliano went to great lengths to explain to Mercurian that he would work diligently to provide the Maronites with proper texts and would even help them improve their literacy. He started with the Maronite envoy that Mihail had sent to Rome, who Eliano claimed "had learned [Arabic] from me on the ship" to Tripoli.[49] He continued that "we judge that it will be necessary [to teach them Arabic] so that all the others can benefit from these Arabic writings; it will especially be necessary to print various things in that language." Lest Mercurian question how this would take place, Eliano explained that "I will dedicate myself to teaching many others this language, because no one knows how to read it."[50]

Eliano's explanation that the Maronites only read Syriac and would only be able to read Arabic texts (e.g., the decrees of the Council of Trent, which he had translated) should he teach them how to do so put the success of the mission squarely on his shoulders. Thus, despite Mercurian's push to diminish the influence of Jewish-lineage Jesuits, this mission would allow Eliano to use his textual prowess honed under his grandfather and knowledge of Arabic learned as the son of a Jewish merchant in Egypt to successfully guide the Maronites in their reforms.

There was one problem with this, however, that impaired this mission from the beginning. While Eliano was the obvious choice to serve on this mission and he was justifiably tasked with the majority of the work, Eliano was not actually the mission's superior. Rather, Mercurian had named Tommaso Raggio as the superior, with Eliano and Amato as his

---

[48] For more on the issue of clerical and general literacy and reform in both Protestant and Catholic contexts, see Jean-François Gilmont, "Protestant Reformations and Reading" (213–37) and Dominique Julia, "Reading and the Counter-Reformation" (238–68), in *A History of Reading in the West*, ed. Guglielmo Cavallo, Roger Chartier, and Lydia G. Cochrane (Amherst: University of Massachusetts Press, 1999).

[49] ARSI, *Gall. 106*, fol. 211r./MPO 1, 69.   [50] Ibid.

assistants.[51] As the next section shows, Raggio quickly proved himself to be an inept leader who did not care for Eliano or the mission. This would have direct implications for Eliano's ability to employ his Jewishness in the reform of the Maronites.

WAYWARD LEADERSHIP AND ELIANO'S FRUSTRATION WITH HIS JUNIOR STATUS

If Raggio were a seasoned administrator (which admittedly Eliano was not), he would have been a fine choice, as it would have freed Eliano to work closely with the Maronites. There is just one problem, namely, it is unclear why Raggio was put in charge: He had no leadership experience, had spent much of the 1570s in secluded Tivoli, had never been to the Ottoman Empire, did not know Arabic, and had been ordained just prior to the mission.[52] In contrast, the other missionary superior that Eliano served, Cristóbal Rodríguez, had years of leadership experience as a theology professor, rector of the college at Valladolid, and vice-provincial of Castile before being named superior of the mission to the Copts in 1561. Selecting the inexperienced and underqualified Raggio makes little sense unless Mercurian's decision, at least in part, stemmed from his view that a former Jew was unfit to lead.

While Mercurian would rely on Eliano's linguistic skills and experience in the Ottoman Empire, it does not appear he was comfortable putting him in charge. Eliano had to navigate his work with the knowledge that any misstep on this mission could be taken as evidence of the crypto-Judaism that compelled Mercurian to go in another direction with leadership. On one hand, fellow Jesuits clearly questioned whether he could be a successful missionary. On the other hand, assisting in the reform of the Maronites could be an opportunity for Eliano to prove that his Jewishness was not only not an obstacle but remained central to his ability to carry out his duties because of his unique textual skills.

If Eliano felt slighted by being overlooked to lead the mission, he did not mention it, at least not initially. It did not take long after having arrived in Lebanon, however, for Eliano to become "very much

---

[51] Amato was born in Geraci, Sicily, in 1543 and joined the Society of Jesus in 1561. He took his vows in 1571. He returned to Lebanon with Eliano in 1581 after Raggio was recalled as superior, and was later in Egypt with Eliano as well, dying in Alexandria in 1584. See *MPO 1*, 456.

[52] For more on Tommaso Raggio, see *MPO 1*, 463.

unsatisfied with the actions of Father Thomaso [*sic*], and I doubt that our uneasy peace, as we have maintained it until now, can last."[53] It was not just that Raggio refused to work on the mission. Rather, "what bothers me most, is that he does not recognize the work I do, as he thinks that I have nothing to do here, as he has said several times that I am here to be his interpreter and that I am to do nothing else."[54] Eliano feared that such a tense relationship with his superior would lead to the mission unraveling: "May Your Paternity, for the love of God, find remedy for my great tribulation ... because I fear that this will not last, and the mission will be impeded if I become melancholy."[55]

Eliano's assertion to Mercurian that Raggio was pulling him into a state of despair gives us a good sense of the frustration Eliano experienced in seeing his skills, which were deemed so necessary to the Society's apostolic ministries in Rome and for this mission, go unappreciated by an inexperienced leader. He knew that the viability of this mission rested on his textual and linguistic skills, and it would be how he could prove his worth to church leaders in Rome and assuage their anxieties concerning his status as a convert. Yet, Raggio viewed him as nothing better than an interpreter. While Eliano does not accuse Raggio of condemning him outright for being a convert, Eliano felt that Raggio did not view him as an equal, or even a worthy subordinate. In the 1560s and early 1570s, his abilities were never questioned; but by 1578, Raggio had strong doubts that Eliano could do anything other than translate, and Eliano feared that others might come to agree. Given the ongoing ostracization of Jesuits of Jewish lineage, such dismissiveness, even if not directly caused by any anti-Jewish prejudice on Raggio's part, was a reminder for Eliano that his Jewishness had taken on new meaning for some and he was clearly not trusted to make decisions.

Such melancholy did not stop Eliano from presenting himself as devoted to the Maronites' reform. While Raggio's diffidence continued to irk him, Eliano reported that the Maronites were "universally confessing to be ignorant (as in effect they are), and that they desire to be taught as disciples," which "gives us great satisfaction and much hope" that they could be thoroughly Catholicized.[56] Central to this process, despite Raggio's claims, would be Eliano. In his discussion of the Maronites' religiosity and desire to reform, he explained that, despite the fact that the Maronites lived "among infidels and so many schismatic nations, God

[53] ARSI, *Gall. 106*, fol. 114r./*MPO 1*, 72.   [54] Ibid.
[55] ARSI, *Gall. 106*, fol. 114r./*MPO 1*, 73.   [56] ARSI, *Gall. 106*, fol. 115r./*MPO 1*, 75.

has preserved 'seven thousand who will never kneel before Baal.'"[57] This scriptural reference (1 Kings 19:18) captures the essence of how Eliano believed that the Maronites would persevere in the face of pressures from the Ottomans as well as "threats and challenges from the Greeks, or Jacobites, or Copts, or Armenians, or Nestorians, all of whom hate [the Maronites] and torment them only because they show obedience to the Roman See."[58] It also requires some elaboration to get a sense of how Eliano positions himself as well as puts his exegetical erudition on display, as Jesuit missionaries often invoked scriptural references in their missionary reports.

While Eliano is engaging in a very common Jesuit practice, the selection of this passage from 1 Kings is of particular note for Eliano as a convert. Eliano knew that his fellow Jesuits, educated as they were in scripture, would remember that it was the prophet Elijah – Eliano's namesake – who led the Jews in their resistance against Baal. Likewise, Jesus claimed that John the Baptist (Eliano's baptismal name – Giovanni Battista) was Elijah renewed, who had been promised in Malachi 4:5 (cf. Matthew 11:14, Mathew 17:11–12, Luke 1:16–17). Eliano's use of 1 Kings here is no coincidence: he positioned himself as a sixteenth-century defender of the faith in the form of Elijah transformed into John the Baptist, come to safeguard the Maronites. Knowing full well the skepticism surrounding Jewish-lineage Jesuits, Eliano needed to seize any opportunity he could to promote himself as a defender of orthodoxy whose religious convictions never wavered. And there would be no better way to do so than to remind fellow Jesuits that he too was an Elijah turned John the Baptist. Eliano shifted the focus of his Jewishness away from potential evidence of crypto-Judaism and religious opportunism toward the biblical legacy of pious Jews and early evangelists who resisted their enemies and protected the orthodoxy of pious communities. To this end, Eliano would lean on the philological skills he mastered under his grandfather. After all, Eliano explained, "not only do [the Maronites] not deny us their books, but they implore us to desire to see them."[59]

While Eliano desired to conduct this textual work for the Maronites while Amato served their spiritual needs, Eliano's relationship with Raggio continued to deteriorate. Raggio showed a thorough inability (or refusal) to understand the Maronites on their own terms. Soon after arriving, Raggio and Eliano reported that there was good reason to

---

[57] ARSI, *Gall. 106*, fol. 115v./*MPO 1*, 77.   [58] Ibid.
[59] ARSI, *Gall. 106*, fol. 115v./*MPO 1*, 78.

believe in the Maronites' desire to "approach the dogmas of the Roman Catholic Church, and totally embrace its traditions and rites." Regarding their liturgy, however, their report states that the Maronites observed "the Greek rite like all the other eastern peoples."[60] This is an incorrect assessment, as their liturgy remained firmly within the West Syrian (or Syro-Antiochene) tradition; it was Greek in neither language nor form.[61] Eliano knew at the very least the rudimentary differences between the various Eastern Rite Christian communities; he also understood quite well that calling them "like the Greeks" was not only inaccurate but deeply offensive to the Maronites. In fact, as we have seen, he enumerated all the sects threatening the Maronites, and he had witnessed firsthand how various Eastern Rite Christians – particularly the Coptic and the Greek religious communities – viewed one another while in Egypt and Cyprus in 1561–63.[62] It is unlikely that Eliano would not have tried to explain this to Raggio. The fact that this letter lumps all Eastern Rite Christians together despite the millennium that these communities had spent in conflict over matters of doctrine and liturgy demonstrates Raggio's ignorance on the subject as well as his refusal to listen to Eliano.

Raggio also seemed distracted from the mission. Eliano explained to Mercurian on 24 July, just a month after their arrival, "I believe that Your Reverence knows that for some time now Father Thomaso [*sic*] has had a great inclination to go to Constantinople to help in the conversion of the Turks and Greeks. And I recall that Your Reverence had asked me about it, that is, if I had any inclination to come here. I responded that I did, but that [Raggio] was inclined to another mission, that is to Constantinople and the Greeks."[63] Eliano's frustration is palpable, as he believed that Mercurian was fully aware that Raggio had no desire to go to Lebanon and had planned from the beginning to go to Constantinople. Why, then, if he knew that Raggio did not want to go to Lebanon in the first place and would put little effort into the mission as a result, did Mercurian put

---

[60] ARSI, *Gall. 106*, fol. 145r./MPO 1, 98.

[61] Leo D. Davis, *The First Seven Ecumenical Councils (325–787): Their History and Theology* (Collegeville, MN: Litrugical Press, 1983). On the Maronites' liturgical trajectory and place within the Syriac tradition, see Peter Galadza, "Eastern Catholic Christianity," in *The Blackwell Companion to Eastern Christianity*, ed. Kenneth Parry (Malden, MA: Blackwell, 2007), 307–8.

[62] ARSI, *Epp. NN 86*, fols. 156r–157v. On the Copts and their place in the larger Ottoman and Christian worlds, especially regarding the Greeks, see Charles A. Frazee, *Catholics and Sultans: The Church and the Ottoman Empire, 1453–1923* (Cambridge: Cambridge University Press, 1983), 61–4.

[63] ARSI, *Gall. 106*, fol. 119r./MPO 1, 82.

Raggio in charge? It seemed that Mercurian would rather entrust the mission to an ambivalent Catholic-born Jesuit than to the dedicated Jewish-born Eliano.

Eliano again attempted to discuss with Raggio his plans to abandon the mission: "I repeated to him that I wondered a lot about what was said [about the mission to Constantinople], and that nothing about it was said to me in Rome, and that the brief from His Holiness made no mention of it."[64] Raggio, furious with Eliano for challenging his authority and his vision for their efforts, purportedly countered that "I did not know anything, and that I have no other role for this mission than to be his interpreter ... and that, as I have finished all that he had commanded of me, I could go back to Rome."[65] Not only was this the second time that Raggio belittled Eliano, but now he was suggesting that he could leave Lebanon because Raggio no longer saw any need for his presence.

Eliano was resolute in his desire to help the Maronites, but he left it up to Mercurian to decide: "Your Paternity can judge how things are." Yet, he reminded Mercurian, abandoning the Maronites at this juncture might "result in damage to their souls: I know for certain that, should these people be helped for some time, all of the [proposed reforms] shall be carried out. Otherwise, they shall remain with their errors, as before."[66] Nevertheless, Eliano made it clear that, so long as Raggio remained in Lebanon, he would feel hamstrung, underutilized, and undervalued. Eliano sardonically lamented that "seeing that I am here for nothing other than to be Father Tomaso's [*sic*] interpreter – and as he is seemingly not even remotely interested in this mission and thinks that he is wasting his time with it – I too have resolved to distance myself from it and do nothing else." He continued that "if no resolution arrives in three or four months, I do not know what I will do; maybe I will go home, to get away from so many pressures and intrigues, in which there is no satisfaction."[67]

Lest Mercurian think that Eliano were the insubordinate junior missionary that Raggio believed him to be – or worse, a resolute crypto-Jew – he did end this letter by explaining that "I certify to Your Paternity that, if you do not give any direction regarding this, we will remain with great confusion. I will strive to have patience and see this out until the end. May Your Paternity deem it right to pray for me, so that I persevere until the end."[68] He pointed to the fact that the mission was failing due to

---

[64] ARSI, *Gall. 106*, fol. 119r./*MPO 1*, 82.   [65] Ibid.
[66] ARSI, *Gall. 106*, fol. 119r./*MPO 1*, 82–3.   [67] ARSI, *Gall. 106*, fol. 119r./*MPO 1*, 83.
[68] Ibid.

a problem with Raggio – whom Mercurian selected over him – and that he was confused on how to handle matters (he was nothing but an interpreter, after all!). Eliano was challenging Mercurian to recognize where the mission might succeed and where it was failing. This is most apparent when this is juxtaposed with Eliano's explanation that the Maronites would surely return to error should the mission fail, as he would no longer be able to provide them with amended books and proper instruction.

By threatening to leave the Maronites to perfidy, Eliano took a risk; but he understood that Raggio's presence would surely doom the mission. He knew as well that he was not alone when it came to Raggio, which would help him convince Mercurian that the mission was in peril, by no fault of his own. For, Mario Amato also found Raggio irascible and intractable: "The cause of [our problems] is that Father Tomase [*sic*] expects to go to Constantinople and leave [this mission] incomplete, saying that there is nothing here that will ever happen; and, as Father Battista has said elsewhere, he said to him that he has no role on this mission and that he came solely to interpret."[69]

While he might have believed that preaching in Constantinople and shutting down Eliano for his apparent insubordination were evidence of his dedication to the faith, these acts – intent notwithstanding – did very little to ingratiate Raggio to his fellow missionaries or to the Maronites. Eliano and Amato believed that the Maronites needed the Jesuits to show a united front in the face of the internal and external threats to the community; the Jesuits could little afford to bicker among themselves or have Raggio jet off to Constantinople, lest the Maronites see such dysfunction as a reason to hedge their bets elsewhere. By the end of July 1578, barely six weeks after their arrival, Eliano and Amato had stopped speaking directly with Raggio, only communicating with him through Giovanni Battista Regolo, the Venetian vice-consul in Tripoli.[70]

Eliano and Amato were further incensed when Raggio began dedicating his time to learning Turkish and planning his voyage to Constantinople. Since Raggio refused to do even the most basic tasks, such as instruct the Maronites in the tenets of the faith or say Mass, Amato carried out most of the day-to-day ministries while Eliano worked on Arabic translations of scripture, a missal, the catechism of Peter Canisius, and Diego de Ledesma's *Christian Doctrine*. And Amato's work

[69] ARSI, *Gall. 106*, fol. 117r./*MPO 1*, 80.   [70] ARSI, *Gall. 106*, fol. 126rv./*MPO 1*, 102.

was essential, as he was both providing spiritual aid and instructing Maronite priests in liturgical orthopraxy.[71] However, if Raggio continued to do nothing, leaving the lion's share of work to Amato and Eliano, both instruction and translation would suffer, and the Maronites would feel inadequately served.

For however obstinate he may have seemed to Eliano and Amato, Raggio was loath to let his fellow missionaries have the final say regarding his actions. He wrote to Mercurian to explain his stance on the mission. While he admitted that the Maronites initially seemed keen to work with the Jesuits, "after such consolation, a bit of desolation followed, caused by the suspicion born in us that they did not walk in truth."[72] According to Raggio, the Maronites resisted their efforts, denied owning certain books, and hid others that he believed were heretical. He also claimed that when he asked Mihail to give certain books to the Jesuits a second time, Mihail told them that "it would be wise if you left the monastery as soon as possible, so that the Turks not find occasion to move against me, given that I have allowed you to be here for some time."[73]

Raggio also had his own take on the dispute with Eliano. While he admitted to Mercurian that he and Eliano disagreed on how to proceed, he felt that, as the superior, he should have the final say. Raggio painted Eliano as a churlish insubordinate and stated again that Eliano's only role was as his interpreter and translator. Beyond that, he felt, Eliano's desire to work with the Maronites was fruitless.[74] He also explained to Mercurian that he had been staying with the Franciscan community in Tripoli because he lost patience with Eliano and Amato. And while Eliano planned to spend the winter translating sections of scripture into Arabic, Raggio hoped to go to Aleppo with Vice-Consul Regolo to see what

---

[71] The translation of spiritual texts was a common practice in early modern Catholicism, especially for the Jesuits, as it promoted the inward reflections that were central to Ignatian spirituality. For an exploration of this in Europe, see Carlos M. N. Eire, "Early Modern Catholic Piety in Translation," in *Cultural Translation in Early Modern Europe*, ed. Peter Burke and R. Hsia (Cambridge: Cambridge University Press, 2007), 83–100. This would eventually be the case with Eastern Rite Christians, as numerous catechisms and devotional texts were translated into Arabic, including Eliano's own catechism. See Giovanni Battista Eliano, *al-ʿItiqād al-Amānah al-urtūdūksiyyah Sacrosanctae Romanae Ecclesiae unitatem venientibus facienda proponitur* (Rome: Typographia Medicea, 1595).

[72] ARSI, *Gall. 106*, fol. 124r./*MPO 1*, 94.

[73] ARSI, *Gall. 106*, fol. 124rv./*MPO 1*, 94–5.

[74] ARSI, *Gall. 106*, fol. 118r./*MPO 1*, 92–3.

benefits would come of it; he also suggested that he might go to Constantinople straight away to preach.[75]

When Eliano learned that Raggio remained staunch in his views, and even wrote to Mercurian to explain to him why the mission was faltering, Eliano felt the need to defend himself against his superior-cum-detractor. Eliano told Mercurian, "because above all Father Thomaso [*sic*] remains firm in his opinion, he perturbs us by saying that we are wasting time," which agitated a young Maronite to the point that "the other day a youth responded to him: 'Why do you say this. . . . Do you not believe that the things that we are doing will be of any use?'"[76] He also feared that Raggio was hiding certain things from him: "I write for myself, without communicating anything with him, because I know that he will have been against me. And even until now, every time that he wrote, he never communicated anything with me."[77] In particular, "I knew that he received various letters from Italy, given the many ships that have come here; yet, [Raggio] has not shown me any [letters] save the letter of Cardinal Caraffa [*sic*] from 20 May."[78] Eliano admitted that it was a difficult, lamentable situation to be in. But he did not see a way to fix matters or convince Raggio to rethink his actions. To make matters worse, Raggio had squandered the Jesuits' money. But because of Raggio's refusal to cooperate, Eliano had to write to Mercurian to ask for more money behind Raggio's back, only fomenting more discord.[79] "And so," Eliano lamented to Mercurian, "here we are . . . divided as far as this mission goes; although, everything else that I support I do not bring up with him, for I am very obedient to him, as God knows."[80]

Eliano's declaration of loyalty to a man with whom he shared little except mutual antipathy demonstrates that Eliano understood exactly how delicate a subject this was to broach given his tenuous position as a Jewish-lineage Jesuit. On one hand, this letter could confirm that Eliano was indeed disobedient and headstrong, as Raggio had suggested. On the other hand, if Eliano could convince Mercurian that he remained dedicated to the mission despite Raggio's secrecy and refusal to see Eliano as anything other than an interpreter, then perhaps Mercurian would

[75] ARSI, *Gall. 106*, fol. 121r./*MPO 1*, 91.
[76] ARSI, *Epp. N.N. 86*, fol. 221r./*MPO 1*, 106.
[77] ARSI, *Epp. N.N. 86*, fol. 221r./*MPO 1*, 106.   [78] Ibid.
[79] ARSI, *Epp. N.N. 86*, fol. 221v./*MPO 1*, 108.
[80] ARSI, *Epp. N.N. 86*, fol. 221r./*MPO 1*, 106–7.

see that it was Raggio – not Eliano – who was responsible for the mission's breakdown.

Eliano also related his troubles with Raggio and their implications for the Maronites to Carafa: "It should not surprise Your Most Illustrious Lordship that I write this without [Raggio's] help, as he has not shown himself to be inclined to this mission."[81] Eliano also told the cardinal that, in front of one of the Maronites who was helping them, Raggio said that "we are wasting time and energy; and he even told me that this youth lacked the spirit to do anything."[82] Eliano explained to Carafa that, despite their issues with Raggio and their ostensible loyalty to him as their superior, he and Amato refused to acquiesce in their work with Mihail and his advisors.

In fact, Eliano declared his desire to "visit the whole [Maronite] nation, which lives in 200 towns and villages; and they live like sheep without shepherds, are separated from the faith of all nations, and desire to obey the Holy See."[83] But Eliano also left Carafa with a warning, one that would both remind the cardinal how dire the situation was but that would also make it clear that Eliano worked in the name of the church: "all of this, if done with charity and diligence, I hope will be worthy work; however, it will be necessary to carry it forth, because, if the cord of this mission is cut and we return [to Rome] without having done everything," the Maronites' struggles would continue.[84] This almost threatening tone conveys just how dire Eliano felt things were, and how he wanted it to be known that it was not he who was stammering about and refusing to follow the desires of Gregory, Carafa, and Mercurian.

The other problem that Eliano feared, beyond the mission's failure, was the potential intervention of the Ottoman authorities. Aside from Raggio's refusal to work with the Maronites and his disdain for Eliano, Eliano also found it troubling that Raggio spent all his time "learning the Turkish language, writing, copying, transferring all things Turkish."[85] Raggio's desire to learn Turkish perturbed Eliano because he knew it was not only fruitless but potentially dangerous. If Raggio were to work with the Latin Christians of Constantinople, as he claimed, Italian or French would suffice. And he certainly would not preach to the city's various Orthodox Christians in Turkish. The fear, however, was that it was not ignorance regarding the ethnolinguistic and religious landscape of

---

[81] ARSI, *Gall. 106*, fol. 130/*MPO 1*, 111.   [82] Ibid.   [83] Ibid.   [84] Ibid.
[85] ARSI., *Gall. 106*, fol. 133r./*MPO 1*, 117.

Constantinople that drove Raggio to study Turkish. Rather, Eliano worried, Raggio was planning to convert Muslims. While this might have been a sincere attempt to express Catholic piety, evangelizing Muslims might lead to his execution at the hands of the Ottomans.[86]

There is also an imbedded message in Eliano's condemnation of Raggio's desire to learn Turkish, namely, Eliano's expertise in the cultural landscape of the Ottoman Empire stemming from his time there before his conversion and during his mission to the Copts. In the latter case, his experiences with accusations that he was a Muslim apostate as well as Coptic Patriarch Gabriel VII's flight after attempting to prevent a Copt from converting to Islam would have resonated with his superiors in Rome.[87] It therefore follows that the very next sentence in this letter censuring Raggio for trying to teach himself Turkish implores Mercurian "to switch Raggio for me [as superior], or to recall him, leaving me here with Mario [Amato], if you deem that we stay, because I hope that I will do much, or even more without him than with him."[88] Such a bold statement – that Raggio's presence in Lebanon was actually hurting the mission and hindering Eliano's efforts – is a reminder that Eliano saw himself as the conduit through which the Maronites would reform themselves; and this was because of his understanding of the dynamics of the Ottoman world and his linguistic and philological erudition.[89]

THE MISSION'S SUSPENSION

By October 1578, Mercurian needed little convincing that the mission had been irrevocably damaged. However, Mercurian did not blame Raggio, at least not initially. Rather, he explained to all three Jesuits that "we have had some displeasure in learning that you have not fully satisfied the goal of the voyage, as was desired, nor have there been the union and peace that with words and writing we had inculcated to you."[90] Mercurian understood that the Jesuits would not come to an agreement and needed to be separated before matters got out of hand.

---

[86] Bruce Masters explains: "Attempts to convert Muslims would result in the execution of the converts and proselytizers alike." Bruce Alan Masters, *Christians and Jews in the Ottoman Arab World: The Roots of Sectarianism* (Cambridge: Cambridge University Press, 2001), 70.

[87] ARSI, *Epp. N.N. 86*, fol. 143r./*MPO 2*, 216. See also Chapter 2.

[88] ARSI., *Gall. 106*, fol. 133r./*MPO 1*, 117.   [89] ARSI, *Gall. 106*, fol.135r./*MPO 1*, 121.

[90] ARSI, *Gall. 106*, fol. 128r./*MPO 1*, 104.

He also realized that the Maronites, especially Mihail, had grown tired of Raggio's refusal to work with them; he knew that Eliano and Amato had done the majority of the work. Finally, he was aware that the Maronites wanted Eliano to stay in Lebanon. Yet, to Eliano's chagrin, Mercurian demanded that all three Jesuits return to Italy once the seas permitted it, without further inquiry. When this letter arrived in Lebanon in late December, Raggio attempted to save the mission and secure his position as its superior. He replied to Mercurian that, since they could not leave Tripoli until at least March due to the onset of winter, he wished to try again with the Maronites. He even hoped to stay beyond March, with Mercurian's approval.[91]

It was too late for Raggio, though. While Raggio agreed to give up plans to travel to Constantinople and expressed some remorse for his actions, at least to Mercurian, Raggio had scandalized others to the point that they no longer wanted to work with him. Fra Bernardino da Basilicata, one of Raggio's Franciscan hosts in Tripoli, had written to Mercurian in November 1578 that Raggio's preference for staying indoors outraged the Latin community of the city, and that he had done very little to aid the city's Christians. Fra Bernardino told Mercurian that, when he brought his concerns to Raggio, "[Raggio] replied to me that if I did not remain quiet he would give me fifty lashings to my ass, as if I were some delinquent."[92] Mihail also explained to Mercurian that "Father Tommaso has only visited us once" since the Jesuits' arrival, and he was dismayed that Raggio "has told you certain things against us, for we know that he did not have the desire to remain in this country, since he does not know our language and he plans to go to Istanbul, as he has told us numerous times."[93]

In the end, Raggio had alienated everyone involved in the mission, even his Franciscan hosts in Tripoli and the Venetian diplomats who would have helped him get to Constantinople. But above all, he belittled the Maronites, insulted Mihail, seemingly lied about what was happening in Lebanon, and snubbed the community's desire to reform. Raggio had repeatedly disobeyed orders, picked fights with fellow Catholics, and had no clue – or did not care – that his actions were endangering the mission. By the time he finally understood what he had done, the Maronites no longer wanted his help. Mercurian's order to recall Raggio predated his

[91] ARSI, *Gall. 106*, fol. 106r./*MPO 1*, 140.
[92] ARSI, *Gall. 106*, fols. 137r–138v/*MPO 1*, 125.
[93] ARSI, *Gall. 95 I*, fol. 40rv./*MPO 1*, 138–9.

knowledge of how much damage Raggio had done, and Raggio began to change his tune. But any hope for reform was dead so long as Raggio was involved in the mission.[94]

   While Raggio's dismissal must have given Eliano a sense of vindication, he was quite dismayed to learn that he was recalled as well. Given the course of events – and with his continued anxiety given the status of Jewish-lineage Jesuits working in the back of his mind – this whole affair was an affront to Eliano's efforts. Eliano felt that there was still much to be done with textual reform; he was likewise pleased by a rumor that there was a centuries-old Arabic Bible kept in a monastery two days' journey from Tripoli.[95] And Eliano's presence in Lebanon was certainly needed – to say nothing of Mihail's desire for his return – to ensure the proper reform of the Maronites. While the Maronites recognized Gregory as the head of the faith and wanted Eliano to assist them, their books, rites, and liturgy were still nowhere near being considered Catholic. It was also feared that, because of clerical shortage and the fact that Maronite bishops and monks were "poor and ignorant" with lax discipline, the community, along with even the most religious of the Maronites, was on the verge of apostasy. Eliano believed that it would only be through his return to Lebanon that the community could be preserved.[96]

   By May 1579, Raggio, Eliano, and Amato were back in Venice, accompanied by two Maronite youths who were sent to study in Rome.[97] When the Jesuits returned to Rome, they gave a full account of the mission. Gregory and Carafa agreed that Eliano would return to Lebanon, this time as superior.[98] They could ill afford to alienate the Maronites any further. While the mission would continue once Eliano returned in 1580, Raggio's treatment of Eliano and Eliano's recall despite his apparent dedication to the mission show that Eliano could never fully escape shadows of scrutiny. Even if not stemming directly from his status as a convert amid fears of crypto-Judaism, ongoing shifts in anti-Jewish policy and Mercurian's role in them were nevertheless underlying factors in the course of this mission. Given how much he dwelled on his Jewishness in the 1560s – when it was anything but an issue for his

---

[94] ARSI, *Fondo Gesuitico* 650a 464/42/MPO *1*, 132.

[95] ARSI, *Epp. N.N. 86*, fol. 224r./MPO *1*, 169.

[96] ASV, *AA.ARM. I–XVIII*, 1765, fol. 1rv./MPO *1*, 182–3.

[97] ARSI, *Epp. N.N. 86*, fol. 271rv./MPO *1*, 164–5.

[98] That full report is inventoried as ASV, *AA.ARM. I–XVIII*, 1765. It can also be found in MPO *1*, 181–7.

superiors – the role that his conversion played in how he constructed a sense of himself surely became more acute.

In this mission and going forward, Eliano did not emphasize his empathy for converts as he had in the 1560s, as institutional fears of the fluidity of conversion and the latent potentiality of recidivism and crypto-religion could render him a problematic Jesuit. Rather, he likened himself to scriptural defenders of the faith and emphasized his skills in Semitic philology, textual exactitude, doctrinal reform, ministry, and understanding Ottoman geopolitics. His expertise in these matters – and Raggio's clear ignorance of them – meant that he believed that his Jewishness put him in a position to lead this mission. It did not help matters that Raggio dismissed him as nothing better than a secretary and interpreter. Eliano had dedicated himself to the apostolic mission of the Society of Jesus for two decades and employed his Jewishness to that end. But the very reason why he was deemed worthy of admission to the order in 1551 was a contributing factor for why he was relegated to a supporting role by 1578: his Jewish birth and conversion were increasingly seen as suspect, and he was cast aside in favor of Raggio.

Raggio's actions show that the myriad skills required for competing for souls were not learned overnight. Jesuit resistance to leadership and conflicts between missionaries were hardly novel, as Raggio, Eliano, and Amato were neither the first nor the last Jesuits whose intentions and methods were scrutinized.[99] As for Raggio, it does not appear he was so much as lightly reprimanded for his actions. He eventually returned to Italy and carried out a successful career in the Society until his death in 1599, even spending some time in the Balkans. But learning Turkish would only be useful to evangelize to the city's Muslims, which would lead to his arrest and execution. And if he did not wish to convert Muslims, Turkish was rather useless, as the city's non-Muslims spoke Arabic, Greek, Armenian, or any number of languages.[100] On this mission, however, Raggio simply could not imagine that his desire to save as

---

[99] For example, see Ines G. Županov, *Disputed Mission: Jesuit Experiments and Brahmanical Knowledge in Seventeenth-Century India* (New York: Oxford University Press, 1999).

[100] Colin Imber, *The Ottoman Empire, 1300–1650: The Structure of Power* (London: Palgrave Macmillan, 2002), 2–8. See also Eric Dursteler, *Venetians in Constantinople: Nation, Identity, and Coexistence in the Early Modern Mediterranean* (Baltimore, MD: Johns Hopkins University Press, 2006), and Ebru Boyar and Kate Fleet, *A Social History of Ottoman Istanbul* (Cambridge: Cambridge University Press, 2010) for more on the diversity of languages and cultures in Constantinople.

many souls as he could might derail the mission; but Eliano knew better because of his experience as both a convert and a Jesuit who aimed to save souls across the Mediterranean.

Eliano's expertise, when contrasted with Raggio's failures, lays bare the anxieties that surrounded the status of converts by the third quarter of the sixteenth century. While not everyone pegged Eliano as a dissimulator or unable to lead because of his Jewish blood – after all, Carafa and Gregory demanded that Eliano return to Lebanon as the mission's superior – others, including Mercurian, had come to suspect Jesuits like him of being crypto-Jewish opportunists, much as his family had; despite his skill set and his experiences, the pervasive anxieties concerning Jewish-lineage Jesuits compelled Mercurian to choose an inexperienced, indifferent leader. And the fact that it took so long for Mercurian to recall Raggio and only replace him with Eliano on Gregory and Carafa's orders highlights they ways in which anxieties about crypto-Judaism informed the decisions of Jesuit superiors. For Eliano, the course of this failed mission was further evidence that, going forward, his efforts as a Jesuit would be counterbalanced by his religious past. He had to be overly zealous, exaggeratedly ambitious in his missionary efforts, and present his Jewishness as the source of a unique missionary toolkit. And he would get his chance when he returned to Lebanon in 1580; he also returned to Egypt in 1582 to work with the Copts (see Chapters 5 and 6) – in both cases as superior. In so doing, his superiors took a risk in charging a convert to be an evangelist, and any failures might cause them to regret their decision. But by presenting himself as the only Jesuit with the skills to see those missions through, he forced his superiors to question whether they had another choice.

CONCLUSION

The events highlighted in this chapter – Eliano's prowess as a confessor; conversionary sermons in Rome; institutional shifts regarding Jewish-lineage Jesuits; skepticism of Eliano because he was born a Jew; Raggio's actions stemming from his zeal, inexperience, and personality conflicts; subsequent Maronite rejection of Raggio; the eventual decision to let Eliano lead – capture the essence of the challenges of conversion and mission as well as the problematic nature of identity construction in the early modern Mediterranean. The actions of Italian and Portuguese Jesuits, institutional marginalization of Jewish-lineage Jesuits, and

Mercurian's selection of Raggio over Eliano expose the pervasive fears concerning religious proximity and fluidity that are the hallmark of conversion. Because Raggio and his family had always been Catholic, it does not seem to have dawned on anyone that Raggio could jeopardize the mission in the way some believed a crypto-Jew might. In fact, Raggio's desire to study Turkish and go to Constantinople was not insubordination or even crypto-religion by any stretch; he simply desired to spread the faith, or die trying, just as Jesuit missionaries were trained to do.[101]

The irony is that Eliano and Raggio wanted to do the same thing: prove their sincerity to their superiors through evangelization. But the Society of Jesus's evolving relationship with its Jewish-lineage members meant Eliano had to recalibrate the nature of his Jewishness if he were to meet his superiors' expectations and assuage their suspicions. The polyvalent religious landscape of the Mediterranean meant that the Jesuits looked for a wide array of tactics in their missionary efforts, ranging from using converts as missionaries to gingerly navigating the religious politics of the Ottoman Empire. For this reason and in the wake of this failed mission, Mercurian recognized that, despite his own anxiety about Jewish-lineage Jesuits, the only way to ensure the proper reform of the Maronites was to entrust the mission to someone who could accurately and efficiently reform the Maronites' beliefs through doctrinal reform and lexicographical exactitude. There was, as we will see in the next chapter, only one Jesuit who fit that bill: the Jewish-born Giovanni Battista Eliano.

---

[101] For more on the martyr-missionary narrative in the Society of Jesus, see Kirstin Noreen, "Ecclesiae Militantis Triumphi: Jesuit Iconography and the Counter-Reformation," *The Sixteenth Century Journal* 29:3 (October 1, 1998): 689–715.

4

Textual Transmission, Pastoral Ministry, and the Re-Fashioning of Eliano's Intellectual Training

I have attached to this letter a piece of paper on which is printed a single psalm, so that you can admire it and rejoice with me the kindness coming from the Holy Father ... this is a model of the imprints. And with both large and small characters, we will print many, many books.[1]

– Giovanni Battista Eliano to Maronite Patriarch Mihail ar-Ruzzy

We have found among this Nation a New Testament in Chaldean on very ancient sheepskin; and according to what is noted at the end of the book in most beautiful script, it is 960 years old. I will send it to Your Most Illustrious Lordship, as I believe that you will be most grateful, so that it be placed in the Vatican or wherever you see most fit.[2]

– Giovanni Battista Eliano to Antonio Carafa

Not long after Eliano's return to Rome, Carafa ordered Eliano to prepare himself at once for a second sojourn to Lebanon. Although Raggio had alienated the Maronites, Mihail and his bishops were willing to allow the Jesuits to conduct another mission. First, Mihail and other leading Maronites still believed that embracing Tridentine reforms would provide their community with the spiritual edification they desired.[3] Second, Mihail saw Catholic reform as an opportunity to consolidate and legitimate his authority given the recurring fears of schism and factionalism.[4] Nevertheless, Mihail was not willing to accept any missionary but Eliano.

---

[1] ARSI, *Gall. 95* I, fol. 193r./*MPO* 1, 198.   [2] ARSI, *Gall. 95* I, fol. 105r./*MPO* 1, 270.

[3] This was necessary even for religious majorities. See Katharine J. Lualdi, "Persevering in the Faith: Catholic Worship and Communal Identity in the Wake of the Edict of Nantes," *The Sixteenth Century Journal* 35:3 (October 1, 2004): 717–34.

[4] For more on the communal decision to sacrifice confessional autonomy – and the tensions that came with it – see Ronald K. Rittgers, *The Reformation of the Keys: Confession,*

But this mission was to be about more than the Maronites wanting to Catholicize through Eliano and what that tells us about their own sense of their religious identities – though there is much to be gleaned in what follows regarding the agency of minority communities such as the Maronites in constructing their religious identities. Rather, the mission provided Eliano with the opportunity to prove to his superiors that he alone could safeguard the Maronites with his textual and lexicographical skills sharpened in his Jewish youth that had become the root of others' skepticism of him. While the Ottomans were not actively pursuing the Maronites' demise, Eliano painted a scene in which he was their savior. Eliano's letters focus on the ways in which he aided the Maronites in their efforts to Catholicize because of his skills in textual translation and his ability to create kinship bonds among the Maronites and between Lebanon and Rome through a synod as well as pastoral visits to the countryside. Eliano's emphasis on textual transmission and translation as well as ministries as opposed to the tortuous journey that typified conversion – which was central to how he employed his Jewishness in Chapters 1 and 2 – centered on the need to downplay the fluidity of conversion given heightened skepticism surrounding Jewish-lineage Jesuits.[5] One on hand, much of his emphasis on text and ministry can be attributed to the fact that the Maronites were anything but Latinized and doctrinally Catholic despite their ostensible loyalty to Rome, and the implementation of orthodoxy and orthopraxy was never that easy.[6] On the other hand, the ways in which Eliano employed his Jewish past

---

Conscience, and Authority in Sixteenth-Century Germany (Cambridge, MA: Harvard University Press, 2004) and Ronald K. Rittgers, "Private Confession and the Lutheranization of Sixteenth-Century Nördlingen," *The Sixteenth Century Journal* 36:4 (December 1, 2005): 1063–85.

[5] On translation as central to cultural exchange, see Sanford Budick and Wolfgang Iser, eds., *The Translatability of Cultures: Figurations of the Space Between* (Stanford, CA: Stanford University Press, 1996); Peter Burke and R. Hsia, eds., *Cultural Translation in Early Modern Europe* (Cambridge: Cambridge University Press, 2007); A. E. B. Coldiron, *Printers without Borders: Translation and Textuality in the Renaissance* (Cambridge: Cambridge University Press, 2015); Rowan Tomlinson and Tania Demetriou, *The Culture of Translation in Early Modern England and France, 1500–1660* (New York: Palgrave Macmillan, 2015); Jane Tylus and Karen Newman, eds., *Early Modern Cultures of Translation* (Philadelphia: University of Pennsylvania Press, 2015).

[6] Marc R. Forster, *The Counter-Reformation in the Villages: Religion and Reform in the Bishopric of Speyer, 1560–1720* (Ithaca, NY: Cornell University Press, 1992); Mary Laven, "Encountering the Counter-Reformation," *Renaissance Quarterly* 59:3 (2006): 706–20; Kathleen M. Comerford, *Reforming Priests and Parishes: Tuscan Dioceses in the First Century of Seminary Education* (Leiden: Brill, 2006); Emily Michelson, *The Pulpit and the Press in Reformation Italy* (Cambridge, MA: Harvard University Press,

in his efforts with the Maronites should also be seen as part and parcel of Eliano's evolving effort to represent his Jewishness as an essential element of his labors as a Jesuit in light of institutional shifts regarding his status within the Society of Jesus and how Jewish-ancestry Catholics were viewed more generally.

PLANNING ELIANO'S RETURN TO LEBANON

Shortly after Antonio Carafa, one of Eliano's ardent supporters, had ordered Eliano to return to the Maronites, the cardinal also dispatched two brief letters to Lebanon, both of which point to the tenuous nature of the mission despite the Maronites' long-standing relationship with Rome. The first was to the secretary of the Ottoman emir to announce Eliano's return to the Levant and to explain his purpose for being in Ottoman territory. Given that Eliano had a reputation that preceded him as far as the Ottomans were concerned because of his arrest under their orders in Egypt in 1562, Carafa deemed it best to let local officials know of Eliano's presence in Lebanon.[7] It also suggests that Carafa knew full well that Raggio's actions and his quite open desire to convert Muslims had jeopardized the Jesuits' standing before the Ottomans.[8] Carafa's second letter, to Mihail and his bishops, was an effort to assuage the Maronites'

2013); Christopher F. Black, "The Public Face of Post-Tridentine Italian Confraternities," *Journal of Religious History* 28:1 (February 1, 2004): 87–101.

[7] On Ottoman imperial growth see, inter alia, C. Max Kortepeter, *Ottoman Imperialism during the Reformation: Europe and the Caucasus* (New York: New York University Press, 1972); Muhammad ʿAdnan Bakhit, *The Ottoman Province of Damascus in the Sixteenth Century* (Beirut: Librairie du Liban, 1982); Rifaʿat Ali Abou-El-Haj, *Formation of the Modern State: The Ottoman Empire, Sixteenth to Eighteenth Centuries* (Albany: State University of New York Press, 1991); Palmira Johnson Brummett, *Ottoman Seapower and Levantine Diplomacy in the Age of Discovery* (Albany: State University of New York Press, 1994); I. Metin Kunt and Christine Woodhead, eds., *Süleyman the Magnificent and His Age: The Ottoman Empire in the Early Modern World* (London: Longman, 1995); Abdul-Rahim Abu-Husayn, *The View from Istanbul: Lebanon and the Druze Emirate in the Ottoman Chancery Documents, 1546–1711* (London: Centre for Lebanese Studies, I.B. Tauris, 2004); Antonis Anastasopoulos, ed., *Provincial Elites in the Ottoman Empire: Halcyon Days in Crete V: A Symposium Held in Rethymno 10–12 January 2003* (Rethymno, Crete: Crete University Press, 2005); Virginia H. Aksan and Daniel Goffman, eds., *The Early Modern Ottomans: Remapping the Empire* (Cambridge: Cambridge University Press, 2007); Tijana Krstić, *Contested Conversions to Islam: Narratives of Religious Change in the Early Modern Ottoman Empire* (Stanford, CA: Stanford University Press, 2011); M. Pinar Emiralioğlu, *Geographical Knowledge and Imperial Culture in the Early Modern Ottoman Empire* (Aldershot: Ashgate, 2014).

[8] ARSI, *Gall. 95 II*, fols. 58r–59v./*MPO 1*, 208–9.

anxieties regarding how Raggio had treated them by inviting them to participate in a synod that Carafa had entrusted Eliano to oversee.[9]

Eliano's stay in Rome was very brief, less than a year. While there, he had little time for rest, as the planning for the synod began as soon as he returned to Rome. On 1 January 1580, Eliano wrote to Mihail that he had not forgotten the promises he had made to the Maronites. Writing in Arabic, rather than Latin, Eliano explained that "the Holy Father has decided that, in the company of an excellent father and brother, neither of whom will be Father Tommaso [Raggio] nor Mario [Amato], I will return to you."[10] Eliano's reassurance that Raggio will not accompany him is significant, as it shows that Eliano understood full well that the Maronites were uneasy about the viability of this mission should Raggio be involved. It also put the mission squarely on him as its leader. Eliano continued, writing that, in addition to serving their spiritual needs, he would "bring with me a number of gifts for your churches, vases and ornaments and molds for hosts and other similar objects, and everything that you have requested from the Pope. And I will stay with you at Qannubin."[11] Given the dearth of accoutrements in the Maronites' churches, Eliano believed that these vessels would be of great help to the Maronites; but this phrase is also a reminder that Eliano understood full well the nature of Catholic orthopraxy and fashioned himself as the one bringing it to the Maronites.

Central to this as well was Eliano's assurance to Mihail that he would serve their intellectual needs via printed books: "Furthermore, [the pope] has ordered that I prepare a book printing house, so that you can print many books for your nation."[12] Lest Mihail doubt Eliano's ability to produce books of the utmost quality for the Maronites, "I have attached to this letter a piece of paper on which is printed a single psalm, so that you can admire it and rejoice with me the kindness coming from the Holy Father."[13] Eliano also told Mihail that this was just a small sample of what he had planned, for "this is a model of the imprints. And with both large and small characters, we will print many, many books, namely the Old and New Testaments, the Large Breviary, the Small Breviary, the Ordinances and a Spiritual Gospel and many others."[14] Eliano's ability to provide the Maronites with printed books for their own use

---

[9] ARSI, *Gall. 106*, fol. 147r./*MPO 1*, 210.   [10] ARSI, *Gall. 95 I*, fol. 193r./*MPO 1*, 198.
[11] Ibid.   [12] ARSI, *Gall. 95 I*, fol. 193r./*MPO 1*, 198.   [13] Ibid.
[14] Ibid. It is unclear what these last two texts are. The critical editor of this letter, Sami Kuri, posits that the Ordinances are perhaps the decrees of Trent. See *MPO 1*, 198n8. The Spiritual Gospel is most likely some sort of devotional work or commentary on the Gospels.

would be a significant step toward their ability to reform themselves. More pointedly, as Eliano's letter concerning his ability to produce Arabic and Syriac books is written in Arabic, Eliano laid bare his linguistic dexterity, philological skills, and technological know-how in setting up a printing press – all of which he mastered as a Jew – as central to ensuring the reform of the Maronites.

After this letter, Eliano began the final preparations for his departure. The exact date of Eliano's departure for Lebanon is unclear, but it was most likely mid-May 1580, as the only clue comes on 7 May with the papal bull *Ex Litteris Tuis*, in which Gregory XIII officially announced the imminent departure of Eliano with his companion Giovanni Bruno (1544–1623) of Abruzzo, an expert in theology who entered the Society of Jesus in 1570.[15] Given his theological acumen, Bruno was to serve as the mission's doctrinal advisor, assist Eliano with the synod, and draft a catechism that Eliano would translate into Arabic and distribute among the Maronite communities. Bruno also possessed a certain dexterity for navigating the eastern Mediterranean (he also had a basic knowledge of Arabic), or at the very least was patient enough to learn, something that Raggio never was.[16]

Carafa shared Eliano's vision for how the mission was to be handled. In addition to the work with textual reform, Carafa believed that the synod should stress the centrality of Maronite bishops and priests promulgating the basic tenets of the Council of Trent, translated copies of which Eliano and Bruno were to distribute.[17] And much as he had hoped to do before, Eliano was to travel to Maronite villages and towns to help these communities implement the synodal reforms. One of the key components of these visits was the distribution of vestments and sacred vessels. Carafa also wanted the pair to instruct Maronites in the Rosary, have them switch to the Gregorian Calendar once it was formally

---

[15] The original copy of this bull seems to have been lost, as it is not inventoried in ASV where it most likely would be housed. There is a copy, in the hand of Eliano, inventoried as ARSI, *Gall. 106*, fol. 147r.

[16] *MPO 1*, 457. See Salvatore Bon, "BRUNO, Giovanni," in *Dizionario biografico degli italiani*, vol. 14, 665–6.

[17] In the epilogue to his study on Trent, John O'Malley discusses the notion of Trent after the Council itself and how Catholic leaders felt the Council could best achieve some staying power. See John W. O'Malley, *Trent: What Happened at the Council* (Cambridge, MA: Belknap Press of Harvard University Press, 2013), 260–75.

implemented,[18] and strive to send to Rome as many as ten youths for instruction at the College of the Neophytes.[19]

Mercurian's instructions, however, lay bare his anxieties concerning Eliano. First and foremost, given Mercurian's ongoing efforts to eradicate any evidence of crypto-Judaism from the Society of Jesus, his selection of Eliano as the superior suggests that Mercurian recognized his previous error when he named the inexperienced and intractable Tommaso Raggio as superior; or, at the very least, he understood that the Maronites admired Eliano and would work with no other man. It was also not fully his call alone to make, for Gregory, Carafa, and Mihail demanded that Eliano lead, as we saw at the end of Chapter 3. Second, while Raggio did prove himself to be a poor leader, Eliano's histrionics from the previous leg of the mission – such as claiming that "seeing that I am here for nothing other than to be Father Tommaso's interpreter ... I too have resolved to distance myself from it and do nothing else"[20] – must have given Mercurian some pause in allowing Eliano too much leeway. On one hand, he knew that the Maronites desired Eliano's help; on the other hand, he simply did not trust him to see the mission through.

Mercurian decided not to take any chances with Eliano. He urged Eliano and Bruno to get along, which must be an indirect reference to Eliano's tensions with Raggio, especially since there seemed to be no tension between Eliano and Bruno: "Flee with every bit of diligence from any occasion of disgust and contention between you, and wholly seek to keep yourselves united through close ties of brotherly charity and love, and to demonstrate toward the superior of this mission, Father Battista Eliano, reverence and obedience in all those things that will be imposed on you by him."[21] He further explained that Eliano was directly responsible for the "health and consolation of his companions, and in particular Father Giovan Bruno."

This clearly delineated who was in control of the mission. Given the Maronites' fear of external threats and internal rivalries, Mercurian was sensible enough to recognize that, Eliano's Jewish birth notwithstanding,

---

[18] This was formally promulgated in Gregory XIII's 24 February 1582 papal bull *Inter gravissimas*. See Vernon Hyde Minor and Brian A. Curran, eds., *Art and Science in the Rome of Gregory XIII Boncompagni (1572–1585)* (Rome: The American Academy in Rome, 2009).

[19] ARSI, *Gall. 95 II*, fols. 67r–68v./*MPO 1*, 205–7.

[20] ARSI, *Gall. 106*, fol. 119r./*MPO 1*, 83.   [21] ARSI, *Gall. 95 II*, fol. 60rv./*MPO 1*, 201.

no one was better positioned to head the mission.[22] At the same time, this was tempered when Mercurian explained that "Father Giovan Bruno must be Father Battista's consultant and advisor," suggesting that Mercurian was not ready to give Eliano unfettered control of the mission despite his expertise and his rapport with the Maronites.[23] And so, directives in hand, Eliano and Bruno set off for Tripoli, arriving on 29 June 1580, with the hope that they could reform the Maronites.

ELIANO'S LEADERSHIP IN THE MARONITE SYNOD

On 18 September, after two solid months of work with the Maronites, Eliano wrote to Carafa to report on his and Bruno's efforts. Upon their arrival in Tripoli, Bishop Georges, the patriarchal envoy who had come to Rome in 1577 to ask Gregory to send missionaries, greeted Eliano and Bruno. After they had arrived at the patriarchal monastery of Qannubin on 19 July, Mihail welcomed the envoys by calling for a ringing of church bells to celebrate the recent arrival of his honored guests. Despite suffering from an illness that kept him bedridden, "as soon as [the patriarch] saw us, he cried from happiness" and professed his love for Gregory and loyalty to Rome.[24] Eliano and Bruno then "showed some of the things that we brought for their nation's churches," namely, "many chalices, vestments, host irons, crowns, books, images, and diverse other things."[25] Beyond liturgical reform and church supplies, Eliano explained that the Maronites were excited about his efforts to eradicate errors from their books and provide them with new ones. Central to this was the fact that "His Holiness in time will have stamped many Catholic books, and the Bible, and breviaries, etc. ... with which their books and those of the whole nation will be corrected or burned."[26]

---

[22] It is possible that Mercurian's views had changed, and his work with Eliano may have caused the shift. As Mercurian died 1 August 1580, and his successor, Claudio Acquaviva, pushed harder toward pressuring former Jews out of the Society, it will forever remain unclear if he eased his view or not. There is no written evidence to suggest he did so, and this is only conjecture on my part. For more on the generalate of Mercurian and his stance on Jews and *conversos*, see Robert A. Maryks, *The Jesuit Order as a Synagogue of Jews: Jesuits of Jewish Ancestry and Purity-of-Blood Laws in the Early Society of Jesus* (Leiden: Brill, 2010), 123–43.

[23] ARSI, *Gall. 95 II*, fol. 60v./*MPO 1*, 201–2.

[24] ARSI, *Gall. 95 I*, fol. 102r./*MPO 1*, 217.

[25] ARSI, *Gall. 95 I*, fol. 102r./*MPO 1*, 217–18.

[26] ARSI, *Gall. 95 I*, fol. 102r./*MPO 1*, 218.

This passage concerning the amendment or destruction of books juxtaposes two elements of Eliano's identity and how his Jewishness remained central to his efforts to assist the Maronites. On one hand, Eliano desired to amend and correct books to be printed and distributed, which would strengthen the claim that he alone could reform the Maronites because of his textual erudition grounded in his Jewish youth. On the other hand, burning books deemed too heretical to save meant that the Maronites were undergoing a purification of sorts, one not at all foreign to Eliano: one needs think only of Eliano's decision to cleanse himself of his Jewish past through fire, when he burned the Talmud in 1553.

But because he knew he could never fully distance himself from that Jewish legacy, as his time in Egypt and the rise of anti-Jewish sentiment within the Society of Jesus had shown, Eliano continued to put his textual skills at the fore, often through thinly veiled self-praise. Regarding the Christian doctrine that Giovanni Bruno had written and Eliano translated into Arabic, the Maronites praised it, and "they all wanted to have one for themselves. This is mainly because of the great manner in which it was made – in the form of a dialogue – as well as because of its print, which was more beautiful than anything they had ever seen. For this, they were so happy, and intended not only to have books for themselves but for the whole Nation."[27] This is more than simply Eliano relaying to Carafa the Maronites' jubilation. Rather, it is the very work that he wished to carry out on the first leg of the mission but could not complete because of his issues with Raggio. Now, however, as the mission's superior, without Raggio's insults and refusal to work with the Maronites, Eliano had the freedom to complete the textual work that he believed was central to reforming the Maronites. It also allowed him to show off his skills in producing Arabic script.

The next step in Eliano and Bruno's work began on 14 August, when a great number of Maronite priests and bishops flocked to Qannubin to celebrate the Feast of the Assumption and participate in the synod. It was at this point that Eliano and Bruno deemed it best to distribute the gifts that they had brought from Rome; when Eliano proclaimed that these were gifts from the Holy See, the Maronite clerics all declared their desire to be "under the faith of the Holy Roman Church, loathing all the other nations and sects." The Maronites who had come from afar then invited

---

[27] ARSI, *Gall. 95 I*, fol. 102r./*MPO 1*, 218.

the Jesuits to visit their villages and be their spiritual guides once the synod concluded.[28]

Everyone moved into the monastery for the convocation of the synod. After the congregants gathered inside, Eliano and Bruno said Mass. Mass ended, Eliano explained why he and Bruno had come, doing so not in Latin, but in colloquial Arabic. It is an obviously pragmatic choice, but it also demonstrates that the Jesuits wanted the Maronites to participate in their own reform and that the Jesuits did not wish to eradicate the basic elements of the Maronites' historical identity. However, Eliano felt the need to tell Carafa that "in their language I spoke to them to give account of why we came here," pointing to Eliano's continued effort to stress to his superiors that he was the perfect leader for this mission because of his linguistic skills.[29] Eliano explained that the Maronites listened attentively "with happiness and a readiness to enact everything that will be imposed by the Apostolic See."[30] After a reflection on the union struck at the Fourth Lateran Council under Pope Innocent III in 1215,[31] all participated in a profession of faith, "which was intoned out loud [by Eliano] and everyone followed him; it was done and read with the contentment of all."[32]

The patriarch next read the oath of confirmation and accepted from Eliano the pallium – a narrow band of cloth that goes over episcopal vestments – as the symbol of papal recognition of his office. Eliano recounted that, upon his acknowledgment of Mihail as a dutiful son of Rome, "everyone was full of such joy that, without knowing what to say, everyone shouted in unison, while all the bells played: 'May all this be done in the honor of the blessed God, Kyrie Eleison.'"[33] Eliano paused to reflect on the congregation's exuberance for the patriarch's coronation. Eliano was awestruck by the manner in which the Maronites presented themselves in the synod: "a people so far from Italy, in these mountains, in the midst of such infidels and schismatics, are with readiness and love to believe and do all that the Holy Roman Church professes."[34] Despite their ignorance, illiteracy, isolation, and poverty, Eliano saw a community that persisted in its devotion to Rome and clung to it as the bedrock

---

[28] ARSI, *Gall. 95 I*, fol. 102r./*MPO 1*, 219.   [29] ARSI, *Gall. 95 I*, fol. 102r./*MPO 1*, 220.

[30] ARSI, *Gall. 95 I*, fol. 102v./*MPO 1*, 220.

[31] On Innocent's universalizing goals, see John C. Moore, *Pope Innocent III (1160/61–1216): To Root Up and to Plant* (Leiden: Brill, 2003).

[32] ARSI, *Gall. 95 I*, fol. 102v./*MPO 1*, 220.

[33] ARSI, *Gall. 95 I*, fol. 102v./*MPO 1*, 220–1.

[34] ARSI, *Gall. 95 I*, fol. 102v./*MPO 1*, 221.

of its identity.[35] While the Maronites originally called for Rome's help because of their immediate concerns regarding schism and factionalism, Eliano could not help but reflect on the religious fervor that pervaded the synod. Clearly, this-worldly pragmatism was in no way incompatible with the Maronites' belief that embracing Rome also provided them with the other-worldly security that they desired.

This preoccupation with achieving some semblance of security through outward expressions of belonging is also apparent for Eliano. With his status as a Jesuit in question given his Jewish birth, his declaration of his efforts in textual reform and in conducting the synod underscores his this-worldly need to secure his position within the Society of Jesus and the Catholic Church. His response to their profession of faith, his leadership in their reform efforts, his acceptance of the patriarch's acknowledgment of papal primacy, his bestowal of the pallium upon Mihail, and his emotive response to their zeal all point toward his effort to convince his superiors that his skills – stemming from his unique status as a Jewish-born Jesuit – were evidence of his ability to reform the Maronites.

Thus, Eliano presented himself as the Elijah of the Maronites, a reference made on his first stint in Lebanon, by repeatedly reminding his superiors of his dedication to the mission, how they would only work with him, and how he alone could keep the Maronites from turning away from the faith.[36] Despite his failures and prison stint in Egypt nearly two decades earlier, his experience with the deterioration of the Coptic community and Jewish retribution for his conversion provided him with certain insights that others lacked. But some might have seen those experiences as proof of how his Jewish birth was at best an obstacle in his efforts and at worst evidence of his inability to convert the Maronites. In turn, he did not downplay his Jewish roots so much as deemphasize religious fluidity and accentuate instead his ability to keep the Maronites from apostasy through the textual erudition groomed in his Jewish past and Catholic orthodoxy learned in his novitiate and apostolic work in Rome

---

[35] It was often the case that religious communities clung to their faith and desired religious purity despite what was perceived as ignorance or rusticity. See Eamon Duffy, *The Stripping of the Altars: Traditional Religion in England, c.1400–c.1580* (New Haven, CT: Yale University Press, 1992); likewise, calls for reform often came from such humble origins. See Mark R. Forster, *Catholic Revival in the Age of the Baroque: Religious Identity in Southwest Germany, 1550–1750* (Cambridge: Cambridge University Press, 2001).

[36] See the previous chapter, where Eliano indirectly describes himself as Elijah and the Maronites as the Israelites who resisted Baal.

in the 1560s and 1570s.[37] Moreover, we should be careful not to see his actions solely in the guise of self-preservation, as none of this diminishes the possibility that he believed he was doing much to help the souls of the Maronites, and therefore securing his own salvation. Eliano's outward acts of self-representation and his inward convictions were not mutually exclusive. Rather, they were just as entangled as were his Jewishness and Catholicity.

Also central to Eliano's efforts with the Maronites was his push to compel Mihail to tackle any perceived heresies in the Maronites' beliefs, particularly regarding their Christology.[38] In a show of solidarity, the Maronite bishops, following Mihail and Eliano's lead, professed their belief in the Chalcedonian formula.[39] The participants of the synod then discussed the necessity of the seven sacraments for salvation. These canons, going into detail concerning the theological significance of each sacrament, also emphasized the necessity of the clergy in their administration. Baptism, for example, was only to be administered by a bishop, priest, or deacon, except in extreme cases when a cleric was not available or death of an unbaptized seemed imminent.[40] The Maronite bishops also accepted the requirement that a priest administer the Eucharist and they agreed to cease giving the Eucharist to newly baptized infants, allowing only youths with the capacity of reason to participate in the reception of the body of Christ.[41]

Theology and doctrine aside, in this canon the most important phrase for understanding Eliano's goals of the synod is "it is permitted in our Church" (*Licet in nostra Ecclesia*). This expression of unity between Eliano and the Maronites – through the use of the first-person plural – lays bare the importance of their shared Catholicism on one hand as well

---

[37] This type of quasi-demagoguery of Jesuits and their individual efforts pervaded the Society of Jesus, such as cults and calls for the canonization of figures such as Francis Xavier. William R. Pinch, "The Corpse and Cult of St. Francis Xavier, 1552–1623," in *Engaging South Asian Religions: Boundaries, Appropriations, and Resistances*, ed. Mathew N. Schmalz and Peter Gottschalk (Albany: State University of New York Press, 2012), 113–31; Pamila Gupta, *The Relic State: St. Francis Xavier and the Politics of Ritual in Portuguese India* (Manchester: Manchester University Press, 2014).

[38] Rather than give a point-by-point summary of the synod, I have decided to continue the narrative and place the synod into the greater context of the missions. An in-depth summary of the synod can be found in Matti Moosa's *The Maronites in History* (Syracuse, NY: Syracuse University Press), 245–55. The discussion of the synod here will focus instead on how the synod should be viewed as a part of the larger culture of conversion rather than its impact on the Maronites alone.

[39] "Synodus Libani" (1580), in *Documents inédits pour servir à l'histoire du Christianisme en Orient*, vol. 1, ed. Antoine Rabbath (Paris: AMS Press, 1905), 154.

[40] Ibid., 158.   [41] Ibid., 161.

as Eliano's preoccupation with placing himself on the right side of orthodoxy on the other. As the author of the canons, Eliano used them both to stress that the Maronites safeguarded their own orthodoxy and to promote himself as the defender of their souls. This comes through in the tenth chapter of the synodal decrees, "De Reformatione," which stresses that the main goal of the synod was to guarantee the Maronites' "soundness of character" and to strive for the "restitution of collapsed church discipline" that would end the risk of apostasy.[42] Discipline was key to reform across all faiths,[43] and penance was often central to Jesuit missions in the early modern Catholic world, so it was unimaginable that such a canon would not have been included.[44] By delegating this responsibility to the community, social discipline would therefore become a process of self-policing and thus further proof that the Maronites' reforms were their own doing.[45]

But the inclusion of such a canon points to Eliano's emphasis on his ability to provide the Maronites with doctrinal and liturgical exactitude, as would have been expected of Jesuit missionaries. Eliano's authorship is thus a reminder that he put himself at the fore of the community's reform and that "reformatione" – if it centers on soundness of character and discipline – was also part and parcel of the individual Jesuit missionary's religious journey. For Eliano, being the figure who preserved the Maronites' Catholicness through textual and doctrinal reform would position him on the right side of the church's anxieties concerning the slippery slope of religious uncertainty; such missionary casuistry – using the

---

[42] Ibid., 165.

[43] For more on social disciplining, see Paolo Prodi, ed. *Disciplina dell'anima, disciplina del corpo e disciplina della società tra medioevo ed età moderna* (Bologna: Società editrice il Mulino, 1994); Katharine Jackson Lualdi and Anne T. Thayer, eds., *Penitence in the Age of Reformations* (Aldershot: Ashgate, 2000); Amy Nelson Burnett, "Basel's Rural Pastors as Mediators of Confessional and Social Discipline," *Central European History* 33:1 (January 1, 2000): 67–85; Raymond A. Mentzer, "Morals and Moral Regulation in Protestant France," *The Journal of Interdisciplinary History* 31:1 (July 1, 2000): 1–20; Ronald K. Rittgers, *The Reformation of the Keys: Confession, Conscience, and Authority in Sixteenth-Century Germany* (Cambridge, MA: Harvard University Press, 2004); Adriano Prosperi, "L'abiura dell'eretico e la conversione del criminale: prime linee di ricerca," *Quaderni Storici* 42:3 (December 2007): 719–29; Abigail Firey, ed., *A New History of Penance* (Leiden: Brill, 2008).

[44] Bernadette Majorana, "Une pastorale spectaculaire: missions et missionnaires jésuites en Italie (XVIe–XVIIIe siècle)," *Annales. Histoire, sciences sociales* 57:2 (March 1, 2002): 297–320.

[45] Wietse de Boer, *The Conquest of the Soul: Confession, Discipline, and Public Order in Counter-Reformation Milan* (Leiden: Brill, 2001); Michel Foucault, *Discipline and Punish: The Birth of the Prison* (New York: Pantheon Books, 1977), 205–16.

Maronites' reform to promote himself – points to the uncertainty of belonging in the early modern church amid fears of crypto-religion and shifting institutional expectations regarding the church's Jewish-lineage members, against which Eliano needed to position himself.[46]

At least partially because of how Eliano and Bruno delivered the decrees and the fact that there was little debate, it has been argued that the effort to reform the Maronites was unequivocally a Roman project that pushed the Maronites headlong into a forced Latinization – in essence, that, on the ground, this was Eliano's authoritarian Catholicizing project.[47] I should emphasize that this is not what I am arguing here. Rather, reform was to center on *both* the Maronites' own efforts *as well as* Eliano's emphasis on his own abilities to guide the Maronites. In other words, Eliano's desires to use this synod for his own ends should in no way take away from the Maronites' desire to reform themselves.

While Eliano depicted himself as in full control of the synod, the synod took all of three days to conclude, with full Maronite support. It would likewise be a stretch to suggest that Eliano could unequivocally compel an entire religious community spread out over a rugged and often impenetrable mountain landscape (with others in Syria and Cyprus) to do much of anything. Eliano needed to correct books and procure vessels for churches long before the Maronite priests could execute the proper church discipline and orthopraxy laid out in the synod, and this would not be complete by the time Eliano left Lebanon – nor by the end of the century for that matter; and such reforms depended upon the willingness of rural communities to open the doors of their churches, monasteries, and libraries to outsiders. Eliano and his superiors simply could not bend the Maronites to their will; their refusal to work with Raggio in 1578 and no one but Eliano thereafter was proof enough of that. Maronite priests were also poorly trained and in short supply, putting in jeopardy the likelihood that any reform in the parishes could take place.

---

[46] Stefania Tutino, *Uncertainty in Post-Reformation Catholicism: A History of Probabilism* (Oxford: Oxford University Press, 2018).

[47] Charles Frazee explains: "This synod of Qannubin was dominated by the Jesuits. A Roman catechism written by Bruno and translated into Arabic by Eliano was proposed and accepted for the religious education of the Maronites. Then a number of canons, based upon the patriarchal propositions and Cardinal Caraffa's instructions, were adopted. Only three days of meeting were required." Charles A. Frazee, *Catholics and Sultans: The Church and the Ottoman Empire, 1453–1923* (Cambridge: Cambridge University Press, 1983), 137–8.

But Eliano surely employed the Maronites' desire to reform for his own ends. This is clear in his decision to send four youths to Rome to be trained by the Jesuits at the Collegio Romano.[48] Eliano's recognition that the Collegio Romano could be key to the Maronites' reforms points to his own novitiate and the Collegio Romano's ability to reform a Jewish convert into the Maronites' Elijah through theological training and engagement with Rome's religious landscape.[49] Thus, much as Eliano wanted to be trusted to conduct a mission far from Rome, the successful implementation of his synod; the continual execution of his reforms throughout Lebanon, Syria, and Cyprus; and the return of Lebanese seminarians from Rome all point to the notion that aspersions need not be cast upon one's Catholicity simply because of the religious failings of one's past.[50] In essence, this synod and the decision to train Maronite seminarians in Rome allowed the Maronites to promote their own Catholicity for their own reasons as well as be able to negotiate what that meant; but it also allowed Eliano to use his efforts with the Maronites

---

[48] ARSI, *Gall. 95 I*, fol. 103r./*MPO 1*, 223. On the Maronites in Rome see, Pierre Raphael, *Le rôle du Collège Maronite Romain dans l'orientalisme aux XVIIe et XVIIIe siècles* (Beyrouth: Université Saint Joseph, 1950); Nasser Gemayel, *Les échanges culturels entre les Maronites et l'Europe: du Collège Maronite de Rome (1584) au Collège de `Ayn-Warqa (1789)* (Beirut: Impr. Y. et Ph. Gemayel, 1984).

[49] On the Jesuits' activities in Rome after Trent, see Thomas Buser, "Jerome Nadal and Early Jesuit Art in Rome," *The Art Bulletin* 58:3 (September 1, 1976): 424–33; Thomas M. Lucas, *Saint, Site, and Sacred Strategy: Ignatius, Rome and Jesuit Urbanism* (Vatican City: Biblioteca apostolica vaticana, 1990); Thomas M. Lucas, *Landmarking: City, Church & Jesuit Urban Strategy* (Chicago: Loyola Press, 1997); Gauvin A. Bailey, *Between Renaissance and Baroque: Jesuit Art in Rome, 1565–1610* (Toronto: University of Toronto Press, 2003); Lance Lazar, *Working in the Vineyard of the Lord: Jesuit Confraternities in Early Modern Italy* (Toronto: University of Toronto Press, 2005). Noteworthy as well is the larger sixteenth- and seventeenth-century project of Roman urbanism in which Maronite seminarians would have been immersed. See Clare Robertson, *Il Gran Cardinale: Alessandro Farnese, Patron of the Arts* (New Haven, CT: Yale University Press, 1992); Gianvittorio Signorotto and Maria Antonella Viscella, eds., *Court and Politics in Papal Rome, 1492–1700* (Cambridge: Cambridge University Press, 2002); Dorothy Metzger Habel, *The Urban Development of Rome in the Age of Alexander VII* (New York: Cambridge University Press, 2002); Nicholas Temple, *Renovatio Urbis: Architecture, Urbanism, and Ceremony in the Rome of Julius II* (London: Routledge, 2011); Dorothy Metzger Habel, *"When All of Rome Was under Construction": The Building Process in Baroque Rome* (University Park: Pennsylvania State University Press, 2013); Jack Freiberg, *Bramante's Tempietto, the Roman Renaissance, and the Spanish Crown* (New York: Cambridge University Press, 2014).

[50] On local reforms and the maintenance of Catholicity beyond the institutional church, see Marc R. Forster, "The Elite and Popular Foundations of German Catholicism in the Age of Confessionalism: The Reichskirche," *Central European History* 26:3 (January 1, 1993): 311–25.

as a means to position his Jewish intellectual training as a pillar of his identity as a doctrinally sound, well-educated, textually exacting Jesuit.

ELIANO'S PASTORAL VISITS IN THE MOUNTAINS OF LEBANON

To further efforts with the Maronites, not long after the synod concluded Eliano and Bruno began their pastoral visitations to Maronite villages, "where we have been very well received and warmly welcomed, and in this we shall collect the fruit of this mission."[51] Eliano was also eager to share how much his textual efforts were beginning to pay off, as "we have distributed our books … and we have given alms in the name of His Holiness to the poor, so that they pray for the health of the Holy Church and the health of all; and here, we see great readiness of spirit from all to desire to do what they are taught."[52]

Eliano also promoted his efforts to tackle the lack of convents for Maronite nuns, who lived with and served the personal needs of the monks. The movement toward monastic enclosure, which hit its apex at the Twenty-Fifth Session of the Council of Trent, stressed the preservation of the nuns' chastity and security.[53] From Rome's perspective, this integration and cohabitation of the sexes threatened the religious' ability to focus on their duties as spiritual models for the community, leaving the laity open to carnal vice. Likewise, it stood in stark contrast to the perceived liberalization of gender dynamics seen in the abolition of convents in former Catholic centers that had adopted Protestantism earlier in the century.[54]

But in the mountains of Lebanon, much like in Europe, the effort to enclose nuns, ostensibly independent of male interference, would have to work according to locals' financial ability – and willingness – to comply.[55]

---

[51] ARSI, *Gall. 106*, fol. 154r./*MPO 1*, 234.   [52] Ibid.

[53] J. Waterworth, ed., *The Canons and Decrees of the Sacred and Oecumenical Council of Trent, Celebrated Under the Sovereign Pontiffs, Paul III, Julius III and Pius IV* (London: C. Dolman, 1848), 240–1. While this would not have been a concern for Eliano, European secular authorities had likewise moved toward enclosure to protect against the erosion of patrician communities. This occurred in Venice and Milan in particular. See Jutta Gisela Sperling, *Convents and the Body Politic in Late Renaissance Venice* (Chicago: University of Chicago Press, 1999); P. Renée Baernstein, *A Convent Tale: A Century of Sisterhood in Spanish Milan* (New York: Routledge, 2002).

[54] Lyndal Roper, *The Holy Household: Women and Morals in Reformation Augsburg.* (Oxford: Oxford University Press, 1989).

[55] The issue of imposing enclosure in the wake of Trent has a wide historiographical reach. In addition to Sperling's and Baernstein's work mentioned in note 53, see, for good case

In turn, Eliano wanted to stress his efforts to implement all of the Tridentine reforms he could while still there, including the cloistering of nuns. Eliano thus told Carafa that he would strive to secure funds necessary to establish convents for Maronite nuns; such efforts on his part would be "of great service to our Lord God, because the people feel terrible that these nuns live in such a way; and this holy work will be a sign to many others that His Holiness works for this nation that is in such need of being helped."[56] Between education and cloistering nuns – between Maronites "taught" and "helped" – Eliano again constellated their reforms around his efforts.

ELIANO'S CONTINUED ANXIETIES ABOUT THE FLUIDITY OF CONVERSION

Despite successfully tackling internal issues that plagued the community, such as monastic reform, pervasive illiteracy, deep-seated heresies, and the types of rivalries seen in the previous chapter, Eliano again had to confront Ottoman inquiries into his presence among Eastern Rite Christians. This was most apparent when, on 27 September, he wrote to Carafa that "certain advisors and confidants were advised that [the patriarch and the Jesuits] were in danger" because of the Ottomans' unease about the Jesuits' presence there.[57] While it remains unclear how perilous the situation was, Eliano and Mihail were worried enough to decide that the patriarch should leave Qannubin, and "it was determined that Father Battista, dressed as a Maronite peasant since he knew the language, would go on this journey with the Patriarch or with one of his bishops to places far from the monastery" and that he would return to Qannubin "every eight or fifteen days to discuss and consult with his companion

studies of the varieties of enclosure, Helen Hills, "Cities and Virgins: Female Aristocratic Convents in Early Modern Naples and Palermo," *Oxford Art Journal* 22:1 (January 1, 1999): 31–54; Thomas Worcester, "'Neither Married nor Cloistered': Blessed Isabelle in Catholic Reformation France," *The Sixteenth Century Journal* 30:2 (July 1, 1999): 457–2; Mary Laven, "Sex and Celibacy in Early Modern Venice," *The Historical Journal* 44:4 (December 1, 2001): 865–88; Silvia Evangelisti, "'We Do Not Have It, and We Do Not Want It': Women, Power, and Convent Reform in Florence," *The Sixteenth Century Journal* 34:3 (October 1, 2003): 677–700; Helen Hills, "The Veiled Body: Within the Folds of Early Modern Neapolitan Convent Architecture," *Oxford Art Journal* 27:3 (January 1, 2004): 271–90.

56 ARSI, *Gall. 106*, fol. 154r./MPO 1, 235.   57 Ibid.

what had occurred" while Eliano was away.[58] First and foremost, Eliano's flight with Mihail while disguised as a Maronite peasant to evade
Ottoman reprisals, the existence of such reprisals notwithstanding, is
eerily reminiscent of his experiences in Egypt – namely, his flight into
the desert with Coptic Patriarch Gabriel and then masquerading as a
Venetian silk merchant so that he could clandestinely flee Jewish-
Ottoman intrigues. Eliano's desire to dress like a Maronite thus suggests
that, despite how much time had passed since his arrest and flight from
Egypt, Eliano still feared for his personal safety and remained anxious
about his reputation in the Ottoman Empire.

That Eliano could pass for a Maronite because of his knowledge of
Arabic is also a reminder that Eliano's shape-shifting abilities still came in
handy despite the anxieties that they caused for his superiors. Likewise,
the fact that Bruno did not come with him and Eliano kept him informed
every week or two because Bruno could not pass for a Maronite should
not be overlooked. It relegates Bruno to an ancillary role on the mission
and puts the mission's success squarely on Eliano's shoulders because of
the very skills that his Jewishness enabled him to possess: textual exactitude, linguistic dexterity, and the ability to navigate and code-switch
between the myriad cultural mores of the eastern Mediterranean.[59]

The Ottomans were not the only group who seemed to imperil the
Maronites through pressures to apostatize. Laurentios, the Greek Orthodox Archbishop of Nicosia "attacked and threatened" the Maronites on
Cyprus by undercharging for baptisms, funerals, and marriages to convince them to accept his authority.[60] While many Cypriot Christians of all
sects converted to Islam after the Ottoman conquest in 1570,[61] the profile
of the island's Greeks had risen, as the Ottomans both aided their commercial ventures and protected them from the ongoing papal-Venetian
rivalry over religious affairs that pervaded the Venetian *Stato da mar*.[62]

---

[58] ARSI, *Gall. 106*, fol. 154v./*MPO 1*, 235.
[59] This is paralleled quite closely in the western Mediterranean by the Moroccan Jew Samuel
Pallache. See Mercedes García-Arenal and Gerard Albert Wiegers, *A Man of Three
Worlds: Samuel Pallache, a Moroccan Jew in Catholic and Protestant Europe*, trans.
Martin Beagles (Baltimore, MD: Johns Hopkins University Press, 2007).
[60] ARSI, *Gall. 106*, fol. 155r./*MPO 1*, 236–7.
[61] In addition to Greeks and Maronites, the island had Catholic and Coptic communities,
the latter of which was mentioned in Chapter 2, in the person of Isaac, the Coptic
archbishop who condemned Patriarch Gabriel's decision to entertain Eliano's efforts
at union.
[62] Ronald C. Jennings, *Christians and Muslims in Ottoman Cyprus and the Mediterranean
World, 1571–1640* (New York: New York University Press, 1993). This tended to be the

Aware of this shift in prospects as well as the discounts that Laurentios was offering, many of the island's Christians, including Maronites, were converting to Greek Orthodoxy out of economic and social expediency.[63] Eliano lamented that "neither [the bishop] nor the nation can live any longer on Cyprus" as the Maronite bishop was unable to find suitable priests to protect the Maronites from the incursions of the Greeks.[64]

While Eliano's reaction to this state of affairs lays bare that he felt that the Maronites on Cyprus were at risk because of these larger geopolitical shifts, it also points to his own ability to navigate the religious vicissitudes of the early modern Mediterranean. First, by stating that the Maronites were "getting mixed in with the Greeks and, if nothing is done, they will remain quite troubled and done in by the Greek sect," Eliano stressed the slippery slope of conversion and how easily the Maronites could be subsumed into the Greek community that surrounded it.[65] Such instances of religious pragmatism were problematic from the perspective of Eliano and the Maronite clerical leadership in Lebanon, as these conversions would have long-term consequences. While these Maronites were converting for financial or social reasons and might have remained Catholics in their hearts and homes, their children would be baptized in Greek baptismal fonts, their loved ones married in Greek churches, and their dead buried in Greek cemeteries; it seemed to Eliano, then, that the Greeks would swallow up the Maronite community on Cyprus within a generation.

But there is something at stake here for Eliano as well, and he does not stop at lamenting the challenges that the Maronites faced because of the Greeks. Rather, Eliano condemned the fluid borders of religious identities themselves – a necessary condemnation of the very fluidity that led to his own conversion – when he castigated the Greeks as not only the "enemy of the Latin nation and of the Maronites" but also as a morally bankrupt nation of renegades that "would rather become Turks than Maronites."[66]

---

case when Ottomans conquered Venetian territories, such as Crete after 1669. See Molly Greene, *A Shared World: Christians and Muslims in the Early Modern Mediterranean* (Princeton, NJ: Princeton University Press, 2000).

[63] Paul Sant Cassia, "Religion, Politics and Ethnicity in Cyprus during the Turkokratia (1571–1787)," *Archives européennes de sociologie*, 27 (1986): 3–28. For more on conversion for social or cultural benefits in the context of Constantinople, see Eric R. Dursteler, *Renegade Women: Gender, Identity, and Boundaries in the Early Modern Mediterranean* (Baltimore, MD: Johns Hopkins University Press, 2011).

[64] ARSI, *Gall. 106*, fol. 155r./MPO *1*, 237.   [65] Ibid.

[66] ARSI, *Gall. 106*, fol. 155r./MPO *1*, 237.

By excoriating the Greeks for their purported fraudulence, religious opportunism, and specious enticement of the Maronites to convert, Eliano distanced himself from the iniquity of renegadism and positioned himself as the ardent defender of the Maronites and the vociferous condemner of the seeming Greeks-qua-Turks.

Eliano determined that it was best to find "the remedy for such a great evil," which, he wrote to Carafa, would be if "Your Lordship or the Most Illustrious Cardinal Santa Severina write to [the Greek] patriarch in Constantinople [Jeremias II], so that he order his Archbishop on Cyprus to cease troubling the Maronites."[67] There was probably little hope of that working, as wounds from the centuries-long schism had come nowhere close to healing, despite efforts to do so at the Council of Florence in the previous century. Eliano nevertheless hoped that putting pressure on the Greeks for violating the religious rites and customs of others, which the Ottomans in theory protected, could lead to at least some solace for Cypriot Maronites, or at the very least convince them that Rome had not forgotten them.[68]

It is also significant in terms of Eliano rearticulating his own experience as a convert that he suggested Giulio Antonio Santoro, the cardinal of Santa Severina and protector of the Oriental Orthodox Churches, write to Jeremias to urge him to call on his clergy to cease their incursions on the Maronites. Turning back to *Roma Sancta*, Gregory Martin explained that, at those conversionary sermons to the Jews of Rome, Santoro was usually there because he was "president of this exercise, as for other causes, especially to keepe the Jewes in awe, and to rebuke them for absence or slacknesse, and to make reporte to his Holinesse of al thinges."[69] As noted in Chapter 3, Eliano may have preached to the Jews; even if not, he was almost certainly there, for "in this Audience the Catechumeni and Neophyti, that is to say, the late converted and the late Baptized Jews, have theyr place among the Christians, in theyr liveries,

---

[67] Ibid. Jeremias II ascended the throne in August 1580. Whether Eliano and Bruno knew by September 1580, when this letter was written, that his predecessor, Metrophanes III, had died is unclear, as he does not mention the patriarch by name.

[68] See Martin Anton Schmidt, "The Problem of Papal Primacy at the Council of Florence," *Church History* 30:1 (March 1, 1961): 35–49; Joseph Gill, *The Council of Florence* (Cambridge: Cambridge University Press, 1961); Henry Chadwick, *East and West: The Making of a Rift in the Church from Apostolic Times until the Council of Florence* (Oxford: Oxford University Press, 2003); Michele Giuseppe D'Agostino, *Il primato della sede di Roma in Leone IX (1049–1054): studio dei testi latini nella controversia greco-romana nel periodo pregregoriano* (Milan: San Paolo, 2008).

[69] Gregory Martin, *Roma Sancta (1581)* (Rome: Edizioni di storia e letteratura, 1969), 77.

they of white, and these of blacke."[70] Given that Santoro's role was to "keepe the Jewes in awe, and to rebuke them" as well as celebrate the successes of converted Jews, his relationship with Eliano must have been on some level an intimate one. It thus makes sense that Eliano believed Santoro should write to Jeremias. Yet, the doubts surrounding Jewish converts and Santoro's efforts to keep them in line also suggest – as we will see more thoroughly in the next two chapters – that their relationship was also a caustic one, oscillating between reliance on Eliano's textual skills on one hand and Santoro's anxieties about Eliano's motivations and ability to be doctrinally accurate on the other.

RECALIBRATING HIS CONVERSIONARY SELF THROUGH DOCTRINAL EXACTITUDE

By late November 1580, Eliano and Bruno had conducted many of their pastoral visits, and Eliano had sent several reports to Rome detailing their efforts. In a letter to Mercurian dated 23 November, Eliano explained that "I began these visitations forty days ago, at first in the companion of the patriarch." Eliano determined, however, that he would be more effective without the oft-ill patriarch, and so "I go about alone from one village to another, accompanied only by the priest of the village."[71] Furthermore, Eliano explained that "on these visits I have never failed to say Mass, outside of one day when I was unwell" and that "everything that the priest says in the Mass, I wrote in their language." The Maronites were, so Eliano said, beginning to perform the Mass "as if in Italy."[72] To expedite this process of reform, Eliano decided "to remain for a day in one of the more important villages, and call for the congregation of the local priests of six or seven villages, and call a little synod" that would ensure that the Maronites were on their way to implementing major aspects of Catholic doctrine.[73]

The issues that Eliano emphasized, such as the inclusion of the *Filioque* in the Creed, correction of prayers such as the *Trisagion*, and the introduction of the Rosary, all reflect Eliano's concern with the Maronites' outward displays of faith that would bring them into unity with Rome and with each other. But they also reflect his continuous effort to place

---

[70] Ibid., 77–8.   [71] ARSI, *Gall. 106*, fol. 157r./*MPO 1*, 239.   [72] Ibid.
[73] ARSI, *Gall. 106*, fol. 157rv./*MPO 1*, 240. Eliano then gives a ten-point list of various reforms that the Maronite priests should institute in their respective villages. These reforms follow closely those of the synod held at Qannubin.

himself at the center of their reforms and how he saw himself as a conduit through which their Latinization would take place. Thus, the push to get the Maronites to come to a consensus on orthopraxy likewise demonstrates that Eliano was cognizant of how he was viewed as a missionary, and he again employed his knowledge of doctrine and his linguistic skills (through translating a Roman missal into Arabic) as mechanisms to this end.[74] Eliano also stressed that his ability to move about on his visitations was often limited. While he had carried out many visits and had conducted the second, minor synod, "these terrible times have forced me to return [to Tripoli, on the coast] ... so this whole winter we will be quite busy: I will read many books and expurgate them, and Father Giovanni will compose other useful things."[75]

Staying positive, Eliano also explained that a recent Ottoman decree, which on the surface of things "is more troubling" than any he could immediately call to mind, could in fact work to the Jesuits' benefit. For as far back as Eliano could remember, all non-Muslim subjects of the Ottoman Empire had been forced to wear turbans of varying colors according to sect to distinguish them from Muslims and Europeans. But this new decree stated that "no Christian nor Jew in the whole of the empire, should dare to wear a turban, but only a beret like that of the Franks – the Jews' shall be red, and the Christians' black."[76] Eliano saw it as a boon, for "before ... when I went about with a turban [that is to say, when he was disguised as a Maronite] it was clear I was a Frank," despite his knowledge of Arabic. However, "I have been experimenting recently ... and now that every [Christian] dresses as a Frank," he found it quite easy to blend in.[77] For Eliano, the liberation from his disguise as a Maronite peasant allowed him to move more freely by shedding his dissimulation. It comes as no surprise, then, when Eliano attributed it to "the singular providence of the Lord toward us, in order to carry out our mission without impediment."[78]

---

[74] Through ritual orthopraxy, Eliano places himself on the right side of Catholicity. It should not be overlooked how important ritual was to the construction of identities and how central participation in them was to building senses of belonging. Edward Muir, *Civic Ritual in Renaissance Venice* (Princeton, NJ: Princeton University Press, 1981); Susan C. Karant-Nunn, *The Reformation of Ritual: An Interpretation of Early Modern Germany* (London: Routledge, 1997); Nicholas Terpstra, ed., *The Politics of Ritual Kinship: Confraternities and Social Order in Early Modern Italy* (Cambridge: Cambridge University Press, 1999).
[75] ARSI, *Gall. 106*, 157v./*MPO 1*, 241.
[76] ARSI, *Gall. 106*, 158r./*MPO 1*, 241. By Franks, he means Latin Catholics from Europe.
[77] ARSI, *Gal. 106*, 158r./*MPO 1*, 242.   [78] ARSI, *Gall. 106*, 158r./*MPO 1*, 241.

THE DEATH OF MERCURIAN

On 9 December, in the midst of his jubilation stemming from the mission's successes, Olivier Mannaerts, who had been the assistant of Germany and was elected as vicar general to oversee the election of the next superior general, wrote to Eliano and Bruno to tell them that Mercurian had died on 1 August 1580 while tending to the sick of Rome during an influenza epidemic. He lauded the pair for their efforts in reforming the Maronites, and even explained that Carafa had told him that "His Holiness remains quite satisfied, and quite excited about continuing this work, and he will give to Your Reverences to this end every aid and favor," despite the transition in leadership within the Society.[79] In his reply, written 11 April 1581, Eliano thanked Mannaerts and explained that "from your letters, we have received great consolation, which to this point we have not felt so warmly, seeing the charity and paternal affection of Your Paternity."[80] Eliano then gave a brief account of their activities, such as his continued visits and Bruno's work with the Maronites. Conspicuously absent in Eliano's letter, however, is any sign of lament regarding Mercurian's death.

Then, on 7 February 1581, Claudio Acquaviva, a thirty-seven-year-old from Abruzzo, was selected to serve as the new father general. As mentioned in Chapter 3, Acquaviva soon proved himself to be more hostile to Jewish-lineage Jesuits than Mercurian had been. Despite this, Eliano knew he had to work with his new superior. In his first letter to Acquaviva, Eliano explained that "we have received with great happiness in the Lord the news that Your Paternity had been elected as our General, for which we all give thanks to divine mercy."[81] Eliano then explained to Acquaviva that he had spent the time since his election editing books and working with the Maronites in Tripoli. His hope over the summer was "to finish my visits, and to see other books, and the errors that we find will be debated in a congregation of the most intelligent of this nation . . . and we hope that they will refute these errors, and embrace the truth, as they have shown themselves to do thus far."[82] Eliano continued the letter by giving an account of his correspondences with Carafa and Santoro.

But like in his letter to Mannaerts, he never mentioned Mercurian's death to Acquaviva, and never seems to have made any effort to mourn. Rather, he was only troubled that some of his letters had arrived in Rome

[79] ARSI, *Venet.* 2, fol. 40r./MPO *1*, 243.   [80] ARSI, *Gall. 106*, fol. 159r./MPO *1*, 256–7.
[81] ARSI, *Gall. 95*, fol. 105v./MPO *1*, 265.   [82] Ibid.

unsealed. Eliano then concluded this first letter to Acquaviva by sharing his hope that "by the grace of god may we all live in union" and stressing his desire that "divine mercy continuously grow, so this mission may continue with his holy favor."[83] The absence of lament over Mercurian's death in Eliano's letters to Mannaerts and Acquaviva suggests much about how Eliano viewed his former boss: given Mercurian's actions against Jewish-lineage Jesuits, how he handled the affair with Raggio, and his continued reluctance to give Eliano unfettered control, it appears that Eliano and Mercurian never reconciled their differences and Eliano did not lament the change in leadership. However, as Acquaviva would soon prove himself to be a staunch opponent of Jewish-lineage Jesuits, Eliano's admiration for his new superior was probably short-lived.

ELIANO'S CONTINUED EFFORTS UNDER CARAFA AND ACQUAVIVA'S LEADERSHIP

Eliano continued his correspondence with Carafa, in addition to the Jesuit leadership. These letters to Carafa also illuminate how Eliano desired to present himself to the Curia and Gregory.[84] On 7 June 1581, Eliano was pleased that "regarding the items and books that Your Most Illustrious Lordship asked us to bring to this nation: they have almost all been distributed, with a great show of gratitude toward His Holiness and Your Most Illustrious Lordship." Eliano was positive that these efforts would only "bear the fruit that they seem to intimate, so much so that we will very much satisfy, with the other items that will come here, the other churches and peoples who have not received anything."[85] Eliano also reassured Carafa that his efforts in teaching Maronite youths were not without success, and that he hoped they would further their education in Rome, "so that so much ignorance no longer remains in this Nation, as was the case in the past." To this end, "we have, with great skill and effort, ensured that some youths of great intelligence will be sent [to Rome]."[86]

---

[83] ARSI, *Gall. 95*, fol. 105v./*MPO 1*, 266.

[84] Part of this is the product of evidence. Whereas Eliano's letters to Carafa have been mostly preserved, numerous letters to Acquaviva seem to have been lost either in transit or over the course of the centuries. It is thus hard to know the true nature of their relationship.

[85] ARSI, *Gall. 95 I*, fol. 104v./*MPO 1*, 267.

[86] ARSI, *Gall. 95 I*, fol. 104v./*MPO 1*, 267–8.

Eliano also implored Carafa to show all of the "vigilance that Your Most Illustrious Lordship has" in overseeing these youths' formation in Rome in preparation for their return to Lebanon. Eliano hammered on the importance of "visiting the said youths and examining them to ensure that they learn," given "how much work and effort it took to separate them from their families, which is a great wonder given how dearly they love their sons." But Eliano believed that this would all but ensure the health of the Maronites' souls, as this education would allow these seminarians "to one day be instruments for helping their Nation."[87]

The parallel to Eliano's own seminary experience is obvious. Just as André des Freux told Ignatius of Loyola that Eliano would be "an instrument for helping others" and should thus be sent to Rome to aid in the Catholic Church's ministries, Eliano used the very same language to describe Maronite seminarians being sent to Rome. Moreover, by emphasizing that family bonds were no obstacle to the educational formation that would render them instruments for helping others, Eliano was also able to textually further himself from the period before his conversion and emphasize that his training at the Collegio Romano, the very education that these Maronite youths were poised to undergo, was also integral to his break from his Jewish past.

Eliano also explained to Carafa that he and Bruno had seen "many principal ecclesiastical books" such as breviaries, missals, and "other particular books for feasts throughout the year. And in these books, many of their errors have been seen and noted, and may Your Most Illustrious Lordship give us the order that such books either be burned or amended."[88] To prevent these errors from returning, Eliano also planned to prepare "a notebook in which [their errors] would be refuted and the truth would be taught. This notebook would be disseminated throughout the Nation, and many copies will be made. And we think this will be enough and it will be a bandage" until long-term reforms and a proper printing press could be established.[89] Eliano also relied on his knowledge of book printing to instruct his superior in the best ways to proceed. Eliano was unsure if amending books was the wisest tack. If they were like books produced in Europe, Eliano noted, "one could note the book, the page, and the line" of the text, which would be enough to allow for redactions and amendments to the text. The Maronites' books, however,

---

[87] ARSI, *Gall. 95 I*, fol. 104v./*MPO 1*, 268.   [88] ARSI, *Gall. 95 I*, fol. 105r./*MPO 1*, 268.
[89] Ibid.

presented a problem that Eliano believed could not be addressed through simple line editing, for "if we wanted to read all their books, and amend them by hand, a lifetime would not be enough, because their books are of diverse forms, and diverse letters, and mixed with other extravagant books."[90]

Instead of Eliano amending by hand, "if we get the other books we requested, they will be added to the others and sent to Rome."[91] Included in this were both books Eliano deemed in need of thorough examination to determine whether they should be destroyed, as well as books that Eliano, in his bibliophilic zeal, deemed trophies that Carafa and others would have coveted. One was a copy of Hebrew Scriptures dating from the Fourth Lateran Council (1215), "for which you will be grateful for its antiquity, as it has handwritten corrections of the Bible," and another an Arabic copy of works of the eighth-century theologian John Damascene,[92] "which we are copying. And it will be among the first things that we can copy for this Nation and the Jacobites, since it deals expressly with the errors that run among them; and it will be accepted most willingly given the authority of such a widely celebrated saint."

The true prize, though, was an edition of the "New Testament in Chaldean on very ancient sheepskin; and according to what is noted at the end of the book in most beautiful script, it is 960 years old. I will send it to Your Most Illustrious Lordship, as I believe that you will be most grateful, so that it will be placed in the Vatican or wherever you see most fit."[93] Eliano is clearly showing off his knowledge of the contents of books that he saw as keys to reforming the Maronites and Jacobites. More pointedly, Eliano is well informed about calligraphy, the history of the book, and book production, as evidenced by his ability to describe in rich detail the nature of the scripts as well as the types of parchment used. This can be attributed to the bibliophilia he shared with Carafa, the former head of the Vatican Library; but Eliano is also employing his past experiences as a Jewish book producer as a tool in his arsenal to reform the Maronites.

---

[90] ARSI, *Gall. 95 I*, fol. 105r./*MPO 1*, 268–9.
[91] ARSI, *Gall. 95 I*, fol. 105r./*MPO 1*, 269.
[92] On John Damascene and his theological legacy, see Andrew Louth, *St. John Damascene: Tradition and Originality in Byzantine Theology* (Oxford: Oxford University Press, 2002).
[93] ARSI, *Gall. 95 I*, fol. 105r./*MPO 1*, 270.

THE ZENITH OF ELIANO'S EFFORTS

By September 1581, Eliano and Bruno had visited most Maronite communities save those in Damascus, Aleppo, and Cyprus. They had also given directives to local priests for performing the Mass and administering the sacraments, and they had distributed numerous Arabic catechisms and missals. Of course, Eliano reminded Carafa, this was still insufficient, as more books were needed, the printing of which, ideally, he and Carafa would oversee. Yet, all of the obstacles that remained would be overcome, for "the patriarch and everyone else deeply desire [these books], knowing that the fruit to be taken by these people will be in having the said books and others like them, corrected by the Apostolic See."[94] Eliano then turned to what he and Bruno had accomplished thus far with the Maronites:

We are now at the point of having accomplished all that has been desired of us on this mission: we have conducted the synod, published a catechism and other books, introduced the sacrament of the chrism and extreme unction, conducted visitations, we have read a great many of their books, and noted errors and made sense of them, and in deep conversation with them we have removed their abuses, and instilled many truths; we put in all their churches the order to observe [these changes], and we taught all the forms and manners of the Sacraments. At our insistence, [the question of] schools in certain places was addressed, and youths were sent to Rome, the end result of which we hope will serve the health of this nation.[95]

The list captures the essence of Eliano's belief that the mission's success verified his Catholicism to his superiors, and that his Jewishness was not an obstacle to his missionary abilities but rather had given him the skills necessary to reform the Maronites. Throughout, Eliano emphasized textual correctness and liturgical orthopraxy as the keys to preserving the Maronites' Catholicity. By highlighting both the changes on one hand, and his role in making those changes happen on the other, Eliano stressed his centrality to the Maronites' reform efforts. While it is certainly true that Eliano included Bruno in his efforts and elucidated all the ways in which the Maronites were reforming themselves – and in fact Eliano knew all too well that Maronite cooperation was essential – Eliano nevertheless represented himself as the catalyst of these reforms and thus as the

---

[94] ARSI, *Gall. 95 I*, fol. 129r./*MPO 1*, 276.
[95] ARSI, *Gall. 95 I*, fol. 129rv./*MPO 1*, 277.

Maronites' Catholic Elijah who saved the Maronites through doctrinal and textual reform.[96]

By the end of 1581, Eliano's efforts to reform the Maronites seemed to be a resounding success. Carafa and Mihail believed that Eliano and Bruno's work benefited both Rome and the Maronites: they had strengthened papal authority in Lebanon and had saved the Maronites from their Ottoman and Christian enemies. And this would continue after Mihail's death on 20 September 1581, with the election of Mihail's brother Sarkis as patriarch. Eliano felt that Sarkis was "a quite worthy person" to succeed his brother because of his deep knowledge of "doctrine, and experience of good governance, since during his brother's life he sustained the work of patriarchal duties," especially during Mihail's myriad illnesses.[97] As Sarkis was one of the signatories of the synod and was a driving force behind its implementation, Eliano knew he would continue the work of reform that Eliano and his brother had begun. Eliano further elaborated on Sarkis: "the following day [after his election], having called a congregation of nearly the whole of the clergy, he clearly and definitively proposed all that we have published, and ordered that everyone accept and distribute them."[98] The excitement in Sarkis's bearing the torch of Maronite reform comes through when Sarkis declared to Eliano and his bishops that "in particular his desire and imperative was to be obedient to the Roman Church, and to conform his faith with ours. We hope with Divine Grace that we have completed this great request, so that he will procure with new fervor the complete execution [of our work], and that this election will result in the great service of Divine Majesty."[99]

Sarkis was not the only Maronite to praise Eliano's efforts and promise to carry through his reforms. The Maronite seminarians sent to Rome were progressing in their studies as well. One pupil named Markos was barely able to withstand his excitement when, in a letter to Eliano,

---

[96] See the previous chapter, where Eliano compares the Maronites to the Israelites and their confessional enemies to the worshippers of the false god Baal, or Hadad. This would thus make Eliano the prophet Elijah.

[97] Eliano praised Sarkis ar-Ruzzy in a letter to Claudio Acquaviva, dated 3 October 1581, just after his election as patriarch. See ARSI, *Ital. 156*, fol. 358r./*MPO 1*, 292–3. The minutes of the election of Patriarch Sarkis ar-Ruzzy were found in Eliano's personal papers, originally written in Arabic with Syriac script (karchuni), save two Latin lines recognizing the presence of Eliano and Bruno at the election. See ARSI, *Gall. 95 I*, fols. 628r–629v./*MPO 1*, 281–6.

[98] ARSI, *Ital. 156*, fol. 358r./*MPO 1*, 293.   [99] ARSI, *Ital. 156*, fol. 358r./*MPO 1*, 293.

he discussed learning Latin.[100] Another, Antonios, explained to Eliano that Cardinal Carafa was a caring spiritual mentor and played such a vital role in his desire to learn and grow as a true member of the faith.[101]

With such positive signs in Rome concerning the training of Maronites at the Collegio Romano, and with a new patriarch poised to guide the Maronites in their continual Latinization, Eliano was an asset who some believed was better employed elsewhere.[102] One such man was Santoro, who had kept a close eye on Eliano's activities ever since it had become the cardinal's duty to oversee the conversion and catechesis of the Jews in Rome. In fact, he had written to Eliano to inquire whether he would work with other Eastern Rite Christians in the Levant (e.g., Jacobites, Armenians, and Assyrians) before Eliano had even left Rome for Lebanon,[103] and he corresponded with Eliano on several occasions during his time there.[104] And once it seemed that the mission to Lebanon was approaching its conclusion, Santoro wrote to Eliano in February 1582 to implore him to consider traveling directly to Egypt from Lebanon to work with the Copts.[105] By June, Acquaviva agreed that Eliano should go to Egypt as soon as possible.[106]

ELIANO'S AMBIVALENCE ABOUT RETURNING TO EGYPT

At first, Eliano was not keen on a return to Egypt, and was vexed by his superiors' decision to send him there without consulting him. In two letters dated 1 August 1582, written to Acquaviva and Santoro, respectively, Eliano made it quite clear that he did not desire to abandon the Maronites, as he felt that it was still far too early for them to continue their reforms without guidance. He explained to Acquaviva that Bruno had already left for Italy against both his and Sarkis's better judgment, whereas Eliano had traveled to Aleppo to visit the city's Maronite community, to meet the Jacobite Patriarch Ignatius Dawud, and to fulfill some of the spiritual needs of Latin merchants in the city.[107] He explained to Santoro that "by order of the Most Illustrious Monsignor Carafa, and by

---

[100] ARSI, *Gall. 95 II*, fol. 141r./*MPO 1*, 301.
[101] ARSI, *Gall. 95 II*, fol. 143r./*MPO 1*, 299.
[102] ARSI, *Venet 2*, fol. 70r./*MPO 1*, 304–5.
[103] ARSI, *Gall. 106*, fols. 148r–149v.; ARSI, *Gall. 95 II*, fols. 69r–70v.
[104] E.g. ARSI, *Gall. 95 II*, fols. 126r–127v. For Eliano's reply, see ARSI, *Gall. 95 I*, fol. 128r.
[105] ARSI, *Gall. 95 II*, fols. 147v–148r./*MPO 1*, 309–10.
[106] ARSI, *Venet. 2*, fol. 86v./*MPO 1*, 316.   [107] ARSI, *Gall. 95 I*, fol. 153r./*MPO 1*, 332.

order of His Holiness, and our father general, unless the Coptic patriarch writes to us and invites us there, we cannot go."[108]

Shortly after he balked at Santoro's request, Acquaviva's 16 June orders for Eliano to travel to Egypt arrived in Tripoli. While it irked Eliano that no one asked him whether the Maronites were ready to continue reforms on their own, he wrote to Acquaviva that "yesterday I received one of your Reverend Father's letters from 16 June, in which you expressly ordered me without delay to travel with Mario [Amato] to Cairo, to which without reply I will carry this out, with the Grace of God; at the first occasion, I will depart either by sea or land."[109] Eliano spent a few more weeks in the Levant, splitting his time between Tripoli and Aleppo. He visited Qannubin one last time to say his farewells to Sarkis and his bishops. Then, on 3 October 1582, he landed in Alexandria and checked in at the residence of the French consul, Paolo Mariani.[110] His time with the Maronites had come to an end.

CONCLUSION

As the next chapter highlights, Eliano's work with the Maronites remained central to his sense of himself while he was in Egypt, for good reason. He and Carafa would continue to work on establishing a printing press for the Maronites. Likewise, Eliano's call to send Lebanese seminarians to Rome eventually laid the groundwork for the Maronite College, a separate establishment opened in 1584 under the authority of the Society of Jesus.[111] The Maronite College was an immediate success. In 1585, one of the Maronite College's first students, Yuhanna al-Hasruni, explained to Eliano that, in addition to their residence, Gregory and Carafa had given them a church with a beautiful garden that was perfect for contemplation and reflection. And on numerous occasions, they wrote to Eliano and Carafa for more books, demonstrating their zeal for their education. The types of books varied: grammars, Arabic medicinal texts, standard devotional works, and the rich

---

[108] ARSI, *Gall. 95 III*, fol. 158r./*MPO 1*, 337.
[109] ARSI, *Gall. 95 I*, fol. 155r./*MPO 1*, 344.
[110] ARSI, *Gall. 98 II*, fol. 64v./*MPO 4*, 26.
[111] For more on the Maronite College, Latin education, and its legacy in the Maronite Church, see Nasser Gemayel, *Les échanges culturels entre les maronites et l'Europe: du Collège Maronite de Rome (1584) au Collège de `Ayn-Warqa (1789)* (Beirut: Impr. Y. et Ph. Gemayel, 1984).

theological works of authors such as Athanasius of Alexandria, Gregory of Nyssa, and Basil of Caesarea.[112] The Maronite youths also never failed to praise everyone involved in providing for them all that they needed during their stay in Rome, such as Gregory and Carafa. But all parties must have recognized how central Eliano was to the intellectual success of Maronite youths.

It is true – and worth repeating – that no Eastern Rite Christians were more amenable to Tridentine Catholicism than the Maronites, to the point that the Syriac Orthodox Patriarch of Antioch Ignatius Dawud told Eliano that the Maronites were "a nation of fools."[113] And the role of the disparate Maronite communities themselves should not be undervalued in light of Eliano's self-praise. By constructing what Catholicism meant for themselves, and desiring that Rome aid them in the first place, the Maronites' efforts should be seen as central to this mission, and the import of collective and grassroots religiosity – what some have called popular or traditional religion – should not be overshadowed by the larger processes of religious reform initiated by the institutions and orders of the Catholic Church.[114] In the case of the Maronites, this is exactly what happened. Continual renewal on the local level would always be needed, just as was the case in the rest of the Catholic world; and the Maronites' gradual movement toward Tridentine Catholicism was hardly complete when the Jesuit Girolamo Dandini arrived there in 1596 and convoked another synod to ensure the longevity of Eliano's reforms.[115]

Nevertheless, Eliano hung this mission's success on his ability to immerse himself in the Maronites' world, instruct them in the faith, and amend their books, all because of his knowledge of Arabic and past experiences of traversing various cultural and religious boundaries of the Mediterranean as a Jew. In other words, Eliano's depictions of his efforts with the Maronites allowed him to affirm his place in the Society of

---

[112] ARSI, *Gall. 95 II*, fol. 179/MPO 3, 121–3.

[113] ARSI, *Gall. 95 I*, fol. 164/MPO 1, 356.

[114] John Bossy, "The Counter-Reformation and the People of Catholic Europe," *Past & Present* 97 (1970): 51–70; Natalie Zemon Davis, *Society and Culture in Early Modern France: Eight Essays* (Stanford, CA: Stanford University Press, 1975); R. W. Scribner, *Popular Cultural and Popular Movements in Reformation Germany* (London: Hambledon Press, 1987); Charles Zika, "Hosts, Processions and Pilgrimages: Controlling the Sacred in Fifteenth-Century Germany," *Past & Present* 118 (1988): 25–64; Eamon Duffy, *The Stripping of the Altars* (New Haven, CT: Yale University Press, 1992).

[115] Carmelo Capizzi, "Un gesuita italiano di fine Cinquecento per i maroniti," *Studi e ricerche sull'oriente cristiano* 1 (1978): 19–36.

Jesus because of his status as its only Jewish-born member. By guiding the Maronites through the synod and conducting his pastoral visits to remote mountain villages, Eliano placed his Jewishness at the center of the Maronites' Catholicization; the Maronites' desire to follow the command of Rome, while sincere and equally a Maronite project, was nevertheless presented in Eliano's letters as his magnum opus. Eliano never missed an opportunity to remind his superiors that he, the Maronites' Elijah, saved the Maronites from the Turk, the Jacobite, the Armenian, the Nestorian, the Greek, and even from themselves; and he knew that he needed to hammer this point home as frequently as possible given the tenuous position of Jewish-lineage Jesuits like himself. Eliano thus went to great lengths to prove that he, a Jewish convert, was responsible for the Maronites' reforms.[116]

As Eliano left Lebanon for Egypt, he saw a second mission to the Copts as another opportunity to rescue yet another Christian group from heresy, to defend the faith, and to expand the borders of early modern Catholicism through textual exactitude and doctrinal reforms via a synod. And given how his last trip to Egypt had ended, he hoped to prove this time around that his Jewishness was not only not an obstacle to his efforts but should be maximized in the name of winning the Copts for Rome. That said, despite how encouraging Eliano's return to Egypt might have seemed at the outset, the next two chapters will show that Eliano's second trip to Egypt ended up much like the first: his work with the Copts failed; then, he wound up in prison at the hands of a Jew. To that story, we now turn.

---

[116] As mentioned in the previous chapter, it was under Acquaviva's leadership that the Society of Jesus would eventually expel all non-professed Jesuits with Jewish ancestry and ban the future admission of novices with Jewish lineage. See Robert A. Maryks, *The Jesuit Order as a Synagogue of Jews: Jesuits of Jewish Ancestry and Purity-of-Blood Laws in the Early Society of Jesus* (Leiden: Brill, 2010), 143–56.

5

Revisiting Eliano's Jewishness on His Return to Egypt

I admit that the greatest difficulty I have had in coming here, so that I not be an obstacle to the mission, was my preoccupation with not being known by the Jews lest I be forced into some entanglement by them as I was last time.[1]

– Giovanni Battista Eliano to Claudio Acquaviva

Because I found [my sister] quite inclined to listen to me without any true danger from the Jews, I no longer deemed it necessary to avoid her. And so, I often would visit her in the company of one of our brothers; but if I realize that I will not find profit with her to the benefit of her soul, I will without doubt desist and I will neither go to see her nor visit her.[2]

– Giovanni Battista Eliano to Claudio Acquaviva

Coming off his successes with the Maronites, Eliano's stock before his superiors was as high as it had been since perhaps his admission into the Society of Jesus in 1551. The conversion of the Copts, which Eliano had failed to achieve in the 1560s after he fled Egypt in duress, had the potential to solidify Eliano's reputation among his peers; and it would not be far-fetched to claim that posterity would have counted him among the most successful Jesuit missionaries of the early modern period. There were surely going to be logistical obstacles: the Copts still possessed centuries-old views that would take numerous rounds of negotiation to reconcile with Catholic teachings;[3] and the Ottomans

---

[1] ARSI, *Gall. 98 I*, fol. 103v./*MPO* 4, 94.

[2] ARSI, *Gall. 98 II*, fol. 129v–130r./*MPO* 4, 139.

[3] For more on the wide array of factors contributing to the tension between Catholic reform and the vicissitudes within the Christian Orient, see Bernard Heyberger, *Les chrétiens du Proche-Orient au temps de la réforme catholique: Syrie, Liban, Palestine, XVIIe–XVIIIe siècles* (Rome: Ecole française de Rome, 1994); Bernard Heyberger, "Polemic Dialogues

were increasingly worried about the ways in which rival European missionaries, diplomats, and merchants conducted themselves in their territories, in turn opening up the possibility of Ottoman intervention in what at first appear to be private disputes – as we will see in the next chapter, this will in fact become an issue for Eliano.[4]

To navigate these issues and ensure that they not hinder the mission, Eliano's first step was ingratiating himself with the European community centered on the French consul to Egypt, Paolo Mariani, who would provide him with a home base. Relations between Venice and Constantinople had soured somewhat after the loss of Cyprus and Venice's pivotal role in the defeat of the Ottomans at Lepanto in 1571.[5] Hoping to benefit from Venice's decline was Henry III of France, the Ottomans' main European ally.[6] Henry thus offered Eliano and Jesuit missions throughout the Ottoman Empire his support in their efforts.[7] Henry's consul, Mariani, would become Eliano's closest ally in Egypt,

---

between Christians and Muslims in the Seventeenth Century," *Journal of the Economic & Social History of the Orient* 55:2/3 (June 2012): 495–516.

[4] Daniel Goffman, *The Ottoman Empire and Early Modern Europe* (Cambridge: Cambridge University Press, 2002); Virginia H. Aksan and Daniel Goffman, eds., *The Early Modern Ottomans: Remapping the Empire* (Cambridge: Cambridge University Press, 2007); Giancarlo L. Casale, *The Ottoman Age of Exploration: Spices, Maps and Conquest in the Sixteenth-Century Indian Ocean* (Oxford: Oxford University Press, 2010). For more on the fear of internal rebellions, see Sam White, *The Climate of Rebellion in the Early Modern Ottoman Empire* (Cambridge: Cambridge University Press, 2011). On Catholic missionary rivalries and Ottoman intervention to maintain peace, see Robert John Clines "Fighting Enemies and Finding Friends: The Cosmopolitan Pragmatism of Jesuit Residences in the Ottoman Levant," *Renaissance Studies* 31:1 (February 2017): 66–86.

[5] Andrew C. Hess, "The Battle of Lepanto and Its Place in Mediterranean History," *Past & Present* 57 (November 1972): 53–73; Roger Crowley, *Empires of the Sea: The Siege of Malta, the Battle of Lepanto, and the Contest for the Center of the World* (New York: Random House, 2008). On the rhetoric in the aftermath of Lepanto, see a recent collection of sources pertaining to the battle: Elizabeth R. Wright, Sarah Spence, and Andrew Lemons, trans., *The Battle of Lepanto* (Cambridge, MA: Harvard University Press, 2014). See also the various contributions to a special edition of the *Journal of Iberian and Latin American Studies* (vol. 24, 2018) on Lepanto.

[6] On Henry, see R. J. Knecht, *Hero or Tyrant? Henry III, King of France, 1574–89* (Aldershot: Ashgate, 2014). Cf. A. Lynn Martin, *Henry III and the Jesuit Politicians* (Geneva: Librairie Droz, 1973).

[7] For more on Jesuit efforts in the sixteenth and seventeenth centuries vis-à-vis the French, see H. Fougueray, "La mission de France à Constantinople durant l'ambassade de M. de Césy," *Études* 113 (1907): 70–101; Charles A. Frazee, *Catholics and Sultans: The Church and the Ottoman Empire, 1453–1923* (Cambridge: Cambridge University Press, 1983), 67–87; Adina Ruiu, "Conflicting Visions of the Jesuit Missions to the Ottoman Empire, 1609–1628," *Journal of Jesuit Studies* 1:2 (2014): 260–80.

and had already written to Eliano while he was still in Lebanon to share his excitement for Eliano's impending arrival and his hope that the Jesuits would find nothing but success.[8]

Yet, despite Mariani's optimism for the mission, Eliano's second foray into evangelizing the Copts compelled him to prove that his work in Lebanon could translate to Egypt. Like he had done in Lebanon, Eliano planned to amend Coptic books and push for doctrinal reform through a synod, which Eliano hoped would prove that his Jewish past was an asset to the Society because it aided in the promotion of orthodoxy among the Copts. However, Egypt was nevertheless the site where he confronted challenges to his religious integrity, and he would again have to revisit his Jewish past. As the next two chapters will show, Eliano had to both promote his textual skills honed during his Jewish youth and downplay his Jewishness when confronted by his family and other Jews who questioned his presence in Egypt. This was necessary given that Acquaviva was increasingly skeptical of the efforts of Jewish-lineage Jesuits like Eliano. The fear was that the mission could unravel at any moment should Eliano's Jewish past become fodder for his rivals who aimed to undermine his efforts. Eliano's second mission to Egypt therefore hinged on his ability to promote his place within the Society of Jesus as its only Jewish-born member by articulating the ways in which his Jewish past played only a positive role in his Jesuit identity.[9] Success or failure notwithstanding, his efforts in Egypt and the challenges that came with them bound Eliano to his pre-conversion identity, the religious and political realities of the Mediterranean world, and evolving views of Jewish converts to Catholicism.

---

[8] ARSI, *Gall. 98 II*, fol. 53r./*MPO 4*, 22–3.

[9] On the political landscape of the Society of Jesus and the challenges that it presented to its members, see A. Lynn Martin, *The Jesuit Mind: The Mentality of an Elite in Early Modern France* (Ithaca, NY: Cornell University Press, 1988); Dauril Alden, *The Making of an Enterprise: The Society of Jesus in Portugal, Its Empire, and Beyond, 1540–1750* (Stanford, CA: Stanford University Press, 1996); Jonathan Wright, *God's Soldiers: Adventure, Politics, Intrigue, and Power: A History of the Jesuits* (New York: Doubleday, 2003); Harro Höpfl, *Jesuit Political Thought: The Society of Jesus and the State, c. 1540–1640* (Cambridge: Cambridge University Press, 2004); Luke Clossey, *Salvation and Globalization in the Early Jesuit Missions* (Cambridge: Cambridge University Press, 2008).

ELIANO'S EARLY STRUGGLES IN EGYPT

Eliano confronted these challenges soon after arriving in Egypt on 3 October 1582. First and foremost were the doctrinal differences between Catholics and Copts. In a letter to Gregory XIII written in late October, Eliano explained that Mariani "has received me in his home and desired that I live there; and with his holy zeal that these people be helped, he has already come to me in person four times" to explain that the Copts were willing to work with him.[10] He likewise explained that Coptic Patriarch John XIV and his advisors "desire to debate with us matters of faith." John had even written to Eliano while the latter was still in Tripoli. Eliano explained to Santoro in late October as well that the patriarch had invited "me to come here, even though I did not receive [his letters], as I had already left."[11] While the patriarch was willing to meet, Eliano told Santoro that he found other Copts quite unwilling to discuss "the two natures, two wills, and two operations [of Christ], and the Council of Chalcedon."[12]

These were perhaps insurmountable obstacles, ones that Eliano had failed to conquer two decades prior; but after just one month in Egypt Eliano could not admit as much, not to Gregory and certainly not to Santoro. In addition to his skepticism of converts, the cardinal protector was a theological hardliner known for his penchant for weeding out heresy, which eventually allowed him to rise to cardinal inquisitor.[13] It would be Santoro, along with the Jesuit theologian Robert Bellarmine,[14] who ordered the famed execution of Giordano Bruno eleven years after Eliano's death in 1600, an execution that took place in Rome's Campo de' Fiori, where Eliano had burned the Talmud in 1553.[15] Knowing Santoro's reputation, Eliano reminded Santoro that

---

[10] ASV, *A.A.Arm. I–XVIII*, 1780./MPO 4, 24.

[11] ARSI, *Gall. 98 II*, fol. 64v./MPO 4, 26.   [12] ARSI, *Gall. 98 II*, fol. 64v./MPO 4, 26.

[13] On Santoro as an inquisitor, see Saverio Ricci, *Il sommo inquisitore: Giulio Antonio Santori tra autobiografia e storia (1532–1602)* (Rome: Salerno Editrice, 2002).

[14] On Bellarmine and his place in the early modern church, see Peter Godman, *The Saint as Censor: Robert Bellarmine Between Inquisition and Index* (Leiden: Brill, 2000); Giovanni Romeo, "Roberto Bellarmino tra Inquisizione e Indice," *Studi Storici* 42:2 (April 1, 2001): 529–35; Sylvio Hermann DeFranceschi, "Le pouvoir indirect du pape au temporel et l'antiromanisme catholique des age pre-infaillibiliste et infaillibiliste," *Revue d'Histoire de l'Eglise de France* 88:220 (January 2002): 103–49; Stefania Tutino, *Empire of Souls: Robert Bellarmine and the Christian Commonwealth* (Oxford: Oxford University Press, 2010).

[15] Michael White, *The Pope and the Heretic: A True Story of Giordano Bruno, the Man Who Dared to Defy the Roman Inquisition* (New York: William Morrow, 2002); Ingrid

his accomplishments in Lebanon – which were the product of his Jewishness – were a roadmap for evangelization in Egypt. Eliano told Santoro that he would leave these issues for later "to deal with them with more ease. May it please Our Lord that the fruit that Your Most Illustrious Lordship and we all desire be done."[16] Eliano also asked Santoro to send copies of the decrees of the Council of Florence,[17] "which will bear fruit, I believe, through the grace of God."[18]

Eliano also wrote to Carafa on 22 October about the Maronite book project, which his orders to travel to Egypt had compelled him to abandon abruptly: "I desired to return [to Rome] as soon as possible, so that we can print many books, as has been generously promised to His Holiness. But since I was interrupted by having come here, I will leave this work to Your Most Illustrious Lordship."[19] In these letters to Gregory, Santoro, and Carafa, Eliano ensured his superiors that he was cognizant of his role in both the Copts' and Maronites' reforms, and that he would dedicate himself to whichever missionary theater his superiors deemed required his skills the most.

With Acquaviva, however, Eliano was much more ambivalent about how he described the Copts. While certain Copts seemed obstinate in their early meetings with Eliano, John and his advisors were more amenable.[20] While "they are so firm in having their books that extensively deal with these things that, frankly, it seems fairly difficult to me that they can be reduced" to Catholicism, if given the opportunity to examine their books and amend them, Eliano could potentially sway them by teasing out

---

D. Rowland, *Giordano Bruno: Philosopher/Heretic* (Chicago: University of Chicago Press, 2008).

[16] ARSI, *Gall. 98 II*, fol. 64v./MPO 4, 25.

[17] On Florence, see Joseph Gill, *The Council of Florence* (Cambridge: Cambridge University Press, 1961); Martin Anton Schmidt, "The Problem of Papal Primacy at the Council of Florence," *Church History* 30:1 (March 1, 1961): 35–49; Alastair Hamilton, *The Copts and the West, 1439–1822: The European Discovery of the Egyptian Church* (Oxford: Oxford University Press, 2006), 49–57.

[18] ARSI, *Gall. 98 II*, fol. 64v/65r./MPO 4, 27.

[19] ARSI, *Gall. 98 II*, fol. 65r./MPO 4, 28–9.

[20] ARSI, *Gall. 98 II*, fol. 56r./MPO 4, 31. Further elaboration on the Nestorian controversy, accompanied by important documents, can be found in John Anthony Cyril McGuckin, *St. Cyril of Alexandria: The Christological Controversy: Its History, Theology, and Texts* (Crestwood, NY: St. Vladimir's Seminary Press, 1994). Also see Susan Wessel, *Cyril of Alexandria and the Nestorian Controversy: The Making of a Saint and of a Heretic* (Oxford: Oxford University Press, 2004).

Catholic beliefs and triangulating them with Coptic understandings of Christology.[21] On one hand, Eliano feared that "no Oriental Christian nation will accept [union],"[22] and he felt that there were obstacles that extended beyond theological differences, which is why he was so willing to return and "work in Rome to finish things with the Maronites so that we not lose the certain for the uncertain."[23] On the other hand, if Acquaviva deemed that he should remain in Egypt, Eliano wanted his superior to know that the theological roadblocks were not his fault, and that he would work to overcome them through the same efforts that resulted in the Maronite synod.

The problem was, as far as Eliano saw it, that Mario Amato was not a good fit for the mission. Much like Eliano had felt hamstrung with Raggio, Amato "has always been discontented, saying that he was sent against his will and that he could go to Naples" instead of remaining in Egypt.[24] Eliano was frustrated that Amato did not want to work with the Copts, as "every day he wracks my brain by saying that they will never do anything and that it would be better to write only that we desire to return [to Italy]. Lastly, in all his actions, he shows only disgust in being here."[25] Eliano requested that "if I have to stay here, you must send a theologian to be my companion, so that we can discuss with [the Copts] the core tenets [of the faith] and craft some treatises in their language and

---

[21] ARSI, *Gall. 98 II*, fol. 56r./MPO 4, 31–2.

[22] ARSI, *Gall. 98 II*, fol. 57r./MPO 4, 34. There had long been a distinction between Eastern Orthodox (those who accepted Chalcedon but not Roman primacy) and Oriental Orthodox (those who rejected both). The Copts, like the Jacobites, were considered Oriental Orthodox. Here, Eliano seems to lump them together without distinction. For more on this distinction, especially regarding the Copts, see Otto Friedrich August Meinardus, *Two Thousand Years of Coptic Christianity* (Cairo: American University in Cairo Press, 1999). For a more elaborate discussion of the division of Christianity and the role of the ecumenical councils in the late antique period, see Leo D. Davis, *The First Seven Ecumenical Councils (325–787): Their History and Theology* (Collegeville, MN: Liturgical Press, 1983); in particular see chapters 5 and 6, which deal with the Councils of Chalcedon and Constantinople II, where monophysitism was one of the central points of contention. See also the contributions in Kenneth Parry, ed., *The Blackwell Companion to Eastern Christianity* (Malden, MA: Blackwell, 2007), which discusses on a case-by-case basis the distinctions between the various Eastern and Oriental Churches, including Eastern Catholic Churches like the Maronites.

[23] ARSI, *Gall. 98 II*, fol. 56v./MPO 4, 32.

[24] Ibid. Naples was a major theater of Jesuit activity in this period. See Jennifer D. Selwyn, *A Paradise Inhabited by Devils: The Jesuits' Civilizing Mission in Early Modern Naples* (Aldershote: Ashgate; Institutum Historicum Societatis Iesu, 2004).

[25] ARSI, *Gall. 98 II*, fol. 56v./MPO 4, 32.

communicate it with them."[26] Eliano also requested that "it will be necessary that the father who comes here bring with him the *Summa* of Saint Thomas [Aquinas] ... and other canonical texts, some books on cases of conscience, the General Councils, and others that will seem better to him, with a Calepino [dictionary]."[27] While this is a fairly standard list as far as textual reform and doctrinal orthodoxy go, his reference to Ambrogio Calepino (1440–1510), the Augustinian polymath whose Latin dictionary first appeared in 1502, is a reminder that Eliano's lexicographical knowledge would be key to his success, much like during his time in Lebanon; but it could be useful only so long as he had a theologian to help him convince the Copts that the texts he aimed to amend were indeed orthodox.

While he knew that he needed to prove to his superiors that he was up to the task of converting the Copts, Eliano realized after one month in Egypt that the forecast for success depended on him, which compelled him to emphasize his textual skills over his ability to debate theology with the Copts. By presenting the Copts' obstinacy as something that he could not tackle alone because his lexicographical skills needed to be complemented by a theologian, Eliano both portrayed himself as central to any success the mission might find while also absolving himself of any culpability should the Copts not accept doctrinal reforms.

His inability to work with the Copts on matters of doctrine comes through after a month of negotiating with John and his theologians. By mid-November, Eliano found them shackled by "their inveterate opinions," and he was convinced that only a true theologian could convince them to abandon their beliefs.[28] While the Copts remained open to debate, they refuted everything he suggested. This back-and-forth did not sit well with the often impatient Eliano: "I find them each time so entrenched and firm in these heresies of theirs, that I dare say that [converting the Copts] will be nearly impossible."[29] Yet, despite his own admission that he did not possess the theological acumen to go toe-to-toe with leading Copts, Eliano did not want his superiors to doubt his dedication or his ability. He then returned to Matthew 3:9, a passage he cited in the 1560s, to show that, despite the Copts' resistance, he would strive to succeed: "as I have said, I do not wish, however, to despair

[26] Ibid.   [27] ARSI, *Gall. 98 II*, fol. 56v./*MPO 4*, 33.
[28] ARSI, *Gall. 98 II*, fol. 60r./*MPO 4*, 35–6.   [29] ARSI, *Gall. 98 II*, fol. 60r./*MPO 4*, 36.

myself of the providence of the Lord and his great mercy, who 'can raise up sons of Abraham from these stones.'"[30]

Emphasizing again his lexicographical skills, Eliano reminded Acquaviva on 19 November that he was willing to return to Rome to oversee the imprinting of Maronite books, as "I am convinced that, if I am not there (which I say with utmost modesty), they will not be printed perfectly, because I am better informed than any other."[31] In the meantime, he would await Acquaviva's decision on how to proceed and would continue to collect Arabic copies of Scripture, which he hoped "can be stamped and disseminated throughout these lands, which will seem to be fruitful alms and of great use, inasmuch as, among the infinite number of Christians who live in these lands, one cannot find even two that have Holy Scripture in their own language. Likewise, these books will help the Collegio Romano, where the Maronites and other nations study."[32]

Clearly, by the end of November 1582, Eliano still remained cautious about debating doctrine with the Copts without a trained theologian, as he knew that the mission's potential failure would fall on him and would raise suspicions about his abilities. His previous time in Egypt was a complete disaster that ended with him in prison on trumped-up charges of apostasy and financial default. So, this was a shot at redemption that could potentially assuage any doubts about his own convictions, especially given Acquaviva's anti-Jewish stance and Santoro's almost militant orthodoxy and role in the conversion of the Jews in Rome. He therefore stressed that his time in Egypt would not be fruitless even if the Copts would not convert, as he would scour books and attempt to amend them, emphasizing time and time again the need for a true theologian to come aid him in reforming the Copts.

By mid-December, despite his best efforts to discuss matters with the Copts, Eliano found himself still unable to counter the Copts' intransigence. In a letter to Acquaviva dated 29 December, Eliano listed ten heresies that the Copts held, ranging from "they still have the Greek heresy concerning the procession of the Holy Spirit [in the Creed]" to their refusal to admit that Confirmation and Last Rites were sacraments.[33] Eliano's emphasis on their heresy, especially when enumerated

---

[30] Ibid. As we saw in Chapter 2, Eliano used the reference to John the Baptist preparing the way for the coming of Christ by preaching to and baptizing the multitude in the wilderness of Jordan to suggest his own ability to evangelize.

[31] ARSI, *Gall. 98 II*, fol. 60r./MPO 4, 36.   [32] Ibid., 36–7.

[33] ARSI, *Gall. 98 II*, fol. 68rv./MPO 4, 43–5.

to such a great length, points not only to his frustrations, but also to his concerns regarding his superiors' views of him. Eliano hyperbolically lambasted the Copts for their intransigence, such as how "the greatest ignorance reigns over all of them . . . and when one of them knows how to read and write well, they take him for a literary genius. The result of this is that there are few capable of reason and of [understanding] the authority of sacred writings."[34] These issues, among others, "are the great difficulties that I have not penetrated so far."[35] Eliano did not wish to lose hope for the mission, but the state of affairs by Christmastide was hardly positive. Eliano suggested again to Acquaviva that, if he deemed converting the Copts far too difficult for two Jesuits to tackle on their own, Eliano would not delay their return to Italy, freeing Eliano to work on the Maronite book project; after all, Eliano reminded his superior, "those poor Maronites await with great desire the printing of their ecclesiastical books that we have amended."[36]

Eliano would not let the Copts' refusal to budge on matters of doctrine render him idle, though. Rather, "while I am here awaiting new orders, I will attend to reading many of their books and noting their errors, as I did with the Maronites," and he would "publish our catechism printed in Rome in Chaldean for the Maronites and provide [the Copts] with copies in Arabic, so that they can accept what they must believe."[37] Eliano also stressed that he would "see to the copying of other Arabic books of Holy Scripture. Since the printing of the Bible is pleasing to God and His Holiness, we should have several exemplars for producing a good Vulgate in Arabic, as in Latin and Greek." Eliano emphasized that this was necessary work, since "all these people and the whole of the East have no knowledge of the Bible except in an abbreviated form, because no one has a complete Bible; some have the Pentateuch, some the books of the prophets, some other books."[38]

While the Copts might have disagreed with Eliano's assessment of their knowledge of scripture, Eliano painted them as ignorant to position himself as the one who could instruct them by providing them with an Arabic translation of the Vulgate and, in turn, the Truth. When triangulated with his list of heresies and his proclamation that "the greatest ignorance reigns over all of them," Eliano's efforts to amend and expand their textual repertoire point to his refashioned Jewishness as grounded in

---

[34] ARSI, *Gall. 98 II*, fol. 68v./MPO 4, 45.   [35] Ibid.
[36] ARSI, *Gall. 98 II*, fol. 68v./MPO 4, 46.   [37] ARSI, *Gall. 98 II*, fol. 68v./MPO 4, 46.
[38] ARSI, *Gall. 98 II*, fols. 68v–69r./MPO 4, 46–7.

textual erudition and lexicographical expertise. Knowing full well of others' skepticism surrounding his Jewish ancestry, Eliano did not want to show any signs of weakness or wavering; he wished only to express his concerns and use the Copts' intransigence – and his vitriol against it – as evidence of his desire to convert them. By January 1583, while he might have chosen to be where he felt he could accomplish something – namely, Lebanon – he humbly, yet pithily, quipped: "I always find myself ready for whatever will be ordained for me, whether I am to return or stay; may it all be for the greater service of God."³⁹

ACQUAVIVA'S GUARDED ACKNOWLEDGMENT OF ELIANO'S CONCERNS

Acquaviva understood that the Copts were not like the Maronites, who had long recognized papal authority, had requested help from Rome, and were more than willing to implement Tridentine reforms. For this reason, on 1 January 1583, Acquaviva wrote to Eliano that "if you have not found any chance of success, the Most Illustrious Caraffa [*sic*] has told me that you can return to Italy immediately." Yet, he explained, if there was even a small chance of success, "you can remain and advise us to the smallest detail of every matter" and that he would do his best to provide what "is judged best for helping the mission."⁴⁰ Despite Eliano's protests and fears of it failing, it was clear that Acquaviva intended for the mission to continue.

That is not to say Acquaviva completely ignored Eliano's requests. Rather, despite his views of Jewish-lineage Jesuits and his distrust of Eliano, Acquaviva recognized that converting the Copts required a theologian who could go toe-to-toe with leading Coptic intellectuals; and so, he decided to send the Neapolitan theologian Francesco Sasso.⁴¹ In addition to his theological aid, Sasso would also bring three papal briefs

---

³⁹ ARSI, *Ital. 157*, fol. 17r./MPO 4, 50.   ⁴⁰ ARSI, *Gall. 98 I*, fol. 70r./MPO 4, 49.

⁴¹ For more on Sasso, see Charles Libois's brief biographical sketch in *MPO* 4, 442. Enrique García Hernán also refers to Sasso as an "expert Jesuit," but an expert of what he does not say. See Enrique García Hernán, "The Holy See, the Spanish Monarchy and Safavid Persia in the Sixteenth Century: Some Aspects of the Involvement of the Society of Jesus," in *Iran and the World in the Safavid Age*, ed. Willem Floor and Edmund Herzig (London: I.B. Tauris, 2012), 186. Likewise, in his very brief discussion of this mission, Alastair Hamilton claims that Sasso was "as rigid a dogmatist as (Cristóbal) Rodríguez." See Alastair Hamilton, *The Copts and the West, 1439–1822: The European Discovery of the Egyptian Church* (Oxford: Oxford University Press, 2006), 69.

that would buttress the Jesuits' work by emphasizing that they were there under Gregory's authority:[42] the first provided general directions for the mission and gave them the authority to convoke and preside over a synod;[43] the second requested that European Catholics in Egypt assist the Jesuits however they could;[44] the third, addressed to John XIV, announced that Gregory had sent the Jesuits to promote the Christian religion.[45]

In the early months of 1583, Sasso's imminent arrival gave the mission a glimmer of promise, as Sasso's theological training would complement Eliano's textual work. Also accompanying Sasso was Francesco Buono of Milan, who would assist with some of the ministries and administrative tasks.[46] Yet, because Sasso and Buono knew little to no Arabic, both would have to rely on Eliano's translations of complex theological works to grasp them fully and would lean on Eliano to interpret in their discussions. Even though Sasso would be the theological architect of the synod, an accord would only occur through Eliano. Acquaviva agreed, by ordering Eliano to translate Sasso's writings and craft treatises in Arabic that stressed the links between the theologies of the two churches.[47] Eliano therefore remained secure as the mission's cardinal figure, as all exchanges and translations – conversational and textual – would run through him. In the meantime, Eliano continued to work with the Copts

---

[42] For more on the give and take of the papacy as both a religious and political institution in the early modern period, see Paolo Prodi, *The Papal Prince* (Cambridge: Cambridge University Press, 1987). Also noteworthy are various contributions to James Corkery and Thomas Worcester, eds., *The Papacy since 1500: From Italian Prince to Universal Pastor* (Cambridge: Cambridge University Press, 2010), in particular Frederic J. Baumgartner, "Julius II: Prince, Patron, Pastor" (pp. 12–28). See also Anthony D. Wright, *The Early Modern Papacy: From the Council of Trent to the French Revolution, 1564–1789* (Harlow: Longman, 2000) and William V. Hudon, "The Papacy in the Age of Reform, 1513–1644," in *Early Modern Catholicism: Essays in Honour of John W. O'Malley, S.J.*, ed. Kathleen M. Comerford, and Hilmar M. Pabel (Toronto: University of Toronto Press, 2001), 46–66. He is also a strong example of the pervading image of the *podestas indirecta* that was central to the political thought of Robert Bellarmine. See Stefania Tutino, *Empire of Souls: Robert Bellarmine and the Christian Commonwealth* (Oxford: Oxford University Press, 2010).

[43] ARSI, *Gall. 98 I*, fols. 89r–90v./*MPO 4*, 59–62.

[44] ASV, *Secr. Brev. 56*, fol. 95rv./*MPO 4*, 64. For more on this infrastructure and its role in shaping Ottoman Cairo, albeit for the seventeenth century, see Raoul Clément, *Les Français d'Égypte aux XVIIe et XVIIIe siècles* (Cairo: Impr. de l'Institut français d'archéologie orientale, 1960).

[45] ARSI, *Gall. 98 II*, fol. 95rv./*MPO 4*, 62. Latin Original. Eliano's Arabic translation is on the inverse.

[46] ARSI, *Neap. 2*, fol. 177r./*MPO 4*, 53.   [47] ARSI, *Gall. 98 I*, fol. 101v./*MPO 4*, 89–90.

and awaited Sasso and Buono's arrival. One of his successes that winter was the conversion of three Copts whom Eliano described as "very honored and esteemed by all." Eliano hoped that John and the rest of the community would look favorably upon these types of conversions.[48]

Despite this, and despite his willingness to address Eliano's concerns, Acquaviva remained apprehensive. On 12 March, Acquaviva wrote to Eliano that he had charged Sasso with "the duty of being consultor, monitor, and Your Reverence's confessor, with the necessary authority, so that with this communication union will be better aided."[49] Such spiritual protection for Eliano would not have been out of place, as it was expected that Jesuit missionaries were to be one another's spiritual guides. However, the subsequent directive extends beyond normal spiritual succor, and points to Acquaviva's unease regarding Eliano's ability to lead the mission: "and if the matters of the past during the other mission were to cause me some discontent, I desire this, my Father: that you succeed in this particular work, and that you lack nothing. I admit that I will be consoled in this desire; because from your words I have promised myself much, and from that of Father Sasso I expect even more."[50] There is a certain ambiguity in Acquaviva's statement, as it is unclear to which "other mission" he is referring: the first mission to the Copts, in which Eliano was arrested, or the troubles he had with Raggio in Lebanon. In either case, Acquaviva was clearly uneasy regarding Eliano's past missionary efforts, which suggests that Eliano's Jewishness perhaps worried Acquaviva to the point that he felt compelled to address it. And it would not take long for Acquaviva's anxieties concerning Eliano and his past to be realized.

THE RESURFACING OF ELIANO'S JEWISH PAST

By mid-March, it had become clear that certain Jews knew of Eliano's presence in Egypt; and as in the 1560s, his family desired to know of his activities. This left him fearful of another conspiracy to have him arrested, which would only make Acquaviva all the more doubtful of Eliano's ability to avoid scandal. While decades had passed since his imprisonment and furtive escape after his father's creditors went after him, he understood that he could not avoid the fact that some saw him as an

---

[48] ARSI, *Gall. 98 I*, fol. 103r./*MPO* 4, 93.   [49] ARSI, *Gall. 98 I*, fol. 101r./*MPO* 4, 89.
[50] ARSI, *Gall. 98 I*, fol. 101rv./*MPO* 4, 89.

opportunistic crypto-Jew; and now potentially included in that number were fellow Jesuits. Rather than downplay the Jews' presence, Eliano explained to Acquaviva on 18 March that "what I feared came upon me. I admit that the greatest difficulty I have had in coming here, so that I not be an obstacle to the mission, was my preoccupation with not being known by the Jews lest I be forced into some entanglement by them as I was last time."[51]

While moving about Cairo, an unidentified Jewish man recognized Eliano. Eliano explained that this Jew approached him and said, "'Are you not that one [who was Jewish]? Your sister is here. She has known of your presence here for some time. . . . She has sent me here, begging me to compel you to come with me to see her.'"[52] Eliano then "went to [Mariani] to tell him everything. He lifted my spirit by saying, 'It should not surprise you that all the Jews who frequent this place (and there are many) know you, as they have spoken to me about you. So, go happily to your sister and console her.'"[53] Forty-five years old and married now, "she stood there for a bit unable to talk, crying, and finally she explained that she had had no other wish but to see me for some time, given that she had not seen me in thirty years."[54] His sister also attempted to assuage his fears concerning other Jews who might still view him as an apostate. She told Eliano that there was no need "to hide from the Jews, who all know of me, and that they are no longer going to give me any trouble, knowing well, as she said, 'you are an important man to the pope and could do great harm or great help to the Jews if [he] wished.'" This calmed him and allowed him to "leave it all to Divine Providence."[55]

While this meeting with his sister in early 1583 must have been a wonderful reconciliation as well as a relief, as it seems to have convinced him a Jewish conspiracy against him was unlikely, Eliano's decision to relay it to Acquaviva in full also points to his need to convince his superior that his Jewish past was not going to be the obstacle that it had been during his previous stint in Egypt. Eliano cast this interaction with his sister and other Jews according to how he needed others to view it. By suggesting that the Jews were not interested in harming him because of his connections in Rome, Eliano attempted to prove to Acquaviva that the mission would not be derailed due to any Jewish plots because they apparently feared papal retribution. And familial recognition of his Catholicness relegates his Jewishness to the past while still rendering it a

---

[51] ARSI, *Gall. 98 I*, fol. 103vJMPO 4, 94.   [52] Ibid.   [53] Ibid.   [54] Ibid.
[55] ARSI, *Gall. 98 I*, fol. 103vJMPO 4, 94–5.

missionary tool rather than an epistemological obstacle to achieving full status as a Jesuit.

His apparent refusal to correct his sister on his relationship with Gregory and standing before his superiors suggests as well that Eliano did not want the Jews to know that some Catholics questioned his loyalty and that he in fact could not simply ask Gregory to persecute Jews. After all, Eliano's position within the Society of Jesus was tenuous for the very reason why his sister claimed that the Jews feared him: The Catholic Church and the Jesuits were actively trying to convert the Jews and were not shy about weeding out crypto-Jews.[56] While he held little influence over Gregory, he was keen to indulge his sister in such a delusion and to keep her and the other Jews ignorant about his superiors' doubts concerning his conversion. Perhaps the Jews would only leave him be so long as they perceived that he could pose a serious threat to them. In both cases – to Catholics and to Jews – Eliano muddled how people viewed his Jewishness to present it in two very different ways depending on the audience.

Eliano's apprehensions were not paranoia, either. In fact, Eliano remained cognizant of the fact that, while at least some may have accepted his conversion, others, Catholics included, could use it against him should he stand in their way. One such figure was Giovanni Paolo Caimo, a monsignor attached to the household of the great Counter-Reformation archbishop, Carlo Borromeo of Milan. On 3 June, Eliano wrote to Acquaviva that Caimo had recently arrived in Egypt with designs to travel to the center of late-antique Egyptian monasticism known as Wadi El Natrun to steal the relics of a fourth-century desert saint called Macarius. Macarius was one of the most venerated of the desert fathers, along with Anthony the Great and Pachomius, legendary figures whom the Copts saw as their forefathers.[57] Relic theft was nothing new in the Mediterranean either, having been a common occurrence throughout the

---

[56] Perez Zagorin, *Ways of Lying: Dissimulation, Persecution, and Conformity in Early Modern Europe* (Cambridge, MA: Harvard University Press, 1990).

[57] James E. Goehring and Janet Timbie, eds., *The World of Early Egyptian Christianity: Language, Literature, and Social Context: Essays in Honor of David W. Johnson* (Washington, DC: Catholic University of America Press, 2007). Words of wisdom attributed to Macarius are included in Benedicta Ward, *The Sayings of the Desert Fathers: The Alphabetical Collection* (Kalamazoo, MI: Cistercian Publications, 1975), 124–38. For more on the development of monasticism and its importance for early Christianity, see Peter H. Görg, *The Desert Fathers: Anthony and the Beginnings of Monasticism* (San Francisco: Ignatius Press, 2011). For a more general discussion of the late antique world and the role of Christianity in it, see Averil Cameron, *The*

Middle Ages.[58] Having Macarius's relics in Milan would have thus provided a boost in prestige for the already powerful Ambrosian Church, which was now under heavy Spanish influence.[59] But because Macarius was so highly venerated among the Copts, Eliano feared that this whole episode was "making these people with their patriarch aliens and enemies of the Franks, which will lead to nothing good for us."[60]

Eliano did all he could to prevent Caimo from seizing the relics, and the Copts also did their part in averting the furtive removal of Macarius's remains. But there was another problem, namely, that Caimo grew angry with Eliano for what he saw as an act of betrayal. This stupefied Eliano, and he grieved to Acquaviva that "thinking that perhaps I was the cause of his failure to get what he wanted … [Caimo] and his companions showed themselves so averse toward me, maybe with the desire to want to lament about me to Your Paternity or to others."[61] While Caimo was eventually unsuccessful in his quest to steal Macarius and never slandered Eliano, Eliano's fear that Caimo might denounce Eliano to his superiors points to a continued confrontation with others' views that he might not be a dedicated Catholic.

ELIANO'S REFRAMING OF HIS JEWISHNESS
IN HIS WORK WITH THE COPTS

Eliano realized that, to assuage these apprehensions surrounding his religious past and his former religious kinsmen's presence in Egypt, he had to stress that his textual work would successfully reform the Copts.

Mediterranean World in Late Antiquity, AD 395–600 (London: Routledge, 1993), particularly pp. 71–5 on "Monks, Ascetics and Holy Men."

[58] For further background on relic theft, see Patrick J. Geary, *Furta Sacra: Thefts of Relics in the Central Middle Ages* (Princeton, NJ: Princeton University Press, 1978). While it is a study of the Holy Land, Oded Peri's *Christianity Under Islam in Jerusalem: The Question of the Holy Sites in Early Ottoman Times* (Leiden: Brill, 2001) is an excellent study of how Christian holy sites fit within Ottoman society. While much of what Peri has to say about sites in the Holy Land does not apply to Christian holy sites in Egypt, the seamless integration of these sites into the Ottoman world is of particular note here.

[59] On Spanish Milan and the Borromeo, see Wietse de Boer, *The Conquest of the Soul: Confession, Discipline, and Public Order in Counter-Reformation Milan* (Leiden: Brill, 2001); Antonio Álvarez-Ossorio Alvariño, "The State of Milan and the Spanish Monarchy," in *Spain in Italy: Politics, Society, and Religion 1500–1700*, ed. Thomas Dandelet and John A. Marino (Leiden: Brill, 2007), 99–132; Stefano D'Amico, *Spanish Milan: A City within the Empire, 1535–1706* (New York: Palgrave Macmillan, 2012).

[60] ARSI, *Gall. 98 II*, fol. 116r./MPO 4, 113–14.

[61] ARSI, *Gall. 98 II*, fol. 116rv./MPO 4, 114.

His hopes for this centered on Paolo Mariani's close relationship with Patriarch John. Because the patriarch trusted Mariani, he welcomed the Jesuits into the community and engaged them in rather amicable theological debates. He also allowed Eliano unfettered access to Coptic libraries.[62] In mid-May 1583, as he remained uneasy about the Jews' knowledge of his presence in Egypt, Eliano explained that "for some time now, I have dealt directly with some intelligent [Copts], and we have settled on matters with which we must deal to reach our end; and so long as the devil and my sins do not impede us, we hope that we will achieve in good measure what is promised."[63] Eliano planned to delve into Coptic books as he had done in Lebanon, as "we have deemed it most expedient to skim through their authentic books, from which we will find Catholic propositions that they deny out of ignorance and for not studying books of the saints. . . . And daily we copy those that we have found thus far."[64] Once his work with these texts was complete and Catholic truths were highlighted as part and parcel of Coptic belief, "in a synod in the presence of the patriarch, his bishops, and other more intelligent theologians, we hope that they will be left convinced and will embrace the faith."[65] Eliano's belief that convoking a synod on the heels of textual study could find success was of course not without precedent, as he had just achieved this in Lebanon – Acquaviva and Santoro would have realized this as well. Securing a synodal accord would be a great triumph for the church, as it would be an important first step in the Catholicization of the historically resistant Copts; and it had the potential to secure Eliano's place within the Society by once again proving that his Jewishness remained integral to his ability to convert Eastern Rite Christians.

It was more than Acquaviva's skepticism, however, that motivated Eliano to emphasize his Jewishness as central to any doctrinal concord. The cardinal protector of the mission, Giulio Antonio Santoro, demanded nothing short of the complete capitulation of the Copts. As discussed in Chapter 3, Eliano and Santoro had an acrimonious past, as Eliano's conversion and labors as a Jesuit were entangled with Santoro's efforts to convert the Jews; but Santoro nevertheless bordered on paranoia regarding the veracity of the very conversions he aimed to procure. By the time Eliano was in Egypt, the micromanagement intimated by his

---

[62] ARSI, *Gall. 98 II*, fol. 106v./MPO 4, 108. Mariani's letter to Eliano is inventoried as ARSI, *Gall. 98 II*, fols. 53r–54v./MPO 4, 22–3.
[63] ARSI, *Gall. 98 II*, fol. 106v./MPO 4, 108.
[64] ARSI, *Gall. 98 II*, fol. 106v./MPO 4, 109.   [65] Ibid.

presence at conversionary sermons in Rome pervaded his approach to this mission. Unlike Antonio Carafa – who had written only six letters to Eliano while he was in Lebanon – Santoro sent Eliano more than twenty lengthy letters of instruction that both showed the cardinal's staunchness as well as ran contrary to how Eliano felt the mission should be conducted. For example, in a verbose, five-page letter sent to Cairo on 10 June 1583, Santoro implored Eliano to put aside niceties and hammer the Copts on doctrinal differences. Santoro explained that, despite "the hardness of [the Copts'] spirit and the antiquity of their abuses and errors," such a hard line would assuredly render them "more manageable and inclined to accept what was proposed to them concerning Catholic truth."[66] Santoro believed that this would liberate a people that "for centuries [were] immersed in errors and the shadows of heresies, and [were] living among infidels."[67]

This is hardly the discretion that Gregory and Acquaviva had stressed, that Carafa had demonstrated with the Maronites, that Mariani employed to secure a meeting with John XIV in the first place, or that Eliano knew would work. Nevertheless, it follows quite well the ways in which Santoro handled matters. And it also put undue pressure on Eliano. While anyone under Santoro's authority faced scrutiny, Eliano was particularly under the microscope given their past relationship as well as his repeated claim that he alone could amend or expurgate Coptic texts because of his Jewish past. If he failed to do the one thing that he alone could purportedly achieve, it could be seen as proof that perhaps his Jewishness was not the uniquely efficacious tool that he had portrayed it to be.

Acquaviva also remained a source of frustration for Eliano because of his cautious optimism for the mission. Always the pragmatist, he recognized that if the mission proved fruitless, there would be little point in continuing. When he finally wrote to Eliano on 12 June, he explained that he should wait until Sasso and Buono arrived before pursuing all avenues with the Copts.[68] The persistent stressor for Acquaviva, however, was Eliano's Jewishness and the ramifications it could have for the mission. On one hand, he understood that Eliano felt safe in Egypt this time around and that a Jewish conspiracy seemed unlikely, thanks to Mariani and the perception among the Jews that Eliano possessed some level of influence with Gregory. On the other hand, Acquaviva was worried

---

[66] ARSI, *Gall. 98 I*, fol. 119r./MPO 4, 115–16.
[67] ARSI, *Gall. 98 I*, fol. 120r./MPO 4, 117.   [68] ARSI, *Gall. 98 I*, fol. 122r./MPO 4, 121.

despite the apparent tranquility, as Ottoman Egypt was the physical setting of "when you felt past dangers in other times" because of his confrontations with Jews, which "leaves us with fear."[69] Despite Eliano's assurances that he was not in danger, Acquaviva nevertheless ordered Sasso to "see that everyone is safe in Cairo, above all Father Battista, who is known by the Jews of that land, and last time was in grave danger."[70] Clearly, Acquaviva had his doubts concerning Eliano, and he stressed to Sasso that his duty, in addition to serving as Eliano's confessor and theological advisor, was to ensure that Eliano's notoriety among the Jews not derail the mission, Eliano's assurances notwithstanding.[71]

Such concerns regarding Eliano's Jewish past must have only added to Eliano's own angst, which compelled him to emphasize his ability to hunt down and analyze Coptic texts as well as to distance himself from the Jews. Regarding the Copts' books, "I will send certain notebooks in Arabic that contain Catholic propositions pulled out of Coptic books." Once this work was carried forth, "I hope they will be convinced" to convert.[72] Eliano also ensured that Acquaviva understood that the patriarch "was pleased by our conversation" regarding his plan to parse out Catholic doctrine from Coptic books. However, Eliano reminded Acquaviva, this would have to wait until Sasso arrived with the apostolic briefs.[73]

Eliano also relayed to Santoro that summer his plan to scour Coptic books and "note many Catholic propositions that they do not consider, because they do not understand them or do not read them." Eliano assured the cardinal that "with the help of the theologian whom I am expecting, [these theological issues] will be made very clear in a synod or in some other manner."[74] Knowing full well of the cardinal's impatience, Eliano reminded Santoro that the lack of progress was not due to a failure in effort. Rather, "we remain quite distressed because we have not received many letters," and because Sasso had yet to arrive.[75] In the meantime, Eliano also reminded those in Rome that, in his efforts to convert the Copts, he could freely move about in Egypt "with great security without any danger; and the Jews, who all know me, honor me above all else."[76] By essentializing the Jews as Other, but an Other that

---

[69] Ibid.   [70] ARSI, *Ven.* 2, fol. 121r./*MPO* 4, 124.
[71] ARSI, *Ven.* 2, fol. 121r./*MPO* 4, 123.   [72] ARSI, *Gall. 98 I*, fol. 108r./*MPO* 4, 125.
[73] Ibid.   [74] ARSI, *Gall. 98 II*, fol. 108r./*MPO* 4, 125.
[75] ARSI, *Gall. 98 II*, fol. 108v./*MPO* 4, 127.
[76] ARSI, *Gall. 98 I*, fol. 108r./*MPO* 4, 125.

does not wish him harm for having converted, Eliano stressed that his Jewishness was grounded in his ability to engage in texts; it did not cause an acrimonious relationship with his quondam religious kin who might want to do him harm, as had happened on the previous mission to Egypt.

SASSO AND BUONO'S ARRIVAL AND THE
REENGAGEMENT WITH THE COPTS

Sasso and Buono finally arrived in Cairo on 12 August 1583. This gave Eliano a partner who would bring much-needed youthful vitality and theological precision to the mission, and an assistant to handle the quotidian logistics of the mission.[77] They wasted no time getting to work. By 18 September, Eliano had found Sasso to be a worthy companion who "has a great desire to aid this mission," and was pleased to finally receive various letters of instruction.[78] In the short term, there was little for Sasso and Buono to accomplish until Eliano finished his theological notebooks, so they traveled to Jerusalem. While they were in the Levant, Eliano planned "to put into order all of the items that I have culled from Coptic books, which they find pleasing, with hope that by such means they will be easily convinced." Eliano intended "to reduce them in good order and have them ready to discuss with them. I will send a translated copy with the Arabic original to Rome, so that Your Paternity and others can be consoled by such beautiful truths that these books contain, which the Copts – out of ignorance and carelessness – do not read or do not consider while reading."[79] Once received in Rome, Santoro and a team of theologians would review and approve the synod in Gregory's name. Eliano believed that this course of action would please both Santoro and the Copts. Building off his experience in Lebanon, Eliano knew full well that the only way for the synod to be successful was if it were collaborative; he also knew it was the only way to prove to his superiors that he was an integral part of the Copts' conversion through his unique ability to communicate with them candidly, scour their books, and lead them to salvation.

Part of this was continuing to stress that the Jews were not a threat and that he would not return to Judaism. That same September, he reminded Acquaviva that he felt safe in Egypt despite the presence of Jews there,

---

[77] ARSI, *Gall. 98 II*, fol. 124r./*MPO* 4, 130.
[78] ARSI, *Gall. 98 II*, fol. 128r./*MPO* 4, 136.
[79] ARSI, *Gall. 98 II*, fol. 128rv./*MPO* 4, 137.

especially since "I had advised Your Paternity last time that I had discovered my sister here, whom I avoided readily, lest I solicit danger from the Jews – which gave me great angst – as had happened on the previous mission."[80] However, not wanting to raise Acquaviva's suspicions because of their constant visits, "because I found her quite inclined to listen to me without any true danger from the Jews, I no longer deemed it necessary to avoid her. And so, I often visit her in the company of one of our brothers; but if I realize that I will not find profit with her to the benefit of her soul, I will without doubt desist and I will neither go to see her nor visit her."[81] Eliano again constructed a gap between himself and the Jews via his sister, one that could be bridged only through Jewish conversion to Catholicism. While he described her as his sister, he nevertheless intimated that their kinship was severed because of his conversion and could be restored only through her decision to follow suit. Eliano stressed that not only were the Jews of Egypt not a threat and not only was he no longer Jewish, but that they – especially his sister – could be his conversionary targets.

ELIANO'S RELATIONSHIP WITH PAOLO MARIANI

Beyond massaging the nature of his relationship with his sister and other Jews, Eliano also stressed that he believed his work with the Copts would continue, due in no small part to Paolo Mariani, the French consul with whom Eliano had developed a close friendship. On 25 September, he wrote to Gregory to laud "the piety and zeal of Paolo Mariani, consul of the Most Christian King in Egypt," concerning the conversion of the Copts.[82] However, there was a slight hiccup regarding Mariani's standing, namely, that Henry III had begun questioning Mariani's loyalty, purportedly because he was Venetian.[83] The root cause of this was Henry's desire to increase his influence and power abroad, which was why he agreed to support this mission in the first place; and it was imperative to have a diplomatic retinue that demonstrated allegiance to Henry.[84] This was especially necessary vis-à-vis his Ottoman ally, as

---

[80] ARSI, *Gall. 98 II*, fol. 129v./*MPO* 4, 139.
[81] ARSI, *Gall. 98 II*, fols. 129v–130r./*MPO* 4, 139.
[82] APF, *Miscellanee Varie* Ia, fol. 506r./*MPO* 4, 143.   [83] Ibid.
[84] While Henry III continued this process, which had begun in earnest under Francis I, it was far from complete. In fact, it would take another one hundred years before this could be thoroughly completed under Louis XIV. See Gillian Weiss, *Captives and Corsairs: France*

Henry was most certainly the junior partner in an uneasy alliance and needed diplomats who would work for him.[85]

Power politics aside, this revelation terrified Eliano, as Mariani's potential recall would mean that the Copts' conversion – and the employment of his Jewishness to that end – might not materialize. Eliano assured his superiors that he had not befriended a dishonest diplomat, for "he has so clearly shown this accusation to be most false, through the testimony of all the merchants, above all the French, who find themselves most satisfied with him and his efforts." More important, Eliano believed that Mariani "has most faithfully served the King, and with much piety promoted and favored matters of our most holy faith in these parts of Egypt."[86] If Henry just asked the French merchants of Egypt, Eliano contended, he would be inundated with praise for Mariani, and would see that Mariani was the best defender of Christian interests in the Ottoman Empire. Eliano implored his superiors, Gregory above all, to write to Henry to convince him not to recall Mariani.[87] Even Patriarch John wrote to Gregory that the accusations of scheming and disloyalty lodged against Mariani were patently false, and that Mariani "has done great work with all sorts of Frankish and Coptic Christians, being very practical in all things, and he knows the state of all men better than almost anyone, and no one can do the good that he does with all Christians because of the compassion he has toward all, and all hearts uniformly love him."[88] On 6 October, Mariani also addressed the accusations, explaining to Santoro that a man named Cristoforo Vento, who had previously held the consulship

---

and Slavery in the Early Modern Mediterranean (Stanford, CA: Stanford University Press, 2011); Junko Thérèse Takeda, Between Crown and Commerce: Marseille and the Early Modern Mediterranean (Baltimore, MD: Johns Hopkins University Press, 2011).

[85] Henry's anxiety concerning renegade diplomats belies the traditional Braudelian notion of a northern invasion of the Mediterranean at the end of the sixteenth century, in which the French, English, and Dutch had infiltrated the space and supplanted the traditional relationships of the Sea. See Fernand Braudel, *The Mediterranean and the Mediterranean World in the Age of Philip II* (New York: Harper & Row, 1972), 626–42; Janet L. Abu-Lughod, *Before European Hegemony: The World System A.D. 1250–1350* (Oxford: Oxford University Press, 1989); Molly Greene, "Beyond the Northern Invasion: The Mediterranean in the Seventeenth Century," *Past & Present* 174 (February 1, 2002): 42–71.

[86] APF, *Miscellanee Varie* Ia, fol. 506r./MPO 4, 143.

[87] APF, *Miscellanee Varie* Ia, fol. 506rv./MPO 4, 143. There is also a letter from Eliano and Sasso to Acquaviva informing him of the situation with Mariani, in which they compel him to ask Gregory to write a letter to Henry III petitioning keeping Mariani as consul to Egypt. See ARSI, *Gall. 98 II*, fol. 134r.

[88] ARSI, *Gall. 95 III*, fol. 204r./MPO 4, 149.

until 1570, was slandering Mariani and actively preventing Henry from learning of Mariani's efforts with the Copts because Vento was a "bad Christian who has relayed some falsehoods to remove me from this consulate," perhaps to reclaim the post.[89]

In either case, the unease surrounding Mariani was a problem for Eliano, as it meant that his main ally might inadvertently ensnare Eliano in a political scandal. A power negotiation centering on who represented the interests of France could have sweeping ramifications for the mission. More to the point, as we will see in the next chapter, it would also affect Eliano's immediate personal security in Egypt and his standing in the Society of Jesus long term. Yet, Mariani was the man who would best position him to employ his Jewishness in the name of converting the Copts. Therefore, Eliano took a risk in defending Mariani, but he did not see that he had another choice. Eliano's stream of letters imploring all parties involved to defend Mariani elucidates that Eliano understood these political intrigues well, and he knew that the possibility of Mariani's recall did not bode well for the outlook of the mission, for his own welfare, or for his standing before his superiors.

CONCLUSION

Given the complications surrounding the future of the French consulship, Eliano's interactions with the Jews, and the Copts' continued intransigence, one would be hard pressed to blame Eliano for wanting to leave Egypt by late 1583. Eliano had other motives for desiring to return to Rome as well: In early November, a Maronite priest arrived in Egypt to remind Eliano of the Maronites' desire to have Eliano lead the Maronite book project in Rome.[90] While this priest trusted Cardinal Carafa, who had been running the printing venture on Eliano's behalf, Carafa did not possess the linguistic dexterity and lexicographical skills that Eliano did. This priest also told Eliano that prominent Maronites felt more secure with him spearheading the project because they knew him personally. Eliano decided that it would be best to leave Egypt, and "if I should return [to Italy], I think that, with Father Sasso remaining here with the Bishop of Sidon [Leonardo Abel] ... they will perfectly complete this mission,

---

[89] ARSI, *Gall. 98 I*, fol. 139r./*MPO* 4, 150–1. Mariani does not name this "mal christiano," but Charles Libois, in his description of this letter, intimates that it was indeed Cristoforo Vento, who at this point was in France actively seeking Mariani's removal.

[90] ARSI, *Gall. 98 II*, fol. 153r./*MPO* 4, 162.

and do everything that I had planned to do."[91] Of course, Eliano also explained that he eagerly awaited instructions, and would remain in Egypt if that were the desire of his superiors. But it was clear that Eliano feared the worst for this mission and believed that the perfect storm of political machinations, the latent fear of Jewish intrigues against him, and the Copts' long-standing refusal to cooperate put him and his legacy in jeopardy.

Then, despite Eliano's expectations for the mission being at their lowest ebb since his arrival, Patriarch John shocked everyone: on 21 November, John "finally resolved himself, with the assent of his advisors and at our behest, to desire to hold a synod at Christmas; and he has already written to his bishops that without delay they should find their way here to discuss matters of the holy faith."[92] While Eliano remained nervous about Mariani's standing and the implications it could have for the mission, his appetite for using his Jewishness to convert the Copts was renewed. As the next chapter will show, coming up with a theological compromise – which the Jesuits and at least some leading Copts seemed to have done – was surprisingly easy, and was ostensibly the ultimate proof of Eliano's ability to use his Jewishness to serve the church. Yet, all of that would be undone when his Jewishness again proved to be a direct challenge to the mission, Eliano's personal security, and his Catholic identity.

---

[91] Ibid. Abel, originally from Malta, was named papal nuncio to the East and worked with the various communities of the Christian Orient. He was named bishop of Sidon, Lebanon, on 20 July 1582. For more on Abel, see *Dictionnaire d'histoire et de géographie ecclésiastiques*, vol. I (Paris: Letouzey et Ané, 1912), 70–1.

[92] ARSI, *Gall. 98 II*, fol. 154r./*MPO* 4, 164.

6

The Coptic Mission, Mediterranean Geopolitics, and the Mediation of Eliano's Jewish and Catholic Identities

On Friday, 21 September, thirty-three years to the day on which I was baptized and entered the Society in Venice ... a band of Turks, with their swords drawn and at the ready, entered our home and church and were accompanied by many other Turks, and a masked spy who led them.[1]

> – Giovanni Battista Eliano to Giovanni Nicola de Notariis,
> Provincial of Italy

We know for certain that David Moze is a Portuguese Marrano, the son of one of the eighteen Marranos who were burned in Ancona under Paul IV. ... This David Moze, in part to vindicate his father, and partly to displease Mariani, at the request of Vento, was the instrument for carrying out this affair.[2]

> – Giovanni Battista Eliano to Claudio Acquaviva

John's decision to convoke a synod gave Eliano and Sasso hope that the mission could be salvaged despite the issues surrounding Mariani's potential removal. As we saw in the previous chapter, Eliano worried that Mariani's removal would hinder the mission, which Eliano continued to see as essential to proving to his superiors the utility of his Jewishness. In this regard, while Sasso planned to write "a beautiful tract concerning our proposals in which he will address everything necessary" for the Copts' acceptance of the Catholic faith, it was important again for Eliano to stress that "that tract will be translated into their language, copied, and distributed to diverse prelates and others," naturally translated by him.

---

[1] ARSI, *Gall. 98 II*, fol. 223v./*MPO* 4, 293.   [2] ARSI, *Gall. 106*, fol. 247r./*MPO* 4, 302.

Eliano also "will see to it that all of the truths culled from their books will be combined" and he intended to have these notebooks distributed prior to the synod.[3] Eliano then planned to send them to Rome for printing and distribution.[4] Eliano's labors in planning this synod, conducting it, and producing books reflecting its decrees point to his continued effort to position himself as the Copts' only savior.

Yet, despite his belief of his own centrality to the mission, Eliano did not believe that there were "any other means by which we can win this nation with ease, if not for [Paolo Mariani]; they are quite obliged to him for the protection he offers them, and for the continual favors that they receive from him."[5] The problem was that, "if [Mariani] were removed from this consulate as some have predicted, and in his place came someone who does not know the language or is not experienced in these matters, and moreover, is a Huguenot heretic, or at the very least someone not so Catholic and zealous as [Mariani] is, things will go badly for us."[6] In particular, given his tenuous status as a Jewish-born Jesuit, things would go very badly for Eliano should this diplomatic dispute disrupt his plans for the mission.

Given the latent anxieties surrounding Mariani, it is unclear why some (but not all) Copts were willing to discuss doctrine and even come to a compromise, rather than distance themselves from Europeans altogether. It is possible, as we will see, that some Coptic bishops distrusted or disliked the patriarch and were looking for leverage against him. Regardless of the Copts' motivations, it is clear that Eliano, Mariani, and the Copts believed that ecumenism would benefit all parties. However, Eliano wanted to expedite the synod and use it as proof of his dedication to the faith, which lays bare his preoccupation with Mariani's removal and its ramifications for how his Jewish past was viewed. Moreover, the eventual fallout of the arrival of Mariani's replacement also points to Eliano's continued need to attend to how his Jewishness informed his Catholic identity. On one hand, convincing the Copts to reach a theological accord would be the ultimate proof that he alone could convert the most obstinate of Eastern Rite Christians because of his unique linguistic and textual skills stemming from his Jewish education. On the other hand, as we will see, his Jewishness yet again became a pretense for an attack on Eliano when a Portuguese renegade accused Eliano of apostasy and inciting war against the Ottomans. While the geopolitical and religious landscapes of

---

[3] ARSI, *Gall. 98 II*, fol. 154r./MPO 4, 164.   [4] Ibid.
[5] ARSI, *Gall. 98 II*, fol. 154r./MPO 4, 165.   [6] Ibid.

the Mediterranean, Catholic missions, and empire building were all potential factors in allowing Eliano to prove that his Jewishness allowed him to excel at converting Eastern Rite Christians, these structures would also always remain obstacles and potential challenges to how he constructed his identity.

ORGANIZING THE SYNOD

Eliano, Sasso, Buono, and Mariani quickly got to work on the synod in hopes of forging an accord before Mariani could be recalled.[7] Also important was their effort to build relationships with leading Copts "who we think can intervene in this synod" on their behalf – namely, particular bishops who believed, for one reason or another, that an alliance with Gregory would serve them.[8] Eliano felt that he would need the help of certain Copts sympathetic to reform to get the synod started and to keep it afloat, for "if we find them to be difficult, certainly we should attribute it in no small part to the fact that they have been mired in these heresies since the time of the Council of Chalcedon, which was more than 1,140 years ago, and perhaps they have just never had the type of help that they have now."[9]

When they all finally convened in late December 1583, some of the Copts rejected the Jesuits' overtures. Most obstinate was John. Given that John had called for the synod, Eliano was bewildered when, in front of his bishops and other prelates, "after a long discourse, [John] got up and, departing, said with anger that he would more readily lose his head" than acquiesce on matters of faith.[10] John's inflexibility threw Eliano into a fit of rage. It was not so much that John needed to be swayed because of his fear of looking like a heretic before his community or his Jacobite and Armenian peers; that was almost expected. Rather, "the worst part is that, he had sworn at [Mariani's] insistence, who was present, that he desired to hold a universal synod, to better discuss things concerning the truth and other matters; but now he has clearly made it known that he does not desire to change anything."[11] Eliano's anger, while surely

---

[7] The date for the synod is given in the final report of the mission, written 28 August 1585, from Rome. ARSI, *Gall. 98 I*, fol. 312r.

[8] ARSI, *Gall. 98 II*, fol. 154r./MPO 4, 164.

[9] ARSI, *Gall. 98 II*, fol. 154r./MPO 4, 165.

[10] ASV, *Fondo Borghese, serie III, 124 D*, fol. 193v./MPO 4, 174.

[11] ASV, *Fondo Borghese, serie III, 124 D*, fol. 193v./MPO 4, 174-5.

reflecting his naïveté and blind faith that the Copts would unequivocally embrace Tridentine Catholicism, also points to his and Sasso's fear that any such disputes carried the risk of preventing or delaying the conclusion of the synod, all the more important given fears that Mariani's days in Egypt were numbered. And if John could backtrack like this in front of Mariani – a man whom John considered a friend – Eliano feared that he would be more intransigent in front of whomever Henry sent to replace Mariani.

Despite John's apparent refusal to budge, by the end of January 1584, Eliano continued to meet with other leading Copts, who seemed equally dismayed that John had pushed the Jesuits away after he had organized the synod in the first place. Eliano reported to Acquaviva that "almost all of the most important and most intelligent" Copts had been swayed "to happily work to promote Catholic Truth among the others." As for John, Eliano rebuked him: "Because of his senility and ignorance, he is so insipid that we cannot accomplish anything with him; what is worse, he is guided by his quite obstinate brother, who is his vicar."[12] Eliano worried that – despite all his, Mariani's, and Sasso's efforts and other Copts' cooperation – the synod was not progressing, and an accord seemed unlikely so long as John lobbied so hard against it. But Eliano also wanted Acquaviva to understand that he had convinced other leading Copts to convert, the truth of this notwithstanding, which was proof that he was doing all he could; thus, just as Patriarch Gabriel refused to convert in 1562 because his bishops were against it, as we saw in Chapter 2, Eliano hoped that, in the face of such institutional pressure, John could not hold out forever, lest he be ostracized and deposed.

Potentially to the mission's detriment, "these difficulties that we find with the patriarch and other less intelligent and obstinate men have caused Father Sasso to want to end matters here and do nothing else, and leave for Italy, as it seems to him that we have done everything we can."[13] Lest his superiors suspect him of the same fatalism, Eliano made it clear that he had not grown weary: "but I am one who has great experience with these Eastern peoples, and I know that there are twelve hours in a day; and as we have already won some of them, with their help we can win the others, and maybe even the patriarch himself!"[14] By leaning on his experience and tireless drive to save souls, Eliano positioned himself

[12] ARSI, *Gall. 106*, fol. 223r./MPO 4, 188–189.
[13] ARSI, *Gall. 106*, fol. 223r./MPO 4, 189.   [14] Ibid.

again as uniquely skilled to convert the Copts. Thus, Eliano planned to wait until the end of September 1584 – a full eight months – to try both to convince John to participate in the synod and to ensure that the patriarch sent youths to study at the Collegio Romano. Eliano's refusal to acquiesce just yet despite John's rebuffs hints at his fear of this mission's potential failure being pinned on him. Given that Eliano's own standing before his superiors remained unsecure, abandoning the mission after so many Copts had already voiced their support was not an option.

Eliano's tenacity paid off. Just as the mission appeared to be at an impasse, Eliano reported on 3 February that a highly esteemed bishop as well as three other high-ranking clerics had grown impatient with John, and requested Eliano to convoke the synod without him. It was, as Eliano described it, "the opportune time to launch another assault [on their faith]."[15] The result of the five-hour meeting was a theological accord. Eliano and Sasso deemed the Copts' declaration that the "two natures united in one person" of Christ to be orthodox and Catholic. While the Copts' fear of being accused of Nestorianism rendered them unwilling to discuss the nature of Christ any further, Eliano and Sasso decided that their acknowledgment that Christ is "true God and true man" was Catholic enough; and the Copts believed they had not given any ground on doctrine.[16] In the proclamation of the accord – written in Latin and Arabic – Eliano and Sasso chose their words carefully. The Copts and Catholics professed in unison that "the eternal Lord is united with the human body, in perfection, [born] from the Virgin Mary," possessing all human characteristics except sin. They stressed their shared belief in "a human God, one Lord, one Christ, God and man together; his humanity was never separated from his divinity, not even for a moment." Furthermore, they affirmed that Jesus possesses "divine and human operations, willfully, without any separation from the moment of conception until the end of time." The Copts might have been uneasy when it came to the nuances of Christ's human and divine wills, natures, and operations. But they could not deny Eliano and Sasso's Christological formula, as doing so would have been Nestorianism. Eliano and Sasso applauded the bishops' acceptance of the synod, something that seemed to signal for Eliano and Sasso – but not for the Copts – a move in the direction toward Coptic acceptance of Catholicism.[17]

Above all, Eliano applauded their own efforts: "As for what our happiness was, we leave it to your Paternity to consider. Since we clearly

---

[15] ARSI, *Gall. 106*, fol. 225r./*MPO* 4, 193–4.
[16] ARSI, *Gall. 106*, fol. 225r./*MPO* 4, 194.   [17] ARSI, *Gall. 106*, fol. 225r./*MPO* 4, 194.

know, that with the removal of this obstacle that had greatly impeded the service of God in this union, we hope to bring to good end this work we have begun ... we pray to Your Paternity that you hold us dearly in your holy sacrifices and prayers." Eliano believed that this synod would be a turning point in both the Copts' religious future and his own, and for this reason "by the grace of the Lord we are all well, desirous of the same for Your Paternity and the other fathers and brothers of the Society."[18] While Sasso crafted the accord, and Mariani facilitated the meeting, Eliano nevertheless signaled to his superiors that his efforts were central to what appeared to be an important step in the full conversion of the Copts.

There was, of course, an important participant missing at the February synod: Patriarch John, who believed – rightly – that he would ultimately be expected to submit to Gregory's authority. Despite the strides made with many other Copts, who seemingly believed that Rome could offer them some solace if not theological leadership, the Jesuits feared that so long as John were patriarch, full Catholicization would remain on hold; or, at the very least, his inflexibility would cause a schism among the Copts, hardly an ideal alternative.[19] Gregory had hoped that Eliano and Sasso could come to some agreement with John before they left, but this now seemed unlikely. One other possibility that stood out for Santoro was John's declining health. Santoro believed that, if one of the bishops who had supported the synod were elected patriarch upon John's death, he would approve the accord and avoid schism.[20] But hanging the mission's success on John's eventually dying was not a particularly efficient way to proceed. That said, all of this points to rifts among Coptic leadership, which perhaps illuminates for us why some Copts asked Eliano to convoke the synod without John. In either case, by February 1584, Eliano and Sasso had won at least some leading Copts over, and they believed – erroneously, as we will see – that the conversion of the Copts was months away.

THE ARRIVAL OF CRISTOFORO VENTO AND THE COLLAPSE OF THE MISSION

For every bit that Eliano was happy about the results of the Coptic synod, he remained troubled by Mariani's unsettled status as consul. Acquaviva also understood the gravity of the situation as early as April 1583, ten

---

[18] ARSI, *Gall. 106*, fol. 225r./MPO 4, 194–5.
[19] ARSI, *Gall. 106*, fol. 229r./MPO 4, 203.   [20] ARSI, *Gall. 98 I*, fol. 195v./MPO 4, 258.

months before the synod, when he had informed Gregory of the accus-ations against Mariani.[21] In response, Gregory wrote letters in support of Mariani to both Henry III and to the papal nuncio in France, Girolamo Ragazzoni.[22] However, by the time these letters arrived in France, Cris-toforo Vento, Mariani's detractor whom we met at the end of the previ-ous chapter, was on his way to Alexandria to replace Mariani by early spring 1584.[23] Ostensibly, Henry's decision to switch consuls need not have been the mission's death knell, as he still desired to convert the Copts for his own reasons; he had even ordered Vento to assist the Jesuits in that regard. This change in diplomats could have been a continuation of Henry's efforts to expand France's influence in the Mediterranean,[24] and did not in theory have to result in the disruption of the Jesuits' efforts with the Copts or their burgeoning relationship with the French in Otto-man lands.[25]

But Eliano also knew that if Mariani – who had strong ties to the Copts and had a personal relationship with John – could not sway the patriarch and others, there was no way Vento could. Combined with the fact that "[the Copts'] poor disposition was fomented by that man, the patriarch's vicar ... we have determined to return to Italy on the first possible ship for Sicily or Venice, so that our efforts be employed fruitfully."[26] Before departing for Italy, Sasso decided on one last pilgrimage to Jerusalem with a few Coptic companions. Eliano planned to remain in Cairo for a

---

[21] ARSI, *Ven. 3*, fol. 1v./*MPO* 4, 231.

[22] Ragazzoni, a Venetian, was coadjutor bishop of Famagusta in Venetian Cyprus from 1561 to 1572. He was apostolic administrator in Cisamus, Crete, until his election as bishop of Novara in 1576. He then moved on to serve as bishop in Bergamo in 1577. He remained in that post until his death, while also serving as papal nuncio to France from 1583 to 1586. For more on his life, see Tarcisio Bottani, *Girolamo Ragazzoni: vescovo di Bergamo* (Bergamo: Corponove, 1994). ARSI, *Gall. 98 I*, fol. 187v./*MPO* 4, 253.

[23] ARSI, *Gall. 98 I*, fols. 187v–188r./*MPO* 4, 253.

[24] Junko Thérèse Takeda, *Between Crown and Commerce: Marseille and the Early Modern Mediterranean* (Baltimore, MD: Johns Hopkins University Press, 2011). For an informative exploration of recent historiography on the French in the Mediterranean, see the recent forum and accompanying articles in *French History* 29:1 (2015).

[25] This trend would continue well into the seventeenth century. See H. Fougueray, "La mission de France à Constantinople durant l'ambassade de M. de Césy," *Études* 113 (1907): 70–101; Charles A. Frazee, *Catholics and Sultans: The Church and the Ottoman Empire, 1453–1923* (Cambridge: Cambridge University Press, 1983), 67–87; Bernard Heyberger, *Les Chrétiens du Proche-Orient au temps de la Réforme catholique: Syrie, Liban, Palestine, XVIIe–XVIIIe siècles* (Rome: Ecole française de Rome, 1994); Adina Ruiu, "Conflicting Visions of the Jesuit Missions to the Ottoman Empire, 1609–1628," *Journal of Jesuit Studies* 1:2 (2014): 260–80.

[26] ARSI, *Gall. 106*, fol. 263r./*MPO* 4, 225.

last-ditch effort to convince John to sign the synodal decree. By the end of April, however, John still had not acknowledged the synod.[27] Further thwarting Eliano's plans was that the first ship for Italy did not depart until the middle of September, leaving him stranded in Alexandria throughout the summer.

The delay in their departure put the Jesuits within the crosshairs of the diplomatic row that was to develop between Vento and Mariani, and that would directly challenge Eliano because of his Jewish birth. On 24 June 1584, Cristoforo Vento landed in Alexandria, bearing a decree from Henry III that deposed Paolo Mariani as French consul in Egypt and named Vento as his replacement. Two days later, a man claiming to be an envoy of Cristoforo Vento arrived at Mariani's residence. Galiazza Stanga, a representative of the English consulate in Egypt, explained that "Mariani did not believe that this man was [Vento's] legitimate envoy and he did not want to listen to his protests, so he did not let himself be known to him." When Vento learned of this, he "sent [the envoy] back, explaining to him that, if he did not protest to Mariani, then it was sufficient to do so to someone in his retinue." But no one in Mariani's retinue was willing to receive the envoy. In turn, "the envoy, thinking that the [Jesuits] who lived in an apartment within Mariani's home where they had their church were his men, went to their home with others from Vento's retinue and intimated that they must accept the protest and then give it to Mariani."[28]

Eliano insisted, however, that the Jesuits "were clerics, and that they were in their own home and not Mariani's, and that they were in a church," hardly the place to adjudicate such matters. Eliano explained that they "could not and must not accept [the document stating Mariani's dismissal] and give it to others at the insistence of anyone."[29] Caring little about the Jesuits' claims, the envoy explained that since their church was attached to Mariani's home, that was good enough for him. He attempted to force upon Eliano Henry's decree deposing Mariani. Eliano was having none of this. He took the decree and "shoved it into the chest pocket of the envoy, who, not wanting to take it back, opened his vest and let the papers fall to the ground. In reply, [Eliano] pointed at the papers with his foot and told [the envoy] to pick them up. But the envy refused. As he was leaving the house and church of the Jesuits, [Eliano] picked them up and tossed them, saying that he should collect his papers."[30] While this was

[27] ARSI, *Gall. 98 II*, fol. 180r./*MPO* 4, 235.
[28] ARSI, *Gall. 98 II*, fol. 238r./*MPO* 4, 250–1.
[29] ARSI, *Gall. 98 II*, fol. 238r./*MPO* 4, 251.   [30] Ibid.

ostensibly Eliano attempting to rise above the diplomatic squabbles that were to ensue between Vento and Mariani, such hotheadedness left Vento will little choice but to see Eliano as an obstructionist living in Mariani's residence. Further, not only did he declare personal loyalty to Mariani, but Eliano also insulted him in his official capacity as representative of Eliano's actual patron, Henry.

Alienating Vento was not the only factor in the mission's unraveling. On 9 July, Eliano learned that Santoro and his team of theologians – including several Jesuits – rejected the synodal accord on the grounds that "the structure and the words that are used in it are expressly contrary to the definition [of the nature of Christ] of the Sacrosanct Council of Chalcedon." To make matters worse, Santoro continued, "It gave me no point of satisfaction; rather I question whether it was nothing more than fraud and deception."[31] On one hand, we are seeing again Santoro's theological intractability, something that Eliano was hardly experiencing for the first time. On the other hand, Santoro's accusation that it was little better than crypto-heresy parading itself as orthodoxy must have alarmed Eliano, who was constantly trying to prove his mettle to his superiors in the face of rising pressures on Jewish-lineage Jesuits.

For months, Eliano had been lauding this theological accord and his linguistic dexterity that made it happen as evidence of his ability to convert the Copts. His lexicographical sharpness and his ability to engage the Copts on their own terms had allowed him to reach a theological harmony that, he thought, was a step toward their conversion. But all of his work was rendered a failure when Santoro declared that Eliano's effort resulted not in true orthodoxy, but instead was little more than a reaffirmation of the Copts' heresy and his and Sasso's collusion in veiling it in a word maze. This would not be the first time Jesuits' methods for conversion would fall under scrutiny for their apparent failure to move far enough away from perceived indigenous beliefs.[32] But this was different for Eliano. Given that many had begun to question whether those of Jewish stock could ever be sincere Catholics, let alone doctrinal hard-liners, Santoro's suggestion that Eliano was either complicit in hiding the

---

[31] ARSI, *Gall. 98 I*, fol. 196v./MPO 4, 260.

[32] Ines G. Županov, "Aristocratic Analogies and Demotic Descriptions in the Seventeenth-Century Madurai Mission," *Representations* 41 (January 1, 1993): 123–48; Ines G. Županov, *Disputed Mission: Jesuit Experiments and Brahmanical Knowledge in Seventeenth-Century India* (New Delhi: Oxford University Press, 1999); R. Po-chia Hsia, *A Jesuit in the Forbidden City: Matteo Ricci, 1552–1610* (Oxford: Oxford University Press, 2010).

Copts' opportunism or not sharp enough to recognize it was all the more biting.

Putting further stress on Eliano's sense of himself and his ability to prove his sincerity was Cristoforo Vento's continued antagonism. In the same letter condemning the synod, Santoro also explained that Eliano needed to be mindful of his personal safety.[33] While his superior's frustrations with the course of the mission must have weighed on Eliano, he had to agree. Not only would Vento not go out of his way to aid the Jesuits, but he also recognized that "he seems to have been offended by me" because of how Eliano reacted to Vento's envoy delivering Henry's deposal of Mariani.[34] Also troubling was the news that Giulio Mancinelli, the head of the Jesuit residence in Constantinople, relayed to Eliano in August:[35] "[Vento] says (but it is false) that I threw his letters to the ground, and all sorts of other things; and this rumor has made its way to Constantinople, and I was advised by [Mancinelli], that we are seen as partial [to Mariani] and that we have no esteem for His Majesty of France." Eliano also learned from Mancinelli that Vento "wants to protest this against me and bring action against me to His Holiness and to the His Christian Majesty, and to Your Reverend Paternity."[36]

Eliano's fear of Vento was palpable and exposed his increasing nervousness in Egypt. Vento, who was officially Henry's representative in Egypt, saw Eliano's refusal to acknowledge his authority as proof that he was Mariani's crony. With the mission in a freefall, in no small part due to Eliano's theological and diplomatic missteps, Mariani attempted to reassure Acquaviva on 20 September that the mission's failure was not caused "by a lack of good will, but because I was not able to help anymore." Likewise, Mariani wrote, "this Coptic nation remains so burdened by the great disturbances of the past few months," namely, in the midst of the mushrooming scandal surrounding Vento's arrival, John

---

[33] ARSI, *Gall. 98 I*, fol. 198r./*MPO* 4, 261–2.

[34] ARSI, *Gall. 98 II*, fol. 219r./*MPO* 4, 284–5.

[35] For more on Mancinelli and his time in Constantinople, see Vincenzo Ruggieri, "Constantinopoli vista da P. Giulo Mancinelli S. J. (1583–1585)," *Revue des études byzantines* 60:1 (2002): 113–31; on the Jesuit presence there, see Eric Dursteler, "Education and Identity in Constantinople's Latin Rite Community, c. 1600," *Renaissance Studies* 18:2 (2004): 287–303; Adina Ruiu, "Conflicting Visions of the Jesuit Missions to the Ottoman Empire, 1609–1628," *Journal of Jesuit Studies* 1:2 (March 12, 2014): 260–80; Robert John Clines, "Fighting Enemies and Finding Friends: The Cosmopolitan Pragmatism of Jesuit Residences in the Ottoman Levant," *Renaissance Studies* 31:1 (February 2017): 66–86.

[36] ARSI, *Gall. 98 II*, fol. 219r./*MPO* 4, 285.

had died and there seemed to be no rush to elect a successor.[37] While Eliano still desired to work with the Copts and push for their reform, his vitriolic exchange with Vento's envoy and Vento's disdain for Eliano put the mission in jeopardy. Combined with Santoro's claim that the synodal decree was duplicitous, Eliano's failure to ingratiate himself to Vento had rendered him a liability. But not even Santoro could have guessed just how much of a liability Eliano had become.

ELIANO'S ARREST AND SUBSEQUENT EFFORTS TO DOWNPLAY HIS JEWISHNESS

On 21 September, the day after Mariani had written to Acquaviva, matters took a dangerous turn. While Eliano was preparing to say Mass for Mariani and his household, the Ottoman governor's security forces burst in, seized the Jesuits, and hauled them off to prison, but not before parading them about in chains with loud declarations that they had been arrested for attempting to incite a Coptic rebellion that would coincide with a Spanish invasion of Egypt.[38] From the perspective of the Ottomans, the Jesuits' alleged plan to help Philip II conquer Egypt was no idle threat given the anxieties stemming from the Ottomans' defeat at the Battle of Lepanto in 1571.[39] At odds with the Habsburgs for much of the sixteenth century, the Ottomans' apprehensions concerning the designs of their European rivals grew more acute after Lepanto. While the defeat of the Ottoman fleet at the hands of John of Austria and the Holy League was only a minor setback in the trajectory of Ottoman power, Europeans rallied behind the victory and celebrated it as the moment in which the political force of Christendom stood up to the perfidy of the Turk and won.[40] Then, in 1580, Philip II became king of

---

[37] ARSI, *Gall. 106*, fol. 242rv./*MPO* 4, 286–7.

[38] Rebellion was a common fear throughout Ottoman lands, especially from the late sixteenth century onward. See Sam White, *The Climate of Rebellion in the Early Modern Ottoman Empire* (Cambridge: Cambridge University Press, 2011).

[39] Bruce Alan Masters, *Christians and Jews in the Ottoman Arab World: The Roots of Sectarianism* (Cambridge: Cambridge University Press, 2001), 68–71.

[40] Andrew C. Hess, "The Battle of Lepanto and Its Place in Mediterranean History," *Past & Present* 57 (November 1972): 53–73. See also John Francis Guilmartin, *Gunpowder and Galleys: Changing Technology and Mediterranean Warfare at Sea in the Sixteenth Century* (Cambridge: Cambridge University Press, 1974), for an examination of the changing nature of naval warfare over the course of the sixteenth century.

Portugal, which also brought with it the Lusitanian overseas holdings in Asia.[41] As the Ottomans and Portuguese had been adversaries in the Indian Ocean for decades, that conflict now became a part of the Ottoman–Habsburg struggle for supremacy.[42] The Ottomans were thus surrounded by the arsenal of Philip II and his allies on their Balkan, Mediterranean, and Indian Ocean frontiers.[43]

Compounding the military threat to their borders were Catholic evangelizing efforts. Although having their minority Christian communities turn to their French allies was perhaps not ideal, it was certainly preferable to letting them fall under the sway of the Habsburgs – invasion or not – which might have potentially rendered Christians in the Ottoman Empire enemies from within.[44] While they only rarely used this as a pretense to oppress Christians in their lands, any inkling of rebellion

---

[41] A. R. Disney, *A History of Portugal and the Portuguese Empire: From Beginnings to 1807*, vol. 1 (Cambridge: Cambridge University Press, 2009), 198–220; Malyn Newitt, *Portugal in European and World History* (London: Reaktion Books, 2009), 82–96.

[42] For more on the maritime rivalry between the Ottomans and Portuguese, see Andrew C. Hess, "The Evolution of the Ottoman Seaborne Empire in the Age of the Oceanic Discoveries, 1453–1525," *The American Historical Review* 75:7 (December 1970): 1892–1919; John Guilmartin, "Ideology and Conflict: The Wars of the Ottoman Empire, 1453–1606," *Journal of Interdisciplinary History* 18:4 (Spring 1988): 721–47; Giancarlo F. Casale, *The Ottoman Age of Exploration: Spices, Maps and Conquest in the Sixteenth-Century Indian Ocean* (Oxford: Oxford University Press, 2010).

[43] C. R. Boxer, *The Church Militant and Iberian Expansion, 1440–1770.* (Baltimore, MD: Johns Hopkins University Press, 1978); Dauril Alden, *The Making of an Enterprise: The Society of Jesus in Portugal, Its Empire, and Beyond, 1540–1750* (Stanford, CA: Stanford University Press, 1996); Ines G. Županov, *Disputed Mission: Jesuit Experiments and Brahmanical Knowledge in Seventeenth-Century India* (New Delhi: Oxford University Press, 1999); Liam Brockey, "'A Vinha Do Senhor': The Portuguese Jesuits in China in the Seventeenth Century," *Portuguese Studies* 16 (January 1, 2000): 125–47; Andreu Martínez d'Alós-Moner, *Envoys of a Human God: The Jesuit Mission to Christian Ethiopia, 1557–1632* (Leiden: Brill, 2015).

[44] For more about the Ottoman understanding of religion and politics as symbiotic loyalties essential to the preservation of the state, see Tijana Krstić, *Contested Conversions to Islam: Narratives of Religious Change in the Early Modern Ottoman Empire* (Stanford, CA: Stanford University Press, 2011). For more on this process over the centuries in early modern Germany, see Joel F. Harrington and Helmut Walser Smith, "Confessionalization, Community, and State Building in Germany, 1555–1870," *The Journal of Modern History* 69:1 (March 1, 1997): 77–101. For Italy, where the missionaries and the pope were from, important work on the trajectory of religious change and how political and religious identities became more intertwined yet more complicated over time include the various contributions in Ronald Delph, Michelle Fontaine, and John Jeffries Martin, eds., *Heresy, Culture, and Religion in Early Modern Italy* (Kirksville, MO: Truman State University Press, 2006), as well as Wietse de Boer, *The Conquest of the Soul: Confession, Discipline, and Public Order in Counter-Reformation Milan* (Leiden: Brill, 2001).

was not taken lightly. When accusations swirled that the Jesuits, who had originally been there under the protection of Henry III, were no longer in the good graces of the Ottomans' ally,[45] but were there to aid in Philip's imperial designs to invade Egypt while the Copts rose up in rebellion, they were arrested and interrogated under pain of death. It of course did not help matters that one of those Jesuits was a former Jew who had already been arrested in Egypt on suspicion of apostasy from Islam. While the accusations of an impending uprising and invasion were baseless, someone – it was at this juncture unclear who – was smart enough to play on the Ottomans' fears concerning the papacy, the Habsburgs, and the potential political resourcefulness of Egypt's Christian minorities.[46]

This jostling of loyalties and concomitant Ottoman concerns pervade Sasso's letter to Acquaviva, which he wrote from prison. He explained that the Ottomans had grown distrustful of foreigners in recent months, "always suspecting them of some revolt," and this latest accusation drove the governor to act. Nevertheless, "knowing how false these accusations were . . . we went confidently, hoping in the Lord, who never abandons his own, and who knows our innocence."[47] Sasso explained that they were interrogated, but when the answers Eliano and Sasso provided did not please the governor, they were thrown into cells. Sasso, fearing the worst, cited 1 Peter 2:21: "For unto this are you called: because Christ also suffered for us, leaving you an example that you should follow his steps." Seemingly in preparation for martyrdom, Sasso closed the letter: "I will say nothing else, only recommending ourselves to the blessed sacrifices and prayers of Your Paternity and all the dearest fathers and brothers of Rome, so that they may impart to us from the Lord true and firm patience."[48]

Eliano too sent a missive from prison, his to Giovanni Nicola de Notariis, the Jesuit Provincial of Italy. With great trepidation, Eliano explained on 3 October that his martyrdom was imminent, "which I have greatly expected and desired. I find myself in the fortress of the Pasha, in hourly danger of expecting my death, such a death that he gives to rebels."[49] Eliano also took time to lament his failures with the Copts,

---

[45] On the Franco-Ottoman alliance, see Christine Isom-Verhaaren, *Allies with the Infidel: The Ottoman and French Alliance in the Sixteenth Century* (London: I.B. Tauris, 2011).
[46] Palmira Johnson Brummett, *Ottoman Seapower and Levantine Diplomacy in the Age of Discovery* (Albany: State University of New York Press, 1994).
[47] ARSI, *Gall. 106*, fols. 244r–244v./MPO 4, 289.
[48] ARSI, *Gall. 106*, fols. 244r–245v./MPO 4, 290.
[49] ARSI, *Gall. 98 II*, fol. 223r./MPO 4, 292.

who "wish to neither speak nor hear about matters of our faith" because
of the Jesuits' arrest; they feared that "they too will be seized and tor-
mented and perhaps killed, along with the confiscation of their property."
Long-term, Eliano dreaded, this whole ordeal would ruin Catholic–
Coptic relations for generations "and no one will have the courage to
send their sons to Rome, as some had had the intention of doing."[50] His
fear was grounded in the governor's accusation that "the pope sent us to
incite local Christians to unite with Franks, and turn this land of the Turk
into a Christian one."[51] He likewise believed that this would be the end
for him, for, as he explained to de Notariis, "my soul finds itself ready for
every evil that may come my way."[52]

Also troubling for Eliano was that he did not know who was behind
this whole conspiracy against him. All he knew was that someone must
have tipped off the governor, most likely the mysterious figure, "a masked
spy," who pointed Eliano out to the Ottoman guards who seized the
Jesuits and ransacked their church and residence. This was no coincidence, Eliano must have thought, for all of this took place on "Friday,
21 September, thirty-three years to the day when I was baptized and
entered the Society in Venice."[53] But who could be behind it? Given his
previous run-ins with the Jews as well as the skepticism surrounding him,
Eliano felt compelled to emphasize that "we know for certain that [our
arrest] was not principally carried out by Jews, because – as I have written
other times – they hold me in good esteem and have continued to show me
every honor." After all, Eliano assured de Notariis, the Jews would be
foolish to risk such a plot, for "they know that we are ministers of His
Holiness, who holds under his jurisdiction a great number of Jews and as
the head of Christians could order a vendetta against them and castigate
all of the Jews in his land." In fact, "many Jews have stated this, fearing
that we would blame them in error."[54] Eliano clearly did not believe that
the Jews would go to such great lengths to attack him because their
relations had improved since the 1560s; or, at the very least, he did not
want his superiors to believe this could be a possibility. Seemingly, it was
"neither a Jew nor a Turk nor a Moor nor some local Christian," all
of whom professed innocence. "Nevertheless," Eliano conjectured,

---

[50] Ibid.   [51] Ibid.   [52] ARSI, *Gall. 98 II*, fol. 224r./*MPO* 4, 293.
[53] ARSI, *Gall. 98 II*, fol. 223v./*MPO* 4, 293.
[54] ARSI, *Gall. 98 II*, fol. 224rv./*MPO* 4, 293.

"the truth will be known and if he will not be punished here, God will not fail to 'avenge the blood of his servants.'"[55]

There is much to unpack in Eliano's prison letter to de Notariis. First and foremost, his refusal to blame the Jews coupled with his continued reference to them stem from his unrelenting obsession with their presence as well as his need to distance himself from them and downplay his Jewish past as a potential complication for the mission. Given that Acquaviva on numerous occasions verbalized his worries about Eliano's personal safety because of the Jews, it is no surprise that Eliano would emphatically refute any claims that the Jews played a role in his arrest. The reason for this – that they accepted him as a Catholic and held him in high esteem – also points to Eliano's use of Revelation 19:2, "avenge the blood of his servants." Still fearing that some saw him as a renegade crypto-Jew who was finally receiving his comeuppance for years of opportunism and dissimulation, Eliano expressed that he was a loyal servant of Christ whose martyrdom, should it come, was to be avenged. Lastly, while it is almost surely happenstance that he was seized thirty-three years to the day of his baptism, his discussion of that coincidence when couched in the language of the ultimate sacrifice to the faith would have signposted to the reader that he positioned himself as a Christlike figure, given the traditional belief that Christ was seized, interrogated, and crucified in his thirty-third year.

The parallels drawn between himself and Christ – two Jews seized, brutalized, and (potentially) sacrificed in the name of the faith – would have resonated with the Jesuits back home. In addition to the martyr-missionary narrative that pervaded Jesuit educational formation, the sacrifice of Christ was a fundamental part of Jesuit spirituality, as evidenced by the centrality of Christ's arrest, imprisonment, and execution in the meditations of the third week of the *Spiritual Exercises*.[56] Furthermore, depictions of the Crucifixion were prevalent in Jesuit art throughout Rome, and could be found in the Collegio Romano as well as in the churches of Santissima Annunziata, Sant'Apollinare, and Santo Stefano. Most important was the Passion Chapel in the Gesù, the mother church of the Society of Jesus, which also had as its main altarpiece a depiction of

---

[55] ARSI, *Gall. 98 II*, fol. 224v./*MPO 4*, 293–4.

[56] Paul John Shore, "'In Carcere; Ad Dupplicium': Jesuit Encounters in Prison and in Places of Execution: Reflections on the Early-Modern Period," *European Review of History* 19:2 (April 2012): 183–200; Ignatius Loyola, *Personal Writings: Reminiscences, Spiritual Diary, Select Letters Including the Text of The Spiritual Exercises* (London: Penguin Books, 1996), 321–6.

the Circumcision, a reminder of Christ's Jewishness.[57] While much of this art, especially that in the Gesù, was created after Eliano's time in Egypt, it nevertheless reflects the centrality in Jesuit spirituality and iconography of Christ's Jewishness and suffering. And Eliano knew full well that his fellow Jesuits would recognize the parallels drawn between himself and Christ and meditate on those images of the Crucifixion as they chewed on Eliano's sufferings. Eliano thus entangled the Jesuit mystical tradition surrounding the life of Christ with his own travails to promote himself as both a true Jesuit *and* Jewish-born lamb sacrificed for the faith.

UNPACKING ANOTHER JEWISH PLOT AGAINST ELIANO

In the end, martyrdom never came; after paying a ransom, Mariani secured the Jesuits' freedom. The next step was attempting to piece together the events leading to their arrest. While they neither liked nor trusted Vento because of his efforts to undermine the mission, going so far as to have them thrown in prison seemed too radical.[58] This explains why, in their joint declaration of what had happened written after their release had been secured, the Jesuits, Mariani, and their allies pinned their arrest on the Ottoman governor's paranoia and tyrannical tendencies. They reiterated that they were only there to provide for the spiritual needs of the Copts, and that the governor's unjustified actions directly put the Copts' souls in jeopardy, as they now feared working with the Jesuits lest the governor persecute them for a nonexistent insurrection.[59] In the 25 October account of their arrest and interrogation sent to Rome, neither Vento nor the Jews were mentioned once.

So, since matters seemed resolved and danger abated, they decided that it would be best to send Sasso back to Rome to elaborate on their

---

[57] Thomas Buser, "Jerome Nadal and Early Jesuit Art in Rome," *The Art Bulletin* 58:3 (1976): 424–33; Leif Holm Monssen, "Rex Gloriose Martyrum: A Contribution to Jesuit Iconography," *The Art Bulletin* 63:1 (1981): 130–7; Kirstin Noreen, "Ecclesiae Militantis Triumphi: Jesuit Iconography and the Counter-Reformation," *The Sixteenth Century Journal* 29:3 (1998): 689–715; Gauvin A. Bailey, *Between Renaissance and Baroque: Jesuit Art in Rome, 1565–1610* (Toronto: University of Toronto Press, 2003); Carol M. Richardson, "Durante Alberti, the Martyrs' Picture and the Venerable English College, Rome," *Papers of the British School at Rome* 73 (2005): 223–63.

[58] ARSI, *Gall. 98 I*, fol. 226r./MPO 4, 294. For more on the transition of the French consulate from Mariani to Vento, as well as Mariani's assumption as English consul, see Prosper Alpini, *Histoire naturelle de l'Egypte, 1581–1584*, vol. I (Cairo: Institut français d'archéologie orientale du Caire, 1979), 110.

[59] ARSI, *Gall. 98 I*, fol. 228r./MPO 4, 296.

imprisonment and the state of the mission. Eliano was to stay in Egypt "because he knows Arabic, with which he can continue to bear fruit with members of the Coptic nation," especially once a new patriarch was elected.[60] This was the practical choice, but there is also an element in which Eliano stayed the course to ensure that his work with the Copts not entirely unravel because of his arrest, much as it had two decades prior. Eliano could thus use his knowledge of Arabic to engage the Copts as well as attempt to ingratiate himself to Vento, with the hope that he could salvage the mission.

By 28 October, however, Eliano had learned that Vento and his associates had played a role in their arrest. At first, Eliano explained, a concerned Vento came to the Jesuits: "'Reverend Fathers, I must tell you, that today after I have arrived here, several Jews told me that you are here to incite the Coptic people against the Turk.'"[61] In response to this, Eliano explained to Acquaviva that "we were stupefied to hear this, knowing how far we were from [such a plot], and that in our instructions we have made particular efforts not to intervene in matters of state."[62] Eliano then put all of his efforts into the larger context of his continual efforts in the Ottoman Empire: "I add that this shocks us that we have come to be thought of in this way, as we were in Syria for more than three years, where we dealt rather freely with matters of the faith with the Maronites and went to visit all places in Mount Lebanon." Furthermore, "we have been here now for two years, working with the Copts in particular. Never, neither in Syria nor here, has any man – neither Jew nor Christian nor Moor – neither said such things to us, nor had any such suspicion."[63]

Nevertheless, Eliano had come to realize that this did not stop Vento from explaining to the Ottoman governor that "Mariani was attempting to incite the Christian population against the Turk at the instigation of King Philip [of Spain], and that he had in his house as corroborators certain priests that were instruments of his plans."[64] While Eliano reiterated how untrue these accusations were – and stressed that his efforts in Lebanon and Egypt showed he was a part of no conspiracy – Vento recognized Mariani's deep personal roots in Egypt and the Jesuits' loyalty to him, and thus decided to rid himself of the Jesuits under spurious

---

[60] ARSI, *Gall. 98 I*, fol. 228rv./*MPO* 4, 296.
[61] ARSI, *Gall. 106*, fol. 246v./*MPO* 4, 300.   [62] ARSI, *Gall. 106*, fol. 246v./*MPO* 4, 300.
[63] Ibid.   [64] Ibid.

means by concocting a plan to implicate Mariani and his allies in a fake conspiracy against Ottoman authority.[65]

But Vento could not let it be known that he was causing a stir for personal reasons. Rather, Eliano learned that Vento claimed that he was only being a good servant to his king, the ally of the sultan, when he relayed to the Ottoman governor a rumor that Mariani and the Jesuits were the purported ringleaders of a planned Coptic rebellion that was part of Philip II's goal to conquer Egypt.[66] The rumor's professed instigator, much to Eliano's dismay, was David Moze, a Portuguese Jew who had been baptized.[67] Eliano slammed Moze: "We know for certain that this David Moze is a Portuguese Marrano," that is to say, a recidivist who had previously converted to Christianity to avoid persecution. Furthermore, Moze was "the son of one of the eighteen Marranos who were burned in Ancona under Paul IV." Thus, "David Moze, in part to vindicate his father, and partly to displease Mariani, at the request of Vento, was the instrument for carrying out this affair, and the masked spy [who had arrested the Jesuits] was also a Marrano."[68] Eliano understood that Moze hated Catholics ever since he had fled Italy in the wake of Popes Julius III's and Paul IV's crackdowns on Jews and *conversos* in the 1550s that included the foundation of ghettos and the destruction of synagogues throughout the Papal States,[69] as well as the Inquisitorial persecutions and executions of suspected crypto-Jews, including Moze's father.[70]

Once he learned of Moze's role in the Jesuits' arrest and his close ties to Vento, Eliano realized two things. First and foremost, it was obvious that Vento was not pursuing what he thought was a veritable threat because of France's alliance with the Ottomans against their common Habsburg

---

[65] Ibid.   [66] ARSI, *Gall. 106*, fol. 246v./MPO 4, 301.

[67] ARSI, *Gall. 106*, fol. 247r./MPO 4, 301.   [68] ARSI, *Gall. 106*, fol. 247r./MPO 4, 302.

[69] David Berger, "*Cum Nimis Absurdum* and the Conversion of the Jews," *The Jewish Quarterly Review* 70:1 (July 1, 1979): 41–9; Daniele Santarelli, *Il papato di Paolo IV nella crisi politico-religiosa del cinquecento* (Rome: Aracne editrice, 2008). On Moze, see *MPO 4, 440.*

[70] On crypto-Judaism, see, Robert Rowland, "New Christian, Marrano, Jew." In *The Jews and the Expansion of Europe to the West, 1450–1800*, ed. Paolo Bernardini and Norman Fiering (New York: Berghahn Books, 2001), 125–48; António José Saraiva, H. P. Salomon, and I. S. D. Sassoon, *The Marrano Factory: The Portuguese Inquisition and Its New Christians 1536–1765* (Leiden: Brill, 2001); Norman Toby Simms, *Masks in the Mirror: Marranism in Jewish Experience* (New York: Peter Lang, 2006); Yirmiyahu Yovel, *The Other Within: The Marranos, Split Identity and Emerging Modernity* (Princeton, NJ: Princeton University Press, 2009).

enemies; rather, Vento was waiting for the right opportunity to attack Mariani and the Jesuits, and he used Moze's false accusations and disdain for Catholics and Jewish converts as the perfect pretext to act. Eventually, Vento did defend the Jesuits and had compelled some French merchants to assist in raising ransom money. But it was only after numerous merchants and diplomats showed up at the governor's palace to demand the Jesuits' release that Vento came to their defense and distanced himself from Moze, at least in public. Eliano retrospectively viewed this as Vento trying to cover up his intrigues once he realized that the Jesuits had plenty of supporters.[71] Ostensibly, anyhow, Vento's turn of heart, even if not sincere, meant that the mission might just be saved after all.

The second, more immediate, problem was David Moze. It seemed too much of a coincidence that a baptized Jew whose renegade father was executed in the same wave of anti-Jewish persecutions that included Eliano's burning of the Talmud in 1553 just happened to be the man who condemned Eliano to the authorities. It seemed, at least from an outsider's perspective, that Eliano's Jewishness had been no small factor in Moze's decision to accuse Eliano of attempting to stir a Coptic rebellion and subsequently orchestrate their arrest and possible execution. Eliano's conversion was the product of the same waves of anti-Judaism that claimed Moze's father. For Moze, Eliano was an agent in the church's larger efforts to eradicate Judaism, as conversion and book burning were as much an assault on Judaism as were the destruction of synagogues and the execution of apostates – like his father – who refused to acquiesce to the demands of inquisitors. Moreover, the revelation that the renegade son of an executed crypto-Jew might have orchestrated his arrest out of revenge was a blow to his struggles to prove to his superiors that his Jewishness was not an obstacle to the mission. Add into the mix the fact that Santoro had eviscerated his theological accord, and Eliano's standing before his superiors surely hit a low ebb. While Moze might have made the accusation against the Jesuits in any case given his long-standing hatred of the church and the Society of Jesus, it is not so much Moze's motivations that mattered, but how a former crypto-Jew attacking the Jewish-born Eliano looked; it was a question of perception over reality. Unsurprisingly, Eliano deemed it necessary to prove that Vento and not Moze had orchestrated the whole ordeal that led to their arrest, and

---

[71] ARSI, *Gall. 106*, fol. 248r./MPO 4, 303–4.

demanded an investigation to clear his name and end any suspicion that his Jewishness was the cause of his arrest.

THE INVESTIGATION OF THE ARREST AND ELIANO'S CONDEMNATION OF VENTO

The inquest was very swift, lasting from 30 October to 3 November 1584. Riccardo da Lecce, the observant Franciscan commissary in Egypt, was charged to take depositions. The first to speak up was Francesco Bongrani, a merchant from Ancona. He explained that Vento was frustrated and bitter that Mariani refused to acknowledge his authority and that the Jesuits defended his rival. Bongrani claimed that Vento was determined to convince the governor to arrest the Jesuits and discredit Mariani.[72] Lorenzo Girardi, a Venetian merchant, concurred. He had overheard Vento telling high-ranking Ottoman officials that Mariani should "lose his head like a rebel" for harboring Habsburg spies (the Jesuits).[73] Marsilio d'Acquisti, a Florentine, claimed that Vento told the governor that Mariani had tried to convince sixty thousand Copts to rise up against the Ottomans as part of Philip's planned invasion. Marino Cocalino, a Venetian, claimed that he had overheard one of Vento's men, a certain Benedetto Armanno, sarcastically ask Mariani whether he had heard the good news, referring to the Jesuits' arrest. Bernardo Veluti, a Florentine, heard Vento say that if Mariani did not remove himself, he would find other means to do so. Paolo Martini da Sorrento witnessed the Ottoman guards take the Jesuits from Mariani's house, and he overheard Vento's men saying that if Mariani did not get out of the way, Vento would ensure that he joined the Jesuits in prison. And finally, the Venetian Nicolò Pelegrini rejected the view that the orders to seize the Jesuits had come from Constantinople, as he was certain that Vento and Moze had invented the Jesuits' role in the fake Spanish invasion and Coptic rebellion.[74]

With the investigation concluded, Eliano immediately sent to Rome a long summary of da Lecce's inquest that was nothing short of a condemnation of Vento, explaining that many merchants refused to accept Vento, as he seemed vain and dishonest, and was only using the consulship for

---

[72] ARSI, *Gall. 98 II*, fol. 240v./*MPO* 4, 310.
[73] ARSI, *Gall. 98 II*, fol. 241r./*MPO* 4, 310.
[74] ARSI, *Gall. 98 II*, fols. 241r–243v./*MPO* 4, 311–17.

political gain. While the Venetian consul refused to stand up against a French diplomat given the Serene Republic's tenuous situation in the Ottoman Empire after the War of Cyprus, many others did. "Not only Mariani," wrote Eliano, "but everyone – Christians, Jews, and Moors among them – including ourselves, who were incarcerated, suspected that the plot had been carried out by Vento."[75] Many claimed that Vento knew of the Jesuits' imprisonment and did nothing to free them, that he instigated the rumor that they were there to start a rebellion, and that he only came to their aid when he realized how many had clamored for the Jesuits' freedom. Eliano also asserted that Vento falsely accused Mariani of choking to death a merchant named Francesco Coronato in hopes that Mariani too would be arrested.[76] Furthermore, Eliano was incensed that, while Vento sent two men to visit him while in prison, "the visit was such, that it was for no other reason than to absolve himself from having carried out the plot." Eliano felt that Vento's visit to them while in prison was for show, "as we so clearly knew it to be a pretense" for hiding Vento's role in their arrest.[77]

Eliano was also mortified to discover that Vento allowed an alleged former crypto-Jew turned recidivist like Moze to live and practice his faith in his home. Eliano reiterated that "the Jews did not orchestrate the plot," but rather "they were middle men in carrying it out, especially that David Moze," because of their ties to the devious Vento.[78] However, Vento continued to play innocent by claiming that he had no idea about the plot and only relayed Moze's message to Ottoman authorities. But "we all wondered: how could it be that Vento allowed David – the man who carried out this plot – to live in his house, as he affirmed" and not have investigated Moze's accusations before turning them over to the Ottomans? Furthermore, if he did know it was a false plot concocted by a renegade angry with Eliano for having converted and he did nothing to stop it, how could he have "denied having played any part in the plot?"[79] After all, refusing to stop Jewish intrigues against a fellow Catholic was surely an act of complicity in said plots. The truth was clear, as far as Eliano was concerned: Vento was the plot's true ringleader, and Moze was not a bitter Jew with an axe to grind against Eliano for what had occurred to his father and the Jews in the 1550s. Rather, he was simply

---

[75] ARSI, *Gall. 98 I*, fols. 246v–247r./*MPO* 4, 319.
[76] ARSI, *Gall. 98 I*, fol. 247v./*MPO* 4, 320.   [77] ARSI, *Gall. 98 I*, fol. 248r./*MPO* 4, 321.
[78] ARSI, *Gall. 98 I*, fol. 249r./*MPO* 4, 322.   [79] Ibid.

one of Vento's pawns; that both Eliano and Moze were born Jews was merely happenstance.

Eliano's condemnation of the Jew-harboring Vento as the true culprit and Moze as simply an instrument in Vento's machinations points to Eliano's need to distance himself from his Jewishness as a source of intrigue. First, he painted Vento as a scoundrel; and Moze was a renegade who aimed to take out Mariani and the Jesuits simply because it was his patron's will. This allowed Eliano to prove that he was sincere in his efforts and that he was an innocent bystander in France's diplomatic maneuverings. Second, Eliano needed to downplay Moze's role given that Moze – a *converso* living openly as a Jew who seemingly wanted retribution for Eliano's decision to convert – had a hand in his arrest. He felt a special need to point out how scandalous it was for Vento not only to house men such as Moze but also to use them as pawns in his own games of diplomatic chess, which rendered him as repugnant as the Jews.[80] The sum of Vento's actions demonstrated for Eliano that Vento was a political opportunist and an enemy of the faith, and this allowed Eliano to distance himself from the accusations of opportunism that always followed him, and to prove that his arrest was not orchestrated by Moze because of his Jewish past but rather was the collateral damage of a diplomatic dispute gone awry. Nevertheless, the whole ordeal was a reminder that Eliano's Jewishness would always remain an obstacle, something that any malcontents could use as potential fodder to attack him or challenge the veracity of his Catholic identity. It is a preoccupation that continued, as we will see in the last chapter.

ELIANO'S SHORT-LIVED REENGAGEMENT WITH THE COPTS

Once it seemed that Vento and Moze's intrigues were behind him, Eliano wished to remain in Egypt, as he believed that the election of a pro-union patriarch could help jump-start the mission, thereby allowing him to assuage any doubts from Santoro. It helped that, by the end of 1584, the court of public opinion believed that Vento was responsible for the arrest, that Mariani and the Jesuits were innocent, and that Mariani appeared to have been a good representative of the French crown.[81]

---

[80] Europeans were often – erroneously or not – suspected of having converted to Judaism. See Martin Mulsow and Richard Henry Popkin, eds., *Secret Conversions to Judaism in Early Modern Europe* (Leiden: Brill, 2004).

[81] ARSI, *Gall. 106*, fol. 248v./MPO 4, 305.

And so Eliano declared his intention to stay in Cairo to try again with the Copts.[82] While his work with the Copts had seemingly stalled, in January 1585 he was able to convert a German Protestant pilgrim to Catholicism after he had spent several days instructing him in matters of the faith.[83]

By 4 February, Eliano's outlook grew worse. Despite his hope for the mission's rebound after his release from prison, "I believe that Your Paternity can well imagine the type of distress I find myself in ... I am here alone in this land of infidels with just one of our brothers. Every day, I anticipate some new snarls, as have been carried out against us until now."[84] Vento also continued to badger Eliano; not only did he deny his role in his arrest but, "what is worse, he and his followers are going about saying that [their arrest] was carried out by Paolo Mariani."[85] Despite his innocence, the arrest hung over his interactions with others. The Copts had distanced themselves from Eliano, and he felt that it would be years before the Copts would trust Catholics again because of the way in which they had been put at the center of the controversy surrounding his arrest. Much of this, Eliano feared, was because "the other day we received all of our letters and briefs with those of the consul [that the Ottomans had seized], except the one regarding the [doctrinal accord] that the Copts made in our presence."[86] While Santoro had rejected it, the Copts feared that the Ottomans were keeping it to potentially use it for further accusations of collusion against Ottoman authority. In Eliano's estimation, the Copts were suspicious and cautious, and the combination of costs, dangers, and doubts meant that they had no desire to risk agitating the Ottomans any further. The other issue was that "still, the [patriarchal] see is vacant, and these Copts do not know when the election of the patriarch will be." That said, "if I am here when [an election] happens ... I will not fail to do whatever I can to promote our mission."[87] Despite the countless setbacks and his clear pessimism, Eliano still wished to remain in Egypt to see the mission through.

Gregory too believed that Eliano should remain in Egypt, as he hoped that if he waited for the election of the patriarch, then perhaps Eliano could sway him in matters of doctrine and the primacy of Rome, especially if he were one of the synod's signatories.[88] Gregory even wrote to the future patriarch – whom Gregory hoped would have been elected

[82] ARSI, *Gall. 98 I*, fol. 250r./*MPO* 4, 327. [83] ARSI, *Gall. 98 I*, fol. 289r./*MPO* 4, 337.

[84] ARSI, *Gall. 98 I*, fol. 250r./*MPO* 4, 342. [85] ARSI, *Gall. 98 I*, fol. 250r./*MPO* 4, 343.

[86] ARSI, *Gall. 98 I*, fol. 250v./*MPO* 4, 344. [87] ARSI, *Gall. 98 I*, fol. 251r./*MPO* 4, 345.

[88] ASV, *Sec. Brev. 62*, fol. 236rv.

before the letter's arrival – imploring him to embrace Eliano as a brother in Christ.[89] But these briefs were written in February, just as Eliano was mulling over whether to renew his dedication to the mission or begin making plans to leave. Since orders like these would not get to Egypt for some time, Eliano had to proceed as if he would stay, while secretly hoping to depart. This caused a rift between what was happening in Egypt and how the mission was viewed from Rome. Despite recognizing the political challenges to the mission as well as the Copts' clear refusal to engage with Eliano, Gregory still did not relinquish his belief in the possibility of Coptic conversion.

By late February, however, Eliano was more frustrated: "I will say nothing else, save that we are here with desire awaiting resolution of what I have to do, whether to stay or to go."[90] In a letter to Sasso, who had returned to Rome, Eliano again showed that he was torn between carrying forward and going home. He also explained to his former companion that, although Vento had failed to incriminate the Jesuits and Mariani, Vento was still seeking other means to undermine them. Eliano also repeated that the Ottomans had seized the copy of the Copts' and Jesuits' theological accord "to make some other intrigue" against him, Mariani, and the Copts on the grounds that theological harmony was the first step toward a Coptic uprising. For this reason, Eliano hoped to know "if I will be allowed to leave here," so that he would be freed of these intrigues against him and Mariani.[91] While there was some hope in April 1585 that there would finally be a new patriarch, perhaps one of the pro-Catholic bishops,[92] the mission on the whole seemed to have slowed to a standstill.

Then, on 10 April 1585, Gregory XIII died. On 24 April, the subsequent conclave quickly elected Felice Peretti di Montalto, who took the name Sixtus V. While he and his successors were more than willing to spend a fortune to turn Rome into a monumental capital of global Catholicism, Sixtus soon proved himself indifferent to converting the Copts, seeing it as just one of Gregory's many unnecessary expenditures that had emptied the papal treasury.[93] This led to a diminished role in the

---

[89] ASV, *Sec. Brev. 62*, fol. 179r.   [90] ARSI, *Gall. 106*, fol. 252r./*MPO 4*, 356.
[91] ARSI, *Gall. 98 II*, fol. 231rv./*MPO 4*, 360.
[92] ARSI, *Gall. 106*, fol. 255r./*MPO 4*, 364.
[93] Italo De Feo, *Sisto V: Un grande papa tra Rinascimento e Barocco* (Milano: Mursia, 1987); Alessandro Zuccari, *I pittori di Sisto V* (Rome: Palombi, 1992); Marcello Fagiolo and Maria Luisa Madonna, *Roma di Sisto V: le arti e la cultura* (Rome: De Luca, 1993); Corinne Mandel, *Sixtus V and the Lateran Palace* (Rome: Istituto poligrafico e zecca dello Stato Libreria dello Stato, 1994); Marcia B. Hall, "Sixtus V: A Program for the Decorum

curia for Santoro as cardinal protector of the Oriental Churches as well.[94] It also meant that Eliano and Buono received orders to come home.[95] They left Egypt some time before 20 May 1585. They arrived in Venice by late August, capping off a three-year mission that had resulted in very little.[96]

As soon as Eliano arrived in Rome, Acquaviva requested an account of the mission. Eliano had few positives to report. Despite his hopes coming out of the synod, the mission was one very expensive failure, capped off by his arrest.[97] Then, in his audience with Sixtus on 18 November, Eliano learned quite forcefully that the new pontiff was little disposed toward what Eliano had to say about any future missions to the Copts.[98] Eliano never left Italy again.

CONCLUSION

The fact that this mission failed in a very similar fashion to Eliano's first mission in Egypt – he was arrested, ostensibly in part because he was a convert – points to the reality that Eliano's Jewishness continued to inform his Catholic identity and the ways in which he performed his missions. Superficially, Eliano was the perfect candidate to lead a Jesuit mission to the Copts. His knowledge of Arabic and understanding of the geopolitics of the Ottoman world had served him well in his efforts with the Maronites. Likewise, his tireless efforts to scour every inch of manuscript and codex in the name of finding Catholic truth where no one

of Images," *Arte cristiana* (1998): 41–8; Leross Pittoni and Gabrielle Lautenberg, *Roma felix: la città di Sisto V e Domenico Fontana* (Rome: Viviani, 2002). This process continued after Sixtus. See Dorothy Metzger Habel, *The Urban Development of Rome in the Age of Alexander VII* (New York: Cambridge University Press, 2002) and Habel, *"When All of Rome Was under Construction": The Building Process in Baroque Rome* (University Park: Pennsylvania State University Press, 2013); Clare Robertson, *Rome 1600: The City and the Visual Arts under Clement VIII* (New Haven, CT: Yale University Press, 2016).

94 Richard P. McBrien, *Lives of the Popes: The Pontiffs from St. Peter to John Paul II* (San Francisco: Harper Collins, 1997), 292–4.

95 ARSI, *Gall. 98 I*, fol. 294r./MPO 4, 372; ARSI, *Gall. 98 I*, fol. 296r./MPO 4, 373.

96 ARSI, *Gall. 98 II*, fol. 300r./MPO 4, 374; ARSI, *Ital. 158*, fol. 163r./MPO 4, 384. Leaving with him was Francesco Buono. Buono's role in the mission is minimal. He is mentioned infrequently in the correspondence and was arrested with Eliano and Sasso. He does not appear to have performed any significant role beyond assisting Eliano in the day-to-day tasks of the mission.

97 ARSI, *Gall. 98 II*, fol. 270rv; 278r./MPO 4, 389–90.

98 ASV, *Liber audientiarum de Card. di Santa Severina*, Armadio 52, vol. 18, fol. 395v.

expected it had resulted in a successful synod in Lebanon. This proved to some, especially Gregory and Carafa, that Eliano should be at the center of the church's efforts to convert Eastern Rite Christians and move Gregory's global vision of the church forward.[99] Even Santoro saw in Eliano the best chance to convert the Copts, despite his reservations.

However, times had changed since men like des Freux, Ignatius, and Laínez embraced Eliano and saw in him a convert who could empathetically guide neophytes through the tortuous challenges and temptations that they might face. First and foremost, Eliano's status as a convert was no longer universally seen as a positive. Rather, some – Mercurian, Acquaviva, Santoro, and others – deemed it a liability. Leading Jesuits now questioned whether men of Jewish ancestry could be successful priests, let along proper Catholics. As the Society of Jesus began marginalizing its Jewish-lineage members, Eliano's status as the only Jewish-born Jesuit meant that there was a heavier burden on him to demonstrate both his loyalty to the faith and his efficacy as a missionary. Since he could not hide his Jewish past, he had to embrace it, reorient its meaning, and reconcile it with his Catholic identity.

Fifty-two years old when this mission began, Eliano was not getting any younger, and his opportunities to contribute to the church were increasingly limited. While his relationship with Acquaviva seems to have improved, he was aware of his superior's policies that targeted Jesuits of Jewish lineage and the larger assessment of church leaders regarding Jewish-lineage Christians. Thus, the Copts' conversion would have been a major step toward proving to Acquaviva and others that Eliano's convictions were real. Furthermore, by glossing over the fluidity of conversionary experiences and stressing that he could convert the Copts once and for all by relying on rigorous textual exactitude and scriptural exegesis, Eliano hoped to prove that his Jewishness provided him with a unique intellectual toolkit and cross-cultural shrewdness that would result in the conversion of even the most intransigent.

But, as this chapter has shown, that never happened. Santoro – already skeptical of Eliano since his days overseeing efforts to convert the Jews in Rome – believed that the theological accord he and Sasso had constructed was insufficient, if not heretical. Even if this did not lead to suspicions that he was an opportunistic crypto-Jew using the Catholic Church for his own ends, Eliano's arrest at the hands of Vento's baptized Jewish

---

[99] Stefania Tutino, *Empire of Souls: Robert Bellarmine and the Christian Commonwealth* (Oxford: Oxford University Press, 2010).

strongman most definitely suggested exactly that. Eliano predictably attempted to blame the mission's failure on anything but his Jewishness: he blamed the Ottoman governor's "Turkish tendencies," Vento's corruption, and John's unyielding refusal to work with him. Given that the Maronites so easily reformed themselves under the same circumstances, at least as far as Eliano believed, this mission's failure had nothing to do with him. That he also went to great lengths to pin the plot on Vento and to downplay David Moze's role in orchestrating his arrest suggests at the very least Eliano's fear that his superiors would think that the mission was sabotaged by a renegade Jew exacting revenge on Eliano for having converted and burned the Talmud in the wave of anti-Jewish sentiments that took Moze's father's life.

By attempting to make sense of the relationship between his dedication to the church and the Society, the positive roles his Jewishness played in his missionary efforts, and the ways in which the geopolitical landscape of the Mediterranean helped or hurt him, Eliano aimed to absolve his Jewishness of any culpability once the mission unraveled. He slammed the Copts as obdurate heretics who feared the Ottomans and presented his arrest as an Ottoman overreaction to Vento's claim that their authority was imperiled.[100] He politicized others' actions and placed his failure with the Copts and his arrest into the larger context of imperial powers, increasingly seeing conversion and religious loyalty as tools of consolidating political authority rather than simply slippery slopes of ambiguous identities.[101]

---

[100] Anton Minkov, *Conversion to Islam in the Balkans: Kisve Bahasi Petitions and Ottoman Social Life, 1670–1730* (Leiden: Brill, 2004); Tijana Krstić, *Contested Conversions to Islam: Narratives of Religious Change in the Early Modern Ottoman Empire* (Stanford, CA: Stanford University Press, 2011). For more on the relationships between the Ottomans and their political rivals, see Daniel Goffman, *The Ottoman Empire and Early Modern Europe* (Cambridge: Cambridge University Press, 2002); Paula S. Fichtner, *Terror and Toleration: The Habsburg Empire Confronts Islam, 1526–1850* (London: Reaktion Books, 2008); Willem Floor and Edmund Herzig, eds., *Iran and the World in the Safavid Age* (London: I.B. Tauris, 2012); Stephen Blake, *Time in Early Modern Islam* (Cambridge: Cambridge University Press, 2013)

[101] Gülru Necipoğlu, "Süleyman the Magnificent and the Representation of Power in the Context of Ottoman-Habsburg-Papal Rivalry," *The Art Bulletin* 71:3 (September 1989): 401–27; Daniel Goffman, *The Ottoman Empire and Early Modern Europe* (Cambridge: Cambridge University Press, 2002); John M. Headley, Hans J. Hillerbrand, and Anthony J. Papalas, eds., *Confessionalization in Europe, 1555–1700: Essays in Honor and Memory of Bodo Nischan* (Aldershot: Ashgate, 2004); Virginia H Aksan and Daniel Goffman, eds., *The Early Modern Ottomans: Remapping the Empire* (Cambridge: Cambridge University Press, 2007).

Eliano downplayed his own role in the mission's failure by painting a political and religious landscape in which conversion was not simply a matter of saving souls but was at the mercy of larger geopolitical shifts that further entangled religious belief and political loyalty. While all of that is certainly true (and Giovanni Botero, a former Jesuit contemporary of Eliano's, did theorize this very thing),[102] we would be remiss to see conversion as simply a zero-sum battle for souls, the battlefields of which, at least in this case, were Christian churches, diplomatic residences, and unforgiving prisons. Rather, converts like Eliano needed to represent their religious identities to others and used others' actions to articulate where they stood in the theater of the everyday. Eliano represented his Jewishness as the source of a skillset that allowed him to evangelize the Maronites and Copts; but he was sure to downplay any of its negative consequences and found other means to justify the mission's demise.

What is apparent over the course of this mission is Eliano's efforts to prove to his superiors that his Jewishness served to help the Society but was never the cause of why he could not. And this all points to Eliano's evolving preoccupation with how his Jewishness was perceived and how he represented his religious identity to fellow Catholics. While the way he portrayed his Jewishness had changed – it was no longer a source of empathy, but rather had allowed him to create a Mediterranean missionary toolkit grounded in textual exactitude, linguistic dexterity, and cultural awareness – it remained central to his struggles to construct a Catholic identity. And this did not stop once he retired in Rome. As we will see in the next and final chapter, in his waning years Eliano strove to safeguard his legacy as the only Jewish-born Jesuit.

---

[102] Giovanni Botero, *The Reason of State* (New Haven, CT: Yale University Press, 1956). Botero's understanding of conversion as statecraft is central to his 1597 *Le Relazioni Universali* as well. On this process, see John M. Headley, "Geography and Empire in the Late Renaissance: Botero's Assignment, Western Universalism, and the Civilizing Process," *Renaissance Quarterly* 53:4 (December 1, 2000): 1119–55.

7

Eliano's Reconciliation with His Jewishness
in His Later Years

I saw coming from afar a great band of people, Turks, Moors, and Jews. Drawing near us, the Jews turned to the Turks and said, "this is the one that we want." Suddenly, they grabbed my hands because they wanted to seize me and drag me to prison. At the same time, the Jews, with anger and threats, were telling me "now is the time that we want to make you burn."[1]

May Your Reverence accept this rough writing, with that sincere spirit, as I have written it, without falsehoods or any exaggeration; which I have done to obey Your Reverence; and if it had not been so directly commanded of me by Your Reverence, I would have never thought to write it. And with what I have finished, I entrust myself to Your Reverence's orations and holy sacrifices, from the Penitentiary [of Saint Peter], 24 January 1588, the day of the conversion of Saint Paul.[2]

– Giovanni Battista Eliano, *Autobiography*

After his audience with Sixtus V on 18 November 1585, Eliano returned to his preaching and teaching duties in Rome. Over the next year, Eliano could also be found at St. Peter's, hearing confessions in any number of languages that he had mastered over the course of his lifetime. In 1587, Sixtus admitted him to the Penitentiary of Saint Peter, where Eliano lived in retirement and occasionally heard confessions.[3] By the time of his retirement, he had been a Jesuit for nearly forty years after having converted at twenty-one years of age. He was a Jesuit for nearly twice as long as he was a Jew. Yet, those first twenty-one years remained central to how

---

[1] ARSI, *Hist. Soc. 176*, fols. 131–2.   [2] ARSI, *Hist. Soc. 176*, fol. 145.
[3] ELIANO, Giovanni Battista, *Dizionario biografico degli italiani*, vol. 42 (Rome: Istituto della Enciclopedia italiana, 1993), 474.

he lived out the subsequent four decades. Eliano had employed his Jewish past as evidence of his unique ability to contribute to the conversion of Eastern Rite Christians. But because of run-ins with family members and renegade Jews, as well as the general shift toward the suppression of Jewish-lineage Jesuits (and Jewish converts to Catholicism more generally), Eliano remained cognizant of the myriad, and often negative, views of his Jewishness. Given his advanced age and declining health, Eliano was no longer able to travel on mission to assuage any anxieties regarding his Jewish past. Rather, in his waning years, Eliano had to reconcile the entangled meanings of his Jewishness and attempt to prove to his superiors once and for all that, despite his failures in Egypt, he remained a loyal Jesuit whose Jewishness was never an obstacle to the ways in which he had contributed to the apostolic mission of the Society of Jesus.

LINGERING PREOCCUPATIONS WITH THE COPTS

After his return to Italy from Egypt, Eliano remained uneasy about his status before his superiors. Given that the mission failed in part because he was imprisoned at the hands of a French diplomat's renegade hatchet man, it could seem to some that Eliano's missionary career ended because of a Jewish intrigue against him. Eliano must have feared that this jeopardized his whole legacy as the Society's only Jewish-born member. To allay any doubts regarding exactly why that mission to the Copts unraveled, Eliano continued to correspond with Paolo Mariani and Paolo's cousin, Mariano Mariani.[4] While the letters that Eliano sent to Egypt are mostly lost, the Mariani cousins' replies to Eliano's letters elucidate that Eliano attempted to prove that Vento and Moze's designs to sabotage the mission were driven not by Eliano's Jewishness but by their thorough corruption and hatred for Mariani.

At the fore of Eliano's concerns were the Copts themselves and his belief that their souls remained in jeopardy. A close second was Paolo Mariani's safety, as the feud with Cristoforo Vento and his henchmen had hardly died down. Their rivalry was especially tense now that Mariani was consul in Egypt on behalf of Elizabeth I, perhaps the only person who could compel Philip II and Henry III to agree on anything.[5] Vento's purported

---

[4] In a letter dated 6 Jan 1586, Paolo explains to Eliano that Mariano is his cousin. Cf. ARSI, *Gall. 98 II*, fol. 341v.
[5] Philip's disdain for Elizabeth, especially after she spurned his nuptial advances, is well known. See R. A. Stradling, *The Armada of Flanders: Spanish Maritime Policy and*

attacks on Mariani's personal networks led the Marianis and Eliano to believe that Vento was using the Anglo-French rivalry as a pretense to continue his intrigues. Facilitating this was the Franco-Ottoman alliance that Vento had successfully exploited to have Eliano arrested. But given that Vento continued these intrigues after Eliano's departure, Eliano saw this as further proof that his attacks on Eliano were driven not by Eliano's Jewishness but because Vento was a corrupt opportunist.[6]

Paolo Mariani explained to Eliano that he would do his best to map out future work with the Copts. He remained pessimistic, however, because of Vento. It is thus probably safe to assume that Eliano would not have taken well to the news of the Copts' intransigence or Vento's attempts to undercut Mariani.[7] At the same time, Eliano was able to absolve himself of guilt by suggesting that anyone would have failed to work with the Copts unless they yielded to Vento's pressures. Mariani was saddened by Eliano's departure and expressed his hope that Eliano could eventually return, and Mariano Mariani held Vento and Moze directly responsible for Eliano's departure and his cousin's issues following his removal from the French consulship and the continual pressures he faced from the French.[8]

But the Marianis' acknowledgment of Moze's role in the conspiracy, even if solely as Vento's accomplice, intimated that the mission failed at least in part because of Eliano's Jewishness. While Eliano's sister had told him in 1583 that he was no longer in danger from attacks by the Jews, the possibility of certain members of the Jewish community wishing to finish what they had started when they had him arrested in 1562 cannot be wholly discounted.[9] And even if this were not the case, it is clear that Eliano's multiple assertions that the Jews were not complicit in his arrest and that Moze did not go after Eliano because of his conversion all point to Eliano's need to prove that the mission's unraveling had nothing to do with his Jewish past.

European War, 1568–1668 (Cambridge: Cambridge University Press, 2002); Garret Mattingly, *The Armada* (Boston: Houghton Mifflin, 2005); Benton Rain Patterson, *With the Heart of a King: Elizabeth I of England, Philip II of Spain, and the Fight for a Nation's Soul and Crown* (New York: St. Martin's Press, 2013); Geoffrey Parker, *Imprudent King: A New Life of Philip II* (New Haven, CT: Yale University Press, 2014). Henry held her in no less disdain, and openly questioned her virginity. See Leonie Frieda, *Catherine de Medici: Renaissance Queen of France* (New York: Harper Perennial, 2006), 179–80.
[6] ARSI, *Gall. 98 II*, fol. 316rv.   [7] ARSI, *Gall. 98 II*, fols. 316v–317r.
[8] ARSI, *Gall. 98 II*, fol. 318rv.   [9] ARSI, *Gall. 98 I*, fol. 103v./MPO 4, 94–95.

To defend Eliano's legacy and prove that this was not just the machin-
ation of the baptized Jew Moze, the Mariani cousins wanted to uncover
exactly how Vento could destroy the mission so easily. Mariano claimed
that the Ottoman governor had long been skeptical of the Jesuits' motives
given his increased fear of the Habsburgs and followed Vento's recom-
mendations as a result.[10] In fact, Mariani lamented that there were still
some who were trying to undermine his position in Egypt by linking him
to further plots against Ottoman authority, which problematized his
relationship with the Copts. With Eliano in Rome, this clearly had nothing to do with him, thereby proving that this was about more than
Eliano's Jewishness. He thus told Eliano that, perhaps one day – maybe
with the election of a new patriarch – relations with the Copts might
improve.[11] Nevertheless, the fact that they continued to wrestle with
whether Eliano's Jewishness was an obstacle or whether the mission
was difficult on its own speaks volumes regarding how much Eliano
preoccupied himself with presenting his Jewishness as beneficial to the
Society only because of how some in Rome viewed converts.

It was for this reason too that Mariani and his associates pushed for
further efforts with the Copts, especially if Eliano were well enough to
travel. Mariano Mariani wanted to help his cousin with the Copts, but
frustrating his efforts in this regard was his inability to speak Arabic, and
he knew that relying on dragomans was perhaps not the best means of
reaching out to the Copts.[12] Others, such as Francesco Bongrani,
the merchant from Ancona who defended Mariani against Vento (see
the previous chapter), believed that the Copts might welcome Eliano
should he return.[13] Bongrani's faith in Eliano's abilities ignores some of
the larger problems any return to Egypt would have faced – namely, the
fact that Santoro called Eliano and Sasso's theological accord fraudulent.
Yet, some remained optimistic regardless of the structural issues that
hindered the mission and continued to emphasize that Eliano's Jewishness
was not a liability but would in fact be an asset to the mission because of
the skills it provided him.

Nevertheless, Vento and his associates continued to undermine Paolo
Mariani's efforts to facilitate another Jesuit mission. In October 1585,
Mariani was frustrated that Vento still worked toward finding a way to
rid himself of the Mariani cousins. As English consul, Mariani felt secure
enough in Egypt; but he was losing allies. In addition to the Copts'

---

[10] ARSI, *Gall. 98 II*, fol. 320r.   [11] Ibid.   [12] ARSI, *Gall. 98 II*, fol. 321v.
[13] ARSI, *Gall. 98 II*, fol. 356r.

diffidence, many of his past associates had abandoned him, and others began to express open disdain for him.[14] By December, Mariani was in trouble. Marsilio D'Acquisti, one of Mariani's ardent defenders in Egypt, wrote to Eliano to explain that Vento had forced Paolo Mariani to flee Cairo for Alexandria.[15] Through spurious means, such as allegedly threatening to undermine the affairs of poorer and less influential merchants should they not support him against Mariani, Vento had won over most of Mariani's connections in Egypt and was trying to gain even more influence. Seeing the writing on the wall, Mariani left Egypt for Constantinople.[16]

From Galata, the European colony in Constantinople, Paolo Mariani continued to write to Eliano. Eliano had replied to Mariani that previous November, and Mariani was pleased that they had maintained their correspondence and that Eliano still believed work with the Copts could be renewed should the circumstances improve.[17] He also explained to Eliano that he hoped that he could sway Santoro and Sixtus to call another mission.[18] Vento had not acquiesced in his pressures, however, and Mariani was convinced that he was not safe in Galata, as Vento "has had all the Most Christian King's favor against me," and was using it to conjure up an attempt on Mariani's life.[19] He likewise feared that Vento would go after any Mariani associates who tried to work with the Copts, and that any new patriarch who could be amenable to Eliano or Mariani could become subject to Vento's intrigues.[20] While all this might have proved that Eliano was not the target of a specific intrigue at the hands of a Jew, but was simply collateral damage in a larger diplomatic spat, it did mean that his time working with the Copts was essentially over.

At this juncture, Paolo Mariani's fears had increased to the point of paranoia. He told Eliano that he believed that Vento and Jacques de Germigny, the French ambassador to Constantinople, were plotting his assassination, presumably on Henry III's orders.[21] He had tried to ingratiate himself to the Venetian bailo, who was increasingly inimical toward the French. Despite this animosity, the Venetians were not interested in something that was, from their perspective, a personal squabble between two foreign nations' diplomats.[22] He did not write to Eliano again until

---

[14] ARSI, *Gall. 98 II*, fols. 322r–324v.   [15] ARSI, *Gall. 98 II*, fols. 337r–338v.
[16] ARSI, *Gall. 98 II*, fols. 341r–346v.   [17] Eliano's letter is now lost.
[18] ARSI, *Gall. 98 II*, fol. 351r.   [19] Ibid.   [20] ARSI, *Gall. 98 II*, fol. 351v.
[21] ARSI, *Gall. 98 II*, fol. 355r.; ARSI, *Gall. 98 II*, fol. 360r.
[22] ARSI, *Gall. 98 II*, fol. 365rv.

March 1588. By that point, Eliano's health had steadily declined. Paolo Mariani was still in Galata, fearing for his life and helplessly watching his associates turn to Vento.[23] The last extant letter that Eliano received was dated 20 April 1588. Its content is much the same as the previous letters: fears, paranoia, intrigue, but always a glimmer of hope.[24] This last letter reflects yet again the need to prove that Vento's intrigues were not about Eliano's Jewishness but constellated around Vento's issues with Mariani and gaining more and more power in Ottoman lands, allegedly for Henry, but certainly for himself. That Eliano got wrapped up in all of this was an unfortunate accident. Latent as well was their staunch belief that, some-how, Eliano could still be central to converting the Copts. While Eliano wished to continue his work with the Copts, Eliano was in declining health. He would need new means to safeguard his legacy.

THE AUTOBIOGRAPHICAL ELIANO

As Eliano's health rendered him unable to leave Rome, he grew worried about his own legacy, as he seemingly no longer had any means to prove to his superiors that his dedication never wavered. An opportunity to do just that came in January 1588, when Claudio Acquaviva commissioned a series of Jesuit biographies and vocational statements that were to serve as a collective record for all of the Jesuits' myriad ministries since the Society's inception.[25] Many of these texts are autobiographical, such as Antonio Possevino's.[26] Others are stylized posthumous vitae or chron-icles, often anonymous, such as a brief encomium of Diego Laínez.[27] In this regard, Eliano's autobiography appears to follow suit, as the intro-duction states that what follows will explore "my vocation to the Faith, and to the holy Religion, and what I experienced in the past 37 years."[28]

But with his legacy on the line amid questions about his Jewish past and its role in his efforts as a Jesuit, Eliano decided to craft a text that deviated from what Acquaviva desired but that would nevertheless address any doubts regarding his status. While his superior asked Eliano

---

[23] ARSI, *Gall. 98 II*, fols. 385r–386v.   [24] ARSI, *Gall. 98 II*, fols. 358r–359v.

[25] The autobiography has appeared in print with a brief sketch of Eliano. José Sola, "El P. Juan Bautista Eliano. Un documento autobiografico inedito," *Archivum Historicum Societatis Iesu*, IV (1935), 291–321.

[26] ARSI, *Hist. Soc. 176*, fols. 183–95.   [27] ARSI, *Hist. Soc. 176*, fol. 225.

[28] ARSI, *Hist. Soc. 176*, fol. 119. Eliano converted in 1551. He wrote the autobiography in 1588. Hence, thirty-seven years.

to write an autobiography in which he discussed his efforts as a Jesuit, Eliano opted instead to explore in depth his Jewish youth, conversion, and experiences with the Jews in Egypt in 1561–62, dedicating only one folio out of twenty-seven to the rest of his life. Because of the ongoing marginalization of Jesuits of Jewish lineage due to the de facto discrimination that would become official policy in 1593, Eliano felt the need to recast yet again the nature of his Jewish past and conversion to Catholicism to secure his place within the Society of Jesus. Eliano's decision to write a conversion narrative rather than explore his career as a Jesuit demonstrates that he was concerned with expressing to Acquaviva that he had irrevocably broken with his Jewish past once he was baptized, and he needed to guide Acquaviva through his conversion and first experiences with his former co-religionists to confirm this reality. In so doing, Acquaviva and other skeptics would see that his conversion was complete upon baptism.

The differences in Eliano's descriptions of his conversion and experiences with the Jews in Egypt in the autobiography as opposed to those found in his missionary letters reflect that Eliano understood that opinions of him had changed. In his letters from the 1560s, his conversion was evidence of his empathy for the conversionary journey, but that was no longer acceptable. Likewise, as his ability to convert the Copts through exegesis and lexicography had also failed, Eliano could no longer use his Jewish intellectual training to prove that he was a sincere Catholic. Instead, Eliano aimed to represent himself according to how institutional expectations had shifted.[29] To achieve this, Eliano depicted himself as neither a struggling convert nor as one who used his past Jewish identity as a tool for evangelization. Rather, he presented himself as a latter-day version of Christianity's most famous Jewish converts turned evangelists, John the Baptist and Paul of Tarsus.[30]

---

[29] The notion of textual reception here does not hinge on how Eliano wanted to be received in an active way or in the sense that he was attempting to make a radical break with institutional norms by representing himself as somehow unique. Rather, how his readers would have received his autobiography hinged on their understandings of his self-representation through contemporaneously existing but nevertheless evolving societal norms and practices. On reception theory, see Hans Robert Jauss, *Toward an Aesthetic of Reception* (Minneapolis: University of Minnesota Press, 1982); Robert Darnton, "Toward a History of Reading," *The Wilson Quarterly* 13:4 (October 1, 1989): 86–102.

[30] Paul also held a significant place in Jesuit thought on conversion and missionary work, in addition to their views of the basic tenets of Catholic doctrine, particularly on the question of original sin and the role of baptism in absolution. See Kirstin Noreen,

The autobiography begins with an account of his travels with his grandfather, including their time in Germany in 1541, where they collaborated with Paul Fagius, as discussed in Chapter 1. It is worth noting again that Eliano here referred to Fagius as "a great heretical preacher," one of many episodes in this text into which Eliano wrote about his Jewishness in Catholic language.[31] The next sequence of events begins with the death of Elijah Levita in 1549 and Eliano's move to Cairo with his parents and sister. There was one holdout, however: Eliano's older brother, Vittorio, who had converted to Christianity by 1546. Eliano said that Vittorio's decision to abandon his family, remain Christian, and not join them in Egypt, as we saw in Chapter 1, "gave us all very great grief."[32]

Two years later, he returned to Venice, where he began his rabbinical studies. At this moment, Eliano emphasizes his resistance to Christianity. Eliano explained that Venice – a city that had vexed him a decade after his conversion while he was there on his way to Egypt – was a difficult city to be in, as "I feared becoming infamous among the Jews" and, as we saw in Chapter 1, his grandfather often drew the ire of Jews for his collaborations with Christians. In turn, Eliano "sought to avoid the overtures of my brother," and dedicated himself to his rabbinical studies. Somehow, Vittorio knew of his arrival, and coaxed his younger brother into joining him in the Benedictine monastery of San Gregorio in Dorsoduro, where Eliano and Vittorio had witnessed their grandfather teach Hebrew to the monks. In this monastery, Eliano began the spiritual deliberations that led

---

"Ecclesiae Militantis Triumphi: Jesuit Iconography and the Counter-Reformation," *The Sixteenth Century Journal* 29:3 (October 1, 1998): 689–715.

[31] ARSI, *Hist. Soc. 176*, fols. 119–20. Levita and Fagius already had an established working relationship. Fagius was the printer for Levita's *Opusculum recens Hebraicum a doctissimo Hebraeo Eliia Leuita Germano grammatico elaboratum, cui titulum fecit Tishbi, id est, Thisbites: in quo 712. uocum, qu[a]e sunt partim Hebraic[a]e, Chaldaicae, Arabic[a]e, Gr[a]ecae & Latinae, qu[a]e[que] in dictionarijs non facilè inueniuntur, & à rabbinis tamen Hebr[a]eoru[m], in scriptis suis passim usurpantur, origo, etymon, & uerus usus doctè ostenditur & explicatur* (Isny im Algau: Paul Fagius, 1541). For more on Fagius and his career as a Hebraist and his relationship with Levita, see Jerome Friedman, *The Most Ancient Testimony: Sixteenth-Century Christian-Hebraica in the Age of Renaissance Nostalgia* (Athens: Ohio University Press, 1983), chapter 5, "Paul Fagius: The Emergence of the Christian Pharisee." See also Frank Rosenthal, "The Study of the Hebrew Bible in Sixteenth-Century Italy," *Studies in the Renaissance* 1 (January 1, 1954): 81–91. Rosenthal explains that the stay in Germany was very brief and that Eliano and Levita returned to Rome where Pope Leo X gave Levita more liberal printing freedom.

[32] ARSI, *Hist. Soc. 176*, fol. 120.

to his conversion.[33] At first, he did not find Christian teachings to be very convincing, and "always resisted [them] with great temerity" because "I was very obstinate."[34]

For many months, Eliano explained, he resisted his older brother's efforts to convert him.[35] In time, however, he began to be swayed. Eliano discussed how he, Vittorio, and other Christians began discussing Isaiah 53, which he claimed, "deals quite clearly with the passion of Christ." But he was unsure, and so Eliano "diligently began to study Isaiah by myself." He wrestled with the text, and "was often stuck by what was the truth." Eventually, these deliberations compelled him to distance himself from other Jews, as "I no longer had the strength to consult rabbis, because I did not want to be rebuked like before." Without their admonitions, Eliano was free "to question if what the Christians were saying was the truth." Further alienating him from the Jewish intellectual community that he knew so well was the fact that "our learned men did not know how to explain parts of scripture."[36]

Because it is an important exegetical text among Christians, Isaiah 53 was a key to how Eliano could present himself to his fellow Jesuits. It was certainly not the only messianic text he had read, nor necessarily *the* text that pushed him to convert. But Isaiah 53 played a central role in Jesuit iconography and spiritual exegesis, and his superiors and any Jesuit would have studied Isaiah 53 during their own novitiates.[37] While we might never know whether Eliano cited the text because he knew Acquaviva would recognize it, it is also impossible to affirm that Eliano's use of Isaiah was just lip service. Rather, employing a famous exegetical text that was also central to his own intellectual and spiritual formation as a Jesuit priest – a formation that he and Acquaviva shared – was a subconscious act to represent himself as a sincere Jesuit and to link his inward sense of himself with how he believed others would receive him. It also allowed him to distance himself from his Jewish self by explaining that, in order to read it as a Catholic would, he had to avoid rabbis.

---

[33] ARSI, *Hist. Soc. 176*, fols. 121–2.   [34] ARSI, *Hist. Soc. 176*, fol. 122.   [35] Ibid.
[36] ARSI, *Hist. Soc. 176*, fols. 122–3.
[37] See Kirstin Noreen, "Ecclesiae Militantis Triumphi: Jesuit Iconography and the Counter-Reformation," *The Sixteenth Century Journal* 29:3 (October 1, 1998): 699. It also has a strong current in Jewish exegesis. See Joel E. Rembaum, "The Development of a Jewish Exegetical Tradition Regarding Isaiah 53," *The Harvard Theological Review* 75:3 (July 1, 1982): 289–311. This is particularly true of Isaiah 53:8: "He was taken away from distress, and from judgment: who shall declare his generation? Because he is cut off out of the land of the living: for the wickedness of my people have I struck him."

By 1 September 1551, Eliano had stopped going to synagogue, had left the Ghetto, and was residing with the Jesuits, where he continued to study scripture under their tutelage. Oddly enough, with the exception of mentioning him prior to his conversion in Venice, Eliano never makes mention of Vittorio as a role model or what role he actually played as he approached conversion. Rather, he focuses solely on Jesuits like des Freux. Despite the Jesuits' hospitality, his struggles remained, as he found himself "in great confusion, seeing myself in a state where I was neither Jewish nor Christian, for having, from one sect and from the other, reasons for and against [each faith]."[38] Causing much of the confusion, Eliano claimed, was the warmth of Christian brotherhood that he experienced while living among the Jesuits. One night, a Jesuit came to him with warm water and offered to wash his feet. Taken aback by this gesture, Eliano asked him why he would want to wash the feet of a Jew. The Jesuit replied, "It is our custom here, that when a stranger comes to us, in the example of Christ, who washed the feet of the disciples, we wash his feet."[39]

In reflection, Eliano interpreted this humbling gesture on the Jesuit's part as proof that he should embrace Christianity. Eliano explained that "I did not sleep at all that night, as I thought about this and ruminated over many truths" that he had begun to accept from the Jesuits.[40] Eliano's reflection on the Jesuits welcoming him into their residence and their ability to move him toward conversion closely parallel his same efforts later in life, many of which occurred under Acquaviva's leadership. There is also another underlying message: the Jesuits welcomed a Jewish Eliano in 1551 and slowly moved him toward conversion and his decades of devotion to the Society; there should therefore be no reason for Acquaviva or any other Catholic to shun a baptized Eliano now.

Eliano then recounted his baptism on 21 September 1551.[41] There is a shift in tone at this point in the autobiography. Whereas he had described himself as mired in a pre-conversion fog that even his Christian brother failed to lift, his baptism provided him with the clarity to realize that his calling was as a devout servant and evangelist of Christ. This was evidenced by his choice for a Christian name: "I reminded myself that I had read in the Gospel that John the Baptist had come in the spirit of the

---

[38] ARSI, *Hist. Soc. 176*, fols. 124–5.   [39] ARSI, *Hist. Soc. 176*, fol. 124.
[40] ARSI, *Hist. Soc. 176*, fol. 124.
[41] Eliano claims this date, the Feast of Saint Matthew, to be the date of his baptism. There is no other extant source that supports this.

prophet Elijah; and since my name was Elijah, I too desired to be named John the Baptist."[42] The day of Eliano's baptism, the Feast of Saint Matthew the Evangelist, continues this theme. First, as tradition holds that Matthew wrote the Gospel that bears his name, Eliano linked himself to Matthew through their shared evangelism. Second, Matthew's traditional birth name is Levi (Mark 2:14; Luke 5:27), suggesting that he was Levitical; as Eliano could claim Levitical status through his grandfather Elijah Levita, Eliano presented himself as a Pauline Levite Elijah in the vein of John the Baptist, a biblical convert turned evangelist. This casts his conversion in a very different light from how he had described it in his missionary letters. Yet, his unique position as a Jewish convert and Christian missionary obtains.

To further remove any doubt regarding his conversion and the weight his Jewish past bore on his Catholic identity, Eliano placed Acquaviva into the text: "I will tell Your Reverence of a situation that consoled me greatly; the morning of St. Matthew, when I was to be baptized, I had such enjoyment and tears of great mercy ... I do not know if in all my life I had had such spiritual happiness as I had had at that moment."[43] Eliano had been recounting what happened and nothing more. But when describing his baptism, he changed his tone completely, addressing the reader, Acquaviva, directly. Through Eliano's evocation of Acquaviva in the text, Acquaviva assumed the role of the confessor, whose duty is to absolve the confessant of his sins.[44] In this evolution and the exposition of his struggles with leaving Judaism for Christianity, Eliano became a sinner undergoing the penitential act. The renewal of his absolution found in baptism continued textually through his admission of his state as a sinner to Acquaviva, who became co-present in the text as his confessor, thus allowing Eliano to prove that his conversion was complete.[45]

---

[42] ARSI, *Hist. Soc. 176*, fol. 126. Cf. Luke 1:13–17.   [43] ARSI, *Hist. Soc. 176*, fol. 126.

[44] For more on the evolution of the confessor and the confessor's role in the path to salvation in the post-Tridentine period, see Wietse de Boer, *The Conquest of the Soul: Confession, Discipline, and Public Order in Counter-Reformation Milan* (Leiden: Brill, 2001), 43–83. In the context of the Jesuits, reform, and social disciplining vis-à-vis penance, see John O'Malley, "Was Ignatius Loyola a Church Reformer? How to Look at Early Modern Catholicism," *The Catholic Historical Review* 77:2 (April 1991): 177–93; O'Malley, *The First Jesuits* (Cambridge, MA: Harvard University Press, 2003), 321–8.

[45] Michael Maher, S.J., "Confession and Consolation: The Society of Jesus and Its Promotion of the General Confession," in *Penitence in the Age of Reformations*, ed. Katharine Jackson Lualdi and Anne T. Thayer (Aldershot: Ashgate, 2000), 184–200. Lualdi further explains in the introduction that "penance reached beyond a concern for

The struggles to leave Judaism are erased through his baptism and then his confession, the two sacraments that lead the believer to the Eucharist; as Eliano explained to Acquaviva: "I needed to be washed of all my sins."[46] Through the purity of his soul in baptism and confession, Eliano cleansed himself of his Jewish legacy and prepared himself to receive, and serve, Christ.[47] Eliano textually transformed himself from irresolute Jew to devout Christian through sacramental acts, a clearly Pauline transformation.[48] And Acquaviva's co-presence in the text serves to show that the Society of Jesus itself was part and parcel of Eliano's abandonment of his Jewish past, and should embrace its Jewish-lineage members rather than ostracize them.[49]

Eliano next turned to his entry into the Society of Jesus and his experience in Egypt in the 1560s. Again, Eliano spoke directly to Acquaviva: "In 1562 I was sent with father Rodríguez to the mission to Cairo; and because Your Reverence knows the reason for that mission, and how it went, without fruit, I will speak about it briefly."[50] After a short discussion of the failed mission, Eliano backtracked chronologically to his experiences with the Jews, delving into his encounter with his mother. He began by explaining that "upon our arrival to Cairo ... I heard that my mother was still alive." He further elaborated:

[S]he requested to see me, hoping that upon seeing her and her speaking to me that I would have stayed in Cairo to return to vomit. We refused at first, but the consul thought it better to appease her so that she not make an issue of it, and so we

---

individual sin and salvation to the heart of Catholic and Protestant self-definition and communal identity" (p. 1), and that "penitence assumed an increasingly prominent and characteristic place in personal piety, catechesis, pastoral care and disciplinary institutions" (p. 2).

[46] ARSI, *Hist. Soc. 176*, fol. 126.

[47] The role of the Eucharist as a unifying element of Catholic belief and belonging is partly discussed in Philip M. Soergel, *Wondrous in His Saints: Counter-Reformation Propaganda in Bavaria* (Berkeley: University of California Press, 1993); see chapter 3, "The Rites of State and the Counter-Reformation Resurgence," where he discusses Corpus Christi processions as a symbol of communal unity.

[48] It is also Augustinian. Augustine as the archetypal convert was, of course, pervasive throughout the church. Augustine also held a position of prominence in Jesuit pedagogy throughout the early modern period, which Eliano would have known well. See Elizabeth Ellis-Marino, "Catechization and Conversion: A Comparison of Two German Jesuit Plays on the Life of St. Augustine," *Journal of Jesuit Studies* 1:2 (March 12, 2014): 212–26.

[49] Carolyn A. Barros, *Autobiography: Narrative of Transformation* (Ann Arbor: University of Michigan Press, 1998). See in particular pp. 1–18, "Narratives of Transformation."

[50] ARSI, *Hist. Soc. 176*, fol. 128. Eliano writes 1562 in the manuscript. This is obviously in error, as Eliano and Rodríguez were there by November 1561.

decided to go talk to her, but not in the Jewish residence, but outside it, in the home of a Christian. Father Rodríguez and I went to satisfy her just this one time ... she did not know how to discern who was her son until I first began to speak and say that I had come to Cairo for certain other duties and also to bring her back to Italy to live with me and my brother, and with Christians. This greatly scandalized her. After speaking for a bit, she said "it does not surprise me that your brother converted, since he was ignorant and lacked judgment. But you were more educated; it really shocks me that you have let yourself be deceived." To this, I replied, "since you have known me so well, you should think that it is not me that has been deceived; but what I have done, I have done with good judgment and for having learned the truth." We finally left her; she remained obstinate, crying with hope that she would have other opportunities to speak with me.[51]

As discussed in Chapter 2, his 1561 letter explained that he and his mother mutually did not wish to meet because she was embarrassed that her sons had converted, and in fact he never told Laínez whether they had. As his struggles with his Jewish past were not seen as a problem in 1561, but rather as evidence of his ability to help potential converts in their spiritual journeys, Eliano did not feel the need to prove to anyone at the time that he had rejected his mother or to downplay the reality that conversion came with temptations of apostasy and longing for one's past.

By 1588, with his legacy on the line, familial bonds could point toward a failed conversion. Thus, the wholesale rejection of maternal supplications was proof that his conversion had been concluded at baptism and that he never came close to complying with his mother's requests to return to Judaism. Perhaps nothing would assuage this tension between anxiety and trust that pervaded the Society's views of its Jewish-lineage members better than recounting the rejection of his mother, especially since the Talmud, the very text he had burned in Rome in 1553, held Judaism to be matrilineal.[52] Furthermore, French Consul Guillaume Gardiolles's insistence that he meet her, his refusal to do so in her own home, and her inability to recognize him on sight all elicit that a Jewish Eliano had become completely inconceivable. Eliano needed to demonstrate to Acquaviva that he had rejected Judaism, his mother, and the rest of his still-Jewish family. The fact that he left his mother in tears, never to see her again, expressed this very sentiment.

Eliano then leapt forward to recount his arrest and flight, which he recast in light of the course of events surrounding Paul's arrest and escape from Jerusalem (Acts 21:27–36). As he, Rodríguez, and Alfonso Bravo were preparing to leave Alexandria, Eliano "saw coming from afar a

---

[51] ARSI, *Hist. Soc. 176*, fol. 131.   [52] Talmud, *Kiddushin* 68b.

great band of people, Turks, Moors, and Jews. Drawing near us, the Jews turned to the Turks and said, 'this is the one that we want.' Suddenly, they grabbed my hands because they wanted to seize me and drag me to prison. At the same time, the Jews, with anger and threats, were telling me 'now is the time that we want to make you burn.'" They took hold of him and carried him to prison.[53]

While describing this turn of events, Eliano again spoke directly to his superior:

Now I want to tell Your Reverence a secret, and it is, that when I was seized, I cannot deny it, I was a bit dumbfounded, and I greatly feared the grave danger that had overcome me; but on the other hand, it came to me, knowing my innocence and their evil, that I was able to calm myself, and in that whole journey I did not think about anything but what was done to Christ our Lord when he was seized. With that, I felt great consolation and happiness, hoping that the Lord would do me the honor of having me die in his holy name.[54]

By evoking Acquaviva again, Eliano renders his superior a witness to his wrestling with and eventual acceptance of his potential martyrdom. This also closely reflects the letter he wrote to Giovanni Nicola de Notariis from prison in October 1583, in which he likened himself to Christ and claimed to be prepared for martyrdom.[55] Much like in the letter to de Notariis, Eliano directly exposed Acquaviva to the textual bifurcation of Eliano's goodness and the Jews' evil. Early-church martyr narratives proliferated in Jesuit seminaries and colleges, serving as exemplars for future Jesuits to embrace death in their service of Christ. This less-than-subtle reference to a major intellectual undercurrent in Jesuit pedagogy enabled Eliano to represent himself on three distinct but intertwined levels: as a convert under pressure from his former co-religionists, a devout Christian, and a dedicated Jesuit. This textual allusion allowed him to remove any doubts concerning his willingness to suffer for and like Christ.[56]

The emphasis on his conscience persists when Eliano expounded that the Jews present at his interrogation exclaimed to the Ottoman judge that "it is so clear that he is Jewish. And if we need more clarity, this you cannot miss, for look and you will see that he is circumcised, like we all are."[57] If a physical characteristic (e.g., blood or circumcision) defined Judaism, then

---

[53] ARSI, *Hist. Soc. 176*, fols. 131–2.   [54] ARSI, *Hist. Soc. 176*, fol. 132.
[55] ARSI, *Gall. 98 II*, fols. 223r–224v./MPO 4, 291–4.
[56] Kirstin Noreen, "Ecclesiae Militantis Triumphi: Jesuit Iconography and the Counter-Reformation," *The Sixteenth Century Journal* 29:3 (October 1, 1998): 689–715.
[57] ARSI, *Hist. Soc. 176*, fol. 133.

Eliano knew that he could never fully become Christian.[58] Eliano countered this sentiment by explaining in the autobiography that Rodríguez, Amato, and numerous European merchants defended Eliano's dedication to the faith by saying that Eliano had frequently said Mass to them and that in his heart he was a true Catholic. This discussion of Eliano's Jewish physicality coupled with his dedication to Christ is reminiscent of Paul's trial before the Sanhedrin (Acts 23:1–11), in which Paul admitted that his heart was Christian even though he had been born a Jew. By emphasizing his Christian spirituality over the physical "reality" of his Judaism, Eliano conveyed in Pauline terms that his conscience and dedication to the faith through desire and action superseded the physicality that his Jewish enemies used to define him. This also countered those within the church, e.g., Acquaviva, who had begun emphasizing purity of blood as a barometer for measuring whether individuals were fit to be a Christian.[59]

The parallels to Acts continued when Eliano underscored the sincerity of his Christian conscience through action, as he relayed to Acquaviva his experiences aboard the Venetian merchant vessel bound for Cyprus:

[B]ecause there were many Jews on the ship, I remained hidden until we had sailed to sea a bit. I then exposed myself, and the Jews feared that I would give them some troubles for my hardships, which they had given me in Alexandria. They saw me and wondered how I had survived. They humbly came to me and explained that they had not been involved in the conspiracy against me, but in fact reproached the others, knowing that I was a good man. And they said to the others that it would be a great danger to the Jews of Christendom if they carried out any harm against me. I looked to them innocently, and said that I forgave them, because they had not caused as much a threat to me, as they had to themselves.[60]

Eliano again presented himself as a good man, in opposition to the Jews. And while they may have once been his kin, they too forgave him for his apostasy, suggesting that even some Jews recognized that a Jewish Eliano

---

[58] This, particularly surrounding blood, was the argument of some. See Albert A. Sicroff, *Les controverses des statuts de 'Pureté de Sang' en Espagne du XVe au XVIIe siècle* (Paris: Didier, 1960).

[59] The emphasis on the conscience as the driving force behind action is central to Ignatian spirituality: "under the name of Spiritual Exercises is understood every method of examination of conscience, of meditation, of contemplation, of vocal and mental prayer, and of other spiritual operations," Ignatius of Loyola, *The Text of the Spiritual Exercises* (Westminster, MD: The Newman Bookshop, 1943), 1. Cf. John M. McManamon, *The Text and Contexts of Ignatius Loyola's Autobiography* (New York: Fordham University Press, 2013).

[60] ARSI, *Hist. Soc. 176*, fols. 136–7.

had been irrevocably washed away through baptism. Likewise, the last line of the foregoing quote demonstrates that Eliano was even willing to go after his former religious kin, should that be necessary in defending himself against them. We have already seen Eliano make such an assertion: In Chapter 5, Eliano refused to correct his sister when she claimed that the Jews would not harm him because of his relationship with Gregory XIII. Here again, Eliano emphasized that even the Jews understood that he was no longer Jewish and that his baptism had definitively rendered him Christian; any attempts to express otherwise would only imperil them.

Such Christian purity despite his Jewish birth comes through in his description of the subsequent shipwreck, when he evokes similar imagery from Paul's own shipwreck near Malta during his voyage to Rome (Acts 27–28):

It was about ten at night, and already everyone or most them were provided for, some with wood, others with a table, others with a barrel … I then saw the extreme danger, and resolved myself as best I could, grasping to a piece of the ship. I began hearing confession from those on board, and since I could not walk about the ship to the many groups, because it had capsized, I stabilized myself, that is to say on a seat, to hear confessions. Almost everyone confessed, outside of the Greeks and Jews; and for not having suitable time, it was necessary to hear confession aloud.[61]

In his 1563 letter to Laínez written from Cyprus, Eliano did explain that he had heard confessions during the shipwreck. In the autobiography, though, Eliano added the bifurcation between himself and the Greeks and the Jews, which reaffirmed that he had distanced himself from his former kin on one hand and was helping to construct a Catholic presence in the Ottoman Empire on the other.

Eliano's effort to present the finite, Pauline nature of conversion through baptism continued in his story of the Jewish youth who had promised to convert should he survive the shipwreck. As discussed in Chapter 2, Eliano had told Diego Laínez in March 1563 that, if left behind in Cyprus, the youth would almost assuredly apostatize; Eliano therefore planned to bring him to Venice to be baptized. However, in the autobiography, Eliano told Acquaviva "of a miracle that happened to a young Jew of about eighteen years old."[62] Having been saved from the waters, the young man purportedly said to Eliano: "'I do not know how

---

[61] ARSI, *Hist. Soc. 176*, fol. 139.   [62] ARSI, *Hist. Soc. 176*, fol. 142.

I have come here, but it seems to me that someone sustained me until I got to land, and so, as I have promised, I desire to be made Christian.'"[63] Eliano then explained that he had baptized the youth in Nicosia and took him to Italy, where he lived out the life of "a good Christian."

This conversion story within Eliano's own Pauline narrative allowed Eliano to reaffirm that his baptism was the moment in which his conversion ended. He linked the two baptisms to each other by placing himself and the completeness of his own conversion at the center of the story. In this sense, Eliano re-evoked his own conversion through this youth's, which Eliano described as miraculous. He likewise placed it amid the Pauline allegory of the shipwreck and within the larger Pauline landscape of evangelization. What is of course important to note here as well is not simply that Eliano used this young Jew's conversion to prove that he could procure converts. Rather, Eliano altered the whole way in which the youth's conversion occurred, as Eliano's 1563 concerns that the young neophyte would Judaize should he be left alone in Cyprus are erased from the autobiography and replaced by his exclamation that the youth's conversion was miraculous and instantaneous.[64] Given that Laínez was a *converso* and Acquaviva had been challenging the status of Jewish-lineage Jesuits, this difference in how Eliano described this conversion to his superiors is all the more stark.

Next, Eliano turned to the winter of 1563 he had spent on Cyprus and then his departure for Venice during Holy Week.[65] Once in Venice, he wrote, he immediately set out for Trent to assist Diego Laínez at the council, which shows yet again that Eliano desired to position himself at the center of the church's reform efforts. Afterward, he returned to Rome to resume teaching Hebrew and Arabic at the Collegio Romano and to serve the spiritual needs of the city's many believers. Eliano then briefly recapped the remaining twenty-five years of his life, the years in which he faced the most skepticism, in just seven lines of text. He then explained that "by the grace of God I continue here in the Penitentiary [of St Peter] where I will finish my life in His holy service."[66]

The autobiography concluded much as it began, with a vocative address to Acquaviva:

---

[63] Ibid.   [64] ARSI, *Hist. Soc. 176*, fol. 142.
[65] In the autobiography Eliano does not give the date, but he had arrived in Venice by 26 June 1563. See ARSI, *Ital. 123*, fol. 49rv.
[66] ARSI, *Hist. Soc. 176*, fol. 145.

May Your Reverence accept this rough writing, with that sincere spirit, as I have written it, without falsehoods or any exaggeration; which I have done to obey Your Reverence; and if it had not been so directly commanded of me by Your Reverence, I would have never thought to write it. And with what I have finished, I entrust myself to Your Reverence's orations and holy sacrifices, from the Penitentiary [of Saint Peter], 24 January 1588, the day of the conversion of Saint Paul.[67]

The closing is rich with supplications, and hinges on Eliano's final effort to prove himself to Acquaviva. Eliano calls the text a "rough writing," when it is obvious – through the many layers of detail and exegesis, not to mention Eliano's stylized calligraphy – that Eliano put great care into constructing the narrative, and probably wrote several drafts.[68] Eliano attempted to convince Acquaviva that he was fulfilling a duty in writing it and would not have written it otherwise. This allowed Eliano to reaffirm the authenticity and finality of his conversion while not presenting the autobiography as overly defensive.

Eliano's reaffirmation of his own memory of events also aimed to prove not only his dedication to the Society of Jesus, but also how his Pauline conversion proved that his Jewishness had no bearing on his Catholic self. This allowed him to be a successful missionary, scholar, teacher, and preacher. By stressing that the autobiography, which presents his conversion as complete at baptism, is "without falsehoods or any exaggeration," Eliano attempted to assuage any anxieties that his conversion might have been a long process that was still ongoing, or worse, could be potentially aborted in some last-ditch death-bed realization that he had been Jewish all along. By constructing the text in this manner, Eliano strove to prove that he had always adhered to the norms of the Society, even if those norms and how he adhered to them had in fact shifted quite dramatically.

Perhaps the most important line in the conclusion is his reminder to Acquaviva that he submitted his autobiography on the day of Paul's conversion, finishing the autobiography with yet another surreptitious suggestion that his conversion was as instantaneous as Paul's, whom Christ had struck down on the road to Damascus, leading to his decision to spread the Word (Acts 22:1–21). By likening himself to arguably the

---

[67] ARSI, *Hist. Soc. 176*, fol. 145.

[68] The aesthetic of Eliano's regular penmanship can only be described as chicken scratch. His typical letters were quickly written, even ones that were official correspondence. A side-by-side comparison of the autobiography with one of his letters demonstrates that he took great care in crafting the final draft of the autobiography.

most important Jewish convert to Christianity, as well as a key figure in Jesuit missionary rhetoric, Eliano elucidated that his Jewishness was not an obstacle to his efforts to promote the apostolic mission of the Catholic Church because it had ceased to exist the moment he was baptized.[69]

By re-casting his conversion as a definitive break, Eliano presented himself in a manner that would convince his superiors that he was a true Catholic. Obviously, Eliano's conversion narrative did not allow him to change the nature of conversion or the role that his Jewishness continued to play in how he constructed his identity; the very need to layer so many elements into his self-defense and to rewrite his conversion experience reflects the very pressures that converts faced and that his conversion had become central to the ways in which he viewed himself. In the end, Eliano aimed to leave to posterity a final statement regarding his conversion and how his Jewishness – what was once evidence of his ability to serve – now had no bearing on his status as a dedicated and sincere servant of the Society, the Catholic Church, and Christ.

CONCLUSION: THE END OF ELIANO'S CONVERSION

While the autobiography might have been an important declaration of his Catholic legacy that he crafted to be definitive, it was not to be his last. Rather, Eliano grappled with his conversion and place within the Society of Jesus until the very end of his life. It was 14 February 1589, and Eliano was on his deathbed. He had recently received the Sacrament of Supreme Unction, often known as Last Rites, the last step in preparing a Christian for death. But rather than just lie there and reflect on the course of his life, Eliano put ink to parchment one last time. In contrast to the autobiography – written in a clear and legible script – this final letter is hastily scribbled with lines of text crossed out and rewritten, reminiscent of Eliano's rushed penmanship that pervades his missionary letters sent to Rome.[70] This letter is not, however, a final statement on his career, nor is it a last-ditch effort to reaffirm what he had written to Acquaviva in his autobiography or to discuss his own actions any further. In fact, this letter is perhaps one of the more selfless texts that Eliano wrote in his whole life:

[69] One of the men known to lecture on Paul was André des Freux, and it is possible that Eliano took his Pauline inspiration from him. See John W. O'Malley, *The First Jesuits* (Cambridge, MA: Harvard University Press, 2003), 107–9.
[70] The letter is inventoried as ARSI, *Gall.* 98 II, fols. 387r–388v; the copy is inventoried as ARSI, *Gall.* 101, fols. 64r–65v.

a defense of Paolo Mariani, lauding him for the great work he had done with the Copts and all that Mariani would continue to do for the church in the future should the Society support him. It is, in essence, a claim that the work that Eliano started should not be aborted and that Vento's actions against him and Mariani continued to undo the work he had achieved with the Copts.

Not everyone was as fond of Mariani as Eliano was. Much of this had to do with Vento systematically destroying Mariani's patronage network that had taken him more than a decade to construct. But Paolo Mariani was no saint. Many, including some Jesuits, had come to see him as a Machiavellian opportunist with a flawed moral compass. Moreover, his inexplicable decision to support the interests of the Protestant Elizabeth I was clear evidence that one should always remember that Mariani put his own interests first. And he was far too talented at drawing the ire of his many enemies, some of whom eventually carried out his murder in 1596 under the clandestine orders of the French ambassador to Constantinople, François Savary de Brèves. But Eliano saw in Mariani, despite his flaws, a devout Christian who desired to protect the Copts in this world and prepare them for the next.[71] One could also claim, some-what skeptically, that Eliano saw Mariani for what he was, but realized that he was the perfect person to use to distance himself from his own failures and the role his Jewishness played in the mission falling apart. Either way, Eliano's fixation on Mariani and the Copts demonstrates that he had come to obsess over converting the Copts as perhaps the ultimate evidence of the sincerity of his own conversion. And his preoccupation with it on his deathbed suggests that he had hardly let it go, as he realized that his failures in Egypt – inextricably linked to his Jewish past, for better or worse – would remain at the fore of how he was viewed.

But Eliano also knew that he was running out of time. While his last letter was not an explicit declaration that he was a good Catholic whose conversion had been complete for decades, it nevertheless lays bare Elia-no's underlying need to uphold the truth of his conversion to Catholicism, which had preoccupied him for the better part of four decades. In one innocuous phrase, "having already received Extreme Unction," Eliano presented his journey to Christ as nearing its completion, a journey that

---

[71] *MPO* 4, 439. In 1596, Mariani tried to return to Egypt, but the French ambassador in Constantinople, François Savary de Brèves, and the Ottoman officials in Egypt had him arrested and hanged from the walls of Cairo. In the end, it turned out, Mariani's suspicions about French officials wanting him dead were not unfounded.

could only take place because he was Christian. Mentioning that he was in a position of grace after having received Extreme Unction demonstrated to Acquaviva that Eliano's soul had been purified and that he spoke from a place of righteousness concerning Mariani. Just as Eliano had placed Acquaviva into the text of the autobiography when he was purified of his sins at baptism, he now reaffirmed his Christianness by mentioning his purification before death when his sins were forgiven through the Sacrament of Penance. Then, through the reception of the Eucharist for the last time – the viaticum, literally "provision for the journey" – Eliano believed that he had completed every step necessary for union with Christ. On 3 March 1589, hoping that his superiors, Jesuit brothers, and fellow Catholics agreed, Eliano died in Rome.

Epilogue

How should we conclude our journey with Eliano? What has his story illuminated about the ways in which individuals lived their conversions and constructed their religious identities in the early modern Mediterranean? After all, I would venture to guess that very few of this book's readers had hitherto heard of him. Yet, the role that his Jewish past played in his conversion, missions, and construction of his Catholic identity reminds us that religion in the early modern Mediterranean never could be simply about one's relationship with God, despite how mystical and introspective that relationship might have been. Religious identities will always be intertwined with the political and cultural conflicts that pervade society as well as how individuals negotiate their interactions with one another. As we have seen over the course of this book, Eliano was a problematic figure for many: Jews saw him as a traitor and opportunist; Christians worried that his conversion was not sincere; even the Ottomans feared he might be a potential insurrectionist. These anxieties concerning who he was meant that Eliano embarked on a lifelong journey to prove the veracity of one fateful decision, to become Catholic; and how he confirmed his belief in a Catholic God had to evolve alongside the expectations placed on him by quite a diverse cast of characters because he was born a Jew.

Clearly, for some of his contemporaries, Eliano's status as a go-between, as someone who traversed all sorts of boundaries that challenged his and others' senses of the way the world worked, rendered him downright petrifying. This notion of Eliano as a go-between is instructive, but not solely in our venture into understanding the nature of religious change and cross-cultural interaction in the early modern Mediterranean.

His story, and the question of whether it unlocks something insightful about more than just his world, reminds me of the famous opening line of the prologue to L. P. Hartley's 1953 novel *The Go-Between*: "The past is a foreign country: they do things differently there."[1] But do they? The professional historian in me says yes, indeed they do. And if the further back we go, the more distant and scary the past becomes, then the ancient historian Keith Hopkins was correct to claim that "Romans were dangerously different."[2]

But to suggest that the past has no resonance beyond understanding the past would be shortsighted, I think. One way to conclude this story is to return to where we started in this book, Eliano's burning of the Talmud on 9 September 1553 at Campo de' Fiori in Rome. Eliano was not the only Jesuit there that day. And he was almost certainly not the only convert. But he was surely the only one who was both. So, then, does this render him what the Italian microhistorian Edoardo Grendi called the "exceptional normal," and if so, what does exceptionally normal even mean?[3] This question of whether his experiences were unique or banal, or somehow both, is what makes Eliano a compelling vehicle for exploring how individuals navigated the construction and performance of religious identities.

The burning of the Talmud is case in point. On 18 September 2011, Rome's Jewish community, led by head rabbi Riccardo Di Segni, inaugurated a plaque placed amid the cobblestones of Campo de' Fiori that commemorated the burning of the Talmud that took place there on Rosh Hashanah in 1553.[4] The words emblazoned on it, "the pages burn, but the letters fly"[5] and "invoke peace for whoever laments your burning,"[6] capture the essence of the futility of erasure and desires to ignore the burden that the past bears on the present. But these quotes also point to the very real ways in which the human experience transcends my inquiries into the cultural and religious landscape of the early modern

---

[1] L. P. Hartley, *The Go-Between* (1953; repr., New York: NYRB Classics, 2002), 17.

[2] Keith Hopkins, "From Violence to Blessing: Symbols and Rituals in Ancient Rome," in *City States in Classical Antiquity and Medieval Italy*, ed. Anthony Molho, Kurt A. Raaflaub, and Julia Emlen (Ann Arbor: University of Michigan Press, 1991), 479–98. The quotation comes on p. 482. I thank Craige B. Champion for this reference, especially this pithy quote.

[3] Edoardo Grendi, "Microanalisi e Storia Sociale," *Quaderni Storici* 35 (1977): 506–20.

[4] Jonatan Della Rocca, "Una targa per non dimenticare il Talmud bruciato in Piazza Campo de' Fiori," http://www.romaebraica.it/rogo-talmud/.

[5] "I fogli bruciano ma le lettere volano."   [6] "Invoca la pace per chi piange il tuo rogo."

Plaque in Campo de' Fiori commemorating 1553 burning of the Talmud.
Author Photo.

Mediterranean. This plaque's link to Eliano can, in fact, inform our understanding of the role of the past in shaping later periods.

As Eliano's story has shown us, proving one's convictions was more than just self-fashioning – it was a fundamental re-articulation of the self. A cynic might still claim, as his detractors did, that Eliano's conversion and how he discussed it throughout his life are nothing but posturing, a master-crafted ruse to hide renegadism; and I suppose it is true that we cannot wholly discount such a possibility, unlikely as I think it is given that Eliano lived in what was after all the golden age of the renegade. But we should under no circumstances underestimate or discount the very raw emotional journeys that individuals undertake in the name of finding meaning, which remains a problem across the modern Mediterranean and beyond.[7] This is why the 2011 commemoration of the Talmud's burning is so poignant. Just as Eliano believed that burning the Talmud proved the veracity of his conversion, modern Rome's Jews usurped this moment from Catholics like Eliano and made it their own by integrating it into their own historical memory: note the inclusion of the date in the lower left corner of the plaque, 5771, the year according to the Jewish calendar when this plaque was inaugurated. It stands in stark contrast to the more common Christian calendar both in its difference and in its antiquity.

---

[7] Peter van der Veer, ed., *Conversion to Modernities: The Globalization of Christianity* (New York: Routledge, 1996); Nadia Marzouki and Olivier Roy, eds., *Religious Conversions in the Mediterranean World* (New York: Palgrave Macmillan, 2013).

The ancient Roman historian Livy reminds us that there is a moral element to all of this, as "the study of history is the best medicine for a sick mind; for in history you have a record of the infinite variety of human experience plainly set out for all to see."[8] While I am neither claiming to be so famous or even the same type of historian of the Mediterranean as Livy was, this quotation points to the fact that what I have partially tried to do in writing about Eliano is to normalize for us the distant experiences and journeys of individuals whose lives had to evolve alongside dynamic shifts ushered in by things that we take for granted, like Renaissance humanism, the printing press, the Reformation, and the nation-state. Doing so helps us to enrich our understanding of the human experience and its relationship with modern challenges such as globalization. But our efforts to understand the present should also give some nod to the afflictions of the past; it should never lose sight of them: for example, what does it mean to be a Jew in twenty-first-century Rome, a city where the monuments of papal power and the legacy of Catholicism's tumultuous relationship with Judaism still loom large?

What happened in the past on one hand and how it is reflected upon, reconstructed, and articulated on the other need not be in concert for them both to possess meaning. And this plaque commemorating the historical legacy of those events in which Eliano participated instructs us that the past deeds of humans are not so foreign after all. The religious changes that struck the early modern Mediterranean are an important part of how modern society constructs its sense of history and how we remember our ancestors. This plaque, much like how Eliano wrote about his conversion to secure his legacy in the face of his detractors, is a reminder that the past is often refashioned to give agency to those who were originally marginalized and persecuted in that history. In essence, the past dwells in the meaning that people give it.

What does come through in Eliano's life – whether we call him exceptional, normal, or exceptionally normal – is that he believed that he lived in an unprecedented age of change, a seemingly scary world that moved faster than the age that came before it. Finding one's place in the world had seemingly never been easier. Travel was more frequent, there were printed books, and there were more faiths to choose from. But it had also never seemed to be so hard, as the stakes were too high for others not to

---

[8] Titus Livy, *The Early History of Rome (Books I–V of The History of Rome from Its Foundations)*, trans. Aubrey De Sélincourt (London: Penguin, 1960), 30.

get up in arms about individuals' life choices. One could proclaim to be something in an instant, but it could take a lifetime to make it stick.

Eliano found that it could be impossible to avoid a moniker – like crypto-Jew, renegade, or opportunist – that he would rather do without. In an age of renegadism, the Inquisition, religious change, empire building, and so forth – the types of structures that for Braudel rendered Eliano simply a pawn in the Middle Sea's intractable *longue durée* – disentangling his Jewishness from his Catholic identity could never be complete solely because Eliano desired it. But he continued to try, even on his deathbed. The fact that I can use his Jewishness as a means of exploring something insightful about the ways in which individuals experienced life in the early modern Mediterranean should at the very least remind us that the Mediterranean never was – and still is not – simply a sea of determinism and structural burdens. It is a space in which individuals not only perform and represent their identities and prove them to others, but they also formulate and construct fuller senses of themselves.

I think it is also important to remember that my exploration of Eliano's religious journey and the weight it bore on his life can be employed in the study of the experiences of other individuals. I hope further work on the place of the individual – replete with those individuals' biases, foibles, misperceptions, blunders, and flaws – follows this book. Even if we look just at the individuals whom Eliano encountered, we see a variety of ways in which people grappled with their identities, outwardly performed their inward senses of themselves, and perceived the actions of others in the theater of the everyday. This should remind us that proving religious convictions was never just the prerogative of converts.

Ethiopian merchants insulted Eliano and his companions on Venetian Zakynthos for their loyalty to Rome. Coptic Patriarch Gabriel risked his life to convince a Copt not to convert to Islam. Coptic monks chased the Jesuits out of their monastery. Eliano's mother voiced her embarrassment in having Christian sons. Certain Jews accused Eliano of apostasy. Italian and Portuguese Jesuits expressed their fear of crypto-Judaism at a general congregation. Mercurian and Acquaviva hounded Jewish-lineage Jesuits to prove that – as fathers general – they took seriously their duty to defend the integrity of the Society. Tommaso Raggio, despite the absurdity of it, wished to turn Constantinople into a Catholic city. Maronite Patriarch Mihail was willing to turn his community over to Eliano in the name of safeguarding his own leadership. Henry III saw converting the Copts as proof that he – not Philip II of Spain – was the true champion of the Catholic faith. David Moze had Eliano imprisoned because he saw him as flesh-and-blood proof that the Catholic Church aimed to eradicate Judaism. Ottoman officials went after apostates and anyone involved in convincing Eastern Christians to disobey Ottoman authority. Church leaders like Pius IV, Gregory XIII, Carafa, and Santoro saw evangelization as evidence that they were the defenders of the faith.

Each of these individuals negotiated and redefined their identities through their interactions with others, which allowed for everyone to grapple with conversion, religious change, and cross-cultural interaction in ways that let others know where they stood. Of course, shifts in collective definition also compelled individuals to redefine themselves, which does anything but solve the problem of capturing who a "believer" is at any one moment.

But just as modern Rome's Jews could use the early modern burning of the Talmud to reaffirm their own sense of belonging, individually and collectively, the key to understanding religious identity – or any type of identity, for that matter – is recognizing its inherently ephemeral and evolutionary nature. It is also imperative that we fully appreciate the relationship between the very introspective nature of religious belief and how those beliefs were informed by interactions with others.[9] This is not to suggest that Braudel is correct (nor, in fairness, wholly wrong) for labeling such human-made artifices foam upon the sea. Rather, it should remind us that individuals' efforts to declare where they stood should be taken seriously and be treated as one of many pillars that make up the dialogue between actors in society that shaped both the overarching societal structures that inform identities on one hand and the beliefs and convictions of the purportedly interpellated on the other.[10] In the end, my hope is that Eliano's journey to reconcile his Jewishness with his Catholicness, something that could never truly be complete, has elucidated for us that the human experience is a rich one, full of variety and color. In essence, what makes Eliano so exceptional, and has made studying him such a worthwhile endeavor for me, is that he is just as normal as everyone else, past and present, trying to make his way as best as he can in an ever-changing world.

[9] Fredrik Barth, ed., *Ethnic Groups and Boundaries: The Social Organization of Culture Difference* (Boston: Little, Brown, 1969).
[10] Louis Althusser, "Ideology and Ideological State Apparatuses (Notes towards an Investigation)," in *Mapping Ideology*, ed. S. Žižek (London: Verso, 1994), 100–40.

Bibliography

ARCHIVAL SOURCES (ABBREVIATIONS)

Archivio di Stato di Roma (ASR)
Archivio di Stato di Venezia (Asve)
Archivio Storico della Propaganda Fide (APF)
Archivum Romanum Societatis Iesu (ARSI)
Archivum Secretum Vaticanum (ASV)
Biblioteca Apostolica Vaticana (BAV)

PUBLISHED SOURCES

A Companhia de Jesus na Península Ibérica nos sécs. XVI e XVII: espiritualidade e cultura: actas do Colóquio Internacional, maio 2004. Porto: Universidade do Porto, Instituto de Cultura Portuguesa da Faculdade da Letras, 2005.

Abé, Takao. *The Jesuit Mission to New France: A New Interpretation in the Light of the Earlier Jesuit Experience in Japan.* Leiden: Brill, 2011.

Abou-El-Haj, Rifa'at Ali. *Formation of the Modern State: The Ottoman Empire, Sixteenth to Eighteenth Centuries.* Albany: State University of New York Press, 1991.

Abou, Sélim. "Le bilinguisme arabe-français au Liban: essai d'anthropologie culturelle." Ph.D. diss., Presses Universitaires de France, 1962.

Abu-Husayn, Abdul-Rahim. *The View from Istanbul: Lebanon and the Druze Emirate in the Ottoman Chancery Documents, 1546–1711.* London: Centre for Lebanese Studies; I.B. Tauris, 2004.

Abu-Lughod, Janet L. *Before European Hegemony: The World System A.D. 1250–1350.* Oxford: Oxford University Press, 1989.

Abulafia, David. *The Great Sea: A Human History of the Mediterranean.* New York: Oxford University Press, 2011.

Adelman, Janet. *Blood Relations: Christian and Jew in the Merchant of Venice*. Chicago: University of Chicago Press, 2008.

Aksan, Virginia H., and Daniel Goffman, eds. *The Early Modern Ottomans: Remapping the Empire*. Cambridge: Cambridge University Press, 2007.

Alden, Dauril. *The Making of an Enterprise: The Society of Jesus in Portugal, Its Empire, and Beyond, 1540–1750*. Stanford, CA: Stanford University Press, 1996.

al-Ghaziri, Bernard Ghobaïra. *Rome et l'Eglise Syrienne-maronite d'Antioche (517–1531): Théses, documents, lettres*. Beirut: Khalil Sarkis, 1906.

Allen, Michael J. B. *The Platonism of Marsilio Ficino: A Study of His Phaedrus Commentary, Its Sources and Genesis*. Berkeley: University of California Press, 1984.

Allen, Michael John Bridgman, Valery Rees, and Martin Davies, eds. *Marsilio Ficino: His Theology, His Philosophy, His Legacy*. Leiden: Brill, 2002.

Alpert, Michael. *Crypto-Judaism and the Spanish Inquisition*. New York: Palgrave, 2001.

Alpini, Prosper. *Histoire naturelle de l'Egypte, 1581–1584*. Cairo: Institut français d'archéologie orientale du Caire, 1979.

Anaissi, Tobias, ed. *Bullarium Maronitarum, complectens bullas, brevia, epistolas, constitutiones aliaque documenta a Romanis pontificibus ad patriarchas Antiochenos Syro-Maronitarum missa. ex tabulario secreto S. Sedis bibliotheca Vaticana, bullariis variis etc*. Rome: M. Bretschneider, 1911.

Anaissi, Tobias, ed. *Collectio documentorum Maronitarum, complectens brevia pontificia, epistolas patriarchales, monumenta historica magni momenti, quibus perpetua inter S. Sedem Apostolicam et nationem Maronitarum realatio probatur: Ex tabulario secreto S. Sedis, bibliotheca Vaticana variisque bibliothecis in Urbe excerpta et juxta temporis seriem disposita*. Rome: Liburni Typ. G. Fabbreschi, 1921.

Anastasopoulos, Antonis, ed. *Provincial Elites in the Ottoman Empire: Halcyon Days in Crete V: A Symposium Held in Rethymno 10–12 January 2003*. Rethymno, Crete: Crete University Press, 2005.

Anderson, Benedict. *Imagined Communities*. London: Verso, 1991.

Aranoff, Deena. "Elijah Levita: A Jewish Hebraist." *Jewish History* 23, no. 1 (March 2009): 17–40.

Arbel, Benjamin. *Cyprus, the Franks and Venice, 13th–16th Centuries*. Aldershot: Ashgate, 2000.

Armanios, Febe. *Coptic Christianity in Ottoman Egypt*. Oxford: Oxford University Press, 2011.

Armstrong, Megan C., and Gillian Weiss, eds. "France and the Early Modern Mediterranean." *French History* 29, no. 1 (March 1, 2015): 1–5.

Baer, Marc David. *Honored by the Glory of Islam: Conversion and Conquest in Ottoman Europe*. New York: Oxford University Press, 2011.

Baernstein, P. Renee. *A Convent Tale: A Century of Sisterhood in Spanish Milan*. New York: Routledge, 2002.

Bailey, Gauvin A. *Between Renaissance and Baroque: Jesuit Art in Rome, 1565–1610*. Toronto: University of Toronto Press, 2003.

Bakhit, Muhammad `Adnan. *The Ottoman Province of Damascus in the Sixteenth Century.* Beirut: Librairie du Liban, 1982.

Balibar, Etienne, and Immanuel Wallerstein. *Race, Nation, Class: Ambiguous Identities.* London: Verso, 1991.

Bangert, William V, and Thomas M. McCoog. *Jerome Nadal, S.J., 1507–1580: Tracking the First Generation of Jesuits.* Chicago: Loyola University Press, 1992.

Barletta, Vincent. *Covert Gestures: Crypto-Islamic Literature as Cultural Practice in Early Modern Spain.* Minneapolis: University of Minnesota Press University, 2005.

Barros, Carolyn A. *Autobiography: Narrative of Transformation.* Ann Arbor: University of Michigan Press, 1998.

Barth, Fredrik, ed. *Ethnic Groups and Boundaries: The Social Organization of Culture Difference.* Boston: Little, Brown, 1969.

Bell, Dean Phillip. *Jewish Identity in Early Modern Germany: Memory, Power and Community.* London: Routledge, 2016.

Bell, Dean Phillip, and Stephen G. Burnett, eds. *Jews, Judaism, and the Reformation in Sixteenth-Century Germany.* Leiden: Brill, 2006.

Benaim, Annette. *Sixteenth-Century Judeo-Spanish Testimonies: An Edition of Eighty-Four Testimonies from the Sephardic Responsa in the Ottoman Empire.* Leiden: Brill, 2012.

Benedict, Philip. *Christ's Churches Purely Reformed: A Social History of Calvinism.* New Haven, CT: Yale University Press, 2002.

Bennassar, Bartolomé, and Lucile Bennassar. *Les chrétiens d'Allah: l'histoire extraordinaire des renégats, XVIe et XVIIe siècles.* Paris: Perrin, 2008.

Benzoni, Gino. *Venezia e i turchi: scontri e confronti di due civiltà.* Milan: Electa, 1985.

Berchet, Guglielmo. *Relazioni dei consoli veneti nella Siria.* Turin: G.B. Paravia, 1866.

Berchet, Jean-Claude. *Le Voyage en Orient: anthologie des voyageurs français dans le Levant au XIXe siècle.* Paris: R. Laffont, 1985.

Berger, David. "*Cum Nimis Absurdum* and the Conversion of the Jews." *The Jewish Quarterly Review* 70, no. 1 (1979): 41–9.

Berger, Harry. *The Absence of Grace: Sprezzatura and Suspicion in Two Renaissance Courtesy Books.* Stanford, CA: Stanford University Press, 2000.

Berger, Harry. *Fictions of the Pose: Rembrandt against the Italian Renaissance.* Stanford, CA: Stanford University Press, 2000.

Bernardini, Paolo, and Norman Fiering. *The Jews and the Expansion of Europe to the West, 1450 to 1800.* New York: Berghahn Books, 2001.

Bernier, Marc André, Clorinda Donato, and Hans-Jürgen Lüsebrink, eds. *Jesuit Accounts of the Colonial Americas: Intercultural Transfers, Intellectual Disputes, and Textualities.* Toronto: University of Toronto Press, 2014.

Bilinkoff, Jodi. *The Avila of Saint Teresa: Religious Reform in a Sixteenth-Century City.* Ithaca, NY: Cornell University Press, 1989.

Bilinkoff, Jodi. *Related Lives: Confessors and Their Female Penitents, 1450–1750.* Ithaca, NY: Cornell University Press, 2005.

Bireley, Robert. *The Counter-Reformation Prince.* Chapel Hill: University of North Carolina Press, 1990.

Bireley, Robert. *The Refashioning of Catholicism, 1450–1700: A Reassessment of the Counter Reformation.* Washington, DC: Catholic University of America Press, 1999.

Bisaha, Nancy. *Creating East and West: Renaissance Humanists and the Ottoman Turks.* Philadelphia: University of Pennsylvania Press, 2004.

Bishai, Wilson B. "The Transition from Coptic to Arabic." *The Muslim World* 53 (1963): 145–50.

Black, Christopher F. *Italian Confraternities in the Sixteenth Century.* Cambridge: Cambridge University Press, 1989.

Black, Christopher F. "The Public Face of Post-Tridentine Italian Confraternities." *Journal of Religious History* 28, no. 1 (February 1, 2004): 87–101.

Blake, Stephen. *Time in Early Modern Islam.* Cambridge: Cambridge University Press, 2013.

Boer, Wietse de. *The Conquest of the Soul: Confession, Discipline, and Public Order in Counter-Reformation Milan.* Leiden: Brill, 2001.

Boer, Wietse de, and Christine Göttler, eds. *Religion and the Senses in Early Modern Europe.* Leiden: Brill, 2013.

Boone, Joseph Allen. *The Homoerotics of Orientalism.* New York: University of Columbia Press, 2014.

Bossy, John. "The Counter-Reformation and the People of Catholic Europe." *Past & Present* 97, no. 47 (1970): 51–70.

Bottani, Tarcisio. *Girolamo Ragazzoni: vescovo di Bergamo.* Bergamo: Corponove, 1994.

Bouwsma, William. *The Waning of the Renaissance, 1550–1640.* New Haven, CT: Yale University Press, 2000.

Boxer, C. R. *The Church Militant and Iberian Expansion, 1440–1770.* Baltimore, MD: Johns Hopkins University Press, 1978.

Boyar, Ebru, and Kate Fleet. *A Social History of Ottoman Istanbul.* Cambridge: Cambridge University Press, 2010.

Braudel, Fernand. *The Mediterranean and the Mediterranean World in the Age of Philip II.* New York: Harper & Row, 1972.

Braudel, Fernand. *The Mediterranean in the Ancient World.* London: Allen Lane, 2001.

Brockey, Liam Matthew. *Journey to the East: The Jesuit Mission to China, 1579–1724.* Cambridge, MA: Belknap Press of Harvard University Press, 2007.

Brockey, Liam Matthew. "'A Vinha Do Senhor': The Portuguese Jesuits in China in the Seventeenth Century." *Portuguese Studies* 16 (January 1, 2000): 125–47.

Broggio, Paolo. *Evangelizzare il mondo: le missioni della Compagnia di Gesù tra Europa e America (secoli XVI–XVII).* Rome: Carocci, 2004.

Broggio, Paolo. "La questione dell'identità missionaria nei gesuiti spagnoli dei xviii secolo." *Mélanges de l'École Française de Rome. Italie et Méditerranée* 115, no. 1 (May 2003): 227–61.

Brotton, Jerry. *The Renaissance Bazaar: From the Silk Road to Michelangelo.* Oxford: Oxford University Press, 2010.

Brummett, Palmira Johnson. *Mapping the Ottomans: Sovereignty, Territory, and Identity in the Early Modern Mediterranean.* Cambridge: Cambridge University Press, 2015.

Brummett, Palmira Johnson. *Ottoman Seapower and Levantine Diplomacy in the Age of Discovery.* Albany: State University of New York Press, 1994.

Buck, Lawrence P. *The Roman Monster: An Icon of the Papal Antichrist in Reformation Polemics.* Kirksville, MO: Truman State University Press, 2014.

Buckser, Andrew, and Stephen D Glazier, eds. *The Anthropology of Religious Conversion.* Lanham, MD: Rowman & Littlefield, 2003.

Budick, Sanford, and Wolfgang Iser, eds. *The Translatability of Cultures: Figurations of the Space Between.* Stanford, CA: Stanford University Press, 1996.

Burckhardt, Jacob. *The Civilization of the Renaissance in Italy.* New York: Harper, 1958.

Burke, Peter. *The Historical Anthropology of Early Modern Italy: Essays on Perception and Communication.* Cambridge: Cambridge University Press, 2005.

Burke, Peter, and R. Hsia, eds. *Cultural Translation in Early Modern Europe.* Cambridge: Cambridge University Press, 2007.

Burkhart, Louise M. *The Slippery Earth: Nahua-Christian Moral Dialogue in Sixteenth-Century Mexico.* Tucson: University of Arizona Press, 1989.

Burnett, Amy Nelson. "Basel's Rural Pastors as Mediators of Confessional and Social Discipline." *Central European History* 33, no. 1 (January 1, 2000): 67–85.

Burns, Loretta T. Johnson. "The Politics of Conversion: John Calvin and the Bishop of Troyes." *The Sixteenth Century Journal* 25, no. 4 (1994): 809–22.

Buser, Thomas. "Jerome Nadal and Early Jesuit Art in Rome." *The Art Bulletin* 58, no. 3 (September 1, 1976): 424–33.

Cacheda Barreiro, Rosa Margarita, and James Nelson Novoa. "Seeing the Turk after Lepanto: Visions of the Ottomans and Islam in Spain and Italy." *Journal of Iberian and Latin American Studies* 24, no. 1 (January 2, 2018): 1–6.

Cameron, Averil. *The Mediterranean World in Late Antiquity, AD 395–600.* London: Routledge, 1993.

Capizzi, Carmelo. "Un gesuita italiano di fine Cinquecento per i maroniti." *Studi e Ricerche Sull'oriente Christiano* 1 (1978): 19–36.

Cappelletti, Silvia. *The Jewish Community of Rome: From the Second Century B.C. to the Third Century C.E.* Leiden: Brill, 2006.

Carayon, Auguste, ed. *Relations inédites des missions de la Compagnie de Jésus a Constantinople et dans le levant au XVIIe siècle.* Poitiers: H. Oudin, 1864.

Casale, Giancarlo L. *The Ottoman Age of Exploration: Spices, Maps and Conquest in the Sixteenth-Century Indian Ocean.* Oxford: Oxford University Press, 2010.

Catlos, Brian A., and Sharon Kinoshita. *Can We Talk Mediterranean?: Conversations on an Emerging Field in Medieval and Early Modern Studies.* Cham, Switzerland: Palgave Macmillan, 2017.

Catto, Michela, Guido Mongini, and Silvia Mostaccio, eds. *Evangelizzazione e globalizzazione: le missioni gesuitiche nell'età moderna tra storia e storiografia.* Rome: Società editrice Dante Alighieri, 2010.

Causey, Matthew, and Fintan Walsh. *Performance, Identity, and the Neo-Political Subject*. London: Routledge, 2013.

Cavallo, Guglielmo, Roger Chartier, and Lydia G. Cochrane, eds. *A History of Reading in the West*. Amherst: University of Massachusetts Press, 1999.

Cavallo, Jo Ann. *The World beyond Europe in the Romance Epics of Boiardo and Ariosto*. Toronto: University of Toronto Press, 2013.

Chadwick, Henry. *East and West: The Making of a Rift in the Church: From Apostolic Times until the Council of Florence*. New York: Oxford University Press, 2003.

Chambers, David, and Pullan, Brian, eds. *Venice: A Documentary History, 1450–1630*. Toronto: University of Toronto Press, 2001.

Chaves, Jonathan. "Inculturation Versus Evangelization: Are Contemporary Values Causing Us to Misinterpret the 16–18th Century Jesuit Missionaries?" *Sino-Western Cultural Relations Journal* 22 (January 2000): 56–60.

Christensen, Mark Z. *Translated Christianities: Nahuatl and Maya Religious Texts*. University Park: Pennsylvania State University Press, 2014.

Clancy-Smith, Julia. "A View from the Water's Edge: Greater Tunisia, France and the Mediterranean before Colonialism." *French History* 29, no. 1 (March 1, 2015): 24–30.

Clément, Raoul. *Les français d'Égypte aux XVIIe et XVIIIe siècles*. Le Caire, Impr. de l'Institut français d'archéologie orientale, 1960.

Clines, Robert John, "By Virtue of the Senses: Ignatian Aestheticism and the Origins of Sense Application in the First Decades of the Gesù in Rome." Master's thesis, Miami University, 2009.

Clines, Robert John. "Fighting Enemies and Finding Friends: The Cosmopolitan Pragmatism of Jesuit Residences in the Ottoman Levant." *Renaissance Studies* 31, no. 1 (February 1, 2017): 66–86.

Clines, Robert John. "Jesuit Thalassology Reconsidered: The Mediterranean and the Geopolitics of Jesuit Missionary Aims in Seventeenth-Century Ethiopia." *Mediterranean Historical Review* 31, no. 1 (January 2, 2016): 43–64.

Clines, Robert John. "The Society of Jesus and the Early Modern Christian Orient." *Jesuit Historiography Online*, December 2016.

Clossey, Luke. *Salvation and Globalization in the Early Jesuit Missions*. Cambridge: Cambridge University Press, 2008.

Cohen, Elizabeth S. "Honor and Gender in the Streets of Early Modern Rome." *The Journal of Interdisciplinary History* 22, no. 4 (1992): 597–625.

Coldiron, A. E. B. *Printers without Borders: Translation and Textuality in the Renaissance*. Cambridge: Cambridge University Press, 2015.

Colombo, Emanuele. "The Watershed of Conversion: Antonio Possevino, New Christians, and Jews." In '*The Tragic Couple': Encounters between Jews and Jesuits*. Edited by James William Bernauer and Robert A. Maryks, 25–42. Leiden: Brill, 2014.

Comerford, Kathleen M. *Reforming Priests and Parishes: Tuscan Dioceses in the First Century of Seminary Education*. Leiden: Brill, 2006.

Comerford, Kathleen M., and Hilmar M. Pabel, eds. *Early Modern Catholicism: Essays in Honour of John W. O'Malley, S.J.* Toronto: University of Toronto Press, 2001.

Cook, Karoline P. *Forbidden Passages: Muslims and Moriscos in Colonial Spanish America.* Philadelphia: University of Pennsylvania Press, 2016.

Copenhaver, Brian, and Daniel Stein Kokin. "Egidio Da Viterbo's Book on Hebrew Letters: Christian Kabbalah in Papal Rome." *Renaissance Quarterly* 67, no. 1 (2014): 1–42.

Copenhaver, Brian, and Charles B. Schmitt. *Renaissance Philosophy.* Oxford: Oxford University Press, 1992.

Corkery, James, and Thomas Worcester, eds. *The Papacy since 1500: From Italian Prince to Universal Pastor.* Cambridge: Cambridge University Press, 2010.

Costantini, Massimo, and Aliki Nikiforou, eds. *Levante veneziano: aspetti di storia delle Isole Ione al tempo della Serenissima.* Rome: Bulzoni, 1996.

Coussemacker, Sophie. "L'ordre de Saint Jerome en Espagne, 1373–1516." Ph.D. diss., Université de Paris X, 1994.

Crespo, José Martínez. "After Lepanto: Turkish and Barbary Corsairs on the Coasts of Galicia in the Seventeenth Century." *Journal of Iberian and Latin American Studies* 24, no. 1 (January 2, 2018): 53–72.

Criado, Pilar Huerga. "Cristianos nuevos de origen ibérico en el Reino de Nápoles en el siglo XVII," *Sefarad* 72, no. 2 (2012): 351–87.

Criado, Pilar Huerga. "La inquisicion romana en Napoles contra los judaizantes (1656–1659)." *Monográfico* 6, no. 9 (2017): 303–22.

Crowley, Roger. *Empires of the Sea: The Siege of Malta, the Battle of Lepanto, and the Contest for the Center of the World.* New York: Random House, 2008.

Cruz, Anne J., and Carroll B. Johnson, eds. *Cervantes and His Postmodern Constituencies.* New York: Garland, 1999.

D'Agostino, Michele Giuseppe. *Il primato della sede di Roma in Leone IX (1049–1054): studio dei testi latini nella controversia greco-romana nel periodo pregregoriano.* Milan: San Paolo, 2008.

D'Amico, Stefano. *Spanish Milan: A City within the Empire, 1535–1706.* New York: Palgrave Macmillan, 2012.

D'Auria, Matthew. "Protean Boundaries: Montesquieu's Europe and the Mediterranean World." *French History* 29, no. 1 (March 1, 2015): 31–45.

Dandelet, Thomas. *Spanish Rome, 1500–1700.* New Haven, CT: Yale University Press, 2001.

Dandelet, Thomas, and John A. Marino, eds. *Spain in Italy: Politics, Society, and Religion 1500–1700.* Leiden: Brill, 2007.

Dandini, Girolamo. *Missione apostolica al Patriarca, e Maroniti del Monte Libano.* Cesena: Neri, 1656.

Darnton, Robert. "Toward a History of Reading." *The Wilson Quarterly* 13, no. 4 (October 1, 1989): 86–102.

Dauverd, Céline. *Imperial Ambition in the Early Modern Mediterranean: Genoese Merchants and the Spanish Crown.* Cambridge: Cambridge University Press, 2016.

Davis, Leo D. *The First Seven Ecumenical Councils (325–787): Their History and Theology.* Collegeville, MN: Liturgical Press, 1983.

Davis, Natalie Zemon. *Society and Culture in Early Modern France: Eight Essays.* Stanford, CA: Stanford University Press, 1975.

Davis, Natalie Zemon. *Trickster Travels: A Sixteenth-Century Muslim Between Worlds.* New York: Hill and Wang, 2006.

Davis, Robert. *Christian Slaves, Muslim Masters: White Slavery in the Mediterranean, the Barbary Coast, and Italy, 1500–1800.* New York: Palgrave Macmillan, 2003.

Davis, Robert. *Holy War and Human Bondage: Tales of Christian-Muslim Slavery in the Early-Modern Mediterranean.* Santa Barbara, CA: Praeger/ABC-CLIO, 2009.

De Feo, Italo. *Sisto V: un grande papa tra rinascimento e barocco.* Milan: Mursia, 1987.

DeFranceschi, Sylvio Hermann. "Le pouvoir indirect du pape au temporel et l'antiromanisme catholique des age pre-infaillibiliste et infaillibiliste." *Revue d'Histoire de l'Eglise de France* 88, no. 220 (January 2002): 103–49.

Della Rocca, Jonatan. "Una targa per non dimenticare il Talmud bruciato in Piazza Campo de' Fiori." Accessed May 16, 2018. http://www.romaebraica.it/rogo-talmud/.

Delph, Ronald, Michelle Fontaine, and John Jeffries Martin, eds. *Heresy, Culture, and Religion in Early Modern Italy.* Kirksville, MO: Truman State University Press, 2006.

Denis-Delacour, Christopher, and Mathieu Grenet. "Building, Enforcing and Subverting Monopoly: France's Compagnie Royale d'Afrique and Eighteenth-Century Mediterranean Trade." *French History* 29, no. 1 (March 1, 2015): 18–23.

Deslandres, Dominique. *Croire et faire croire: les missions françaises au XVIIe siècle (1600–1650).* Paris: Fayard, 2003.

Dib, Pierre. *History of the Maronite Church.* Detroit: Maronite Apostolic Exarchate, 1971.

Dictionnaire d'histoire et de géographie ecclésiastiques. Paris: Letouzey et Ané, 1912.

Dimmock, Matthew. *Mythologies of the Prophet Muhammad in Early Modern English Culture.* Cambridge: Cambridge University Press, 2013.

Disney, A. R. *A History of Portugal and the Portuguese Empire: From Beginnings to 1807.* 2 vols. Cambridge: Cambridge University Press, 2009.

Ditchfield, Simon. "Thinking with Saints: Sanctity and Society in the Early Modern World." *Critical Inquiry* 35, no. 3 (2009): 552–84.

Ditchfield, Simon, and Helen Smith, eds. *Conversions: Gender and Religious Change in Early Modern Europe.* Manchester: Manchester University Press, 2017.

Dizionario biografico degli italiani. Rome: Istituto della Enciclopedia italiana, 1960–.

Donnelly, Jonn Patrick. "Antonio Possevino and Jesuits of Jewish Ancestry." *Archivum Historicum Societatis Iesu* 55 (1986): 3–31.

Donnelly, John Patrick, ed. *Jesuit Writings of the Early Modern Period, 1540–1640.* Indianapolis: Hackett, 2006.

Duffy, Eamon. *The Stripping of the Altars: Traditional Religion in England, c.1400–c.1580.* New Haven, CT: Yale University Press, 1992.

Dursteler, Eric. "Education and Identity in Constantinople's Latin Rite Community, c. 1600." *Renaissance Studies* 18, no. 2 (2004): 287–303.

Dursteler, Eric. *Renegade Women: Gender, Identity, and Boundaries in the Early Modern Mediterranean.* Baltimore, MD: Johns Hopkins University Press, 2011.

Dursteler, Eric. *Venetians in Constantinople: Nation, Identity, and Coexistence in the Early Modern Mediterranean.* Baltimore, MD: Johns Hopkins University Press, 2006.

Edelheit, Amos. *Ficino, Pico and Savonarola: The Evolution of Humanist Theology 1461/2–1498.* Leiden: Brill, 2008.

Eire, Carlos M. N. *Reformations: The Early Modern World, 1450–1650.* New Haven, CT: Yale University Press, 2016.

Eisenstein, Elizabeth L. *The Printing Press as an Agent of Change: Communications and Cultural Transformations in Early Modern Europe.* Cambridge: Cambridge University Press, 1979.

El-Leithy, Tamer. "Coptic Culture and Conversion in Medieval Cairo, 1293–1524 A.D." Ph.D. diss., University of Michigan, 2005.

Eldem, Edhem, Daniel Goffman, and Bruce Masters, eds. *The Ottoman City Between East and West: Aleppo, Izmir, and Istanbul.* Cambridge: Cambridge University Press, 1999.

Eliano, Giovanni Battista. *al-'Itiqād al-Amānah al-urtūdūksiyyah Sacrosanctae Romanae Ecclesiae unitatem venientibus facienda proponitur ...* Rome: In Typographia Medicea, 1595.

Ellis-Marino, Elizabeth. "Catechization and Conversion: A Comparison of Two German Jesuit Plays on the Life of St. Augustine." *Journal of Jesuit Studies* 1, no. 2 (March 12, 2014): 212–26.

Emiralioğlu, M. Pinar. *Geographical Knowledge and Imperial Culture in the Early Modern Ottoman Empire.* Farnham: Ashgate, 2014.

Émonet, Pierre. *Ignatius of Loyola: Legend and Reality.* Translated by Thomas M. McCoog. Philadelphia, PA: Saint Joseph's University Press, 2016.

Evangelisti, Silvia. "'We Do Not Have It, and We Do Not Want It': Women, Power, and Convent Reform in Florence." *The Sixteenth Century Journal* 34, no. 3 (October 1, 2003): 677–700.

Fagiolo, Marcello, and Maria Luisa Madonna, eds. *Sisto V.* Rome: Istituto poligrafico e zecca dello Stato: Libreria dello Stato, 1992.

Fichtner, Paula S. *Terror and Toleration: The Habsburg Empire Confronts Islam, 1526–1850.* London: Reaktion Books, 2008.

Field, Arthur. *The Intellectual Struggle for Florence: Humanists and the Beginnings of the Medici Regime, 1420–1440.* Oxford: Oxford University Press, 2017.

Field, Arthur. *The Origins of the Platonic Academy of Florence.* Princeton, NJ: Princeton University Press, 1988.

Firey, Abigail, ed. *A New History of Penance.* Leiden: Brill, 2008.

Firpo, Luigi, ed. *Relazioni di ambasciatori veneti al Senato: XIII–XIV, Costantinopoli.* Turin: Bottega d'Erasmo, 1965.

Floor, Willem, and Edmund Herzig, eds. *Iran and the World in the Safavid Age.* London: I.B. Tauris, 2012.

Formica, Marina. *Lo specchio turco: immagini dell'altro e riflessi del sé nella cultura italiana d'età moderna.* Rome: Donzelli, 2012.

Forrestal, Alison, and Seán Alexander Smith, eds. *The Frontiers of Mission: Perspectives on Early Modern Missionary Catholicism.* Leiden: Brill, 2016.

Forster, Marc R. *Catholic Revival in the Age of the Baroque: Religious Identity in Southwest Germany, 1550–1750.* Cambridge: Cambridge University Press, 2001.

Forster, Marc R. *The Counter-Reformation in the Villages: Religion and Reform in the Bishopric of Speyer, 1560–1720.* Ithaca, NY: Cornell University Press, 1992.

Forster, Marc R. "The Elite and Popular Foundations of German Catholicism in the Age of Confessionalism: The Reichskirche." *Central European History* 26, no. 3 (January 1, 1993): 311–25.

Foucault, Michel. *Discipline and Punish: The Birth of the Prison.* New York: Pantheon Books, 1977.

Fouqueray, Henri. *Histoire de la Compagnie de Jésus en France des origines à la suppression (1528–1762).* Paris: A. Picard et Fils, 1910.

Fouqueray, Henri. "La mission de France à Constantinople durant l'ambassade de M. de Césy." *Études* 113 (1907): 70–101.

Franco Llopis, Borja. "Turks, Moriscos, and Old Christians: Cultural Policies and the Use of Art and Architecture as a Means to Control the Faith before and after Lepanto. Some Reflections on the Valencia Area." *Journal of Iberian and Latin American Studies* 24, no. 1 (January 2, 2018): 73–91.

Frazee, Charles A. *Catholics and Sultans: The Church and the Ottoman Empire, 1453–1923.* Cambridge: Cambridge University Press, 1983.

Freiberg, Jack. *Bramante's Tempietto, the Roman Renaissance, and the Spanish Crown.* Cambridge; New York: Cambridge University Press, 2014.

Freiberg, Jack. "The Lateran Patronage of Gregory XIII and the Holy Year 1575." *Zeitschrift Für Kunstgeschichte* 54, no. 1 (1991): 66–87.

Frieda, Leonie. *Catherine de Medici: Renaissance Queen of France.* New York: Harper Perennial, 2006.

Friedman, Jerome. *The Most Ancient Testimony: Sixteenth-Century Christian-Hebraica in the Age of Renaissance Nostalgia.* Athens: Ohio University Press, 1983.

Fromont, Cécile. *The Art of Conversion: Christian Visual Culture in the Kingdom of Kongo.* Chapel Hill: University of North Carolina Press, 2014.

Fuchs, Barbara. *Mimesis and Empire: The New World, Islam, and European Identities.* Cambridge: Cambridge University Press, 2001.

Fuchs, Barbara, and Emily Weisbourd, eds. *Representing Imperial Rivalry in the Early Modern Mediterranean.* Toronto: University of Toronto Press, 2015.

Fusaro, Maria, Colin Heywood, and Mohamed-Salah Omri, eds. *Trade and Cultural Exchange in the Early Modern Mediterranean: Braudel's Maritime Legacy.* London: Tauris Academic Studies, 2010.

García Martín, Pedro, Emilio Solá Castaño, and Germán Vázquez, eds. *Renegados, viajeros y tránsfugas: comportamientos heterodoxos y de frontera en el siglo XVI.* Madrid: Fugaz, 2000.

García Villoslada, Ricardo. *Storia del Collegio romano dal suo inizio (1551) alla soppressione della Compagnia di Gesù (1773).* Rome: Pontificia Università Gregoriana, 1954.

García-Arenal, Mercedes, and Fernando Rodríguez Mediano, eds. *The Orient in Spain: Converted Muslims, the Forged Lead Books of Granada, and the Rise of Orientalism*. Leiden: Brill, 2013.

Garcia-Arenal, Mercedes, and Gerard Albert Wiegers, eds. *The Expulsion of the Moriscos from Spain: A Mediterranean Diaspora*. Leiden: Brill, 2014.

García-Arenal, Mercedes, and Gerard Albert Wiegers. *A Man of Three Worlds: Samuel Pallache, a Moroccan Jew in Catholic and Protestant Europe*. Translated by Martin Beagles. Baltimore, MD: Johns Hopkins University Press, 2007.

Geanakoplos, Deno J. "The Council of Florence (1438–1439) and the Problem of Union between the Greek and Latin Churches." *Church History* 24, no. 4 (December 1, 1955): 324–46.

Geary, Patrick J. *Furta Sacra: Thefts of Relics in the Central Middle Ages*. Princeton, NJ: Princeton University Press, 1978.

Geertz, Clifford. *The Interpretation of Cultures: Selected Essays*. New York: Basic Books, 1973.

Gemayel, Nasser. *Les échanges culturels entre les Maronites et l'Europe: du Collège Maronite de Rome (1584) au Collège de `Ayn-Warqa (1789)*. Beirut: Impr. Y. et Ph. Gemayel, 1984.

Georgopoulou, Maria. *Venice's Mediterranean Colonies: Architecture and Urbanism*. Cambridge: Cambridge University Press, 2001.

Gerber, Haim. "Jews and Money-Lending in the Ottoman Empire." *The Jewish Quarterly Review*, New Series, 72, no. 2 (October 1, 1981): 100–118.

Giddens, Anthony. *The Constitution of Society: Outline of the Theory of Structuration*. Berkeley: University of California Press, 1984.

Gill, Joseph. *The Council of Florence*. Cambridge: Cambridge University Press, 1961.

Gilmore, David D, ed. *Honor and Shame and the Unity of the Mediterranean*. Washington, DC: American Anthropological Association, 1987.

Ginsburg, Christian D, ed. and trans. *Jacob Ben Chajim Ibn Adonijah's Introduction to the Rabbinic Bible*. New York: Ktav Pub. House, 1968.

Gibsburg, Christian D., ed. and trans. *Masoret Ha-Masoret: Jacob ben Chajim ibn Adoniah's Introduction to the Hebrew Bible and Massoreth Ha-Massoreth of Elias Levita*. New York: Ktav Pub. House, 1968.

Ginzburg, Carlo. *The Cheese and the Worms: The Cosmos of a Sixteenth-Century Miller*. Baltimore, MD: Johns Hopkins University Press, 1980.

Godman, Peter. *The Saint as Censor: Robert Bellarmine Between Inquisition and Index*. Leiden: Brill, 2000.

Goehring, James E., and Janet Timbie, eds. *The World of Early Egyptian Christianity: Language, Literature, and Social Context: Essays in Honor of David W. Johnson*. Washington, DC: Catholic University of America Press, 2007.

Goffman, Daniel. *Izmir and the Levantine World, 1550–1650*. Seattle: University of Washington Press, 1990.

Goffman, Daniel. *The Ottoman Empire and Early Modern Europe*. Cambridge: Cambridge University Press, 2002.

Gómez-Menor, José. "La progenie ebrea del Padre Pedro de Ribadeneyra S.I." *Sefarad* 36 (1976): 307–32.

Bibliography 239

Gooren, Henri Paul Pierre. *Religious Conversion and Disaffiliation: Tracing Patterns of Change in Faith Practices.* New York: Palgrave Macmillan, 2010.

Görg, Peter H. *The Desert Fathers: Anthony and the Beginnings of Monasticism.* San Francisco: Ignatius Press, 2011.

Graf, Tobias. *The Sultan's Renegades: Christian-European Converts to Islam and the Making of the Ottoman Elite, 1575–1610.* Oxford: Oxford University Press, 2017.

Graizbord, David L. *Souls in Dispute: Converso Identities in Iberia and the Jewish Diaspora, 1580–1700.* Philadelphia: University of Pennsylvania Press, 2013.

Greenblatt, Stephen. *Renaissance Self-Fashioning: From More to Shakespeare.* Chicago: University of Chicago Press, 1980.

Greene, Molly. "Beyond the Northern Invasion: The Mediterranean in the Seventeenth Century." *Past & Present*, no. 174 (February 1, 2002): 42–71.

Greene, Molly. *A Shared World: Christians and Muslims in the Early Modern Mediterranean.* Princeton, NJ: Princeton University Press, 2000.

Greer, Allan. *Mohawk Saint: Catherine Tekakwitha and the Jesuits.* Oxford; New York: Oxford University Press, 2005.

Grell, Ole Peter, and R.W. Scribner, eds. *Tolerance and Intolerance in the European Reformation.* Cambridge: Cambridge University Press, 1996.

Grendi, Edoardo. "Microanalisi e storia sociale." *Quaderni storici* 35 (1977): 506–20.

Grendler, Paul F. *The University of Mantua, the Gonzaga & the Jesuits, 1584–1630.* Baltimore, MD: Johns Hopkins University Press, 2009.

Grootveld, Emma. "Trumpets of Lepanto: Italian Narrative Poetry (1571–1650) on the War of Cyprus." *Journal of Iberian and Latin American Studies* 24, no. 1 (January 2, 2018): 135–54.

Grove, A. T, and Oliver Rackham. *The Nature of Mediterranean Europe: An Ecological History.* New Haven, CT; London: Yale University Press, 2001.

Grözinger, Karl-Erich, and Joseph Dan. *Mysticism, Magic, and Kabbalah in Ashkenazi Judaism: International Symposium Held in Frankfurt a.M. 1991.* Berlin: De Gruyter, 1995.

Gruen, Erich S. *Diaspora: Jews amidst Greeks and Romans.* Cambridge, MA: Harvard University Press, 2002.

Guicciardini, Luigi. *The Sack of Rome.* Translated by James H. McGregor. New York: Italica Press, 2008.

Guilmartin, John Francis. *Gunpowder and Galleys: Changing Technology and Mediterranean Warfare at Sea in the Sixteenth Century.* Cambridge: Cambridge University Press, 1974.

Guilmartin, John F. "Ideology and Conflict: The Wars of the Ottoman Empire, 1453–1606." *Journal of Interdisciplinary History* 18, no. 4 (Spring 1988): 721–47.

Gupta, Pamila. *The Relic State: St Francis Xavier and the Politics of Ritual in Portuguese India.* Manchester: Manchester University Press, 2014.

Habel, Dorothy Metzger. *The Urban Development of Rome in the Age of Alexander VII.* New York: Cambridge University Press, 2002.

Habel, Dorothy Metzger. *"When All of Rome Was under Construction": The Building Process in Baroque Rome.* University Park: Pennsylvania State University Press, 2013.

Hamilton, Alastair. *The Copts and the West, 1439–1822: The European Discovery of the Egyptian Church.* Oxford: Oxford University Press, 2006.

Hamilton, Michelle, ed. *In and of the Mediterranean: Medieval and Early Modern Iberian Studies.* Nashville, TN: Vanderbilt University Press, 2015.

Hankins, James. *Humanism and Platonism in the Italian Renaissance.* Rome: Edizioni di storia e letteratura, 2003.

Hanlon, Gregory. *Confession and Community in Seventeenth-Century France.* Philadelphia: University of Pennsylvania Press, 1993.

Harrington, Joel F., and Helmut Walser Smith. "Confessionalization, Community, and State Building in Germany, 1555–1870." *The Journal of Modern History* 69, no. 1 (March 1, 1997): 77–101.

Harris, A. Katie. *From Muslim to Christian Granada: Inventing a City's Past in Early Modern Spain.* Baltimore, MD: Johns Hopkins University Press, 2007.

Harris, William V., ed. *Rethinking the Mediterranean.* Oxford: Oxford University Press, 2004.

Harris, William W. *Lebanon: A History, 600–2011.* New York: Oxford University Press, 2012.

Hartley, L. P. *The Go-Between.* 1953. Reprint, New York: NYRB Classics, 2002.

Harvey, L. P. *Muslims in Spain, 1500 to 1614.* Chicago: University of Chicago Press, 2005.

Headley, John M. "Geography and Empire in the Late Renaissance: Botero's Assignment, Western Universalism, and the Civilizing Process." *Renaissance Quarterly* 53, no. 4 (2000): 1119–55.

Headley, John M., Hans J. Hillerbrand, and Anthony J. Papalas, eds. *Confessionalization in Europe, 1555–1700: Essays in Honor and Memory of Bodo Nischan.* Aldershot: Ashgate, 2004.

Hegyi, Ottmar. *Cervantes and the Turks: Historical Reality versus Literary Fiction in La Gran Sultana and El Amante Liberal.* Newark, DE: Juan de la Cuesta, 1992.

Henke, Robert, and Eric Nicholson, eds. *Transnational Mobilities in Early Modern Theater.* Farnham: Ashgate, 2014.

Hernández, Marie Theresa. *The Virgin of Guadalupe and the Conversos: Uncovering Hidden Influences from Spain to Mexico.* New Brunswick, NJ: Rutgers University Press, 2014.

Hershenzon, Daniel. *The Captive Sea: Slavery, Communication, and Commerce in Early Modern Spain and the Mediterranean.* Philadelphia: University of Pennsylvania Press, 2018.

Herzfeld, Michael. "Honour and Shame: Problems in the Comparative Analysis of Moral Systems." *Man* 15 (1980): 339–51.

Herzfeld, Michael. *Poetics of Manhood: Contest and Identity in a Cretan Mountain Village.* Princeton, NJ: Princeton University Press, 1985.

Hess, Andrew C. "The Battle of Lepanto and Its Place in Mediterranean History." *Past & Present* 57 (November 1972): 53–73.

Hess, Andrew C. "The Evolution of the Ottoman Seaborne Empire in the Age of the Oceanic Discoveries, 1453–1525." *The American Historical Review* 75, no. 7 (December 1970): 1892–1919.

Heyberger, Bernard, ed. *Chrétiens du monde arabe: un archipel en terre d'Islam.* Paris: Autrement, 2003.

Heyberger, Bernard. *Les Chrétiens du Proche-Orient au temps de la reforme catholique: Syrie, Liban, Palestine, XVIIe–XVIIIe siècles.* Rome: Ecole française de Rome, 1994.

Heyberger, Bernard. "Entre Byzance et Rome: l'image et le sacré au Proche-Orient au XVIIe siècle." *Histoire, économie et société* 8, no. 4 (1989): 527–50.

Heyberger, Bernard. "Les nouveaux horizons méditerranéens des Chrétiens du Bilād Al-Šām (XVIIe–XVIIIe siècle)." *Arabica* 51, no. 4 (October 1, 2004): 435–61.

Heyberger, Bernard. "Polemic Dialogues between Christians and Muslims in the Seventeenth Century." *Journal of the Economic & Social History of the Orient* 55, no. 2/3 (June 2012): 495–516.

Hills, Helen. "Cities and Virgins: Female Aristocratic Convents in Early Modern Naples and Palermo." *Oxford Art Journal* 22, no. 1 (January 1, 1999): 31–54.

Hills, Helen. "The Veiled Body: Within the Folds of Early Modern Neapolitan Convent Architecture." *Oxford Art Journal* 27, no. 3 (January 1, 2004): 271–90.

Hindmarsh, D. Bruce. *The Evangelical Conversion Narrative: Spiritual Autobiography in Early Modern England.* Oxford; New York: Oxford University Press, 2012.

Hinz, Manfred, and Danillo Zardin, eds. *I gesuiti e la Ratio Studiorum.* Rome: Bulzoni Editore, 2004.

Homsy, Basile. *Les Capitulations et la protection des chrétiens au Proche-Orient aux XVIe, XVIIe et XVIIIe siècles.* Harissa, Lebanon: Librarie Orientaliste P. Gauthner, 1956.

Homza, Lu Ann. *Religious Authority in the Spanish Renaissance.* Baltimore, MD: Johns Hopkins University Press, 2000.

Hook, Judith. *The Sack of Rome, 1527.* 2nd ed. New York: Palgrave Macmillan, 2004.

Höpfl, Harro. *Jesuit Political Thought: The Society of Jesus and the State, c. 1540–1640.* Cambridge: Cambridge University Press, 2004.

Horan, Joseph. "King Cotton on the Middle Sea: Acclimatization Projects and the French Links to the Early Modern Mediterranean." *French History* 29, no. 1 (March 1, 2015): 93–108.

Horden, Peregrine, and Sharon Kinoshita, eds. *A Companion to Mediterranean History.* Malden, MA: Wiley Blackwell, 2014.

Horden, Peregrine, and Nicholas Purcell. *The Corrupting Sea: A Study of Mediterranean History.* Oxford; Malden, MA: Blackwell, 2000.

Horn, Jeff. "Lessons of the Levant: Early Modern French Economic Development in the Mediterranean." *French History* 29, no. 1 (March 1, 2015): 76–92.

Horodowich, Elizabeth. *Language and Statecraft in Early Modern Venice.* New York; Cambridge: Cambridge University Press, 2011.

Hsia, R. Po-chia. *A Jesuit in the Forbidden City: Matteo Ricci, 1552–1610.* Oxford: Oxford University Press, 2010.

Hsia, R. Po-Chia. *The World of Catholic Renewal, 1540–1770.* 2nd ed. Cambridge: Cambridge University Press, 2005.

Hsia, R. Po-chia, and Hartmut Lehmann, eds. *In and Out of the Ghetto: Jewish-Gentile Relations in Late Medieval and Early Modern Germany.* Washington, DC: German Historical Institute; Cambridge: Cambridge University Press, 1995.

Huerga Criado, Pilar. "Cristianos nuevos de origen ibérico en el Reino de Nápoles en el siglo XVII." *Sefarad* 72, no. 2 (2012): 351–87.

Hughes-Freeland, Felicia, and Mary M. Crain. *Recasting Ritual: Performance, Media, Identity.* London; New York: Routledge, 1998.

Iappelli, Filippo, ed. *Alle origini dell'Università dell'Aquila: cultura, università, collegi gesuitici all'inizio dell'età moderna in Italia meridionale: Atti del convegno internazionale ... L'Aquila, 8–11 Novembre 1995.* Rome: Institutum Historicum S.I., 2000.

Imber, Colin. *The Ottoman Empire, 1300–1650: The Structure of Power.* 2nd ed. New York: Palgrave Macmillan, 2002.

Ingram, Kevin, ed. *The Conversos and Moriscos in Late Medieval Spain and Beyond.* Leiden: Brill, 2009.

Ingram, Kevin. "Secret Lives, Public Lies: The Conversos and Socio-Religious Non-Conformism in the Spanish Golden Age." Ph.D. diss., University of California, San Diego, 2006.

Isom-Verhaaren, Christine. *Allies with the Infidel: The Ottoman and French Alliance in the Sixteenth Century.* London: I.B. Tauris, 2011.

Israel, Jonathan Irvine. *Diasporas within a Diaspora: Jews, Crypto-Jews and the World Maritime Empires (1540–1740).* Leiden: Brill, 2002.

Jardine, Lisa. *Worldly Goods: A New History of the Renaissance.* New York: Nan A. Talese, 1996.

Jauss, Hans Robert. *Toward an Aesthetic of Reception.* Minneapolis: University of Minnesota Press, 1982.

Jennings, Ronald C. *Christians and Muslims in Ottoman Cyprus and the Mediterranean World, 1571–1640.* New York: New York University Press, 1993.

Kaplan, Benjamin J. *Divided by Faith: Religious Conflict and the Practice of Toleration in Early Modern Europe.* Cambridge, MA: Belknap Press of Harvard University Press, 2007.

Karant-Nunn, Susan C. *The Reformation of Feeling: Shaping the Religious Emotions in Early Modern Germany.* Oxford: Oxford University Press, 2010.

Karant-Nunn, Susan C. *The Reformation of Ritual: An Interpretation of Early Modern Germany.* London: Routledge, 1997.

Karapidakis, Nicolas. *Civis fidelis: l'avènement et l'affirmation de la citoyenneté corfiote (XVIème–XVIIème siècles).* Frankfurt: P. Lang, 1992.

Knecht, R. J. *Hero or Tyrant? Henry III, King of France, 1574–89.* Aldershot: Ashgate, 2014.

Kortepeter, C. Max. *Ottoman Imperialism during the Reformation: Europe and the Caucasus.* New York: New York University Press, 1972.

Kristeller, Paul Oskar. *Marsilio Ficino and His Work after Five Hundred Years.* Florence: Leo S. Olschki, 1987.

Krstić, Tijana. *Contested Conversions to Islam: Narratives of Religious Change in the Early Modern Ottoman Empire.* Stanford, CA: Stanford University Press, 2011.

Krstić, Tijana. "The Elusive Intermediaries: Moriscos in Ottoman and Western European Diplomatic Sources from Constantinople, 1560s–1630s." *Journal of Early Modern History* 19, no. 2–3 (April 21, 2015): 129–51.

Krstić, Tijana. "Illuminated by the Light of Islam and the Glory of the Ottoman Sultanate: Self-Narratives of Conversion to Islam in the Age of Confessionalization." *Comparative Studies in Society and History* 51, no. 1 (2009): 35–63.

Kunt, I. Metin. *The Sultan's Servants: The Transformation of Ottoman Provincial Government, 1550–1650.* New York: Columbia University Press, 1983.

Kunt, I. Metin, and Christine Woodhead, eds. *Süleyman the Magnificent and His Age: The Ottoman Empire in the Early Modern World.* London: Longman, 1995.

Laven, Mary. "Encountering the Counter-Reformation." *Renaissance Quarterly* 59, no. 3 (2006): 706–20.

Laven, Mary. "Sex and Celibacy in Early Modern Venice." *The Historical Journal* 44, no. 4 (December 1, 2001): 865–88.

Lazar, Lance. *Working in the Vineyard of the Lord: Jesuit Confraternities in Early Modern Italy.* Toronto: University of Toronto Press, 2005.

Lea, Henry Charles. *The Inquisition in the Spanish Dependencies: Sicily, Naples, Sardinia, Milan, the Canaries, Mexico, Peru, New Granada.* Cambridge: Cambridge University Press, 2010.

Lee, Rosemary. "Theologies of Failure: Islamic Conversion in Early Modern Rome." *Essays in History* (January 2012): 59–74.

Legrand, Emile. *Relation de l'establissement des PP. de la Compagnie de Jésus en Levant.* Paris: Maisonneuve, 1869.

Lehmann, Matthias B. "Rethinking Sephardi Identity: Jews and Other Jews in Ottoman Palestine." *Jewish Social Studies,* New Series, 15, no. 1 (October 1, 2008): 81–109.

Leone, Massimo. *Religious Conversion and Identity: The Semiotic Analysis of Texts.* London; New York: Routledge, 2004.

Levi Della Vida, Giorgio, ed. *Documenti intorno alle relazioni delle chiese orientali con la S. Sede durante il pontificato di Gregorio XIII.* Vatican City: Biblioteca apostolica vaticana, 1948.

Levi Della Vida, Giorgio, ed. *Secondo elenco dei manoscritti arabi islamici della Biblioteca vaticana.* Vatican City: Biblioteca apostolica vaticana, 1965.

Levita, Elijah. *Opusculum recens Hebraicum a doctissimo Hebraeo Eliia Leuita Germano grammatico elaboratum, cui titulum fecit Tishbi, id est, Thisbites: in quo 712. uocum, qu[a]e sunt partim Hebraic[a]e, Chaldaicae, Arabic[a]e, Gr[a]ecae & Latinae, qu[a]e[que] in dictionarijs non facilè inueniuntur, & à rabbinis tamen Hebr[a]eoru[m], in scriptis suis passim usurpantur, origo, etymon, & uerus usus doctè ostenditur & explicatur.* Isny im Algau: Paul Fagius, 1541.

Litterae quadrimestres ex universis, praeter Indiam et Brasiliam. Tomus primus (1546–1552). Rome: Monumenta Historica Societatis Iesu, 1894.

Little, Donald P. "Coptic Conversion to Islam under the Baḥrī Mamlūks, 692–755/1293–1354." *Bulletin of the School of Oriental and African Studies* 39 (1976): 552–69.

Livy, Titus. *The Early History of Rome (Books I–V of The History of Rome from Its Foundations).* Translated by Aubrey De Sélincourt. London: Penguin, 1960.

Longino, Michèle. *Orientalism in French Classical Drama.* Cambridge: Cambridge University Press, 2002.

Lopes de Barros, Maria Filomena, and José Alberto Rodrigues da Silva Tavim. "Cristãos(ãs)-novos(as), mouriscos(as), judeus e mouros. Diálogos em trânsito no Portugal moderno (séculos XVI–XVII)." *Journal of Sefardic Studies* 1 (2013): 1–45.

Lotz-Heumann, Ute. "The Concept of 'Confessionalization': A Historiographical Paradigm in Dispute." *Memoria y civilización* 4 (2001): 93–114.

Lotz-Heumann, Ute, and Matthias Pohlig. "Confessionalization and Literature in the Empire, 1555–1700." *Central European History* 40, no. 1 (March 1, 2007): 35–61.

Louth, Andrew. *St John Damascene: Tradition and Originality in Byzantine Theology: Tradition and Originality in Byzantine Theology.* Oxford: Oxford University Press, 2002.

Loyola, Ignatius of. *The Constitutions of the Society of Jesus.* St. Louis, MO: Institute of Jesuit Sources, 1970.

Loyola, Ignatius of. *Counsels for Jesuits: Selected Letters and Instructions of Saint Ignatius Loyola.* Chicago: Loyola University Press, 1985.

Loyola, Ignatius of. *Personal Writings: Reminiscences, Spiritual Diary, Select Letters Including the Text of The Spiritual Exercises.* London: Penguin Books, 1996.

Loyola, Ignatius of. *The Text of the Spiritual Exercises.* Westminster, MD: The Newman Bookshop, 1943.

Lualdi, Katharine J. "Persevering in the Faith: Catholic Worship and Communal Identity in the Wake of the Edict of Nantes." *The Sixteenth Century Journal* 35, no. 3 (October 1, 2004): 717–34.

Lualdi, Katharine J., and Anne T. Thayer, eds. *Penitence in the Age of Reformations.* Aldershot: Ashgate, 2000.

Lucas, Thomas M. *Landmarking: City, Church & Jesuit Urban Strategy.* Chicago: Loyola Press, 1997.

Lucas, Thomas M. *Saint, Site, and Sacred Strategy: Ignatius, Rome and Jesuit Urbanism.* Vatican City: Biblioteca apostolica vaticana, 1990.

Luebke, David Martin, ed. *The Counter-Reformation: The Essential Readings.* Blackwell Essential Readings in History. Malden, MA: Blackwell, 1999.

Lukács, Ladislaus, ed. *Monumenta Paedagogica Societatis Iesu.* 7 vols. Rome: Monumenta Historica Societatis Iesu, 1965.

Luria, Keith P. "Conversion and Coercion: Personal Conscience and Political Conformity in Early Modern France." *The Medieval History Journal* 12, no. 2 (July 1, 2009): 221–47.

Luria, Keith P. *Sacred Boundaries: Religious Coexistence and Conflict in Early-Modern France*. Washington, DC: Catholic University of America Press, 2005.

Luria, Keith P. "Separated by Death? Burials, Cemeteries, and Confessional Boundaries in Seventeenth-Century France." *French Historical Studies* 24, no. 2 (Spring 2001): 185–222.

MacCulloch, Diarmaid. *The Reformation*. New York: Viking, 2004.

MacDonnell, Joseph, ed. *Gospel Illustrations: A Reproduction of the 153 Images Taken from Jerome Nadal's 1595 Book, Adnotationes et Meditationes in Evangelia*. Fairfield, CT: Fairfield Jesuit Community, 1998.

MacLean, Gerald. *Looking East: English Writing and the Ottoman Empire Before 1800*. New York: Palgrave Macmillan, 2007.

Maddox, Donald. *Fictions of Identity in Medieval France*. Cambridge: Cambridge University Press, 2006.

Majorana, Bernadette. "Une pastorale spectaculaire: missions et missionnaires jésuites en Italie (XVIe–XVIIIe Siècle)." *Annales. Histoire, sciences sociales* 57, no. 2 (March 1, 2002): 297–320.

Mallett, Michael Edward, and Christine Shaw. *The Italian Wars 1494–1559: War, State and Society in Early Modern Europe*. New York: Routledge, 2012.

Maltezou, Chrysa, ed. *Venezia e le Isole Ionie*. Venice: Istituto Veneto di scienze, lettere ed arti, 2005.

Mandel, Corinne. *Sixtus V and the Lateran Palace*. Rome: Istituto poligrafico e zecca dello Stato Libreria dello Stato, 1994.

Martin, A. Lynn. *Henry III and the Jesuit Politicians*. Geneva: Librairie Droz, 1973.

Martin, A. Lynn. *The Jesuit Mind: The Mentality of an Elite in Early Modern France*. Ithaca, NY: Cornell University Press, 1988.

Martin, Francis Xavier, and John E Rotelle. *Friar, Reformer and Renaissance Scholar: Life and Work of Giles of Viterbo, 1469–1532*. Villanova, PA: Augustinian Press, 1992.

Martin, Gregory. *Roma Sancta (1581)*. Rome: Edizioni di storia e letteratura, 1969.

Martin, John Jeffries. *Myths of Renaissance Individualism*. New York: Palgrave Macmillan, 2004.

Martin, John Jeffries. *Venice's Hidden Enemies: Italian Heretics in a Renaissance City*. Berkeley: University of California Press, 1993.

Martínez d'Alós-Moner, Andreu. *Envoys of a Human God: The Jesuit Mission to Christian Ethiopia, 1557–1632*. Leiden: Brill, 2015.

Maryks, Robert A., ed. *A Companion to Ignatius of Loyola: Life, Writings, Spirituality, Influence*. Leiden: Brill, 2014.

Maryks, Robert A. *The Jesuit Order as a Synagogue of Jews: Jesuits of Jewish Ancestry and Purity-of-Blood Laws in the Early Society of Jesus*. Leiden: Brill, 2010.

Marzouki, Nadia, and Olivier Roy, eds. *Religious Conversions in the Mediterranean World*. New York: Palgrave Macmillan, 2013.

Masters, Bruce Alan. *Christians and Jews in the Ottoman Arab World: The Roots of Sectarianism*. Cambridge: Cambridge University Press, 2001.

Matar, Nabil. "'Abdallah Ibn 'Aisha and the French Court, 1699–1701: An Ambassador without Diplomacy." *French History* 29, no. 1 (March 1, 2015): 62–75.

Mattingly, Garrett. *The Armada*. Boston: Houghton Mifflin, 2005.

Mazur, Peter. *Conversion to Catholicism in Early Modern Italy*. London: Routledge, 2016.

Mazur, Peter. *The New Christians of Spanish Naples: 1528–1671: A Fragile Elite*. New York: Palgrave Macmillan, 2013.

Mazur, Peter, and Abigail Shinn, eds. "Conversion Narratives in the Early Modern World." *Journal of Early Modern History* 17, no. 5–6 (2013): 427–595.

McBrien, Richard P. *Lives of the Popes: The Pontiffs from St. Peter to John Paul II*. San Francisco: Harper Collins, 1997.

McCluskey, Phil. "'Les ennemis du nom chrestien': Echoes of the Crusade in Louis XIV's France." *French History* 29, no. 1 (March 1, 2015): 46–61.

McCoog, Thomas M. *The Mercurian Project: Forming Jesuit Culture, 1573–1580*. Rome: Institutum Historicum Societatis Iesu; Saint Louis, MO: Institute of Jesuit Sources, 2004.

McGuckin, John Anthony. *St. Cyril of Alexandria: The Christological Controversy: Its History, Theology, and Texts*. Crestwood, NY: St. Vladimir's Seminary Press, 1994.

McJannet, Linda. *The Sultan Speaks: Dialogue in English Plays and Histories about the Ottoman Turks*. New York: Palgrave Macmillan, 2006.

McKee, Sally. *Uncommon Dominion: Venetian Crete and the Myth of Ethnic Purity*. Philadelphia: University of Pennsylvania Press, 2000.

McManamon, John M. *The Text and Contexts of Ignatius Loyola's Autobiography*. New York: Fordham University Press, 2013.

Meinardus, Otto Friedrich August. *Two Thousand Years of Coptic Christianity*. Cairo: American University in Cairo Press, 1999.

Melammed, Renée Levine. *Heretics or Daughters of Israel?: The Crypto-Jewish Women of Castile*. New York: Oxford University Press, 2002.

Melammed, Renée Levine. *A Question of Identity: Iberian Conversos in Historical Perspective*. New York: Oxford University Press, 2004.

Mentzer, Raymond. "Morals and Moral Regulation in Protestant France." *The Journal of Interdisciplinary History* 31, no. 1 (July 1, 2000): 1–20.

Mentzer, Raymond, and Andrew Spicer, eds. *Society and Culture in the Huguenot World: 1559–1685*. Cambridge: Cambridge University Press, 2002.

Meserve, Margaret. *Empires of Islam in Renaissance Historical Thought*. Cambridge, MA: Harvard University Press, 2008.

Michelson, Emily. "Conversionary Preaching and the Jews in Early Modern Rome." *Past & Present* 235, no. 1 (May 2017): 68–104.

Michelson, Emily. *The Pulpit and the Press in Reformation Italy*. Cambridge, MA: Harvard University Press, 2013.

Minkov, Anton. *Conversion to Islam in the Balkans: Kisve Bahasi Petitions and Ottoman Social Life, 1670–1730*. Leiden: Brill, 2004.

Minor, Vernon Hyde, and Brian A. Curran, eds. *Art and Science in the Rome of Gregory XIII Boncompagni (1572–1585)*. Rome: American Academy in Rome, 2009.

Miola, Robert S. *Early Modern Catholicism: An Anthology of Primary Sources.* Oxford: Oxford University Press, 2007.

Molho, Anthony, Kurt A. Raaflaub, and Julia Emlen, eds. *City States in Classical Antiquity and Medieval Italy.* Ann Arbor: University of Michigan Press, 1991.

Molina, J. Michelle. *To Overcome Oneself: The Jesuit Ethic and Spirit of Global Expansion, 1520–1767.* Berkeley: University of California Press, 2013.

Montaigne, Michel de. *The Complete Essays.* Translated by M. A. Screech. London: Penguin Classics, 1993.

Montaigne, Michel de. *Complete Works: Essays, Travel Journal, Letters.* Stanford, CA: Stanford University Press, 1958.

Monumenta Proximi-Orientis (MPO). 6 vols. Rome: Monumenta Historica Societatis Iesu, 1989.

Moore, John C. *Pope Innocent III (1160/61–1216): To Root Up and to Plant.* Leiden: Brill, 2003.

Moosa, Matti. *The Maronites in History.* Syracuse, NY: Syracuse University Press, 1986.

Moran, J. F. *The Japanese and the Jesuits: Alessandro Valignano in Sixteenth-Century Japan.* London: Routledge, 1993.

Muccillo, Maria. *Platonismo ermetismo e "Prisca theologia": ricerche di storiografia filosofica rinascimentale.* Florence: L.S. Olschki, 1996.

Muir, Edward. *Civic Ritual in Renaissance Venice.* Princeton, NJ: Princeton University Press, 1981.

Muir, Edward. *Mad Blood Stirring: Vendetta & Factions in Friuli during the Renaissance.* Baltimore, MD: Johns Hopkins University Press, 1993.

Mulsow, Martin, and Richard Henry Popkin, eds. *Secret Conversions to Judaism in Early Modern Europe.* Leiden: Brill, 2004.

Naaman, Paul, and Antonius Faustus Naironus. *Essai sur les maronites: leur origine, leur nom et leur religion: par Fauste Nairon de bane maronite, Rome 1679.* Kaslik, Lebanon: Universite Saint Esprit de Kaslik, 2006.

Nadal, Gerónimo. *Annotations and Meditations on the Gospels.* Philadelphia: Saint Joseph's University Press, 2003.

Nadal, Gerónimo. *Epistolae P. Hieronumi Nadal Societatis Jesu, Ab Anno 1546 Ad 1577.* 5 vols. Rome: Monumenta historica Societatis Iesu, 1898.

Newitt, Malyn. *Portugal in European and World History.* London: Reaktion Books, 2009.

Noreen, Kirstin. "Ecclesiae Militantis Triumphi: Jesuit Iconography and the Counter-Reformation." *The Sixteenth Century Journal* 29, no. 3 (October 1, 1998): 689–715.

Nye, Robert A. *Masculinity and Male Codes of Honor in Modern France.* Berkeley: University of California Press, 1998.

O'Malley, John W. *The First Jesuits.* Cambridge, MA: Harvard University Press, 1993.

O'Malley, John W. *Giles of Viterbo on Church and Reform.* Leiden: Brill, 1968.

O'Malley, John W. *Trent: What Happened at the Council.* Cambridge, MA: Belknap Press of Harvard University Press, 2013.

O'Malley, John W. "Was Ignatius Loyola a Church Reformer? How to Look at Early Modern Catholicism." *The Catholic Historical Review* 77, no. 2 (April 1991): 177–93.

Oberholzer, Paul, S.J., ed. *Diego Laínez (1512–1565) and His Generalate: Jesuit with Jewish Roots, Close Confidant of Ignatius of Loyola, Preeminent Theologian of the Council of Trent.* Rome: Bibliotheca Instituti Historici Societatis Iesu, 2015.

Oberman, Heiko Augustinus, and Dennis D. Martin. *Masters of the Reformation: The Emergence of a New Intellectual Climate in Europe.* Cambridge: Cambridge University Press, 2008.

Ocker, Christopher, Michael Printy, Peter Starenko, and Peter Wallace, eds. *Politics and Reformations: Communities, Polities, Nations, and Empires.* Leiden: Brill, 2007.

Oldrati, Valentina. "Renegades and the Habsburg Secret Services in the Aftermath of Lepanto: Haci Murad and the Algerian Threat as a Case Study." *Journal of Iberian and Latin American Studies* 24, no. 1 (January 2, 2018): 7–26.

Omasta, Matt, and Drew Chappell. *Play, Performance, and Identity How Institutions Structure Ludic Spaces.* London: Routledge, 2015.

Paiva, José Pedro. "Vescovi ed ebrei/nuovi cristiani nel Cinquecento portoghese." In *Riti di passaggio, storie di giustizia.* Edited by Vincenzo Lavenia and Giovanna Paolin. Pisa: Edizioni della Normale, 2011, 67–85.

Papademetriou, Tom. *Render unto the Sultan: Power, Authority, and the Greek Orthodox Church in the Early Ottoman Centuries.* Oxford: Oxford University Press, 2015.

Pardo, Osvaldo F. *The Origins of Mexican Catholicism: Nahua Rituals and Christian Sacraments in Sixteenth-Century Mexico.* Ann Arbor, MI: University of Michigan Press, 2006.

Parker, Charles H. *Global Interactions in the Early Modern Age, 1400–1800.* Cambridge: Cambridge University Press, 2010.

Parker, Charles H., and Jerry H. Bentley, eds. *Between the Middle Ages and Modernity: Individual and Community in the Early Modern World.* Lanham, MD: Rowman & Littlefield, 2007.

Parker, Geoffrey. *Imprudent King: A New Life of Philip II.* New Haven, CT: Yale University Press, 2014.

Parker, Geoffrey. *The Thirty Years' War.* London: Routledge & Kegan Paul, 1984.

Parker, Geoffrey, and Lesley M. Smith. *The General Crisis of the Seventeenth Century.* London: Routledge & Kegan Paul, 1978.

Parry, Kenneth, ed. *The Blackwell Companion to Eastern Christianity.* Malden, MA: Blackwell, 2007.

Pastore, Stefania. *Un'eresia spagnola: spiritualità conversa, alumbradismo e inquisizione (1449–1559).* Florence: L.S. Olschki, 2004.

Patterson, Benton Rain. *With the Heart of a King: Elizabeth I of England, Philip II of Spain, and the Fight for a Nation's Soul and Crown.* New York: St. Martin's Press, 2013.

Peri, Oded. *Christianity under Islam in Jerusalem: The Question of the Holy Sites in Early Ottoman Times.* Leiden: Brill, 2001.

Perry, Mary Elizabeth. *The Handless Maiden: Moriscos and the Politics of Religion in Early Modern Spain.* Princeton, NJ: Princeton University Press, 2005.

Pettegree, Andrew. *Reformation and the Culture of Persuasion.* Cambridge: Cambridge University Press, 2005.

Pirri, Pietro. "Sultan Yahya e P. Claudio Acquaviva." *Archivum Historicum Societatis Iesu* 13 (1944): 62–76.

Pittoni, Leros, and Gabrielle Lautenberg. *Roma felix: la città di Sisto V e Domenico Fontana.* Rome: Viviani, 2002.

Prodi, Paolo, ed. *Disciplina dell'anima, disciplina del corpo e disciplina della società tra medioevo ed età moderna.* Bologna: Società editrice il Mulino, 1994.

Prodi, Paolo. *The Papal Prince.* Cambridge: Cambridge University Press, 1987.

Prosperi, Adriano "L'abiura dell'eretico e la conversione del criminale: prime linee di ricerca." *Quaderni storici* 42, no. 3 (December 2007): 719–29.

Prosperi, Adriano. *Il Concilio di Trento: una introduzione storica.* Turin: Einaudi, 2001.

Prosperi, Adriano. "L'Europa cristiana e il mondo: alle origini dell'idea di missione." *Dimensioni e problemi della ricerca storica* 2 (December 1992): 189–220.

Prosperi, Adriano. *Tribunali della coscienza: inquisitori, confessori, missionari.* Turin: G. Einaudi, 1996.

Prosperi, Adriano. *La vocazione: storie di gesuiti tra cinquecento e seicento.* Turin: Einaudi, 2016.

Rabbath, Antoine, ed. *Documents inédits poir servir à l'histoire du Christianisme en Orient (XVI – XIX Siècle).* 2 vols. Paris: AMS Press, 1905.

Rambo, Lewis R. *Understanding Religious Conversion.* New Haven, CT: Yale University, 1993.

Raphael, Pierre. *Le rôle du Collège Maronite Romain dans l'orientalisme aux XVIIe et XVIIIe siècles.* Beirut: Université Saint Joseph, 1950.

Rastoin, Marc. "Les chrétiens d'origine juive dans la Compagnie naissante." *Christus* 211 (2006): 357–63.

Rawlings, Helen. *The Spanish Inquisition.* Malden, MA: Blackwell, 2006.

Ray, Jonathan. *After Expulsion: 1492 and the Making of Sephardic Jewry.* New York: New York University Press, 2013.

Raymond, Andre. "Soldiers in Trade: The Case of Ottoman Cairo." *British Journal of Middle Eastern Studies* 18, no. 1 (1991): 16–37.

Raz-Krakotzkin, Amnon. *The Censor, the Editor, and the Text: The Catholic Church and the Shaping of the Jewish Canon in the Sixteenth Century.* Philadelphia: University of Pennsylvania Press, 2007.

Redolfi, Maddalena. *Venezia e la difesa del Levante: da Lepanto a Candia 1570–1670.* Venice: Arsenale, 1986.

Rega Castro, Iván. "The 'New Lepanto'? John V of Portugal and the Battle of Matapan (1717)." *Journal of Iberian and Latin American Studies* 24, no. 1 (January 2, 2018): 93–106.

Reinhard, Wolfgang. "Gegenreformation als Modernisierung? Prolegomena einer Theorie des konfessionellen Zeitalters." *Archiv Für Reformationsgeschichte* 68 (1977): 226–51.

Reinhard, Wolfgang. "Gelenkter Kulturwandel im Siebzehnten Jahrhundert: Akkulturation in den Jesuitenmissionen als universalhistorisches Problem." *Historische Zeitschrift* 223, no. 3 (December 1976): 529–90.

Reinhard, Wolfgang. "Reformation, Counter-Reformation, and the Early Modern State a Reassessment." *The Catholic Historical Review* 75, no. 3 (July 1, 1989): 383–404.

Reites, James W. *St. Ignatius of Loyola and the Jews.* St. Louis, MO: American Assistancy Seminar on Jesuit Spirituality, 1981.

Reites, James, W. "St. Ignatius of Loyola and the Jews," *Studies in the Spirituality of the Jesuits* 13, no. 4 (1981): 13–17.

Rembaum, Joel E. "The Development of a Jewish Exegetical Tradition Regarding Isaiah 53." *The Harvard Theological Review* 75, no. 3 (July 1, 1982): 289–311.

Restrepo, D., S.J., and Joannes Vilar, S.J., eds. *Patris Petri de Ribadeneira, Societatis Iesu sacerdotis, confessiones, epistolae aliaque scripta inedita.* Vol. 1. Madrid: La editorial ibérica, 1920.

Rey, Eusebio. "San Ignacio de Loyola y el problema de los 'cristianos nuevos,'" *Razón y Fe* 153 (1956): 173–87.

Ribadeneira, Pedro de. *The Life of Ignatius of Loyola.* Translated by Claude Nicholas Pavur. Saint Louis, MO: The Institute of Jesuit Sources, 2014.

Ribadeneyra, Pedro de. *Vita del P. Ignatio Loiola Vita Del P. Ignatio Loiola fondatore della religione della Compagnia di Giesù ... nuovamente tradutta dalla spagnuola nell'italiana da Giovanni Giolito de' Ferrari.* Venice, 1586.

Ricci, Giovanni. *Ossessione turca: in una retrovia cristiana dell'Europa moderna.* Bologna: Il mulino, 2002.

Ricci, Saverio. *Il sommo inquisitore: Giulio Antonio Santori tra autobiografia e storia (1532–1602).* Rome: Salerno Editrice, 2002.

Richardson, Carol M. "Durante Alberti, the Martyrs' Picture and the Venerable English College, Rome." *Papers of the British School at Rome* 73 (2005): 223–63.

Rittgers, Ronald K. "Private Confession and the Lutheranization of Sixteenth-Century Nördlingen." *The Sixteenth Century Journal* 36, no. 4 (December 1, 2005): 1063–85.

Rittgers, Ronald K. *The Reformation of the Keys: Confession, Conscience, and Authority in Sixteenth-Century Germany.* Cambridge, MA: Harvard University Press, 2004.

Robertson, Clare. *Il Gran Cardinale: Alessandro Farnese, Patron of the Arts.* New Haven, CT: Yale University Press, 1992.

Robertson, Clare. *Rome 1600: The City and the Visual Arts under Clement VIII.* New Haven, CT: Yale University Press, 2016.

Robichaud, Denis J.-J. *Plato's Persona: Marsilio Ficino, Renaissance Humanism, and Platonic Traditions.* Philadelphia: University of Pennsylvania Press, 2018.

Romeo, Giovanni. "Roberto Bellarmino tra Inquisizione e Indice." *Studi Storici* 42, no. 2 (April 1, 2001): 529–35.

Roncaglia, Martiniano Pellegrino, ed. *La République de Venise et les lieux saints de Jérusalem: documents inédits du XVe aux XIXe S. tirés des archives privées du Couvent de St. François-De-La-Vigne de Venise.* Beirut: Dar Al-Kalima, 1972.

Rondot, Pierre. *Les institutions politiques du Liban: des communautés traditionnelles à l'état moderne.* Paris: Institut d'études de l'Orient contemporain, 1947.

Roper, Lyndal. *The Holy Household: Women and Morals in Reformation Augsburg.* Oxford: Oxford University Press, 1989.

Rosen, Mark. *The Mapping of Power in Renaissance Italy: Painted Cartographic Cycles in Social and Intellectual Context.* Cambridge: Cambridge University Press, 2015.

Rosenthal, Frank. "The Study of the Hebrew Bible in Sixteenth-Century Italy." *Studies in the Renaissance* 1 (January 1, 1954): 81–91.

Rostagno, Lucia. *Mi faccio turco: esperienze ed immagini dell'Islam nell'Italia moderna.* Rome: Istituto per l'Oriente C.A. Nallino, 1983.

Roth, Norman. *Conversos, Inquisition, and the Expulsion of the Jews from Spain.* Madison: University of Wisconsin Press, 2002.

Rothman, E. Natalie. "Becoming Venetian: Conversion and Transformation in the Seventeenth-Century Mediterranean." *Mediterranean Historical Review* 21, no. 1 (June 1, 2006): 39–75.

Rothman, E. Natalie. *Brokering Empire: Trans-Imperial Subjects Between Venice and Istanbul.* Ithaca, NY: Cornell University Press, 2012.

Rothman, E. Natalie. "Dragomans and 'Turkish Literature': The Making of a Field of Inquiry." *Oriente moderno* 93, no. 2 (2013): 390–421.

Rothman, E. Natalie. "Interpreting Dragomans: Boundaries and Crossings in the Early Modern Mediterranean." *Comparative Studies in Society and History* 51, no. 4 (October 1, 2009): 771–800.

Rowland, Ingrid D. *Giordano Bruno: Philosopher/Heretic.* Chicago: University of Chicago Press, 2008.

Ruderman, David B. *Early Modern Jewry: A New Cultural History.* Princeton, NJ: Princeton University Press, 2010.

Ruggieri, Vincenzo. "Constantinopoli vista da P. Giulo Mancinelli S. J. (1583–1585)." *Revue des études byzantines* 60, no. 1 (2002): 113–31.

Ruiu, Adina. "Conflicting Visions of the Jesuit Missions to the Ottoman Empire, 1609–1628." *Journal of Jesuit Studies* 1, no. 2 (March 12, 2014): 260–80.

Ruiz, Teofilo F, Geoffrey Symcox, and Gabriel Piterberg. *Braudel Revisited: The Mediterranean World, 1600–1800.* Toronto: University of Toronto Press, 2010.

Rummel, Erika. *The Confessionalization of Humanism in Reformation Germany.* Oxford: Oxford University Press, 2000.

Salibi, Kamal S. "The Maronites of Lebanon under Frankish and Mamluk Rule (1099–1516)." *Arabica* 4, no. 3 (September 1957): 288–303.

Salibi, Kamal S. "The Muqaddams of Bšarrī: Maronite Chieftains of the Northern Lebanon 1382–1621." *Arabica* 15, no. 1 (February 1968): 63–86.

Sangalli, Maurizio. *Università, accademie, gesuiti: cultura e religione a Padova tra Cinque e Seicento.* Trieste: LINT, 2001.

Sansovino, Francesco. *Venetia Città Nobilissima (Venice, 1581).* Farnborough: Gregg, 1968.

Sant Cassia, Paul. "Religion, Politics and Ethnicity in Cyprus during the Turkokratia (1571–1787)." *Archives européennes de sociologie* 27 (1986): 3–28.

Santarelli, Daniele. *Il papato di Paolo IV nella crisi politico-religiosa del Cinquecento*. Rome: Aracne editrice, 2008.

Santoro, Giulio Antonio. *Cardinal Giulio Antonio Santoro and the Christian East: Santoro's Audiences and Consistorial Acts*. Edited by John Krajcar. Rome: Pont. Institutum Orientalium Studiorum, 1966.

Santosuosso, Antonio. "Religious Orthodoxy, Dissent and Suppression in Venice in the 1540s." *Church History* 42, no. 4 (December 1973): 476–85.

Sanz, Enrique. "Los Laínez y la limpieza de sangre." *Perficit* 17 (1993): 65–71.

Saraiva, António José, H. P Salomon, and I. S. D Sassoon. *The Marrano Factory: The Portuguese Inquisition and its New Christians 1536–1765*. Leiden: Brill, 2001.

Scaraffia, Lucetta. *Rinnegati: per una storia dell'identità occidentale*. Rome: Laterza, 2002.

Schatz, Klaus. *Papal Primacy: From Its Origins to the Present*. Collegeville, MN: Liturgical Press, 1996.

Schilling, Heinz. *Religion, Political Culture, and the Emergence of Early Modern Society: Essays in German and Dutch History*. Leiden: Brill, 1992.

Schmalz, Mathew N., and Peter Gottschalk, eds. *Engaging South Asian Religions: Boundaries, Appropriations, and Resistances*. Albany: State University of New York Press, 2012.

Schmidt, Martin Anton. "The Problem of Papal Primacy at the Council of Florence." *Church History* 30, no. 1 (March 1, 1961): 35–49.

Schmitt, Jean-Claude, and Alex J Novikoff. *The Conversion of Herman the Jew Autobiography, History, and Fiction in the Twelfth Century*. Philadelphia: University of Pennsylvania Press, 2013.

Scribner, Robert W. *Popular Culture and Popular Movements in Reformation Germany*. London: Hambledon Press, 1987.

Scully, Robert E., S.J. *Into the Lion's Den: The Jesuit Mission in Elizabethan England and Wales, 1580–1603*. St. Louis, MO: Institute of Jesuit Sources, 2011.

Selwyn, Jennifer D. *A Paradise Inhabited by Devils: The Jesuits' Civilizing Mission in Early Modern Naples*. Aldershote: Ashgate; Institutum Historicum Societatis Iesu, 2004.

Shore, Paul John. "'In Carcere; Ad Dupplicium': Jesuit Encounters in Prison and in Places of Execution. Reflections on the Early-Modern Period." *European Review of History* 19, no. 2 (April 2012): 183–200.

Shoulson, Jeffrey S. *Fictions of Conversion: Jews, Christians, and Cultures of Change in Early Modern England*. Philadelphia: University of Pennsylvania Press, 2013.

Sicroff, Albert A. *Les controverses des statuts de "pureté de sang" en Espagne du XVe au XVIIe siècle*. Paris: Didier, 1960.

Signorotto, Gianvittorio, and Maria Antonella Viscella, eds. *Court and Politics in Papal Rome, 1492–1700*. Cambridge: Cambridge University Press, 2002.

Simms, Norman Toby. *Masks in the Mirror: Marranism in Jewish Experience*. New York: Peter Lang, 2006.

Simonsohn, Shlomo. *The Jews in the Duchy of Milan: A Documentary History of the Jews of Italy.* Jerusalem: Israel Academy of Sciences and Humanities, 1982.

Sluhovsky, Moshe. *Becoming a New Self: Practices of Belief in Early Modern Catholicism.* Chicago: University of Chicago Press, 2017.

Smith, Ian. *Race and Rhetoric in the Renaissance: Barbarian Errors.* New York: Palgrave Macmillan, 2009.

Smith, Jeffrey Chipps. *Sensuous Worship: Jesuits and the Art of the Early Catholic Reformation in Germany.* Princeton, NJ: Princeton University Press, 2002.

Snyder, Jon R. *Dissimulation and the Culture of Secrecy in Early Modern Europe.* Berkeley: University of California Press, 2012.

Soergel, Philip M. *Wondrous in His Saints: Counter-Reformation Propaganda in Bavaria.* Berkeley: University of California Press, 1993.

Solá Castaño, Emilio, and José F. de la Peña. *Cervantes y la Berbería: (Cervantes, mundo turco-berberisco y servicios secretos en la época de Felipe II).* Madrid: Fondo de Cultura Economica, 1996.

Solá Castaño, Emilio. *Un Mediterráneo de piratas: corsarios, renegados y cautivos.* Madrid: Tecnos, 2004.

Sola, José. "El P. Juan Bautista Eliano. Un documento autobiografico inedito." *Archivum Historicum Societatis Iesu* IV (1935): 291–321.

Sorce, Francesco. "Astraea at Lepanto: Lattanzio Gambara's Frescoes in Palazzo Lalatta, Parma." *Journal of Iberian and Latin American Studies* 24, no. 1 (January 2, 2018): 107–34.

Soyer, François. *The Persecution of the Jews and Muslims of Portugal: King Manuel I and the End of Religious Tolerance (1496–7).* Leiden: Brill, 2007.

Soykut, Mustafa. "The Development of the Image 'Turk' in Italy Through 'Della Letteratura De' Turchi' of Giambattista Dona." *Journal of Mediterranean Studies* 9, no. 2 (November 1999): 175–203.

Soykut, Mustafa. *Image of the "Turk" in Italy: A History of the "Other" in Early Modern Europe, 1453–1683.* Berlin: K. Schwarz, 2001.

Sperling, Jutta Gisela. *Convents and the Body Politic in Late Renaissance Venice.* Chicago: University of Chicago Press, 1999.

Stanivukovic, Goran V., ed. *Remapping the Mediterranean World in Early Modern English Writings.* New York: Palgrave Macmillan, 2007.

Steensgaard, Niels. "The Seventeenth-Century Crisis and the Unity of Eurasian History." *Modern Asian Studies* 24, no. 4 (October 1, 1990): 683–97.

Stow, Kenneth R. "The Burning of the Talmud in 1553, in Light of Sixteenth-Century Catholic Attitudes Toward the Talmud." *Bibliothèque d'Humanisme et Renaissance* 34, no. 3 (1972): 435–59.

Stow, Kenneth R. *Jewish Life in Early Modern Rome: Challenge, Conversion, and Private Life.* Aldershot: Ashgate, 2007.

Stow, Kenneth R. "The Papacy and the Jews: Catholic Reformation and Beyond." *Jewish History* 6, no. 1/2 (January 1, 1992): 257–79.

Stow, Kenneth R. *Theater of Acculturation: The Roman Ghetto in the Sixteenth Century.* Seattle: University of Washington Press, 2001.

Stradling, R. A. *The Armada of Flanders: Spanish Maritime Policy and European War, 1568–1668. Cambridge*; New York: Cambridge University Press, 1992.

Subrahmanyam, Sanjay. "Connected Histories: Notes towards a Reconfiguration of Early Modern Eurasia." *Modern Asian Studies* 31, no. 3 (July 1, 1997): 735–62.

Subrahmanyam, Sanjay. *Three Ways to Be Alien: Travails and Encounters in the Early Modern World.* Waltham, MA: Brandeis University Press, 2011.

Szpiech, Ryan. *Medieval Exegesis and Religious Difference: Commentary, Conflict, and Community in the Premodern Mediterranean.* New York: Fordham University Press, 2016.

Tabak, Faruk. *The Waning of the Mediterranean, 1550–1870: A Geohistorical Approach.* Baltimore, MD: Johns Hopkins University Press, 2008.

Takeda, Junko Thérèse. *Between Crown and Commerce: Marseille and the Early Modern Mediterranean.* Baltimore, MD: Johns Hopkins University Press, 2011.

Takeda, Junko Thérèse. "French Mercantilism and the Early Modern Mediterranean: A Case Study of Marseille's Silk Industry." *French History* 29, no. 1 (March 1, 2015): 12–17.

Temple, Nicholas. *Renovatio Urbis: Architecture, Urbanism, and Ceremony in the Rome of Julius II.* London; New York: Routledge, 2011.

Terpstra, Nicholas. *Lay Confraternities and Civic Religion in Renaissance Bologna.* Cambridge: Cambridge University Press, 1995.

Terpstra, Nicholas, ed. *The Politics of Ritual Kinship: Confraternities and Social Order in Early Modern Italy.* Cambridge: Cambridge University Press, 1999.

Testa, Luca. *Fondazione e primo sviluppo del Seminario Romano (1565–1608).* Rome: Pontificia Università Gregoriana, 2002.

Tiepolo, Maria, ed. *I greci a Venezia.* Venice: Istituto veneto di scienze, lettere ed arti, 2002.

Tomlinson, Matt. *Ritual Textuality, Pattern, and Motion in Performance.* New York: Oxford University Press, 2014.

Tomlinson, Rowan, and Tania Demetriou. *The Culture of Translation in Early Modern England and France, 1500–1660.* New York: Palgrave Macmillan, 2015.

Trexler, Richard. *Public Life in Renaissance Florence.* New York: Academic Press, 1980.

Trinkaus, Charles Edward. *In Our Image and Likeness: Humanity and Divinity in Italian Humanist Thought.* Chicago: University of Chicago Press, 1970.

True, Micah. *Masters and Students: Jesuit Mission Ethnography in Seventeenth-Century New France.* Montreal: McGill-Queen's University Press, 2015.

Tsang, Rachel, and Eric Taylor Woods. *The Cultural Politics of Nationalism and Nation-Building: Ritual and Performance in the Forging of Nations.* London: Routledge, 2014.

Tuan, Yi-fu. *Space and Place: The Perspective of Experience.* Minneapolis: University of Minnesota Press, 1977.

Tutino, Stefania. *Empire of Souls: Robert Bellarmine and the Christian Commonwealth.* Oxford: Oxford University Press, 2010.

Tutino, Stefania. *Shadows of Doubt: Language and Truth in Post-Reformation Catholic Culture.* Oxford: Oxford University Press, 2014.

Tutino, Stefania. *Uncertainty in Post-Reformation Catholicism: A History of Probabilism.* Oxford: Oxford University Press, 2018.

Tylus, Jane, and Karen Newman, eds. *Early Modern Cultures of Translation.* Philadelphia: University of Pennsylvania Press, 2015.

Upton, Dell. "Architecture in Everyday Life." *New Literary History* 33, no. 4 (2002): 707–23.

van Boxel, Piet. *Jewish Books in Christian Hands: Theology, Exegesis and Conversion under Gregory XIII (1572–1585).* Vatican City: Biblioteca Apostolica Vaticana, 2016.

Varriale, Gennaro. "Tra il Mediterraneo e il fonte battesimale: Musulmani a Napoli nel XVI secolo." *Revista de historia Moderna. anales de La Universidad de Alicante* 31 (2013): 91–108.

Varriale, Gennaro. *Arrivano li turchi: guerra navale e spionaggio nel Mediterraneo (1532–1582).* Novi Ligure: Città del silenzio, 2014.

Vatin, Nicolas. "The Ottoman View of France from the Late Fifteenth to the Mid-Sixteenth Century." *French History* 29, no. 1 (March 1, 2015): 6–11.

Vaumas, Etienne de. *La répartition de la population au Liban introduction à la géographie humaine de la république libanaise.* Cairo: Impr. de l'Institut français d'archéologie orientale, 1953.

Veer, Peter van der, ed. *Conversion to Modernities: The Globalization of Christianity.* New York: Routledge, 1996.

Vitkus, Daniel J., ed., *Piracy, Slavery, and Redemption: Barbary Captivity Narratives from Early Modern England.* New York: Columbia University Press, 2001.

Vitkus, Daniel J., ed. *Three Turk Plays from Early Modern England: Selimus, A Christian Turned Turk, and The Renegado.* New York: Columbia University Press, 2000.

Vitkus, Daniel J. *Turning Turk: English Theater and the Multicultural Mediterranean, 1570–1630.* New York: Palgrave Macmillan, 2003.

Vitkus, Daniel J. "Turning Turk in Othello: The Conversion and Damnation of the Moor." *Shakespeare Quarterly* 48, no. 2 (July 1, 1997): 145–76.

Walton, Michael T., and Phyllis J. Walton. "In Defense of the Church Militant: The Censorship of the Rashi Commentary in the Magna Biblia Rabbinica." *The Sixteenth Century Journal* 21, no. 3 (October 1, 1990): 385–400.

Ward, Benedicta. *The Sayings of the Desert Fathers: The Alphabetical Collection.* Rev. ed. Kalamazoo, MI: Cistercian Publications, 1975.

Waterworth, J., ed. *The Canons and Decrees of the Sacred and Oecumenical Council of Trent, Celebrated under the Sovereign Pontiffs, Paul III, Julius III and Pius IV.* London: C. Dolman, 1848.

Weil, Gérard E. *Élie Lévita humaniste et massorète (1469–1549).* Leiden: Brill, 1963.

Weiss, Gillian. *Captives and Corsairs: France and Slavery in the Early Modern Mediterranean.* Stanford, CA: Stanford University Press, 2011.

Werner, Michael, and Bénédicte Zimmermann. "Beyond Comparison: Histoire Croisée and the Challenge of Reflexivity." *History and Theory* 45, no. 1 (February 1, 2006): 30–50.

Wessel, Susan. *Cyril of Alexandria and the Nestorian Controversy: The Making of a Saint and of a Heretic.* Oxford: Oxford University Press, 2004.

White, Michael. *The Pope and the Heretic: A True Story of Giordano Bruno, the Man Who Dared to Defy the Roman Inquisition.* New York: William Morrow, 2002.

White, Sam. *The Climate of Rebellion in the Early Modern Ottoman Empire.* Cambridge: Cambridge University Press, 2011.

Wilkinson, Robert J. *Orientalism, Aramaic, and Kabbalah in the Catholic Reformation: The First Printing of the Syriac New Testament.* Leiden: Brill, 2007.

Wilson, Bronwen. *The World in Venice: Print, the City and Early Modern Identity.* Toronto: University of Toronto Press, 2005.

Wilson, Peter. *The Thirty Years War: Europe's Tragedy.* Cambridge, MA: Harvard University Press, 2009.

Winter, Michael. *Egyptian Society Under Ottoman Rule, 1517–1798.* London: Routledge, 1992.

Winter, Michael, and Amalia Levanoni, eds. *The Mamluks in Egyptian and Syrian Politics and Society.* Leiden: Brill, 2004.

Winter, Stefan. *The Shiites of Lebanon Under Ottoman Rule, 1516–1788.* Cambridge: Cambridge University Press, 2010.

Wojciehowski, Hannah Chapelle. *Group Identity in the Renaissance World.* Cambridge: Cambridge University Press, 2011.

Worcester, Thomas, ed. *The Cambridge Companion to the Jesuits.* Cambridge: Cambridge University Press, 2008.

Worcester, Thomas. "'Neither Married nor Cloistered': Blessed Isabelle in Catholic Reformation France." *The Sixteenth Century Journal* 30, no. 2 (July 1, 1999): 457–72.

Wright, Anthony D. *The Early Modern Papacy: From the Council of Trent to the French Revolution, 1564–1789.* Harlow: Longman, 2000.

Wright, Elizabeth R. *The Epic of Juan Latino: Dilemmas of Race and Religion in Renaissance Spain.* Toronto: University of Toronto Press, 2016.

Wright, Elizabeth R., Sarah Spence, and Andrew Lemons, trans. *The Battle of Lepanto.* I Tatti Renaissance Library. Cambridge, MA: Harvard University Press, 2014.

Wright, Jonathan. *God's Soldiers: Adventure, Politics, Intrigue, and Power: A History of the Jesuits.* New York: Doubleday, 2003.

Yovel, Yirmiyahu. *The Other Within: The Marranos: Split Identity and Emerging Modernity.* Princeton, NJ: Princeton University Press, 2009.

Zaborowski, Jason R. *The Coptic Martyrdom of John of Phanijōit: Assimilation and Conversion to Islam in Thirteenth-Century Egypt.* Leiden: Brill, 2005.

Zagorin, Perez. *Ways of Lying: Dissimulation, Persecution, and Conformity in Early Modern Europe.* Cambridge, MA: Harvard University Press, 1990.

Zika, Charles. "Hosts, Processions and Pilgrimages: Controlling the Sacred in Fifteenth-Century Germany." *Past & Present* 118 (1988): 25–64.

Zimmer, Eric. "Jewish and Christian Hebraist Collaboration in Sixteenth Century Germany." *The Jewish Quarterly Review,* New Series, 71, no. 2 (October 1, 1980): 69–88.

Žižek, Slavoj, ed. *Mapping Ideology.* London: Verso, 1994.

Županov, Ines G. "Aristocratic Analogies and Demotic Descriptions in the Seventeenth-Century Madurai Mission." *Representations* 41 (January 1, 1993): 123–48.

Županov, Ines G. *Disputed Mission: Jesuit Experiments and Brahmanical Knowledge in Seventeenth-Century India.* New Delhi: Oxford University Press, 1999.

Index